A Certain Magical Index 16

ORIGINAL STORY: KAZUMA KAMACHI

CHARACTER DESIGN: KIYOTAKA HAIMURA

CHUYA KOGINO

A CERTAIN MAGICAL INDEX 16 TABLE OF CONTENTS
Index Librorum Prohibitorum

#92 THE QUEEN'S FLEET ⑤ — 003

#93 ROSARY OF THE APPOINTED TIME ① — 033

#94 ROSARY OF THE APPOINTED TIME ② — 059

#95 ROSARY OF THE APPOINTED TIME ③ — 093

#96 THEIR HOMEWARD JOURNEYS — 125

#97 MIKOTO'S PUNISHMENT GAME — 161

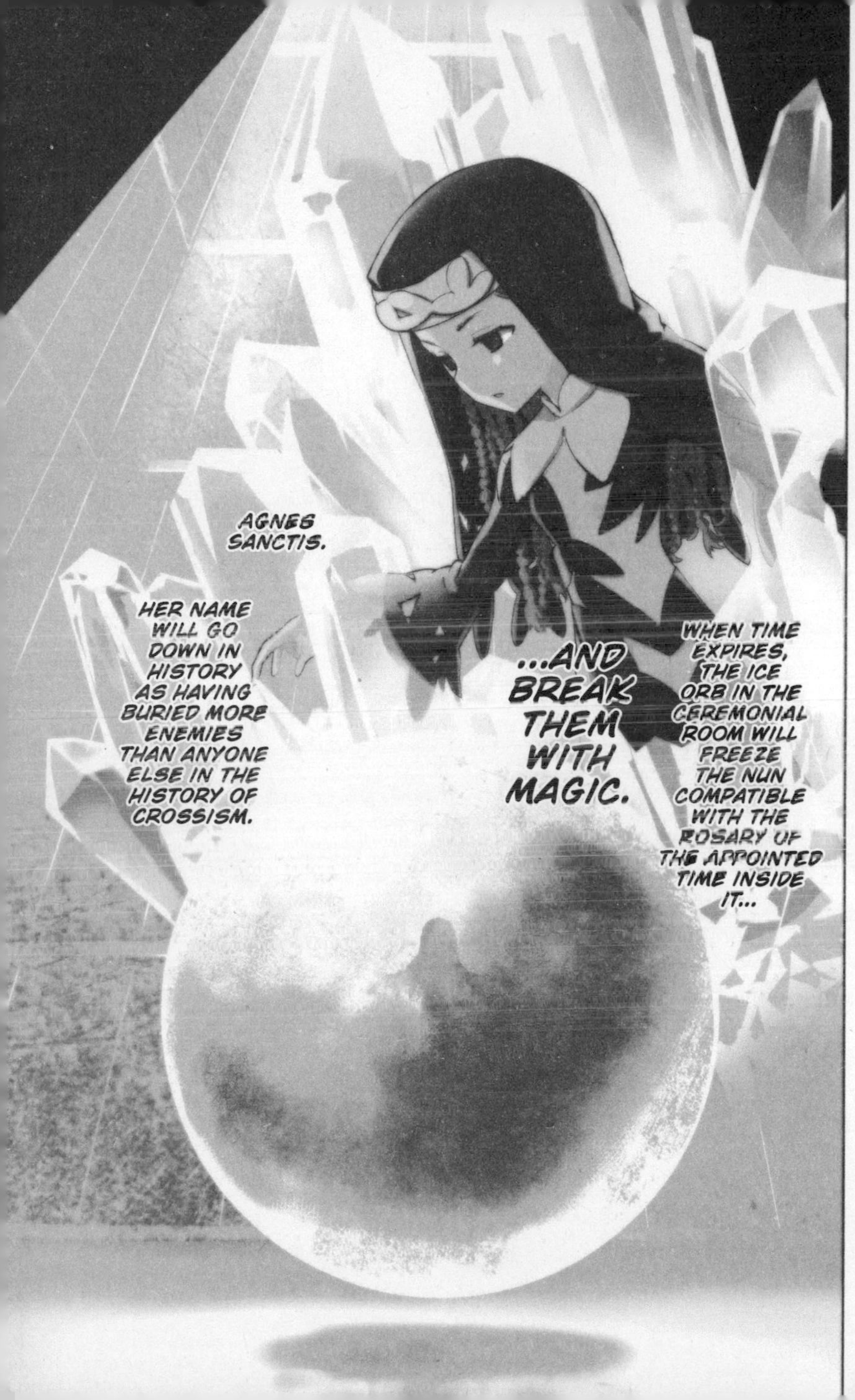
WHEN TIME EXPIRES, THE ICE ORB IN THE CEREMONIAL ROOM WILL FREEZE THE NUN COMPATIBLE WITH THE ROSARY OF THE APPOINTED TIME INSIDE IT...
...AND BREAK THEM WITH MAGIC.
AGNES SANCTIS.
HER NAME WILL GO DOWN IN HISTORY AS HAVING BURIED MORE ENEMIES THAN ANYONE ELSE IN THE HISTORY OF CROSSISM.

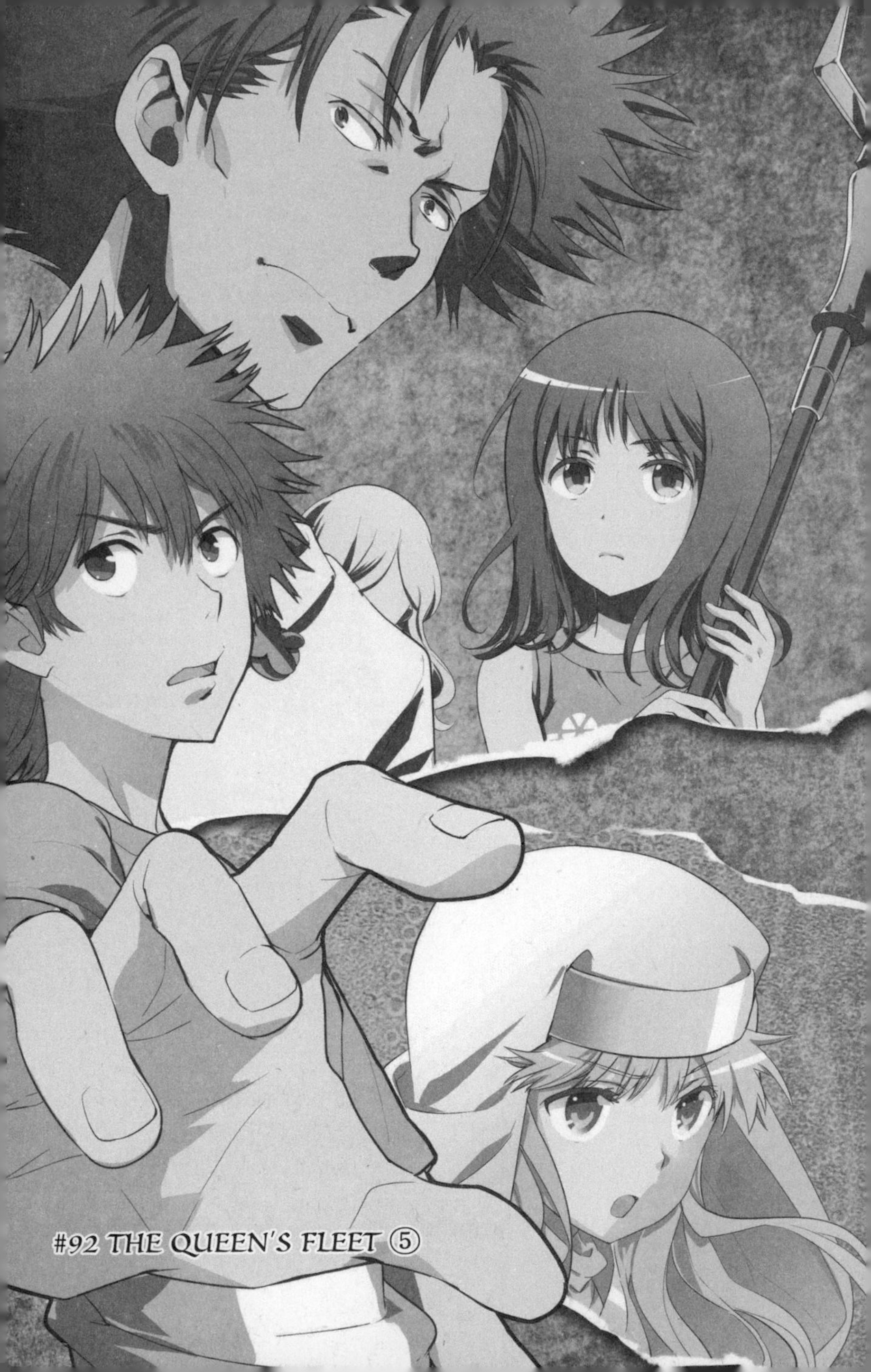
#92 THE QUEEN'S FLEET ⑤

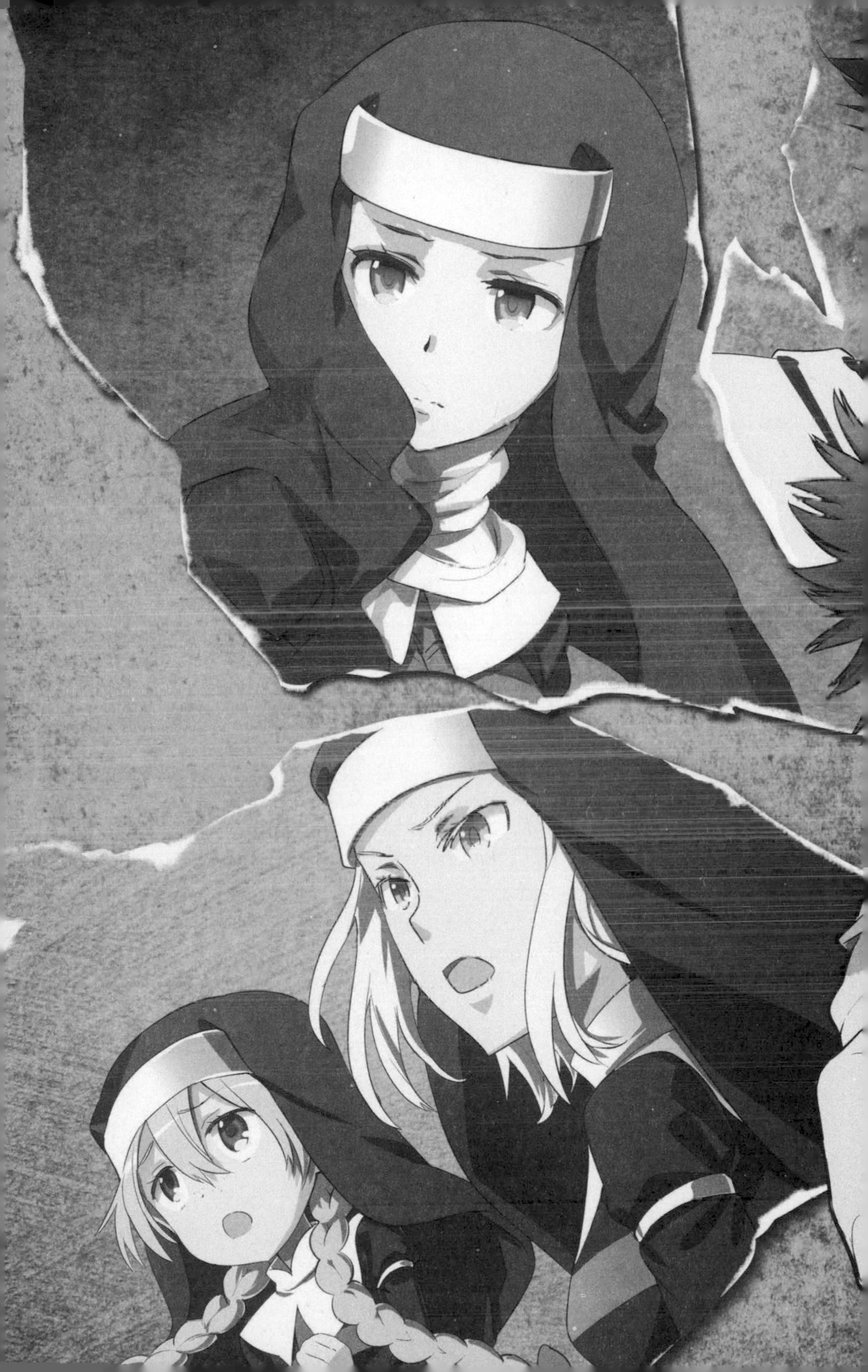

A Certain Magical Index

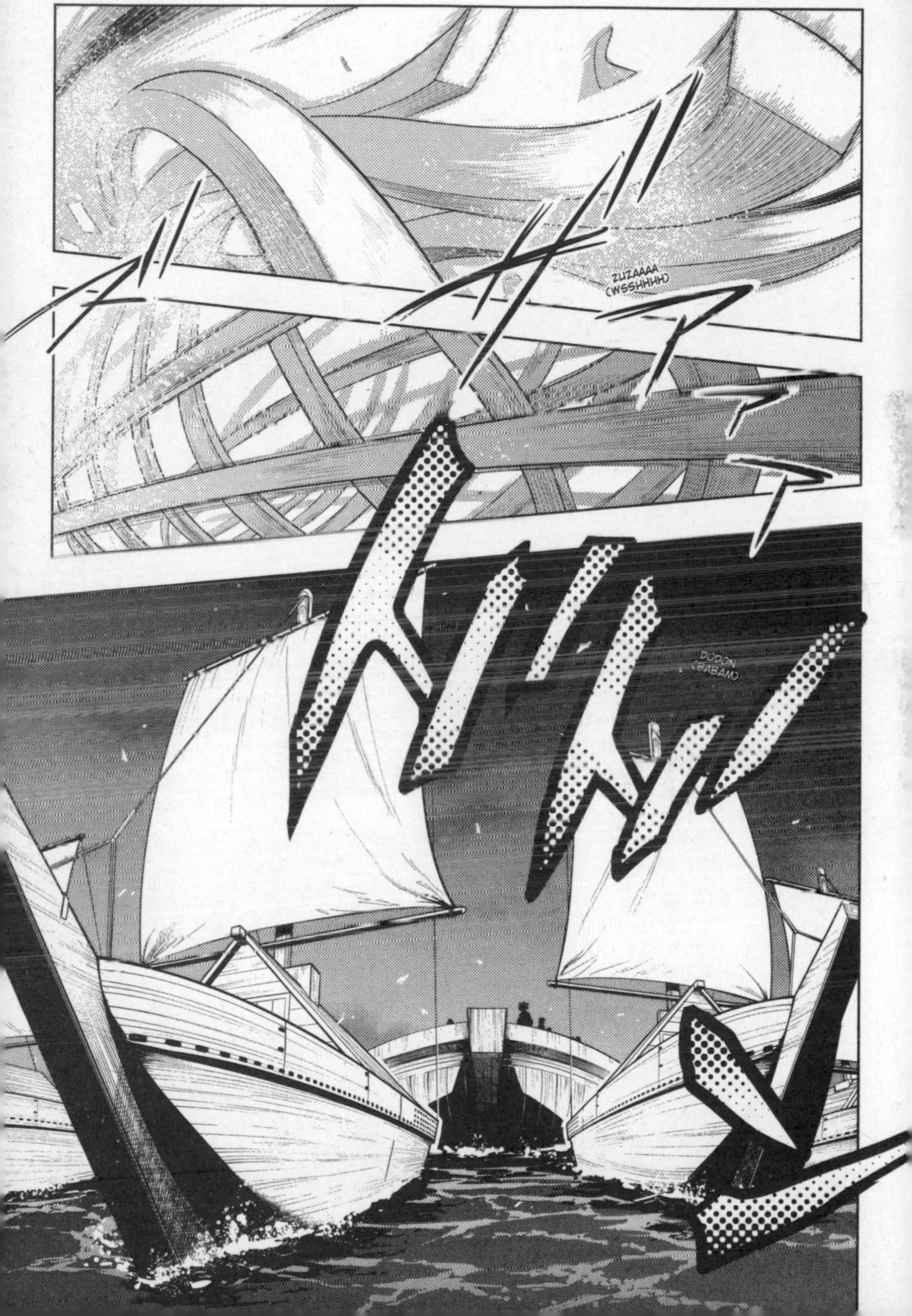
ZUZAAAA
(WSSHHHH)
DODON
(BABAM)

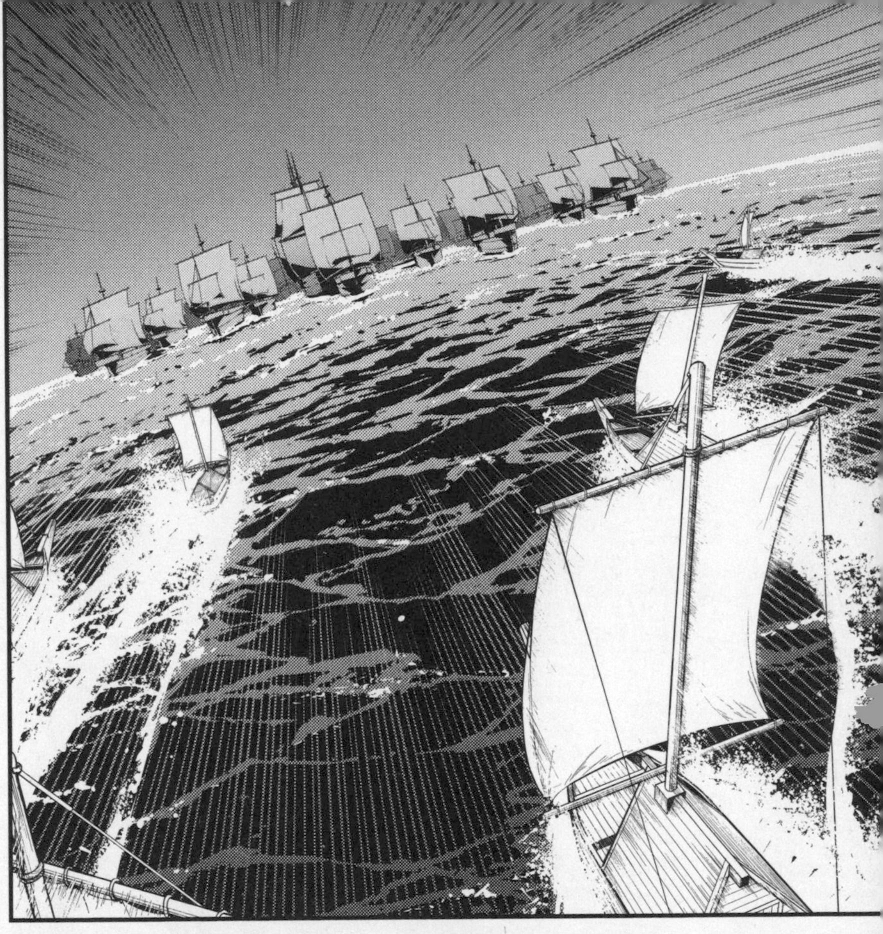

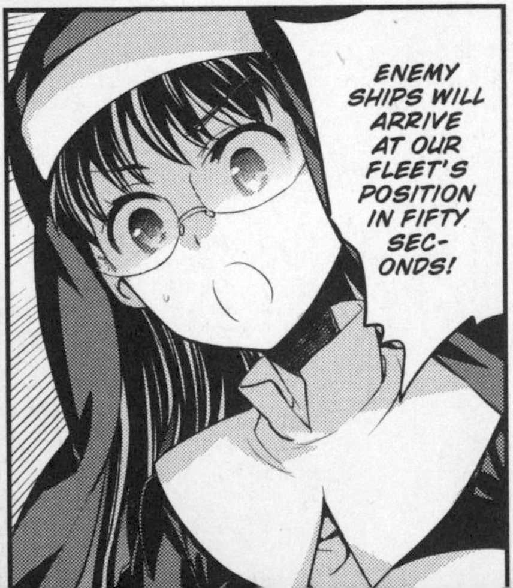
ENEMY SHIPS WILL ARRIVE AT OUR FLEET'S POSITION IN FIFTY SEC-ONDS!

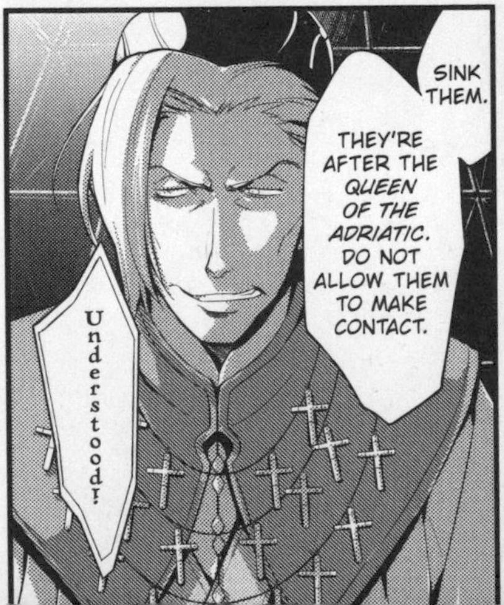
SINK THEM.
THEY'RE AFTER THE *QUEEN OF THE ADRIATIC.* DO NOT ALLOW THEM TO MAKE CONTACT.
Understood!

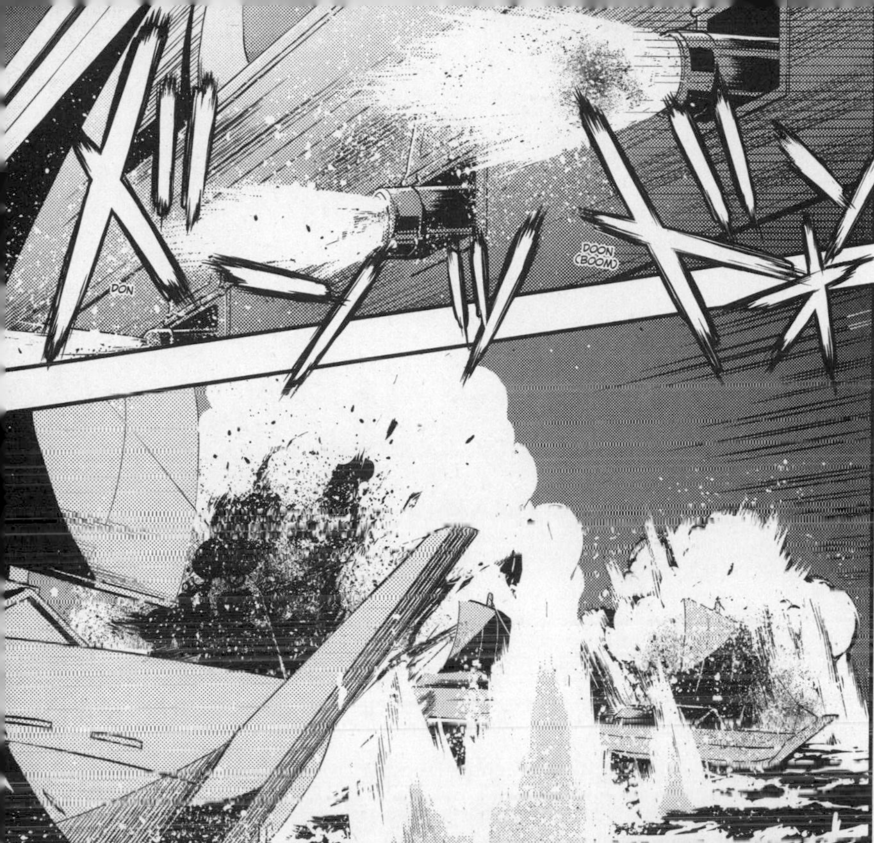
DOON (BOOM)
DON

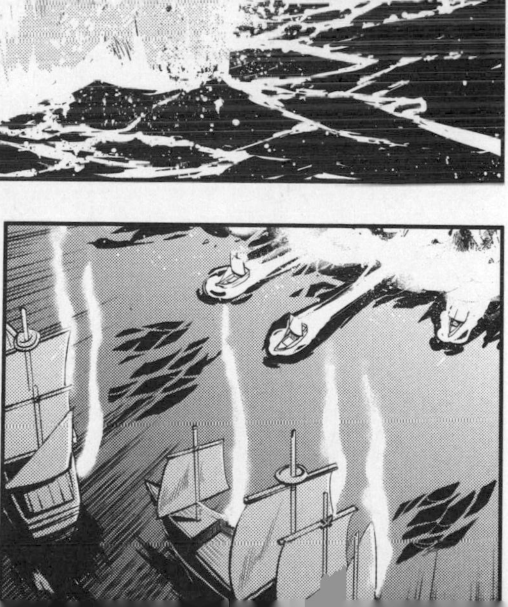

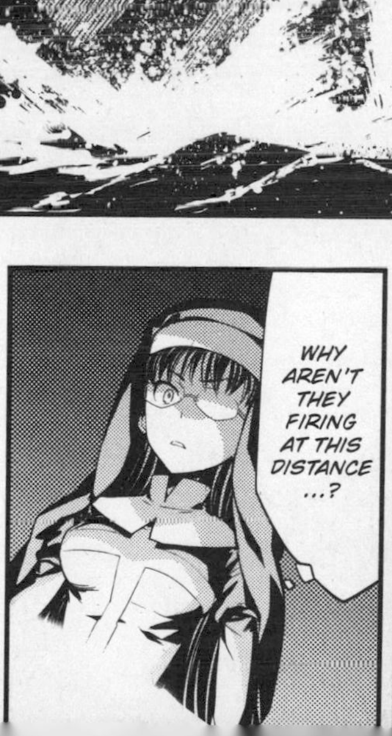
WHY AREN'T THEY FIRING AT THIS DISTANCE ...?

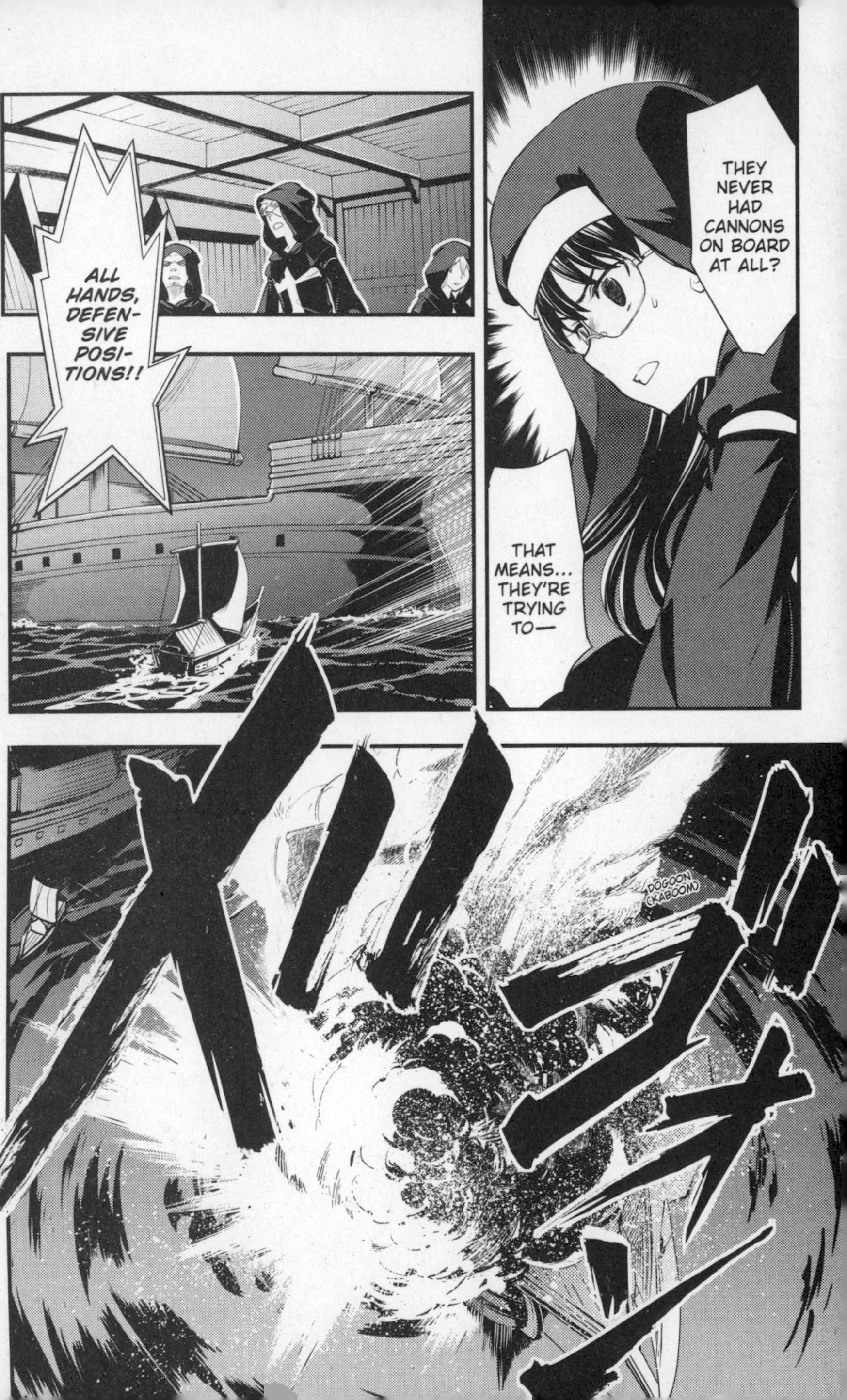
THEY NEVER HAD CANNONS ON BOARD AT ALL?
THAT MEANS... THEY'RE TRYING TO—
ALL HANDS, DEFENSIVE POSITIONS!!
DOGOON (KABOOM)

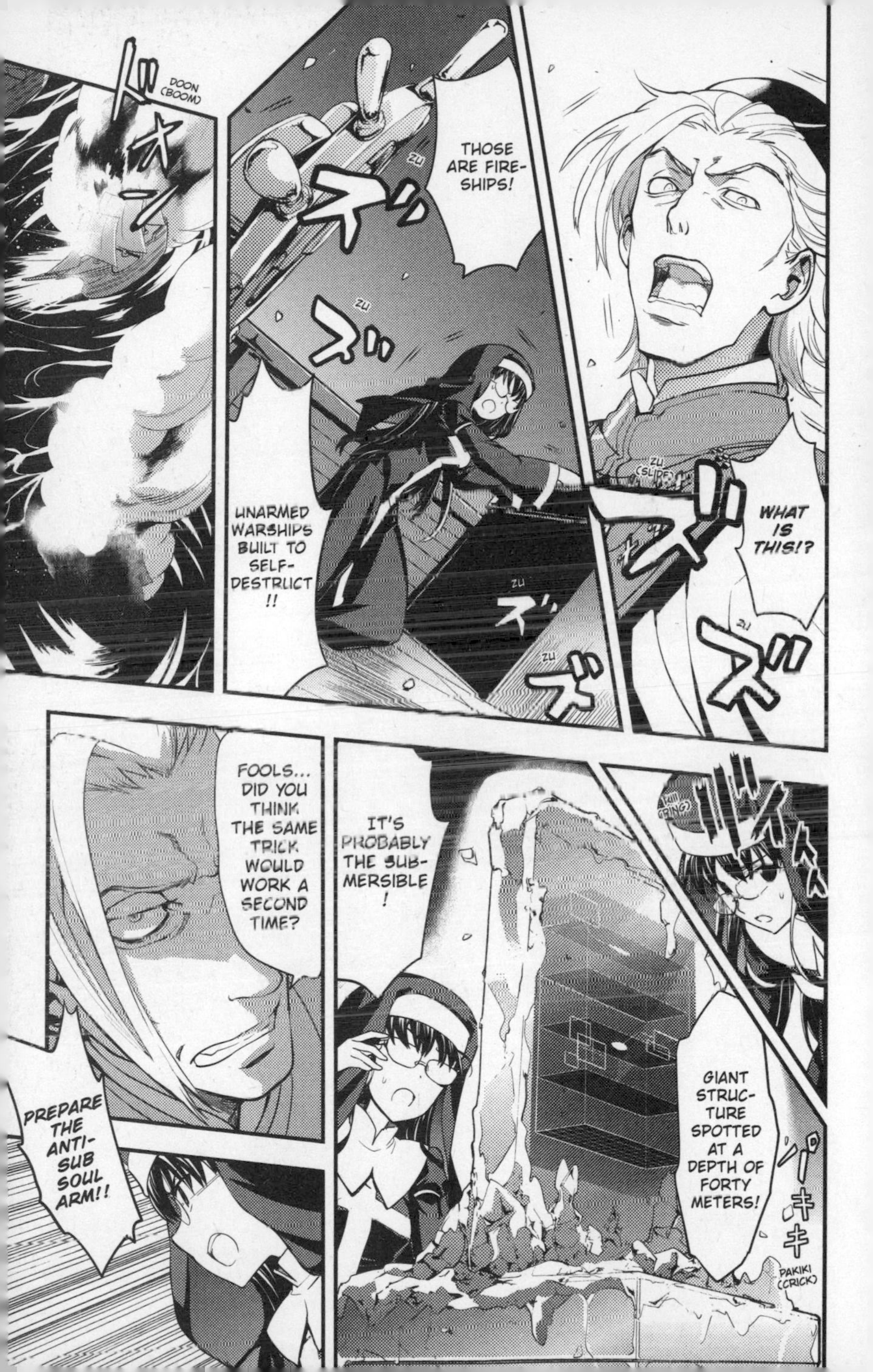
ZU (SLIDE)
WHAT IS THIS!?
ZU
THOSE ARE FIRE-SHIPS!
ZU
ZU
UNARMED WARSHIPS BUILT TO SELF-DESTRUCT!!
ZU
ZU
DOON (BOOM)
(RING)
GIANT STRUCTURE SPOTTED AT A DEPTH OF FORTY METERS!
PAKIKI (CRICK)
IT'S PROBABLY THE SUBMERSIBLE!
FOOLS... DID YOU THINK THE SAME TRICK WOULD WORK A SECOND TIME?
PREPARE THE ANTI-SUB SOUL ARM!!

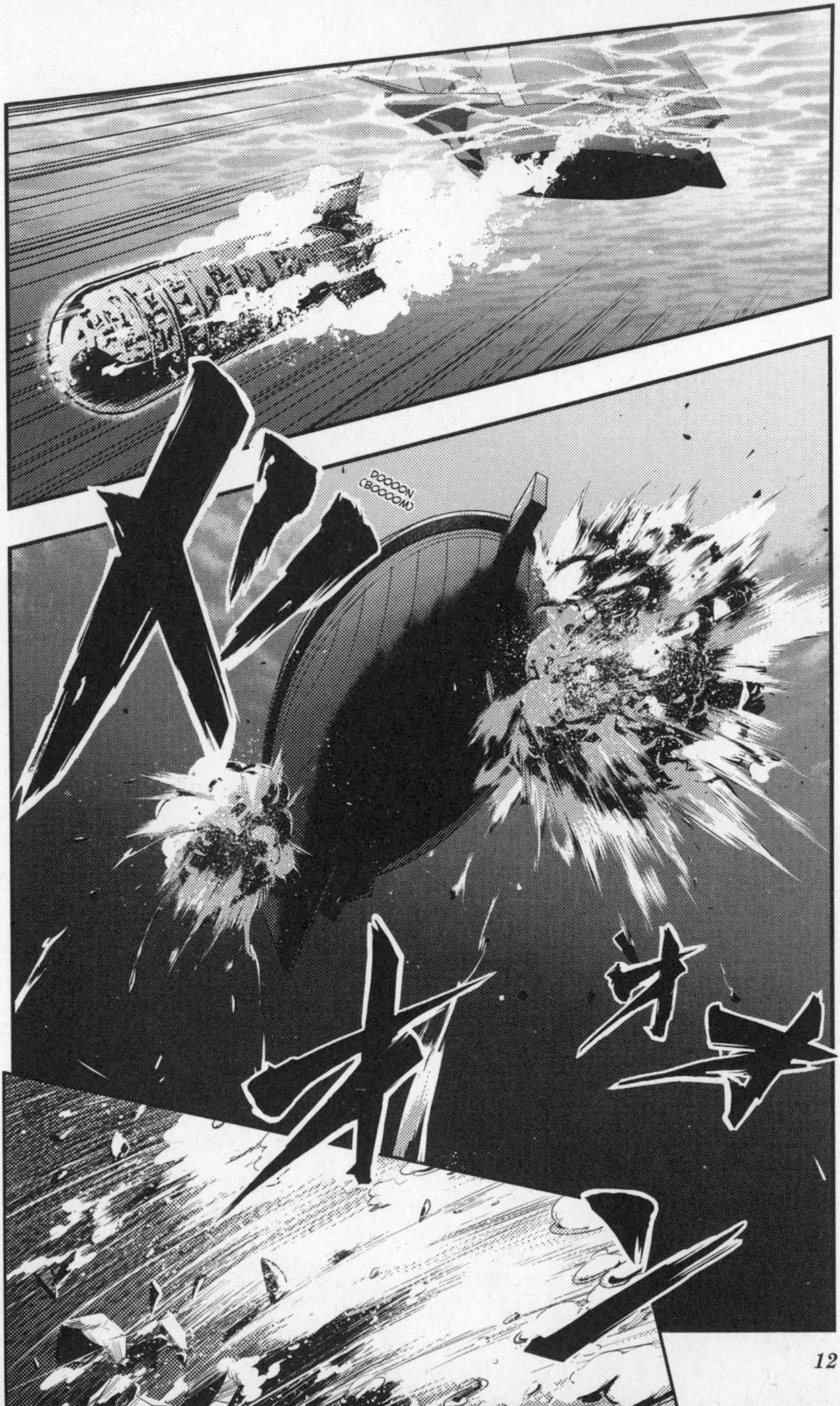
DOOOON
(BOOOOM)

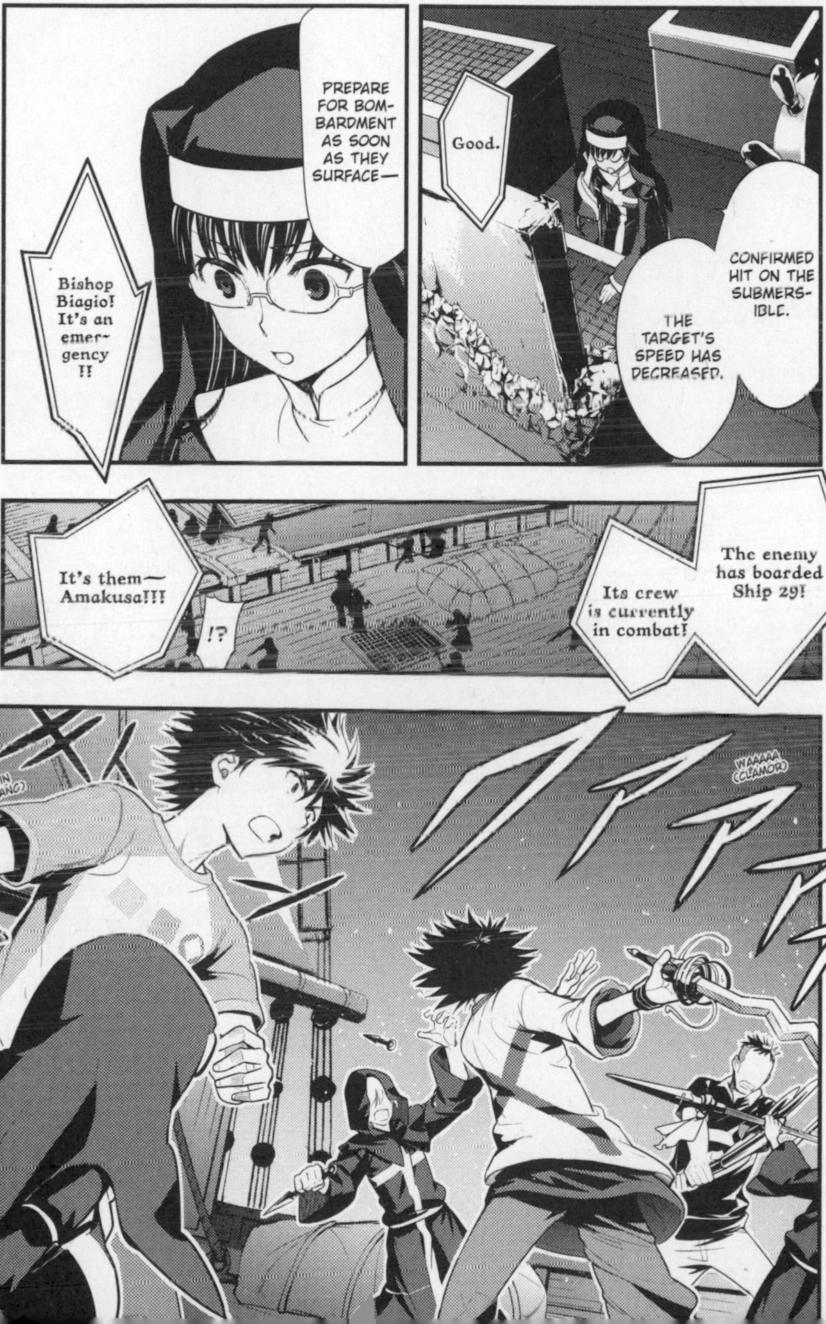
CONFIRMED HIT ON THE SUBMERSIBLE.
THE TARGET'S SPEED HAS DECREASED.
Good.
PREPARE FOR BOMBARDMENT AS SOON AS THEY SURFACE—
Bishop Biagio! It's an emergency!!
The enemy has boarded Ship 29!
Its crew is currently in combat!
!?
It's them— Amakusa!!!
WAAAAA (CLAMOR)
KIIN (CLANG)

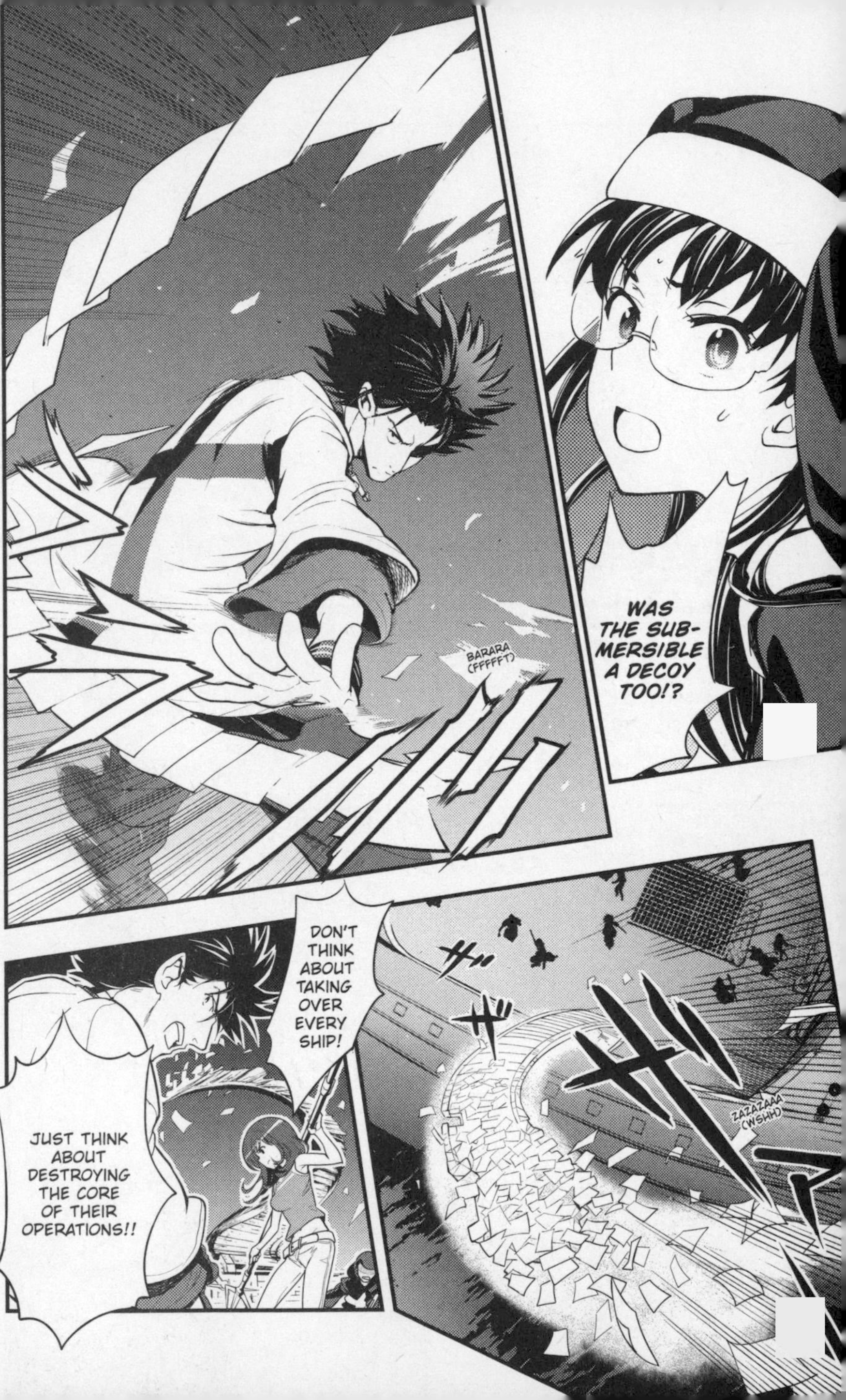
WAS THE SUB-MERSIBLE A DECOY TOO!?
BARARA (FFFFFT)
ZAZAZAAA (WSHH)
DON'T THINK ABOUT TAKING OVER EVERY SHIP!
JUST THINK ABOUT DESTROYING THE CORE OF THEIR OPERATIONS!!

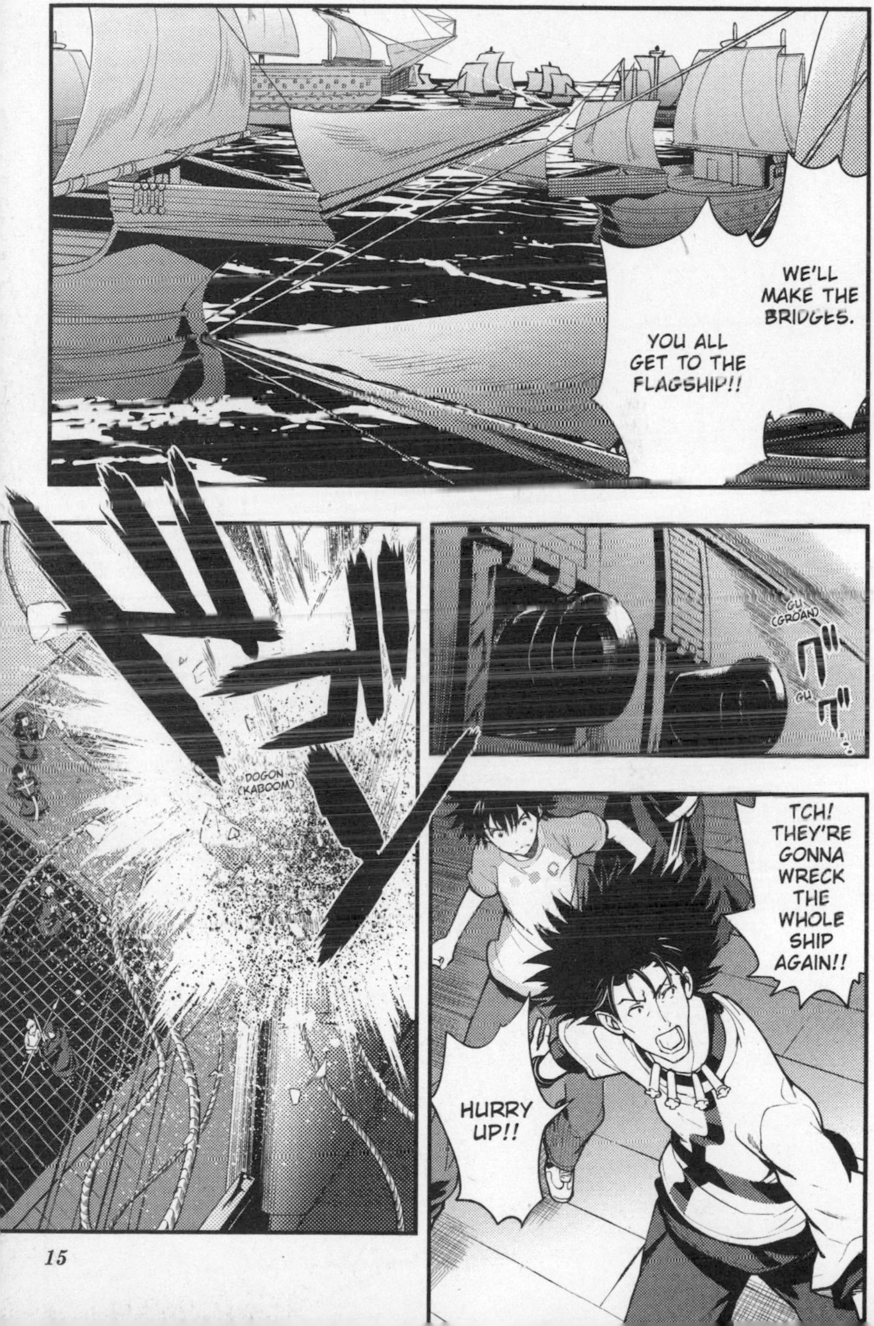
WE'LL MAKE THE BRIDGES.
YOU ALL GET TO THE FLAGSHIP!!
GU (GROAN)
GU
TCH! THEY'RE GONNA WRECK THE WHOLE SHIP AGAIN!!
HURRY UP!!
DOGON (KABOOM)

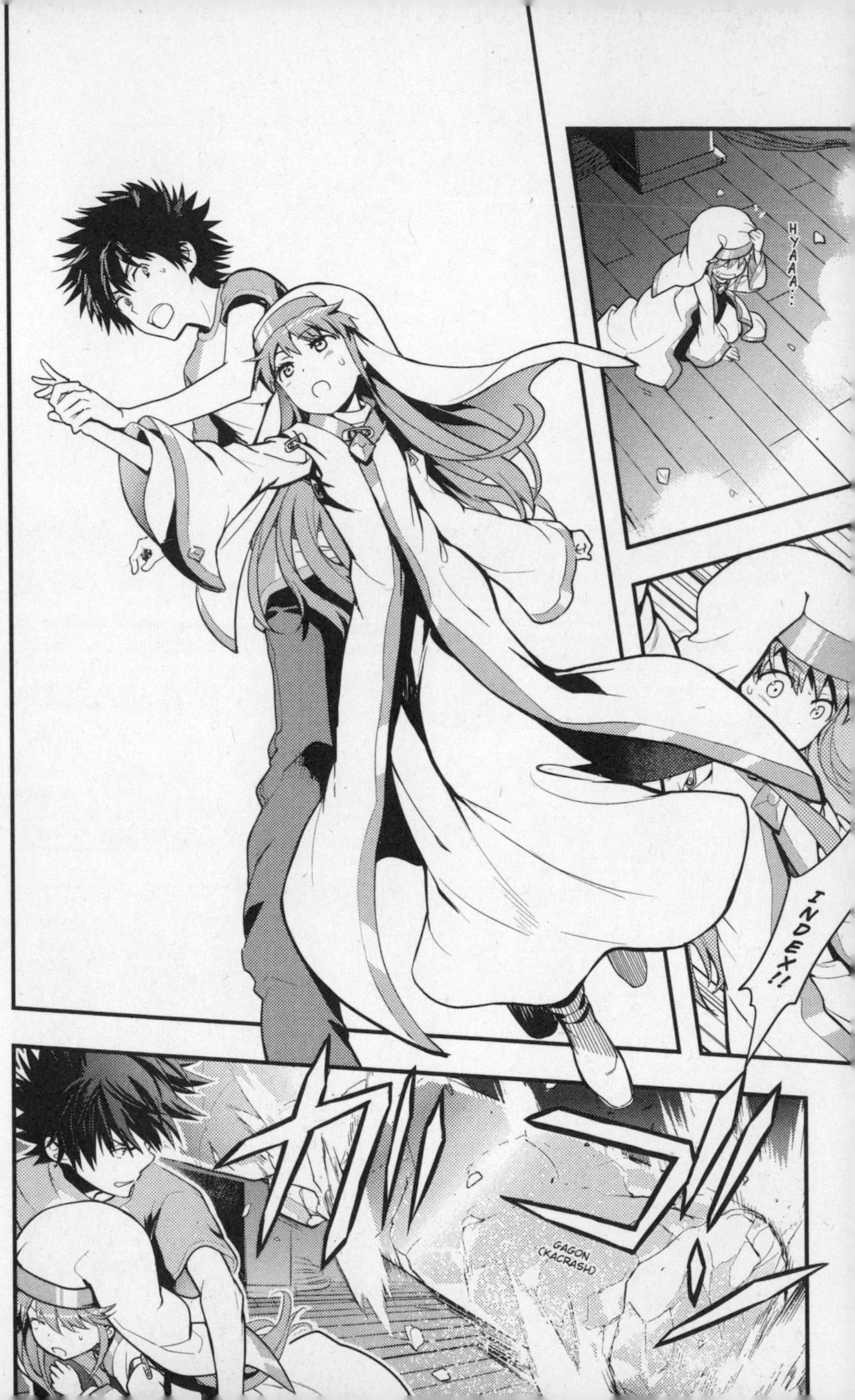
HYAAA...
INDEX!!
GAGON (KACRASH)

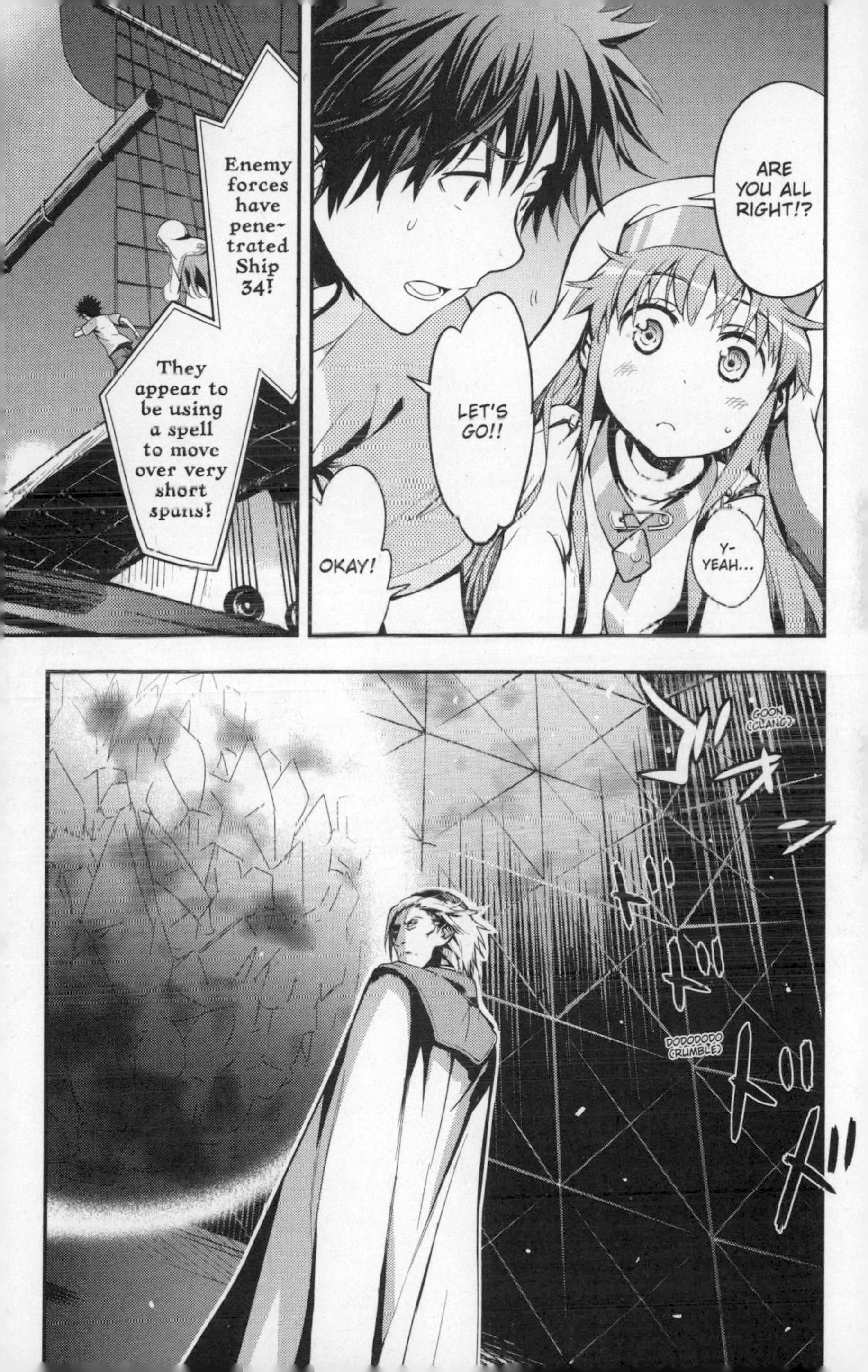
ARE YOU ALL RIGHT!?
Y-YEAH...
LET'S GO!!
OKAY!
Enemy forces have pene-trated Ship 34!
They appear to be using a spell to move over very short spans!
GOON (CLANG)
DODODODO (RUMBLE)

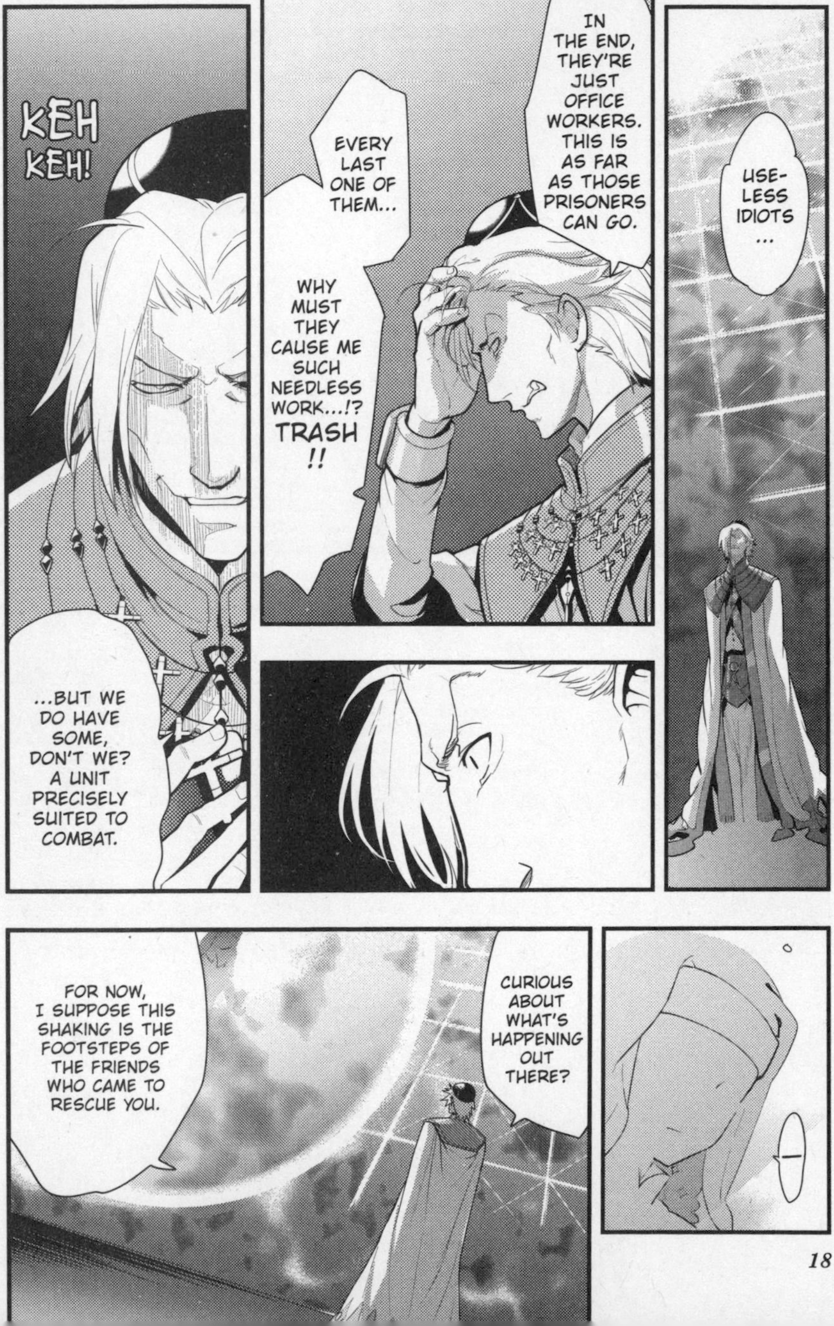
USE-LESS IDIOTS ...
IN THE END, THEY'RE JUST OFFICE WORKERS. THIS IS AS FAR AS THOSE PRISONERS CAN GO.
EVERY LAST ONE OF THEM...
WHY MUST THEY CAUSE ME SUCH NEEDLESS WORK...!? TRASH!!
KEH KEH!
...BUT WE DO HAVE SOME, DON'T WE? A UNIT PRECISELY SUITED TO COMBAT.
—
CURIOUS ABOUT WHAT'S HAPPENING OUT THERE?
FOR NOW, I SUPPOSE THIS SHAKING IS THE FOOTSTEPS OF THE FRIENDS WHO CAME TO RESCUE YOU.

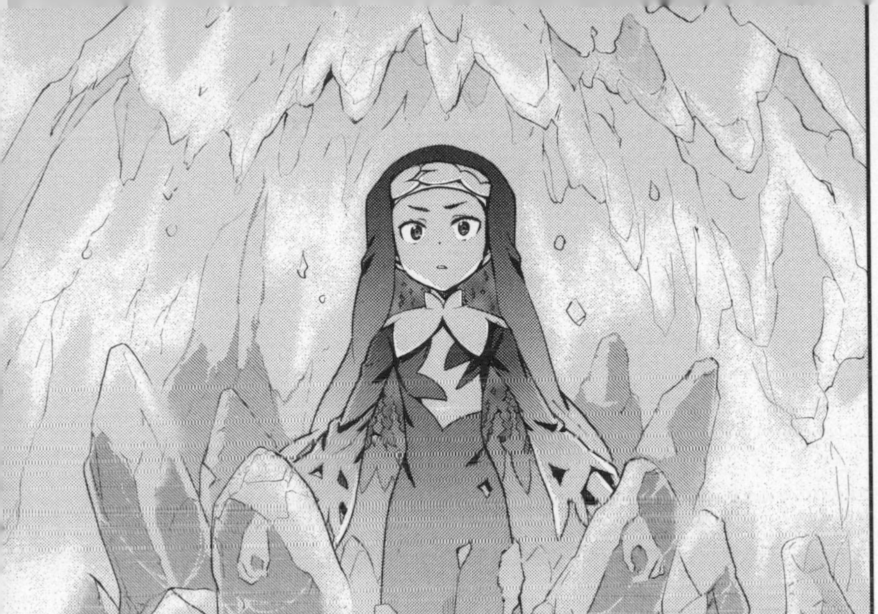

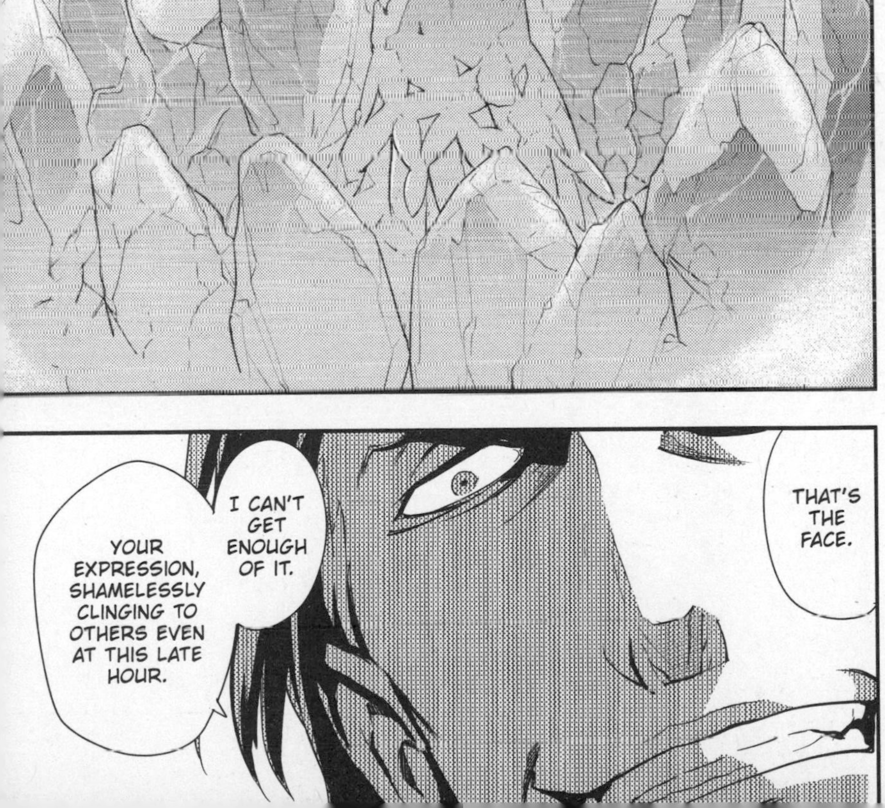
THAT'S THE FACE.
I CAN'T GET ENOUGH OF IT.
YOUR EXPRESSION, SHAMELESSLY CLINGING TO OTHERS EVEN AT THIS LATE HOUR.

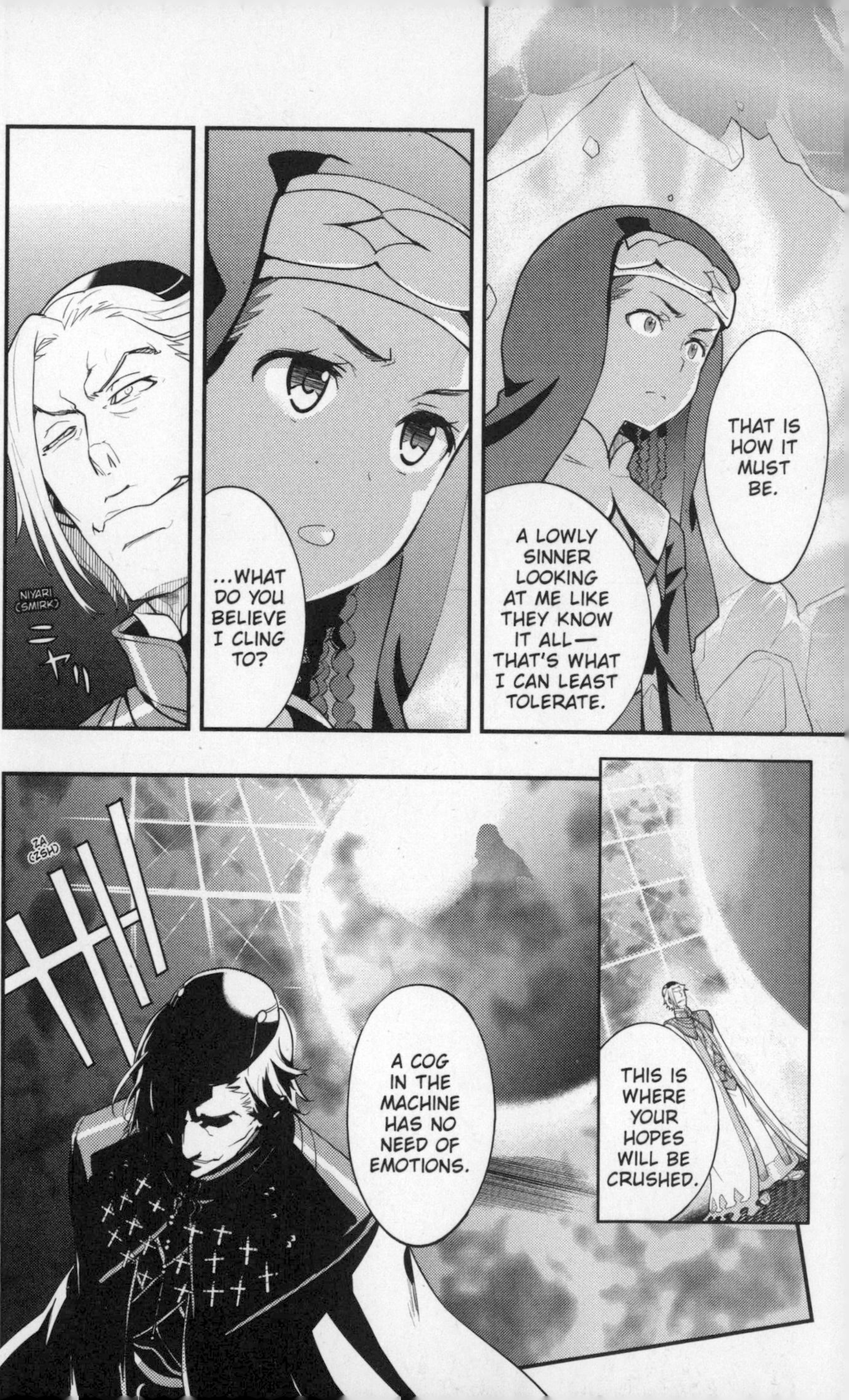
THAT IS HOW IT MUST BE.
A LOWLY SINNER LOOKING AT ME LIKE THEY KNOW IT ALL— THAT'S WHAT I CAN LEAST TOLERATE.
...WHAT DO YOU BELIEVE I CLING TO?
NIYARI (SMIRK)
THIS IS WHERE YOUR HOPES WILL BE CRUSHED.
ZA (ZZSH)
A COG IN THE MACHINE HAS NO NEED OF EMOTIONS.

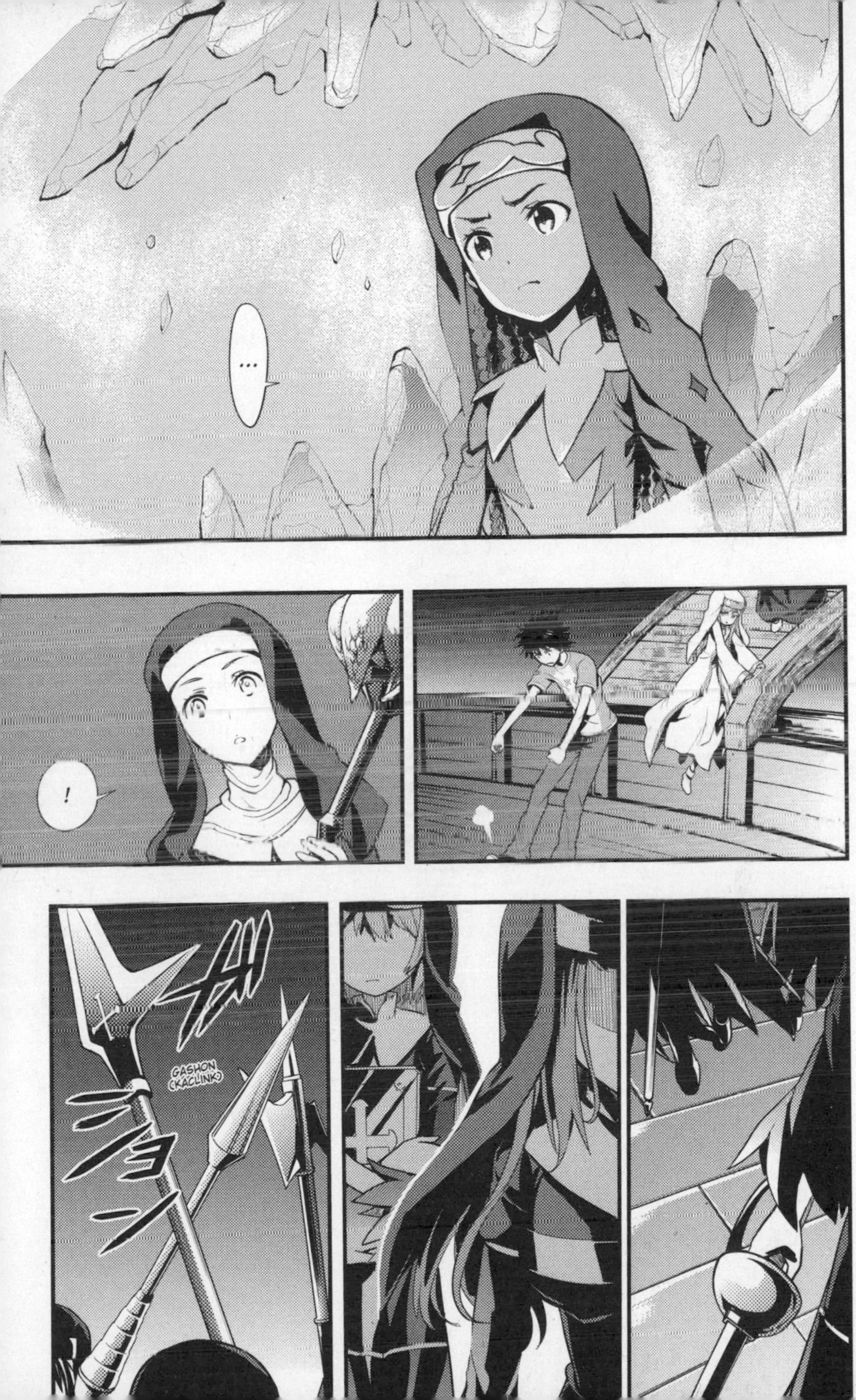
...
!
GASHON (KACLINK)

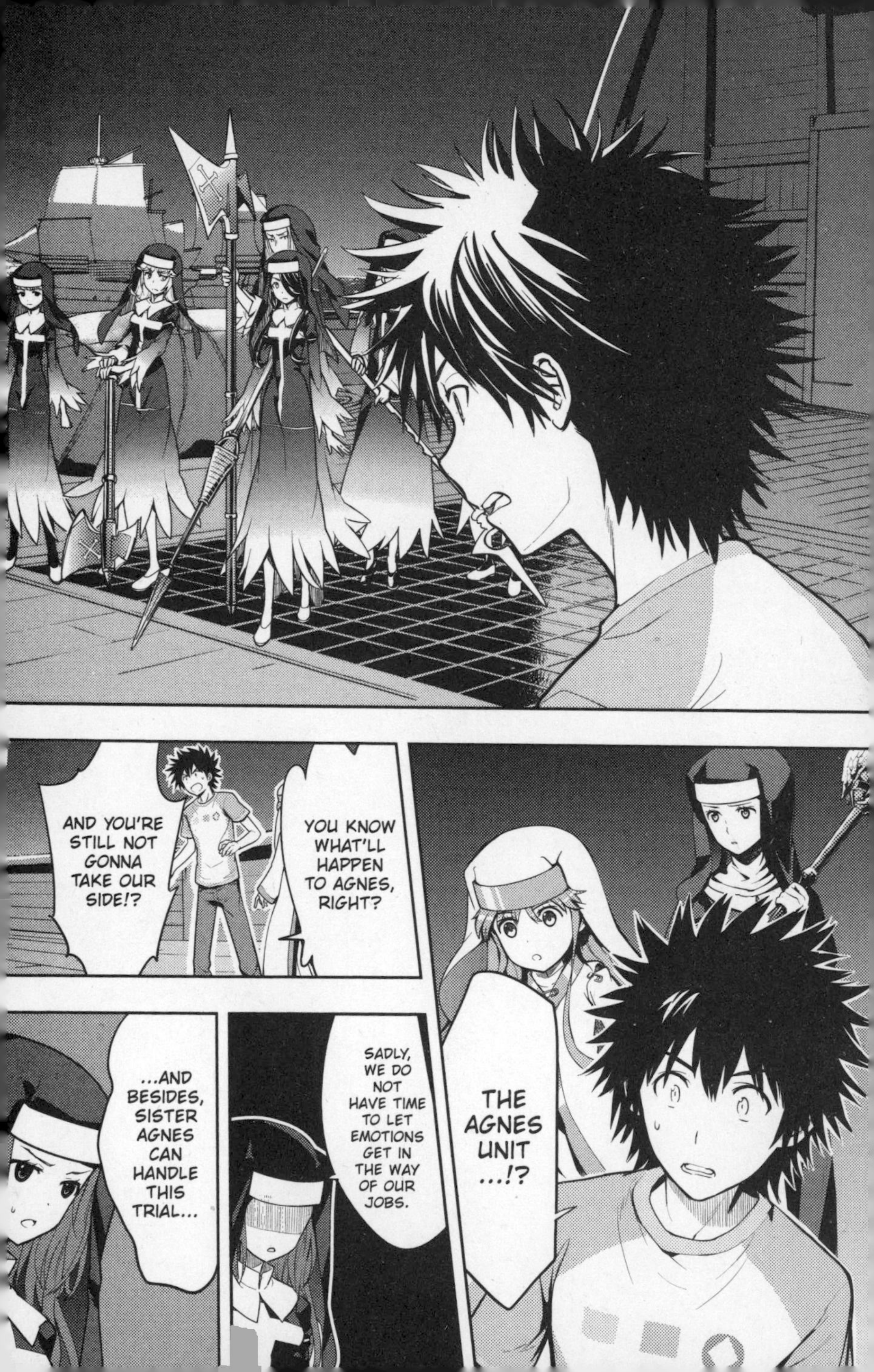
THE AGNES UNIT ...!?
YOU KNOW WHAT'LL HAPPEN TO AGNES, RIGHT?
AND YOU'RE STILL NOT GONNA TAKE OUR SIDE!?
SADLY, WE DO NOT HAVE TIME TO LET EMOTIONS GET IN THE WAY OF OUR JOBS.
...AND BESIDES, SISTER AGNES CAN HANDLE THIS TRIAL...

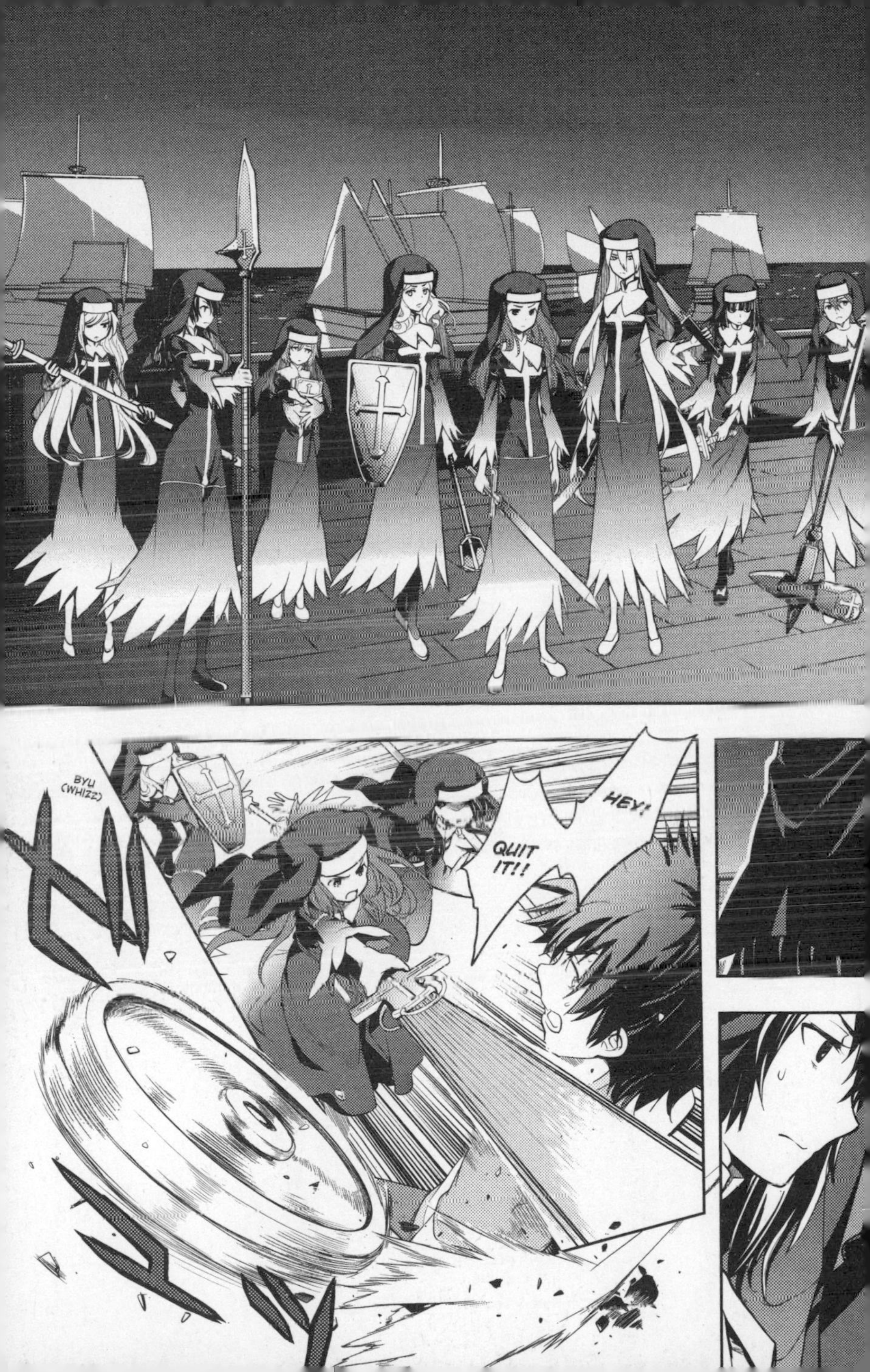
HEY!
QUIT IT!!
BYU (WHIZZ)

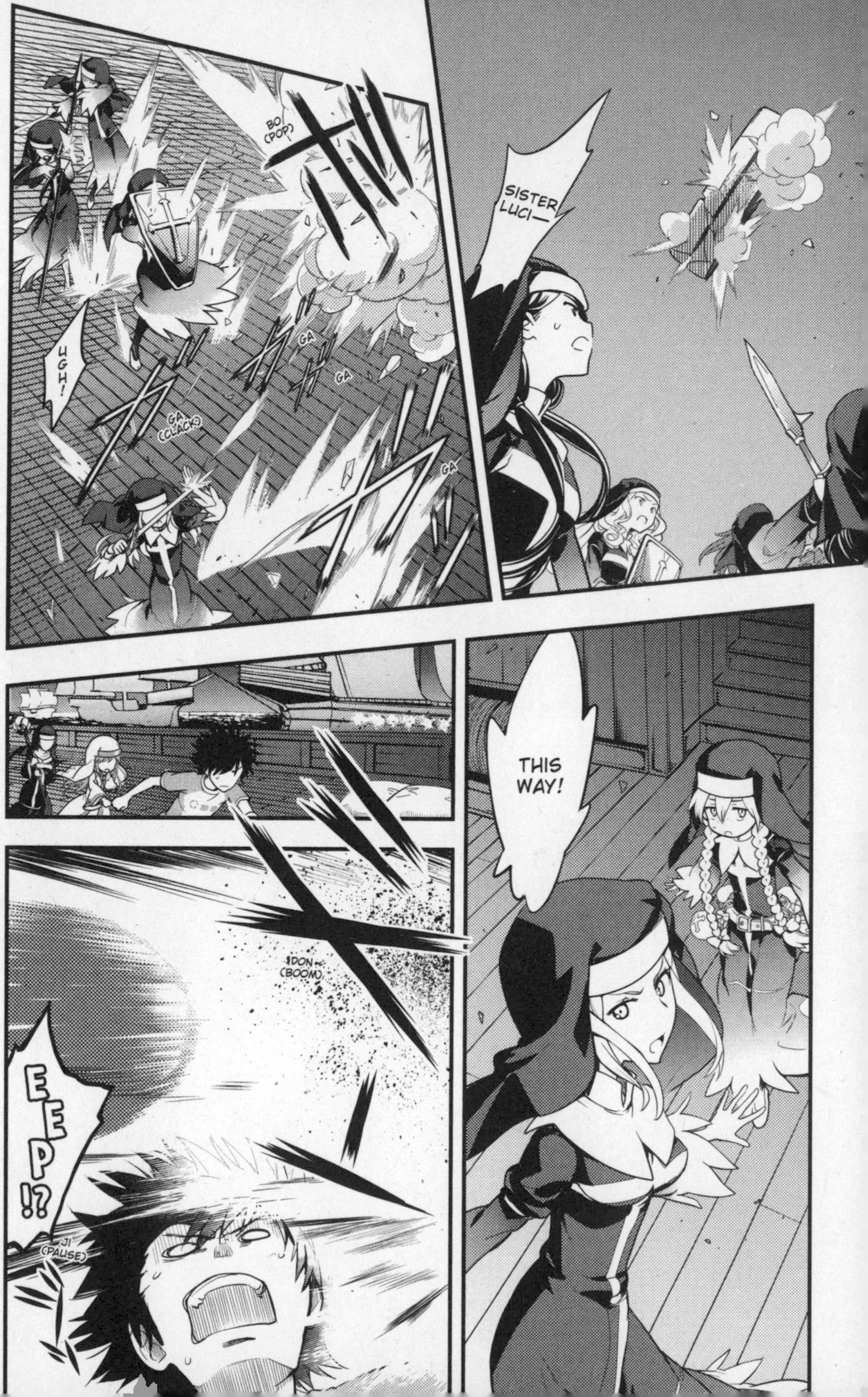
SISTER LUCI—
BO (POP)
UGH!
GA
GA
GA (CLACK)
GA
THIS WAY!
DON (BOOM)
EEP!?
JI (PAUSE)

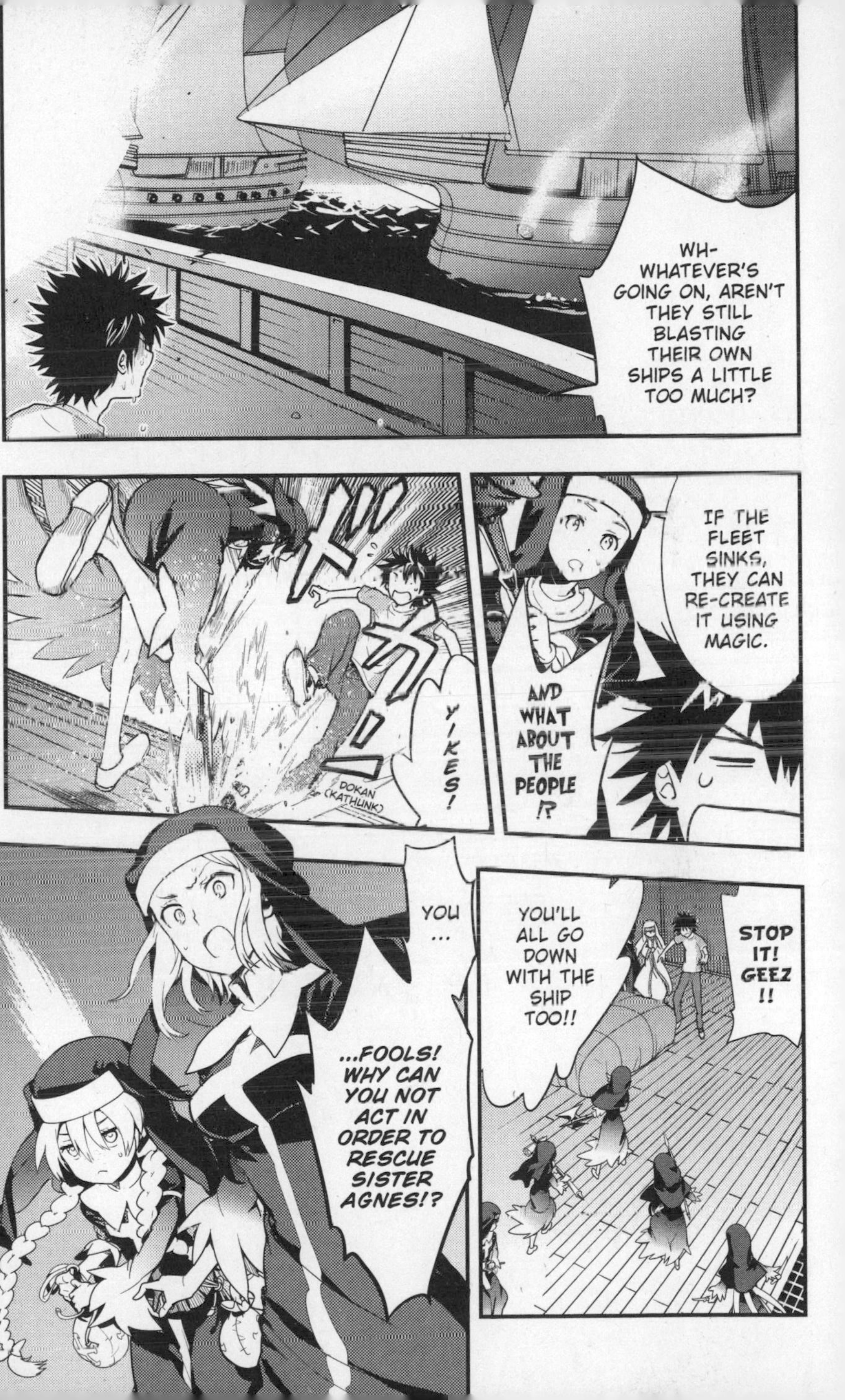
WH-WHATEVER'S GOING ON, AREN'T THEY STILL BLASTING THEIR OWN SHIPS A LITTLE TOO MUCH?
IF THE FLEET SINKS, THEY CAN RE-CREATE IT USING MAGIC.
AND WHAT ABOUT THE PEOPLE!?
YIKES!
DOKAN (KATHUNK)
STOP IT! GEEZ!!
YOU'LL ALL GO DOWN WITH THE SHIP TOO!!
YOU ...
...FOOLS! WHY CAN YOU NOT ACT IN ORDER TO RESCUE SISTER AGNES!?

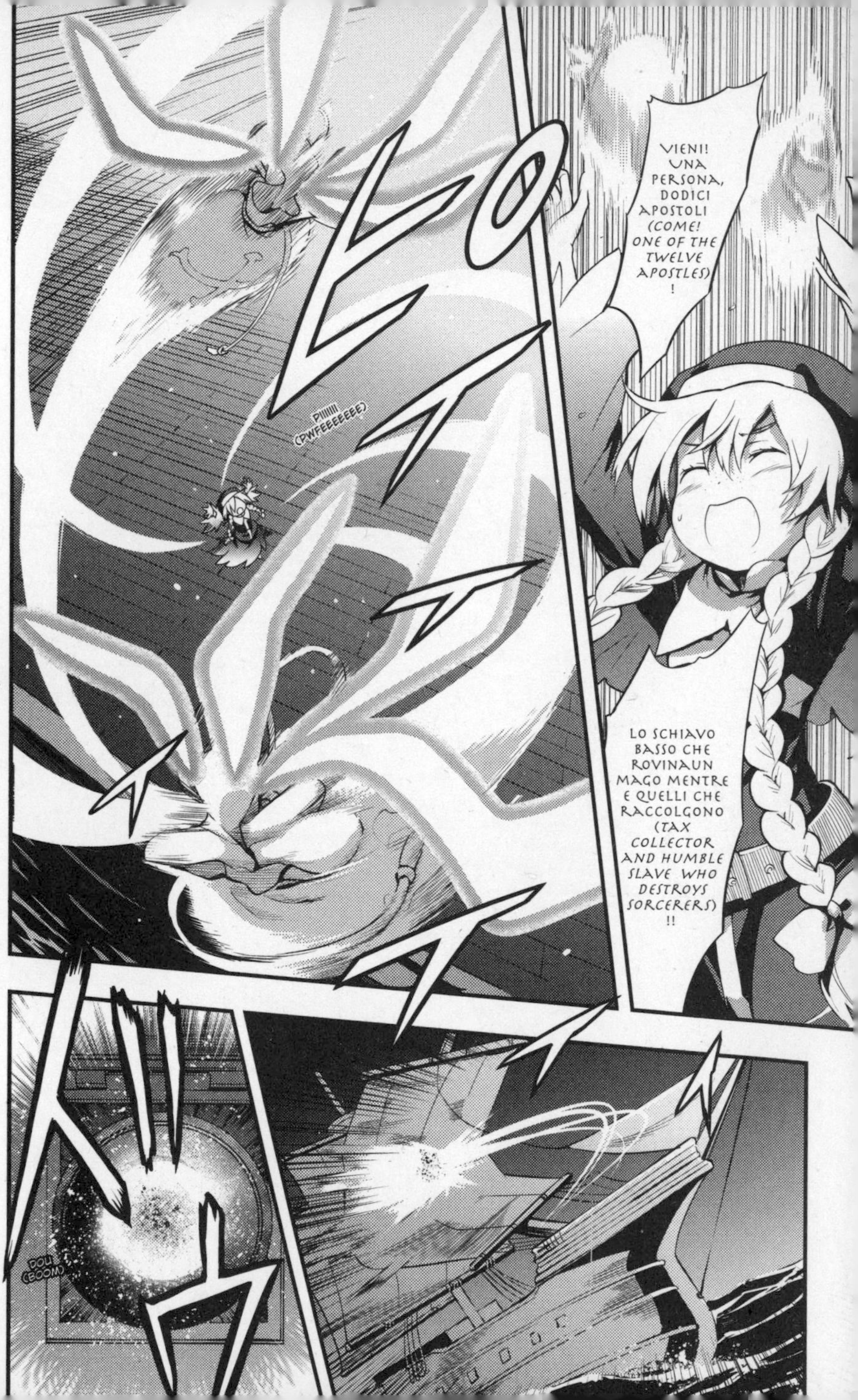
VIENI! UNA PERSONA, DODICI APOSTOLI (COME! ONE OF THE TWELVE APOSTLES) !
LO SCHIAVO BASSO CHE ROVINAUN MAGO MENTRE E QUELLI CHE RACCOLGONO (TAX COLLECTOR AND HUMBLE SLAVE WHO DESTROYS SORCERERS) !!
PIIIIIII (PWFEEEEEEEE)
DOU (BOOM)

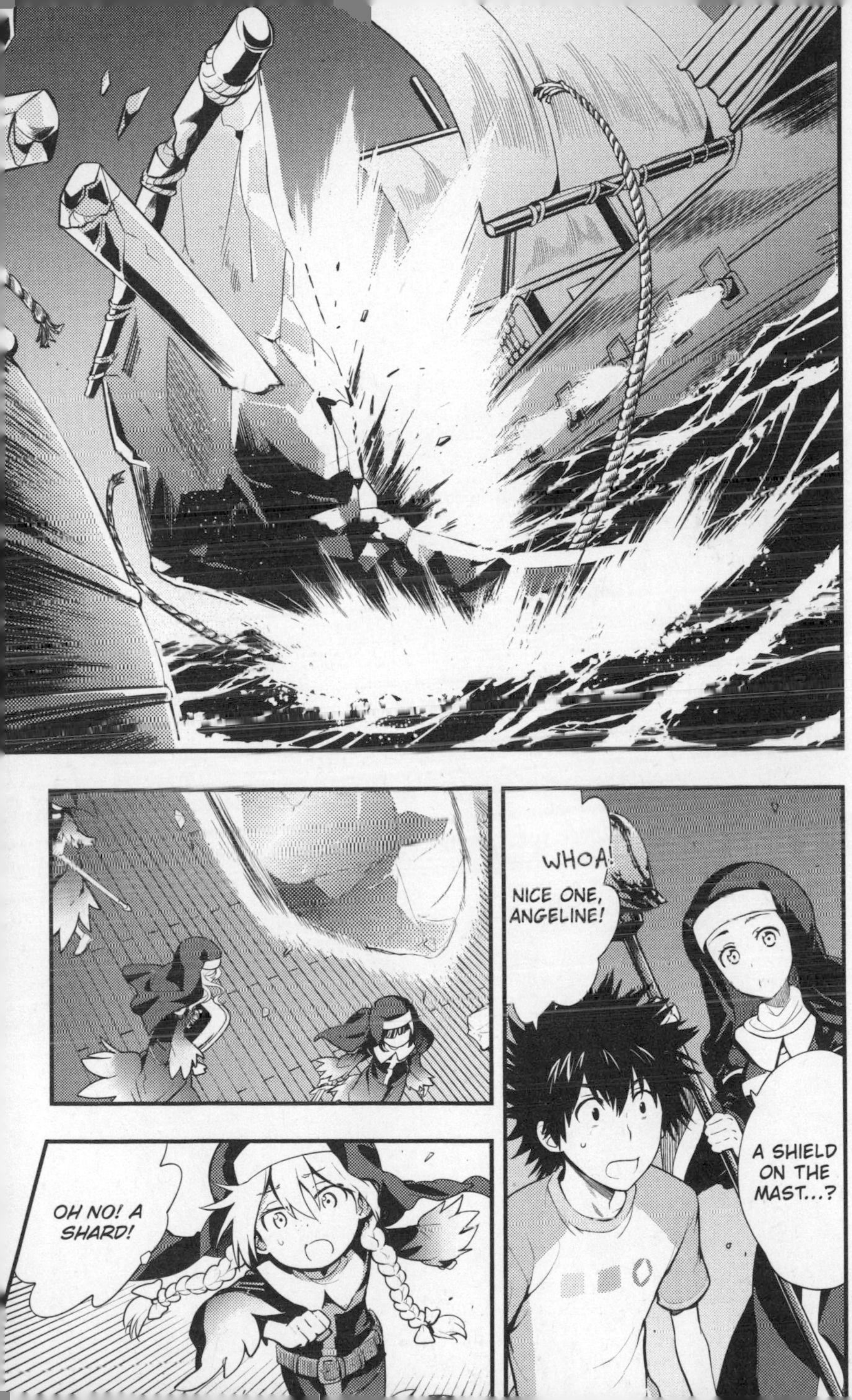
WHOA!
NICE ONE, ANGELINE!
A SHIELD ON THE MAST...?
OH NO! A SHARD!

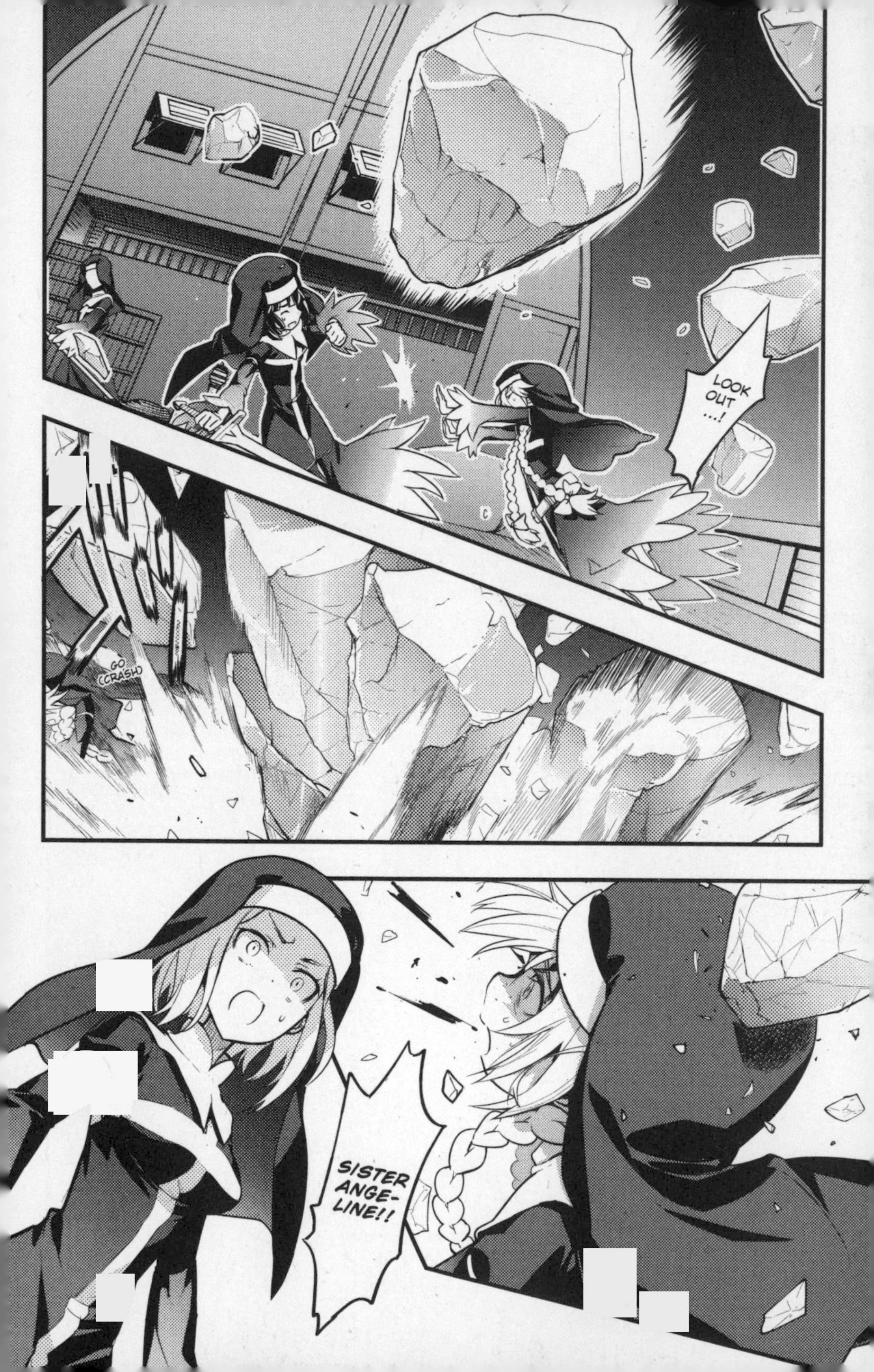
LOOK OUT ...!
GO (CRASH)
SISTER ANGE-LINE!!

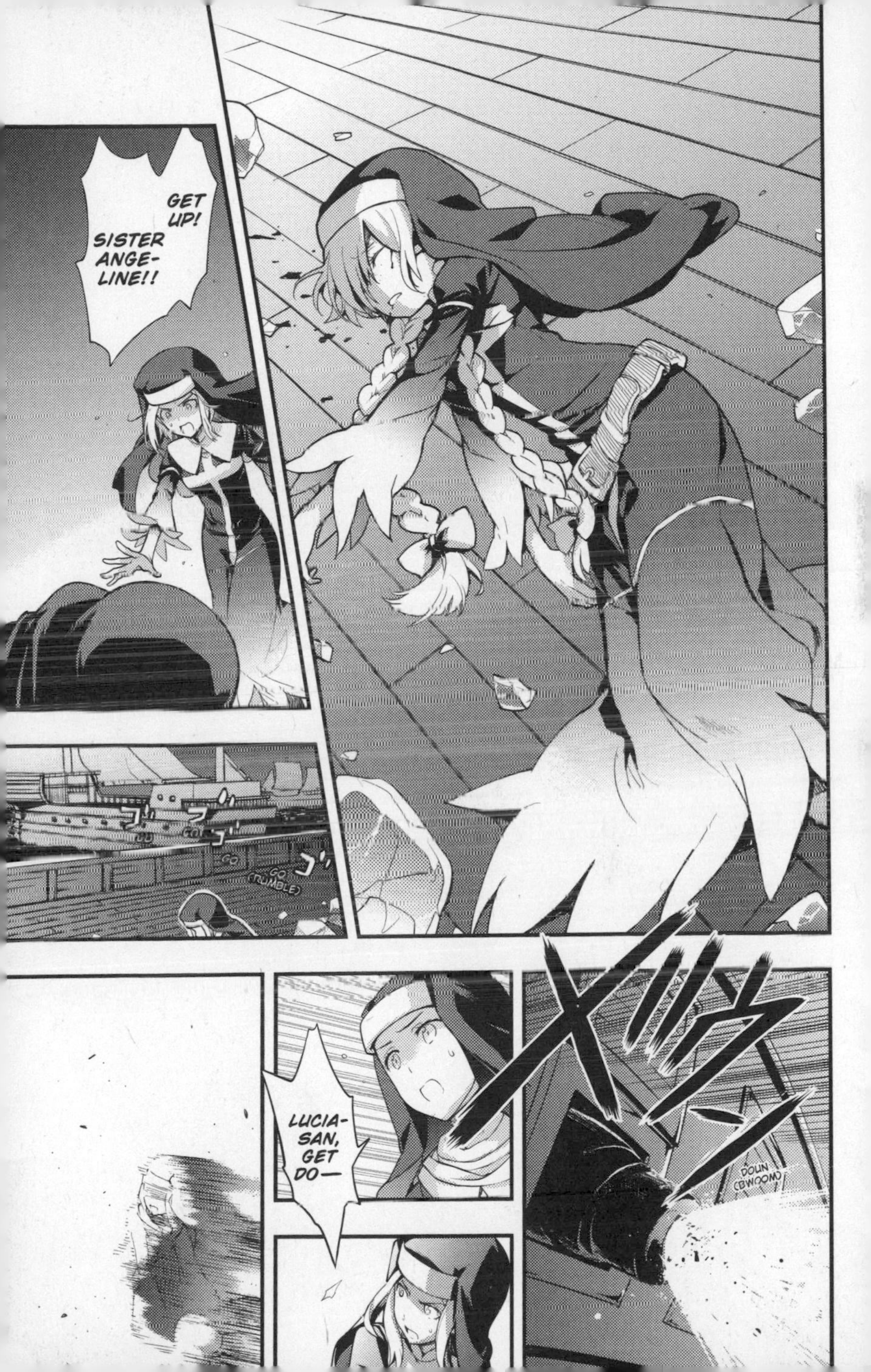
GET UP! SISTER ANGE-LINE!!
GO
GO (RUMBLE)
DOWN (BWOOM)
LUCIA-SAN, GET DO—

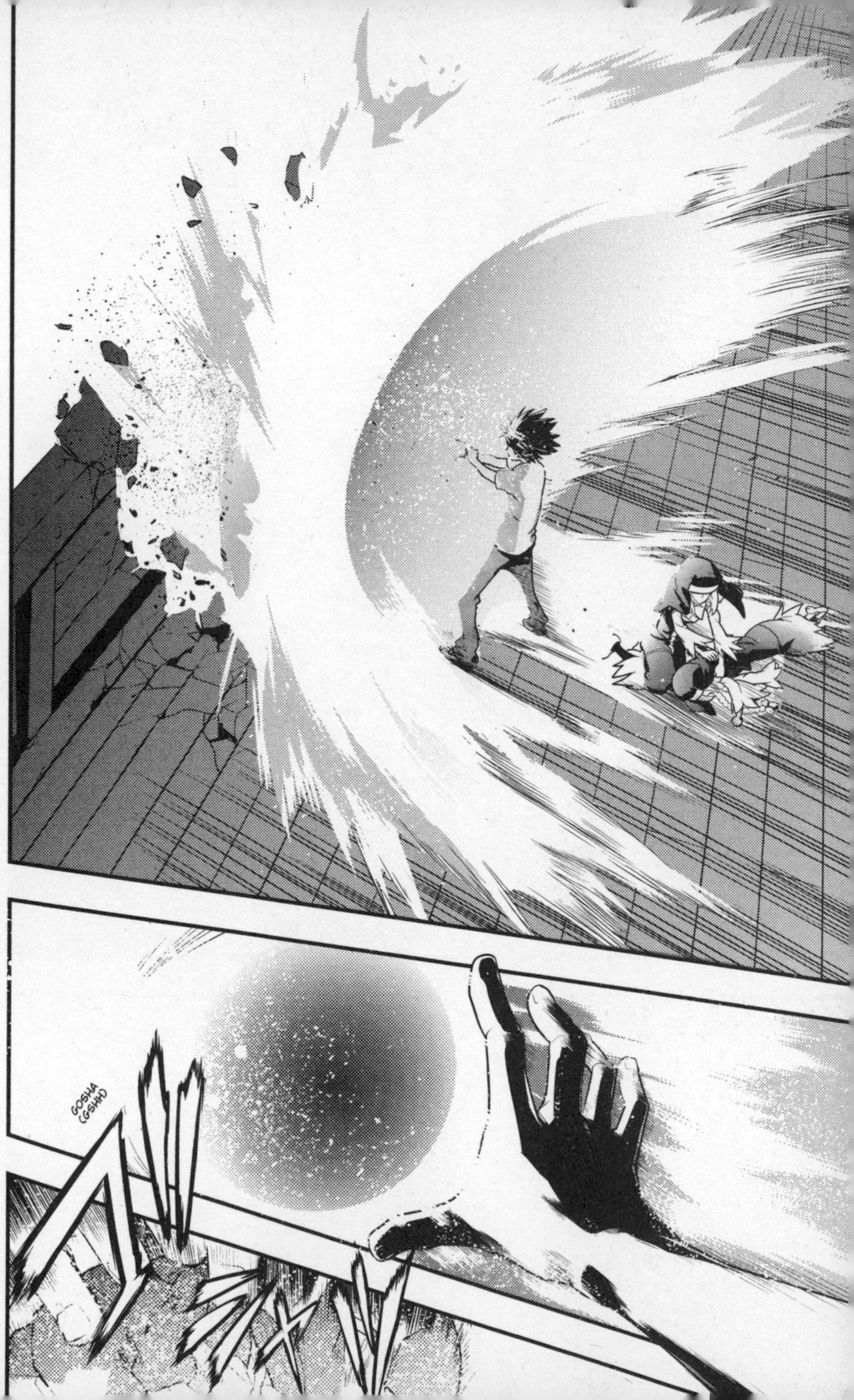
GOSHA
(GSHH)

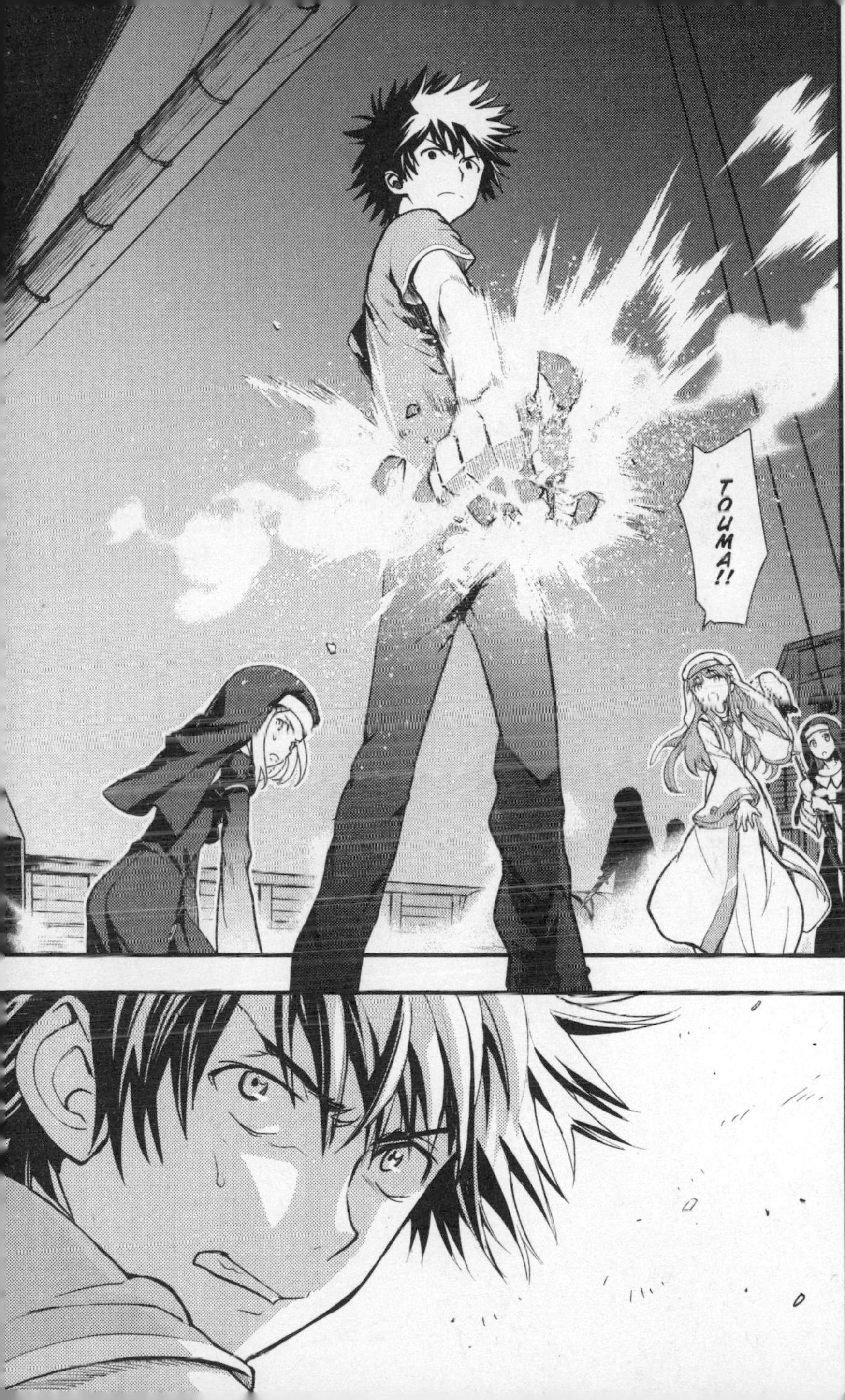
TOUMA!!

A Certain Magical Index

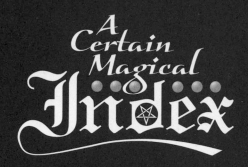

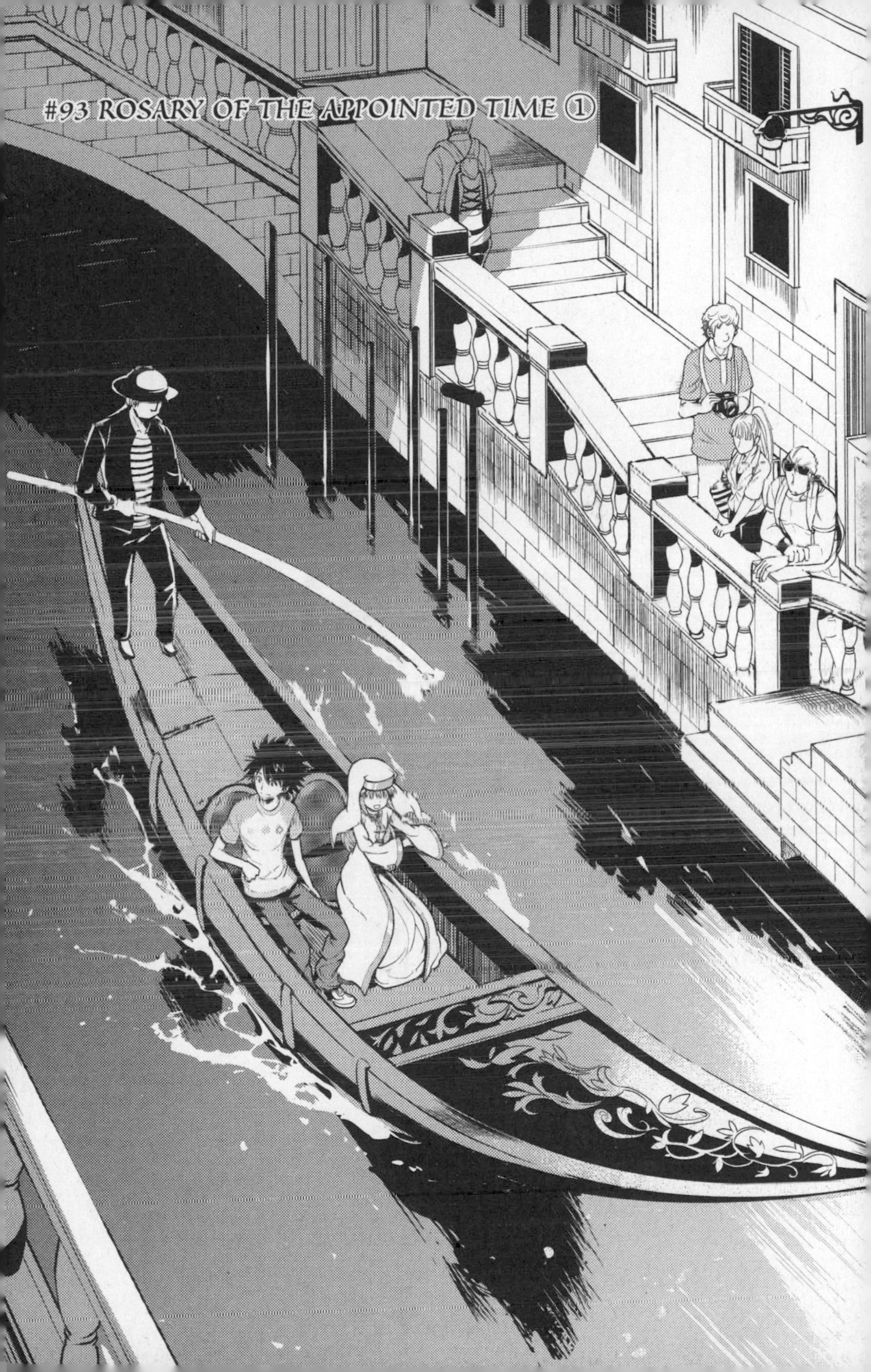
#93 ROSARY OF THE APPOINTED TIME ①

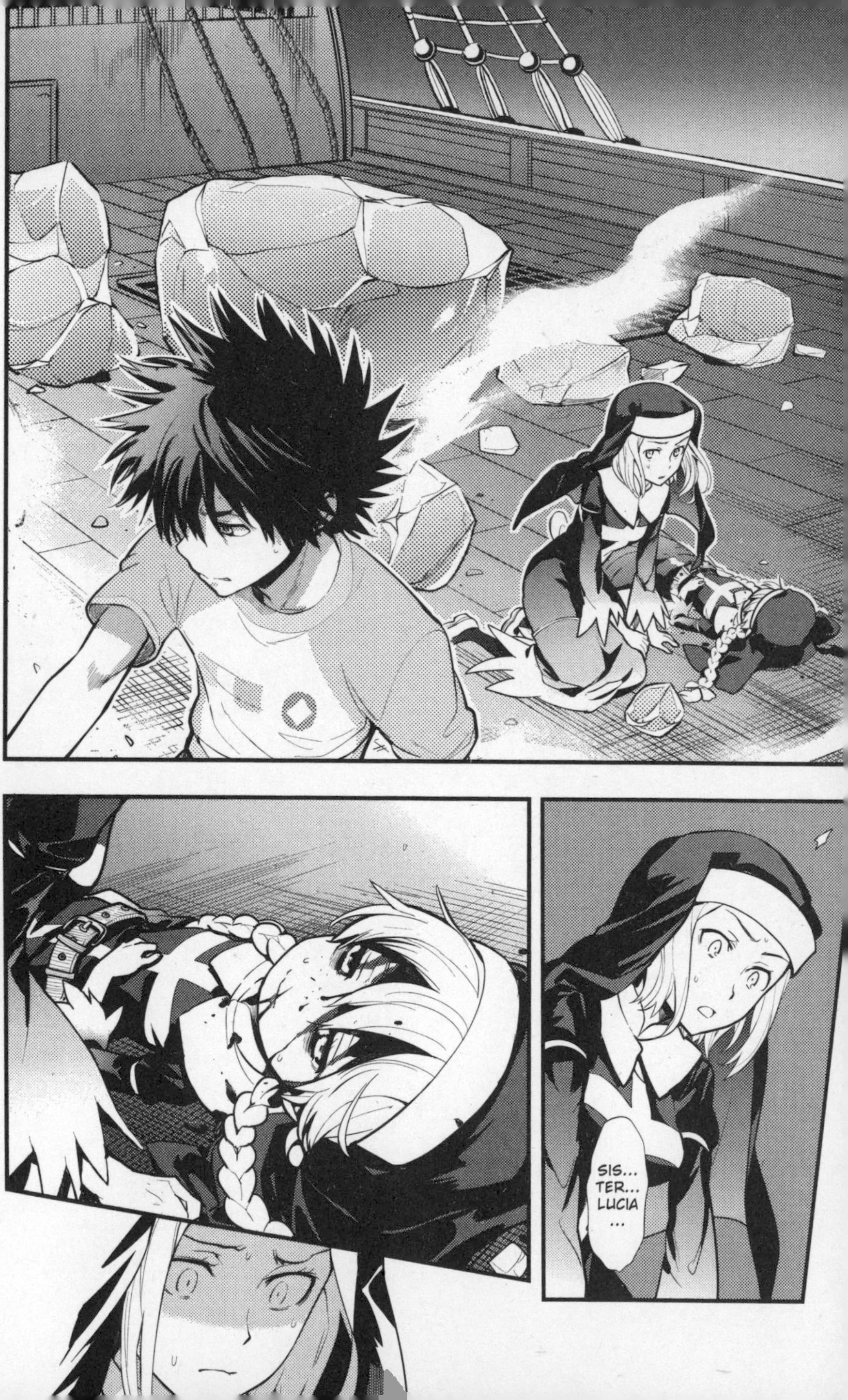
SIS... TER... LUCIA ...

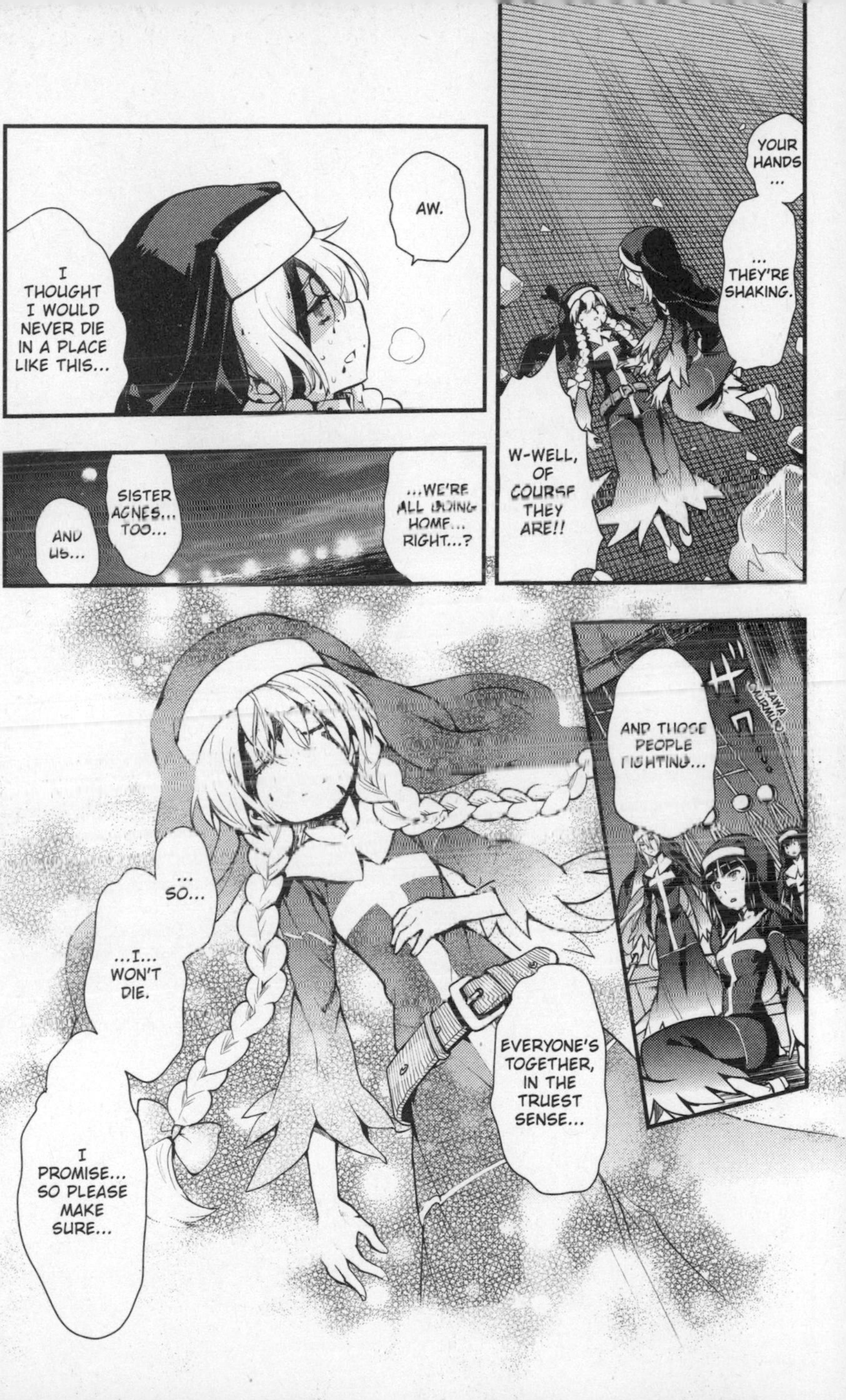
YOUR HANDS ...
... THEY'RE SHAKING.
W-WELL, OF COURSE THEY ARE!!
AW.
I THOUGHT I WOULD NEVER DIE IN A PLACE LIKE THIS...
...WE'RE ALL GOING HOME... RIGHT...?
SISTER AGNES... TOO...
AND US...
AND THOSE PEOPLE FIGHTING...
ZAWA MURMUR
EVERYONE'S TOGETHER, IN THE TRUEST SENSE...
... SO...
...I... WON'T DIE.
I PROMISE... SO PLEASE MAKE SURE...

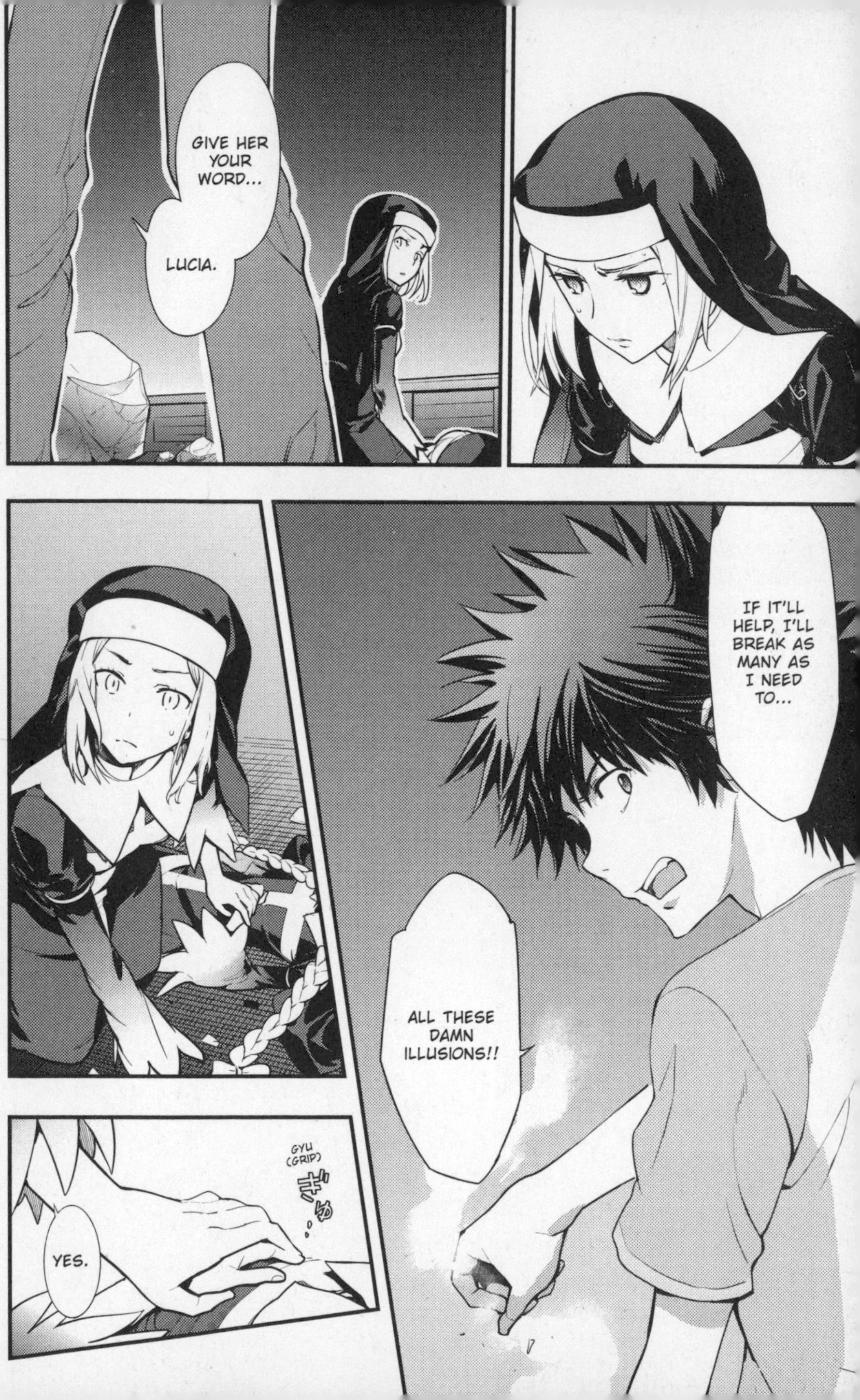
GIVE HER YOUR WORD...
LUCIA.
IF IT'LL HELP, I'LL BREAK AS MANY AS I NEED TO...
ALL THESE DAMN ILLUSIONS!!
GYU (GRIP)
ぎゅ
YES.

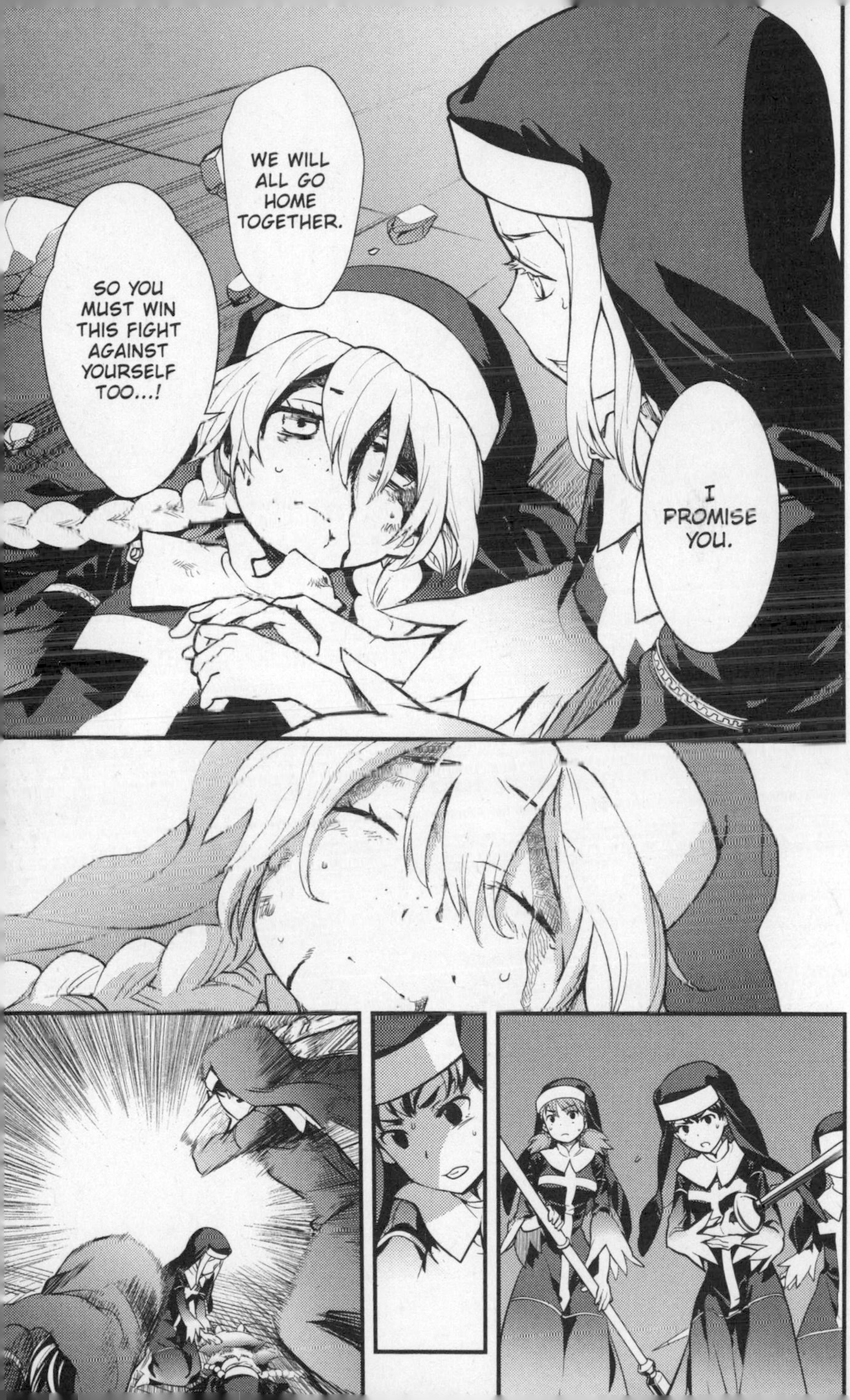
I PROMISE YOU.
WE WILL ALL GO HOME TOGETHER.
SO YOU MUST WIN THIS FIGHT AGAINST YOURSELF TOO...!

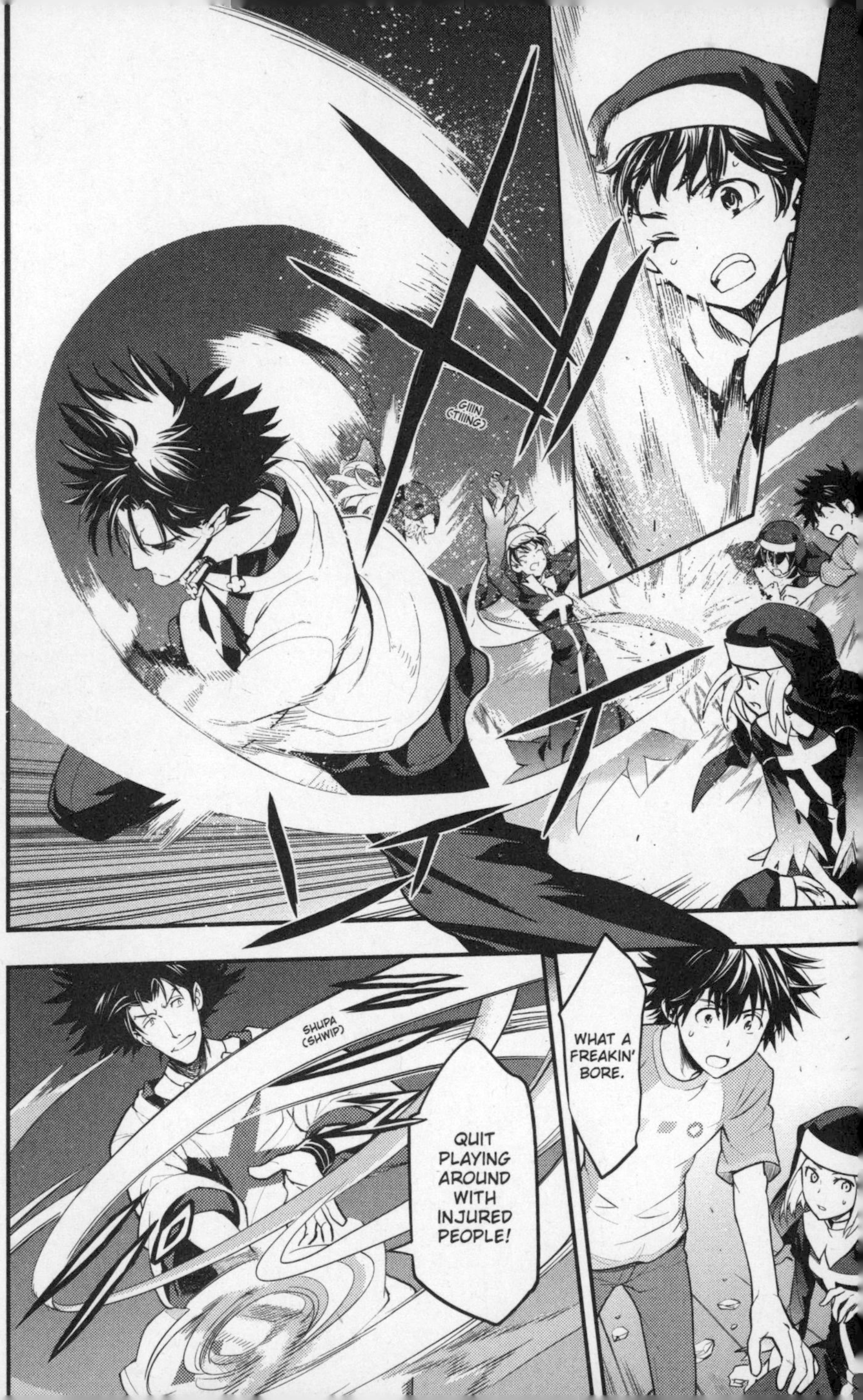
GIIIN (TIIING)
WHAT A FREAKIN' BORE.
QUIT PLAYING AROUND WITH INJURED PEOPLE!
SHUPA (SHWIP)

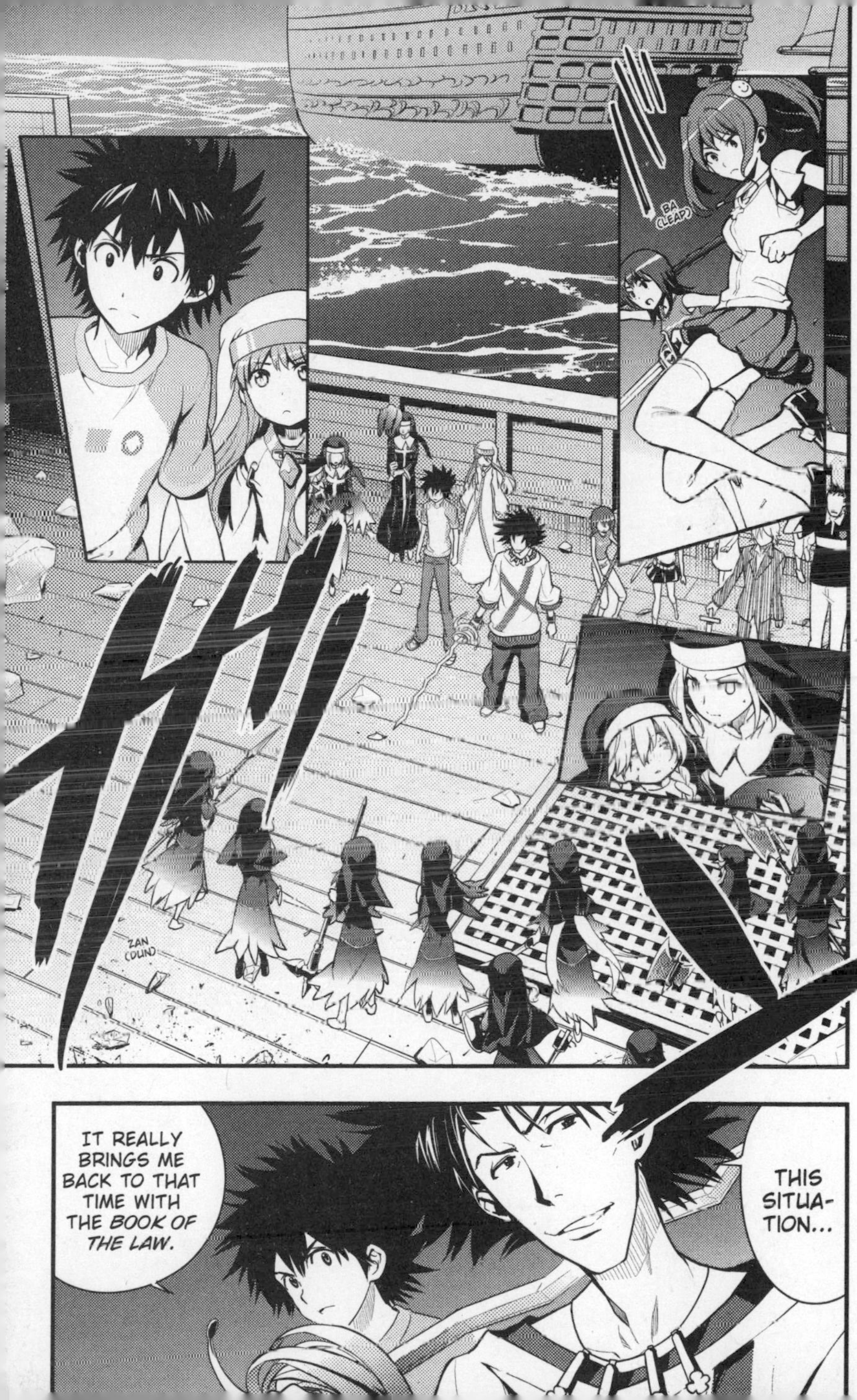
BA (LEAP)
ZAN (DUN)
THIS SITUATION...
IT REALLY BRINGS ME BACK TO THAT TIME WITH THE *BOOK OF THE LAW*.

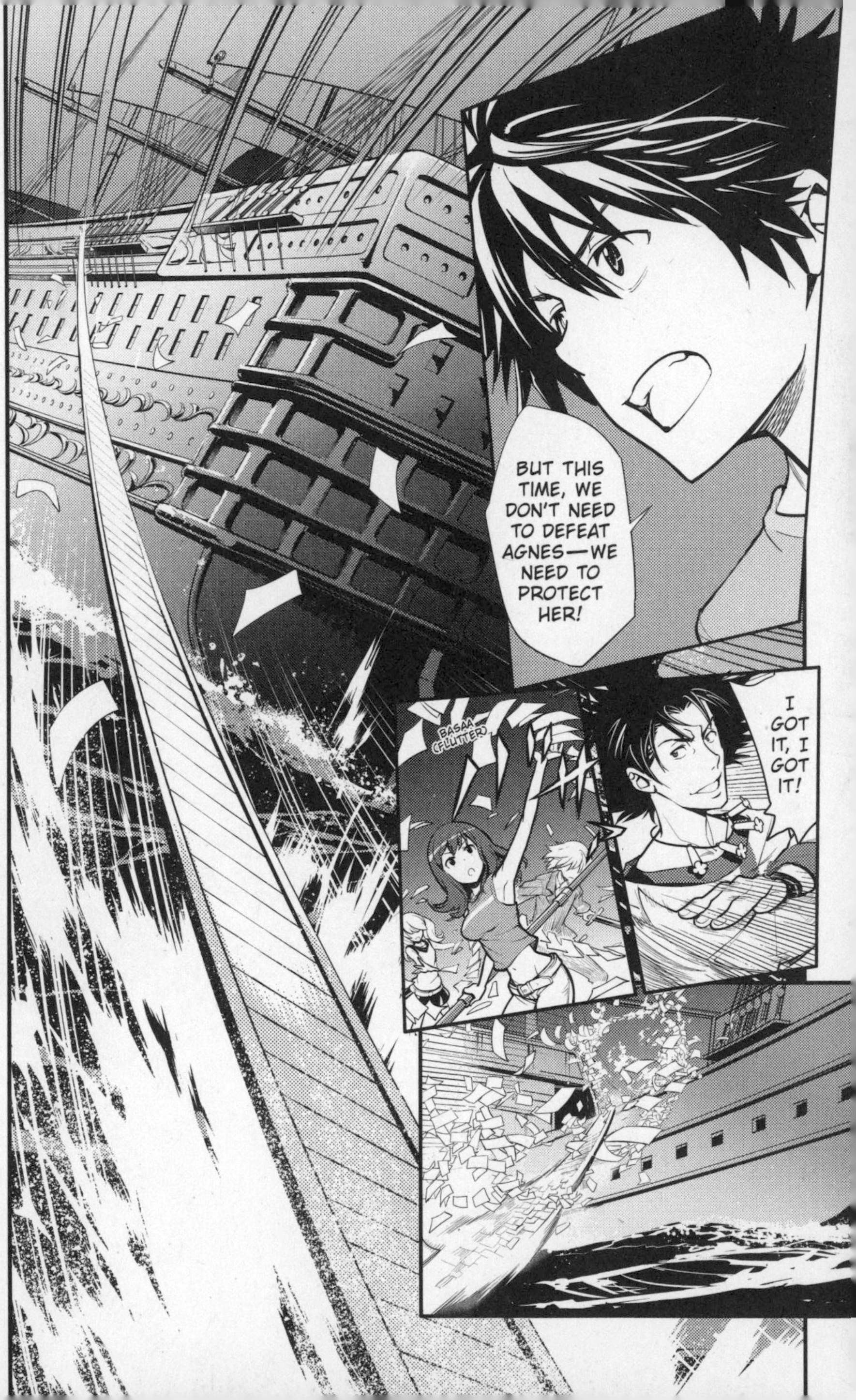
BUT THIS TIME, WE DON'T NEED TO DEFEAT AGNES—WE NEED TO PROTECT HER!
I GOT IT, I GOT IT!
BASAA (FLUTTER)

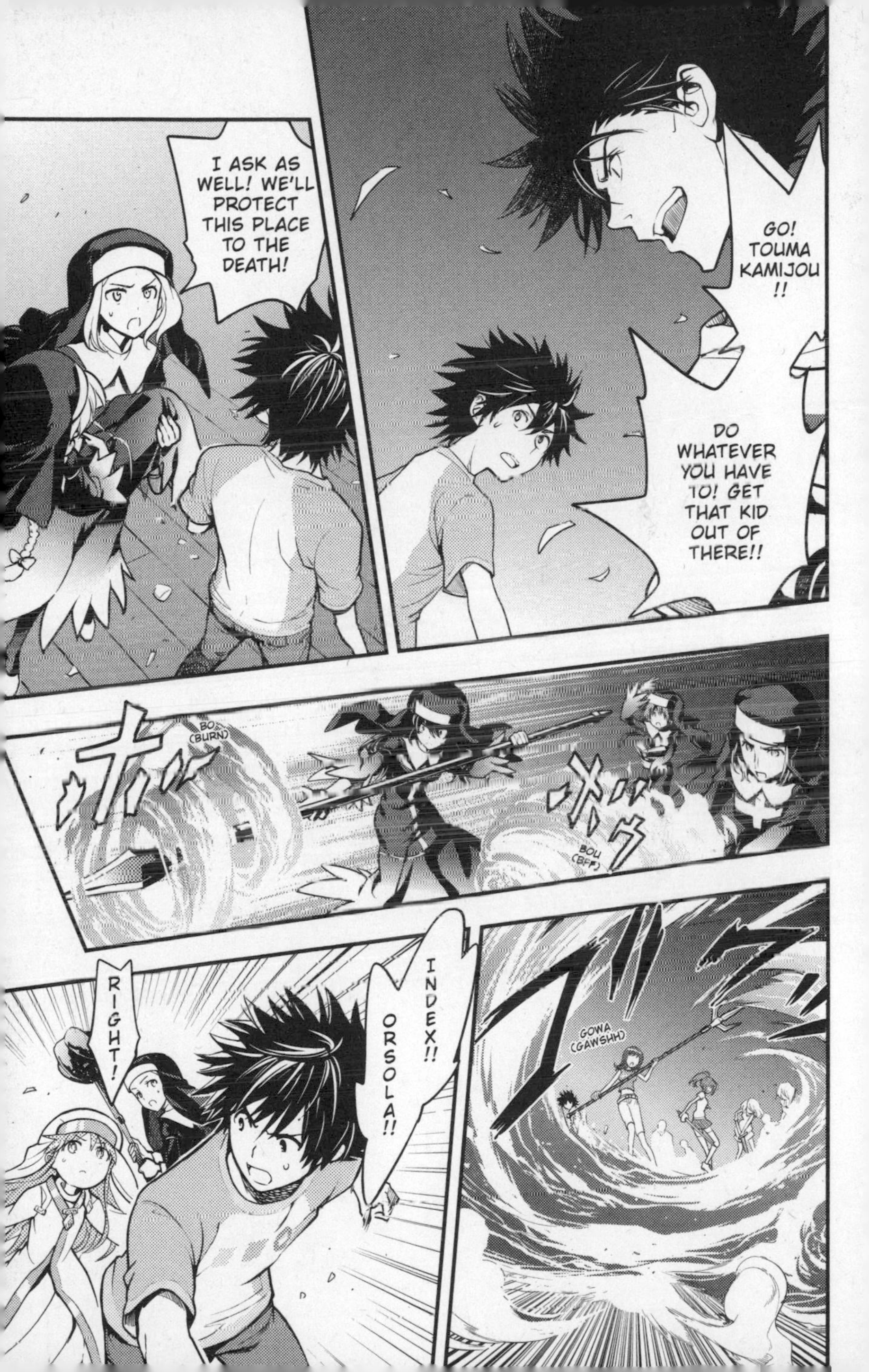
GO! TOUMA KAMIJOU!!
DO WHATEVER YOU HAVE TO! GET THAT KID OUT OF THERE!!
I ASK AS WELL! WE'LL PROTECT THIS PLACE TO THE DEATH!
BOU (BFF)
BO (BURN)
GOWA (GAWSHH)
INDEX!! ORSOLA!!
RIGHT!

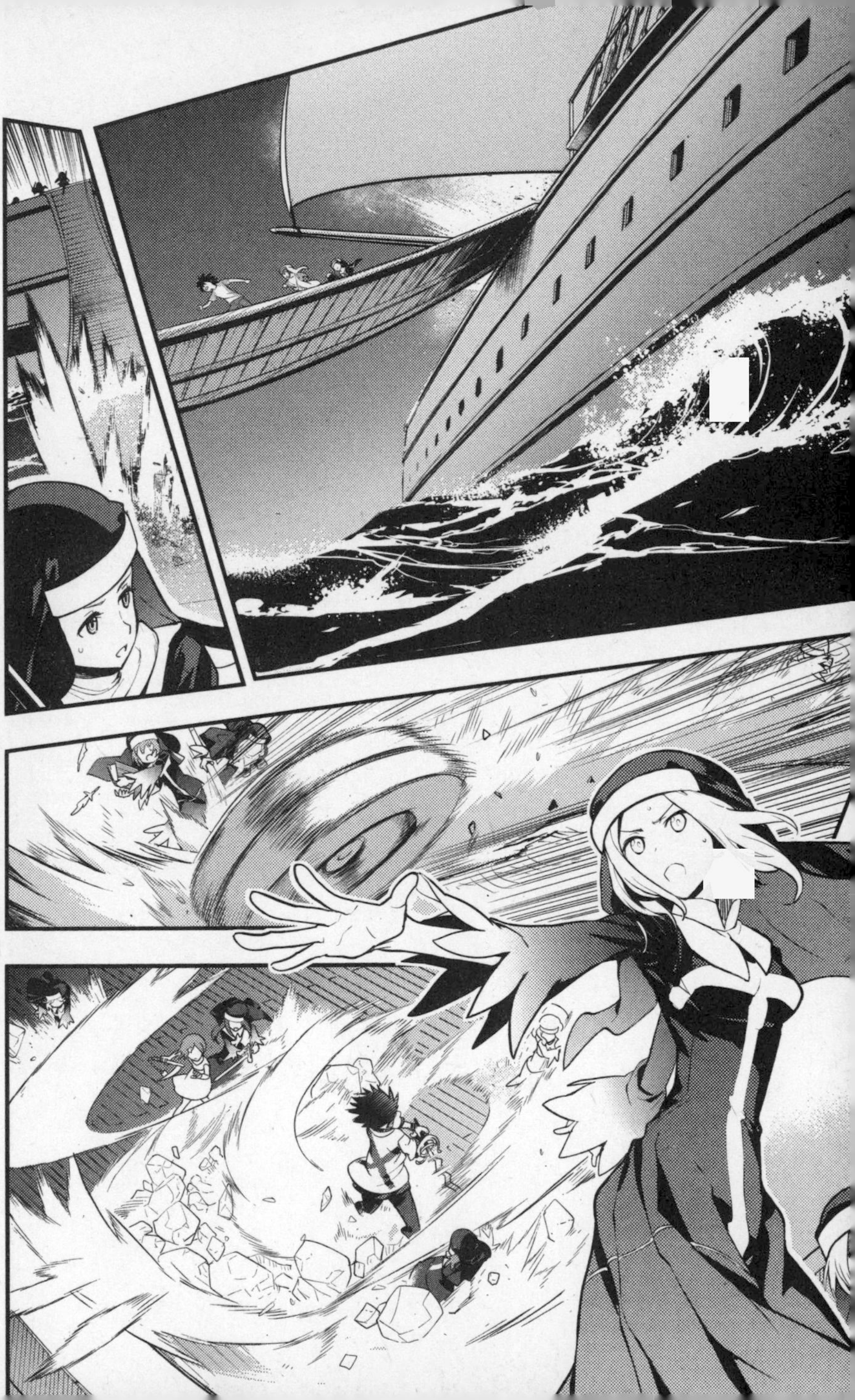

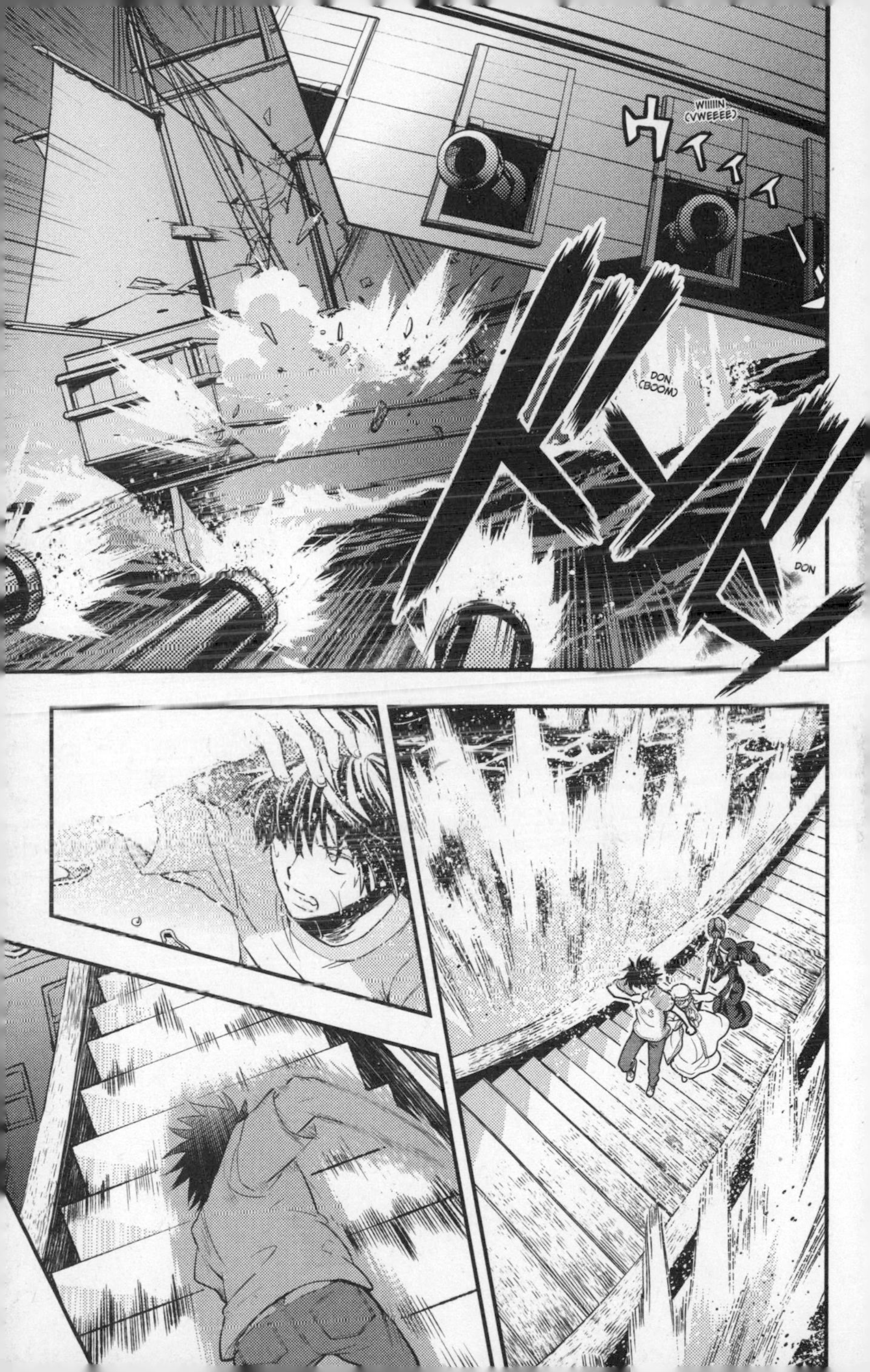
WIIIIN
(VWEEEE)
DON
(BOOM)
DON

GOOON
(GROAN)

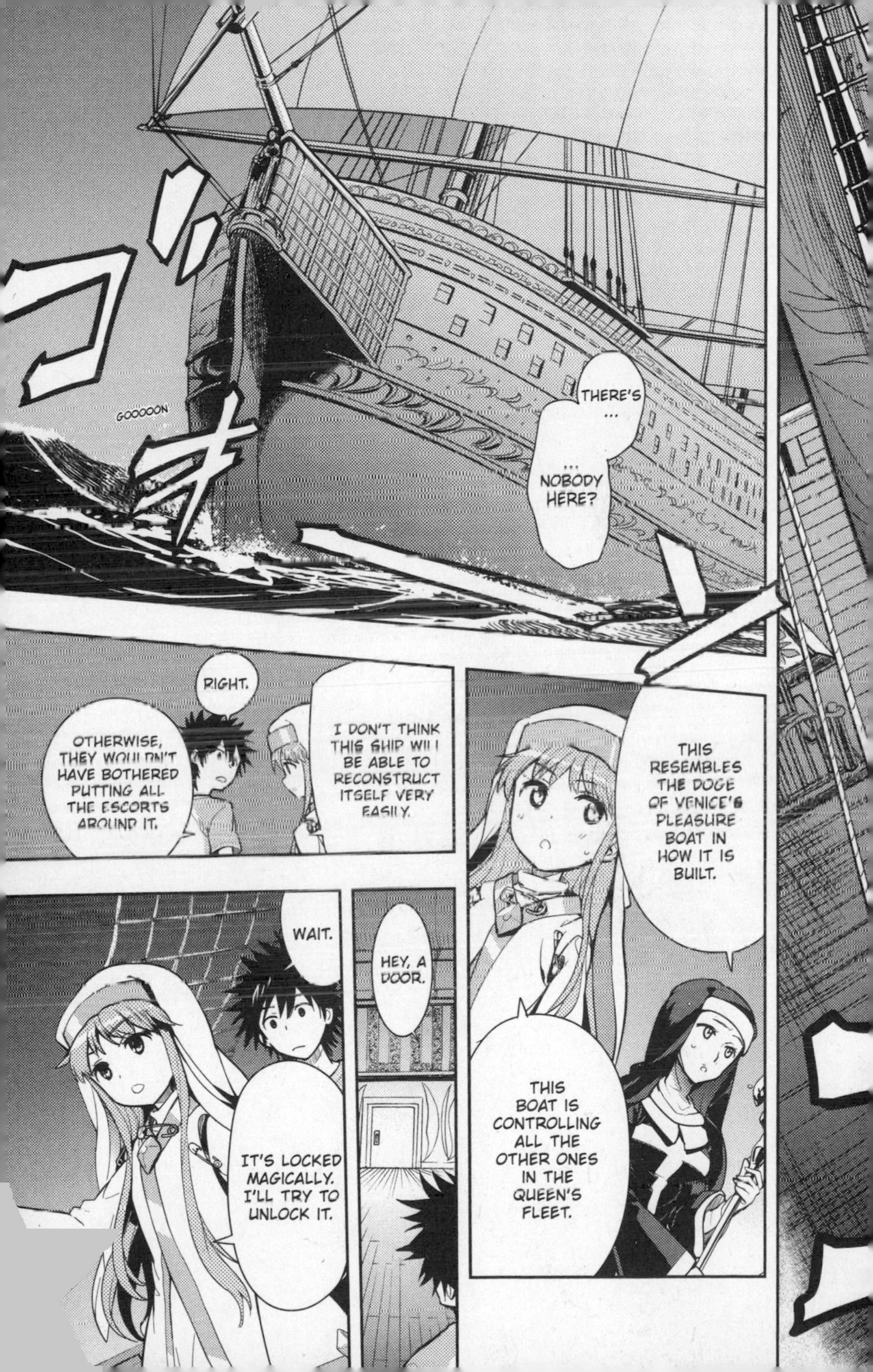
GOOOOON
THERE'S ...
... NOBODY HERE?
THIS RESEMBLES THE DOGE OF VENICE'S PLEASURE BOAT IN HOW IT IS BUILT.
THIS BOAT IS CONTROLLING ALL THE OTHER ONES IN THE QUEEN'S FLEET.
I DON'T THINK THIS SHIP WILL BE ABLE TO RECONSTRUCT ITSELF VERY EASILY.
RIGHT.
OTHERWISE, THEY WOULDN'T HAVE BOTHERED PUTTING ALL THE ESCORTS AROUND IT.
HEY, A DOOR.
WAIT.
IT'S LOCKED MAGICALLY. I'LL TRY TO UNLOCK IT.

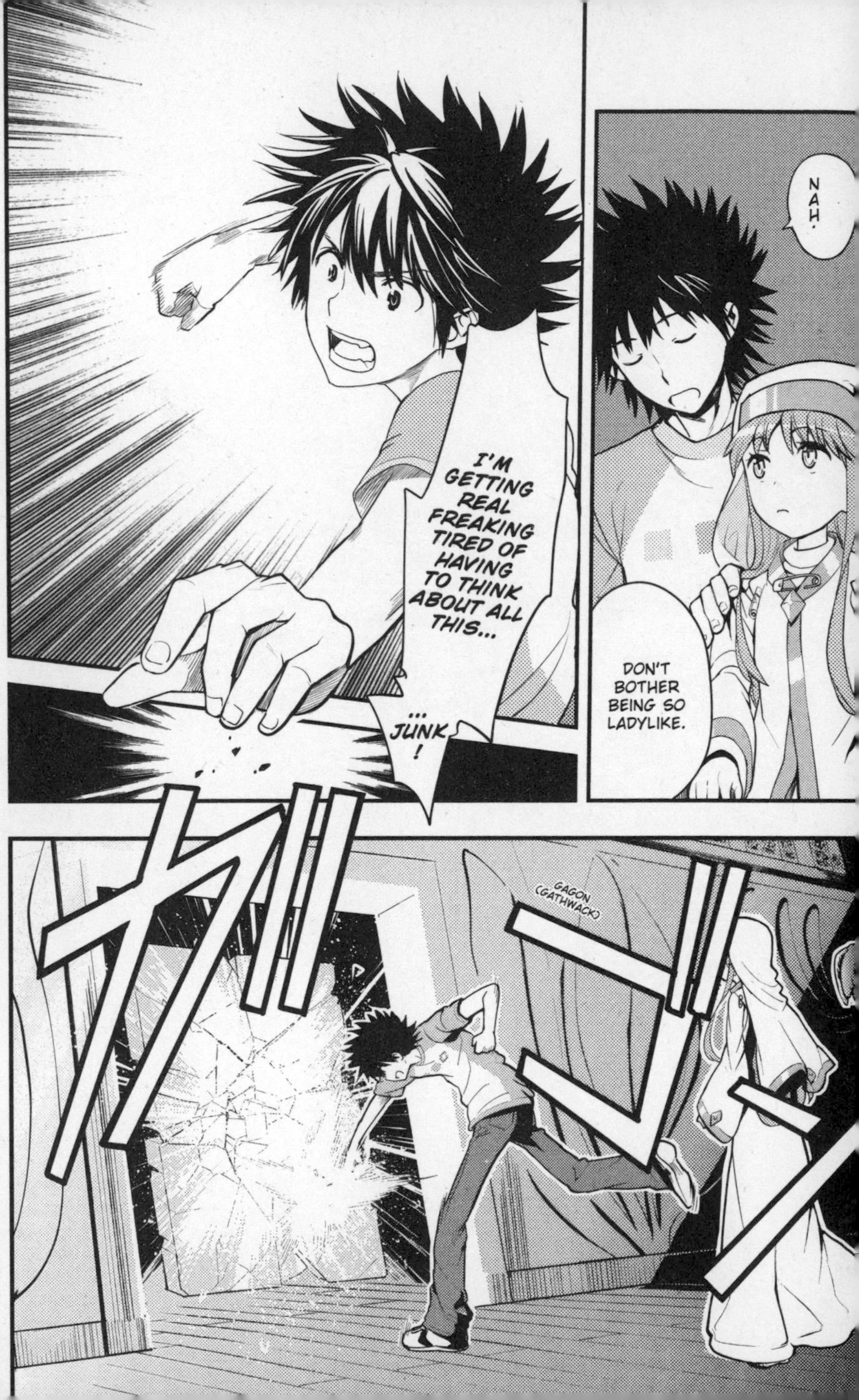
NAH.
DON'T BOTHER BEING SO LADYLIKE.
I'M GETTING REAL FREAKING TIRED OF HAVING TO THINK ABOUT ALL THIS...
...JUNK!
GAGON (GATHWACK)

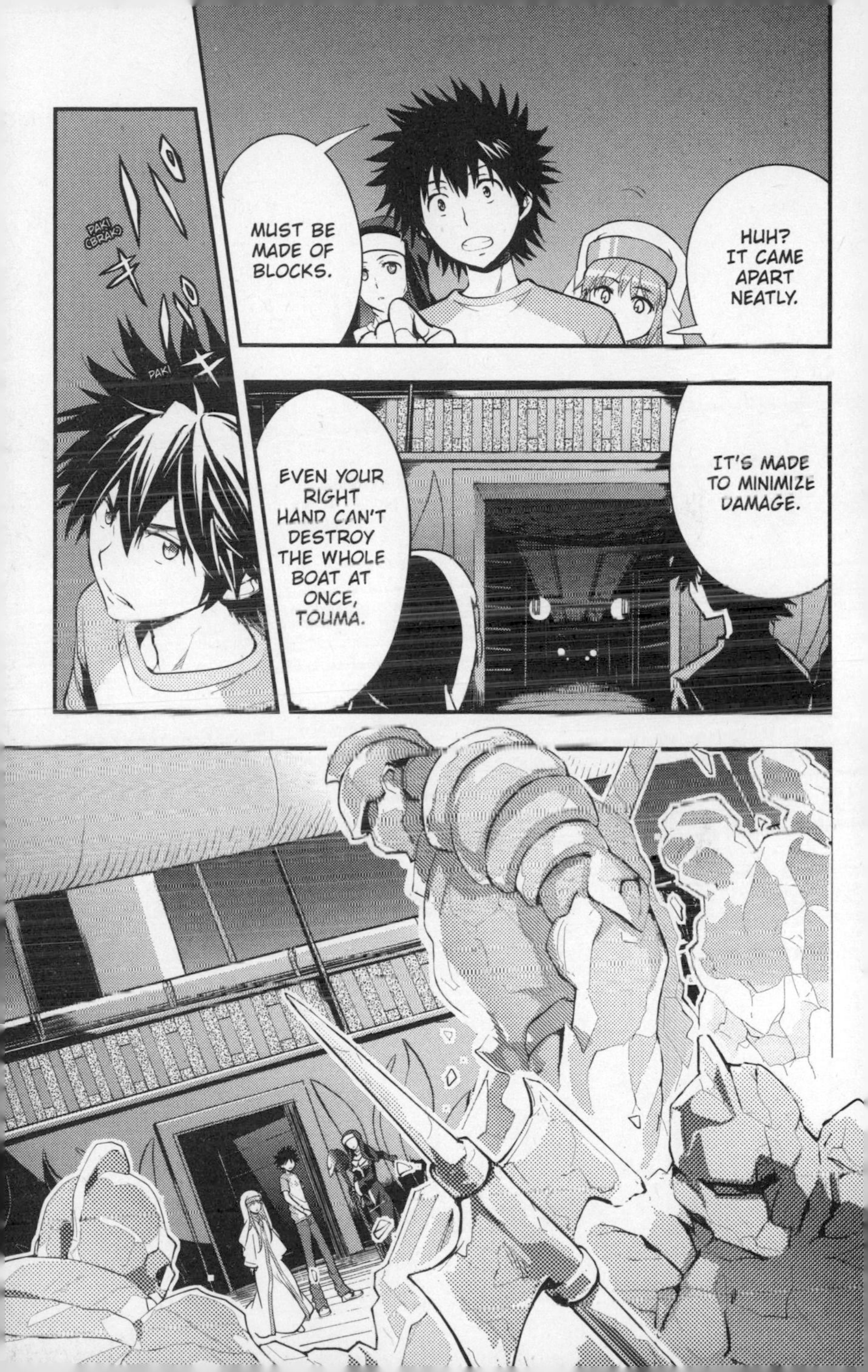
HUH? IT CAME APART NEATLY.
MUST BE MADE OF BLOCKS.
IT'S MADE TO MINIMIZE DAMAGE.
EVEN YOUR RIGHT HAND CAN'T DESTROY THE WHOLE BOAT AT ONCE, TOUMA.
PAKI (BRAK)
PAKI

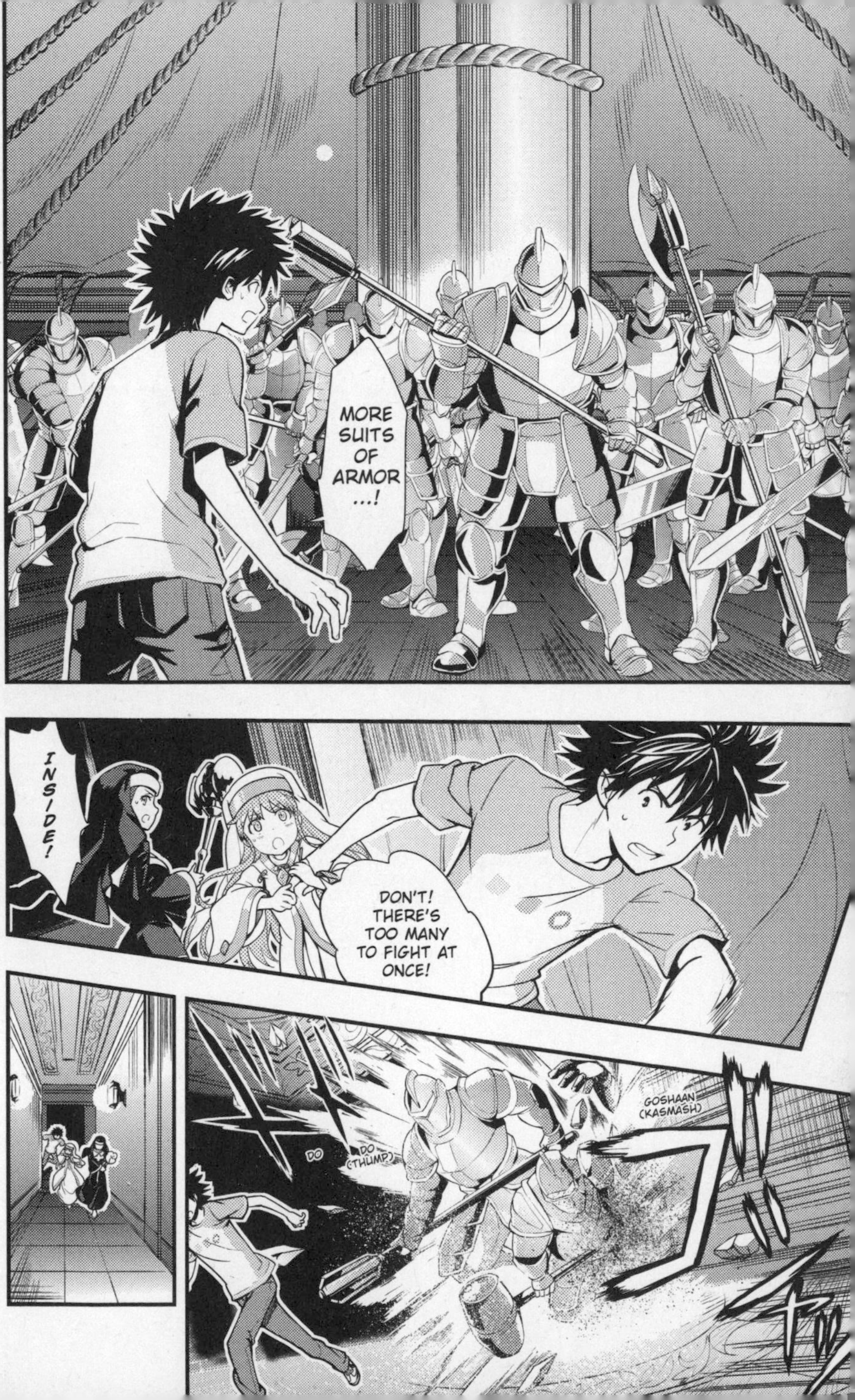
MORE SUITS OF ARMOR ...!
DON'T! THERE'S TOO MANY TO FIGHT AT ONCE!
INSIDE!
GOSHAAN (KASMASH)
DO (THUMP)
DO

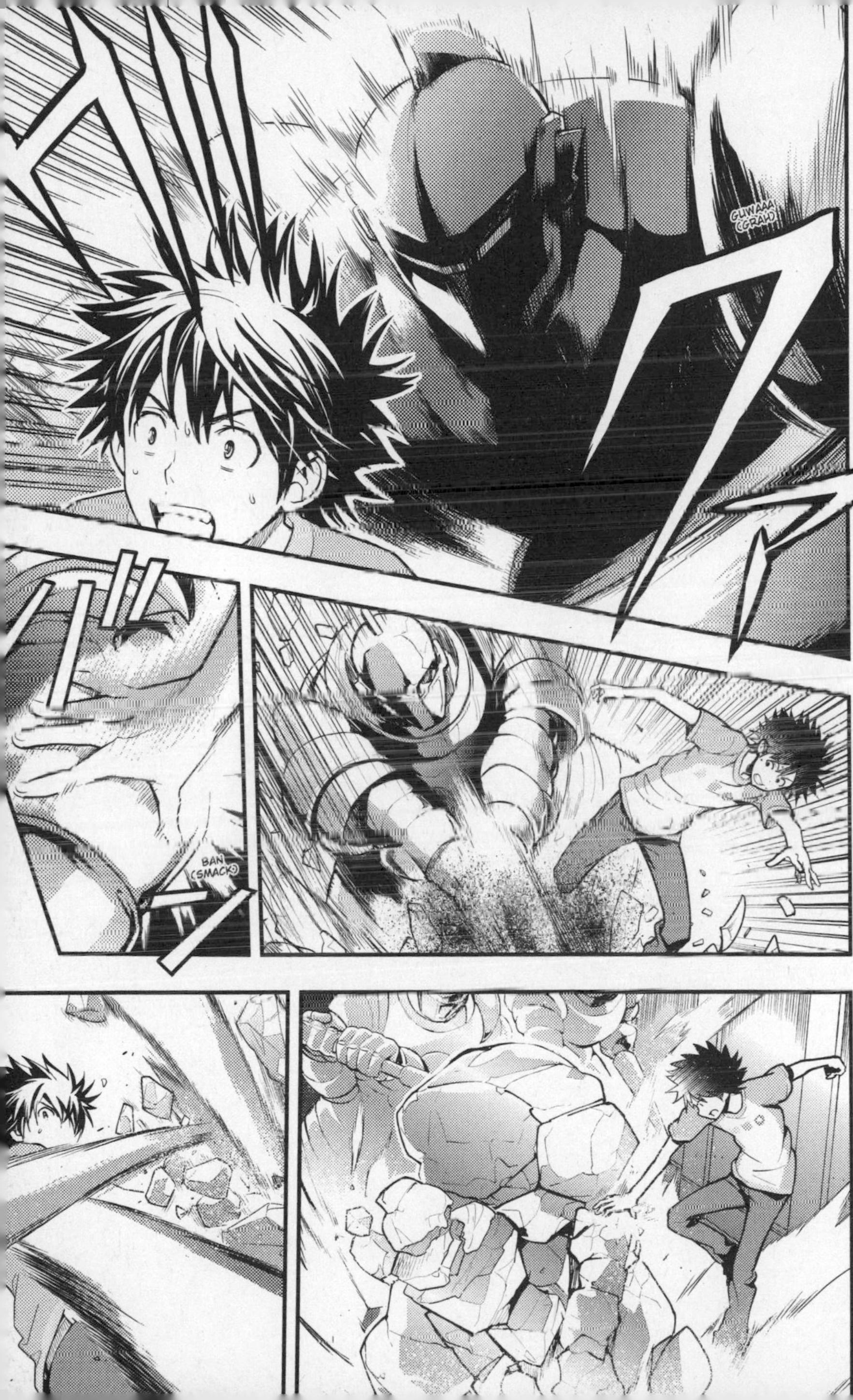
GUWAAA (GRAH)
BAN (SMACK)

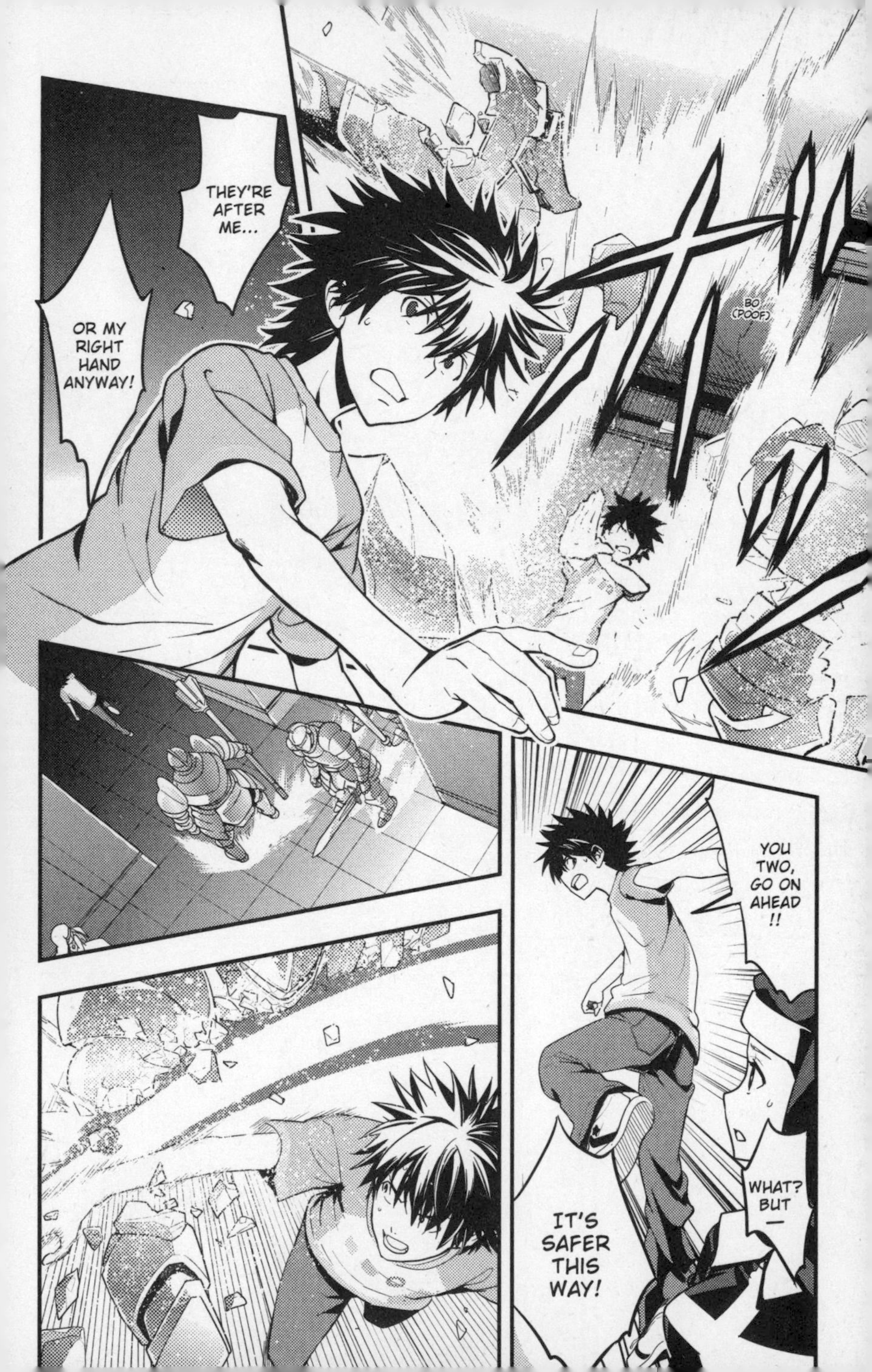
BO (POOF)
THEY'RE AFTER ME...
OR MY RIGHT HAND ANYWAY!
YOU TWO, GO ON AHEAD!!
WHAT? BUT—
IT'S SAFER THIS WAY!

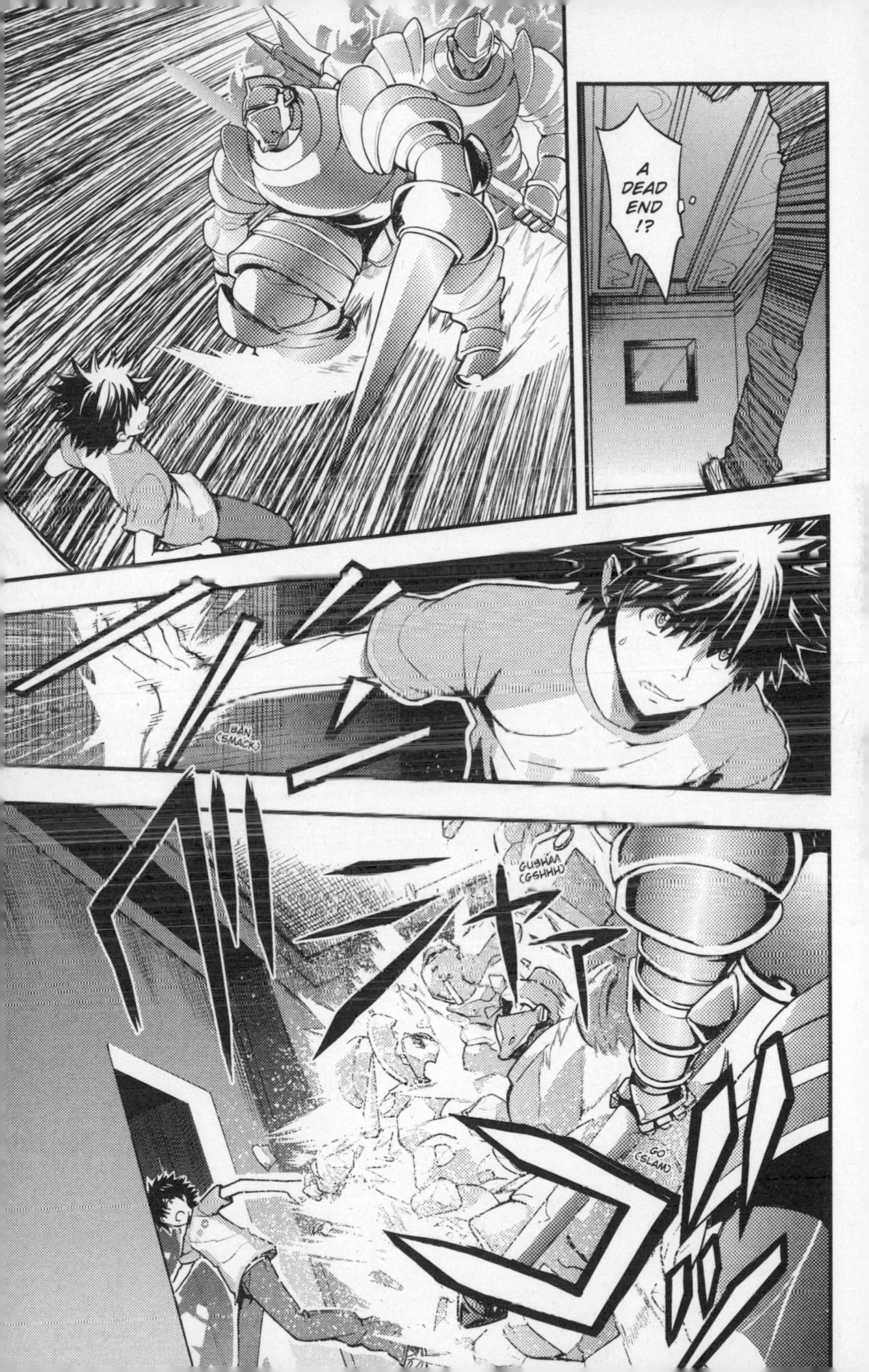
A DEAD END !?
BAN (SMACK)
GUSHAA (GSHHH)
GO (SLAM)

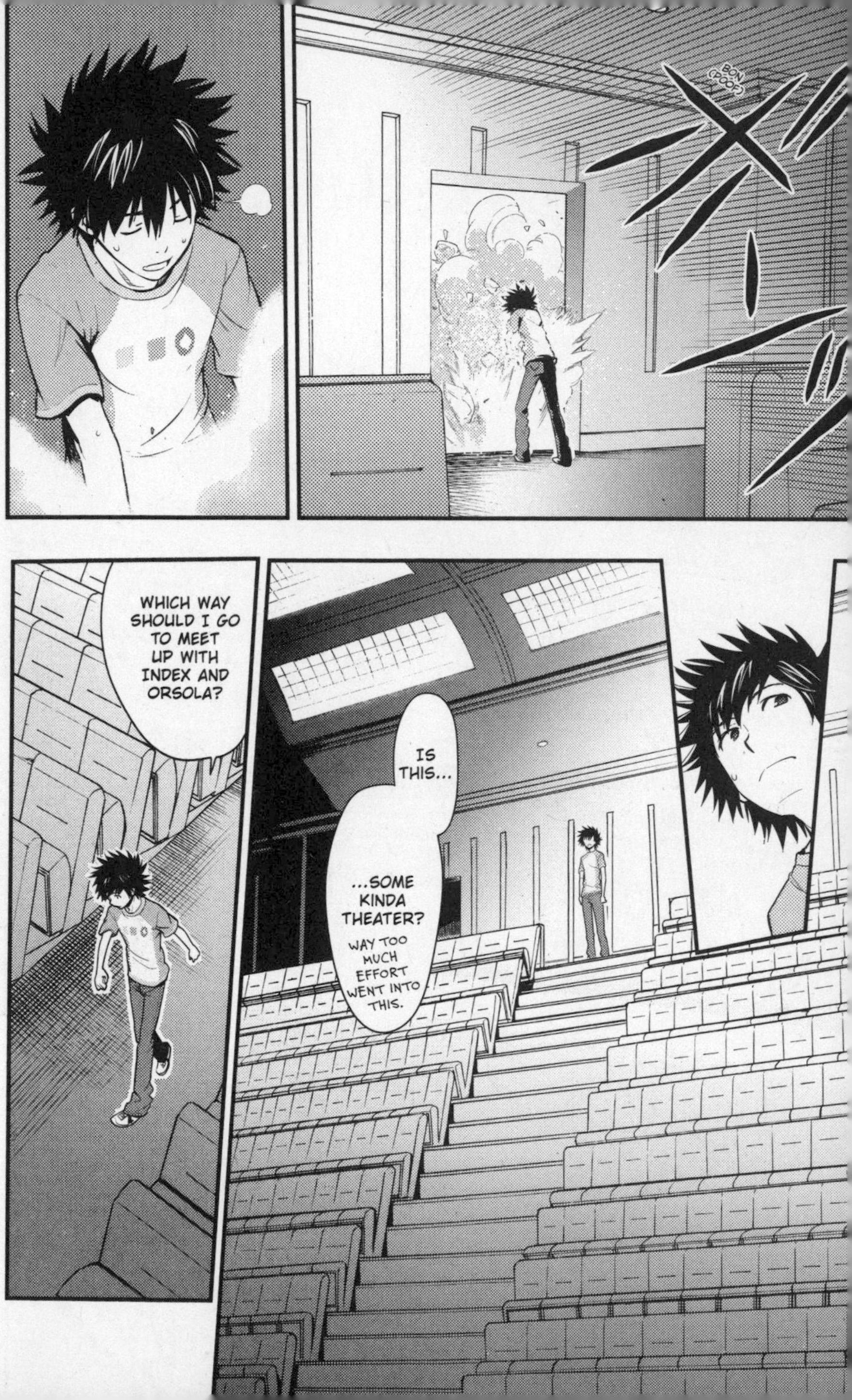
BON (POOF)
IS THIS...
...SOME KINDA THEATER?
WAY TOO MUCH EFFORT WENT INTO THIS.
WHICH WAY SHOULD I GO TO MEET UP WITH INDEX AND ORSOLA?

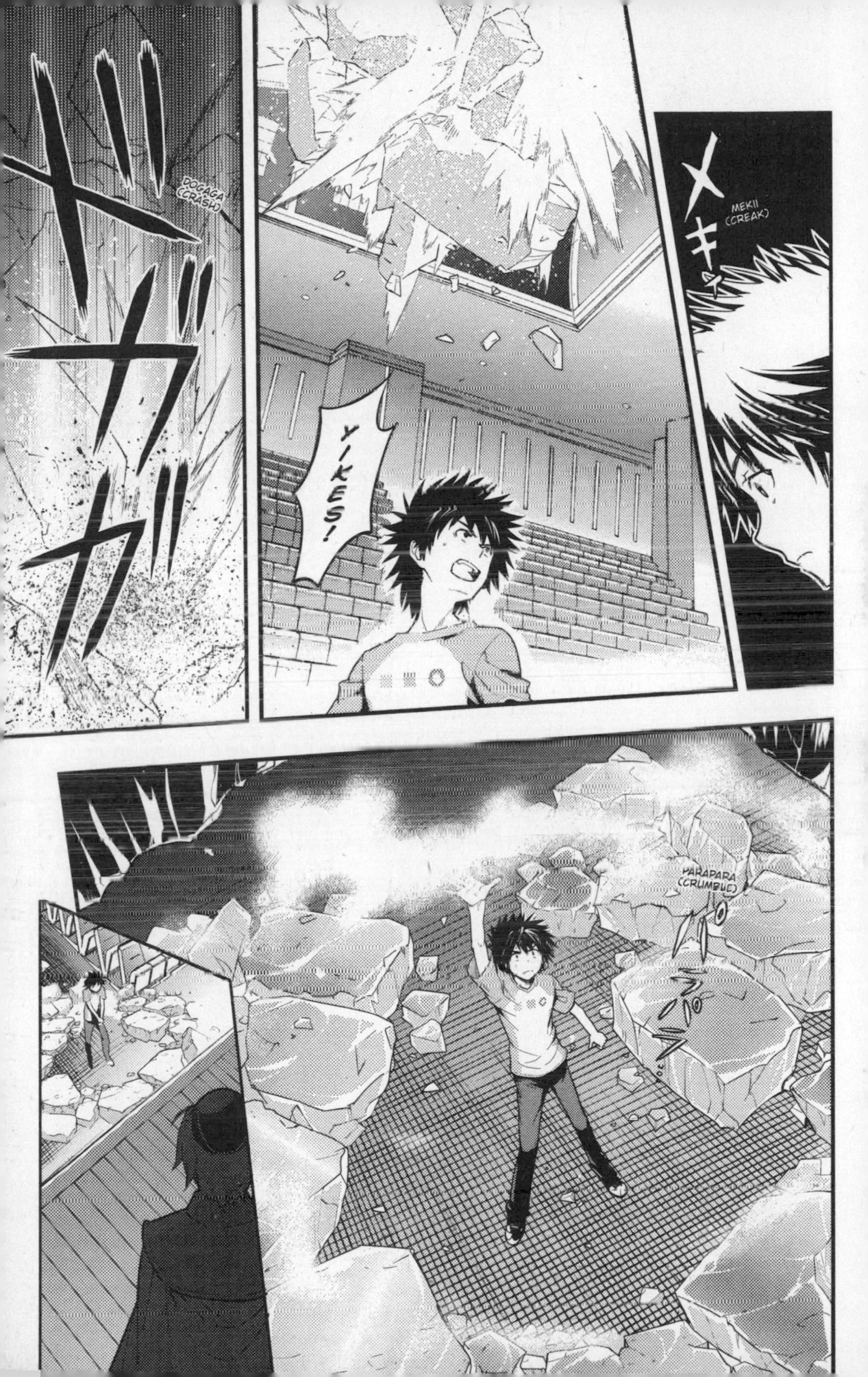
MEKII (CREAK)
YIKES!
DOGAGA (CRASH)
PARAPARA (CRUMBLE)

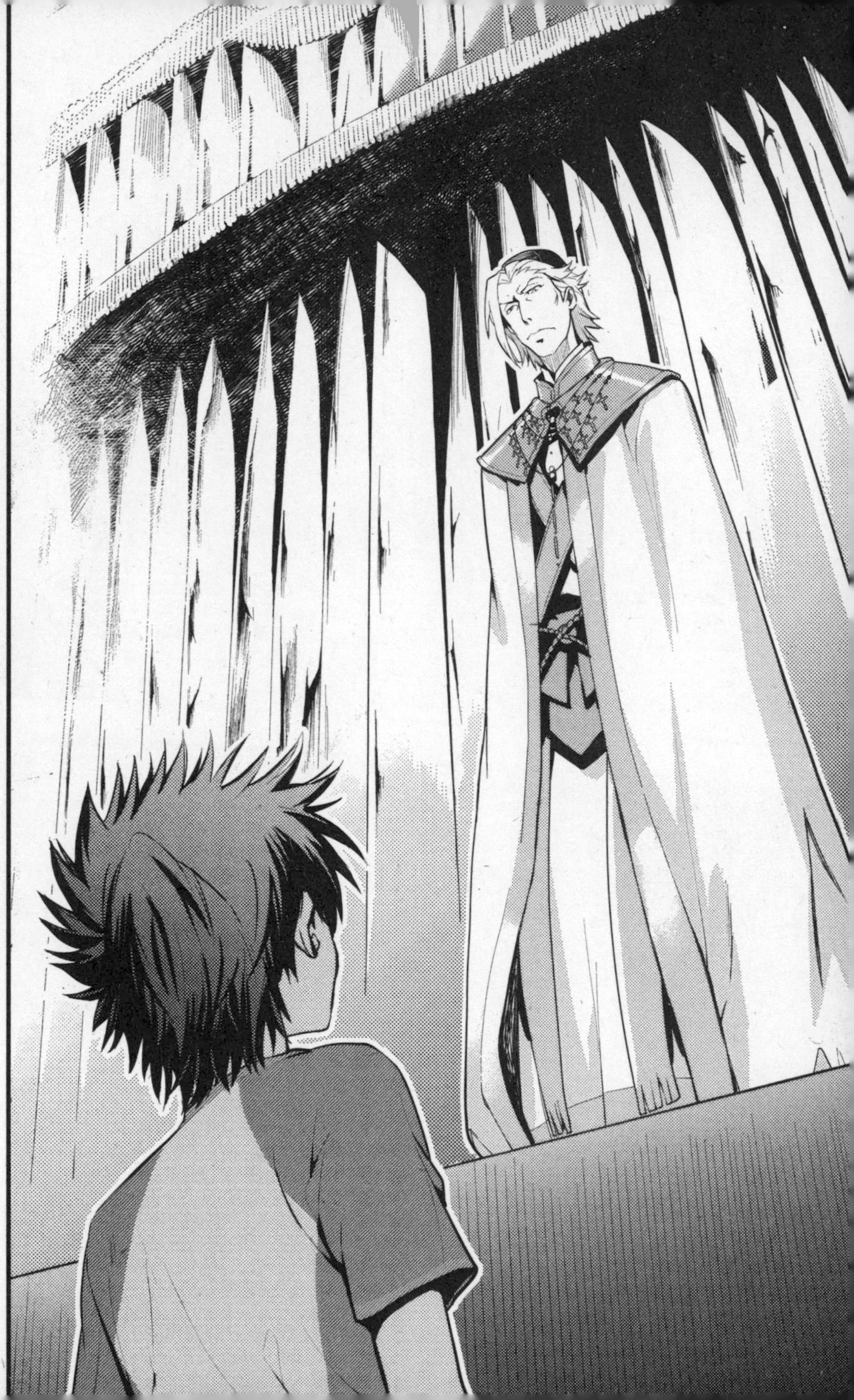

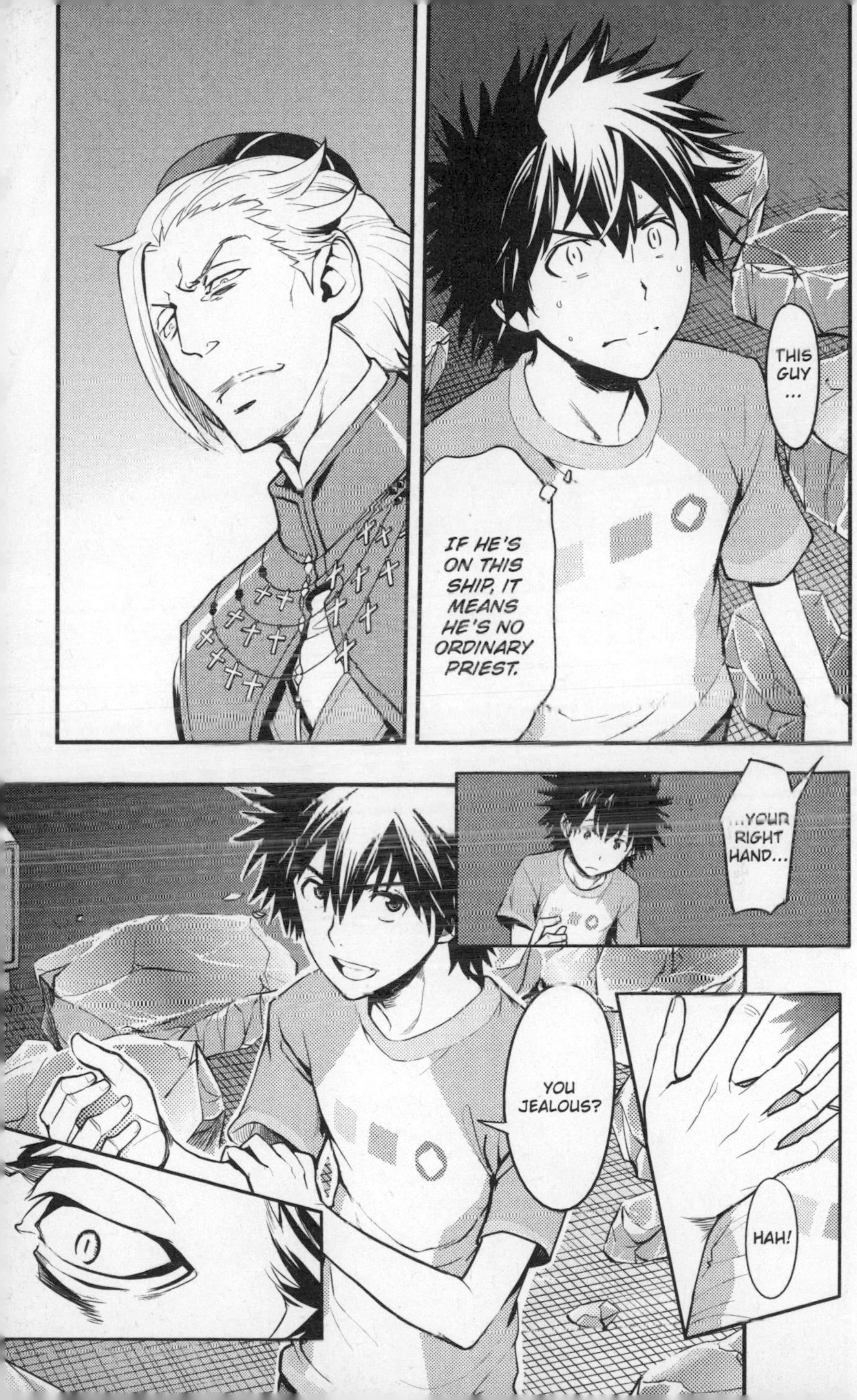
THIS GUY ...
IF HE'S ON THIS SHIP, IT MEANS HE'S NO ORDINARY PRIEST.
...YOUR RIGHT HAND...
YOU JEALOUS?
HAH!

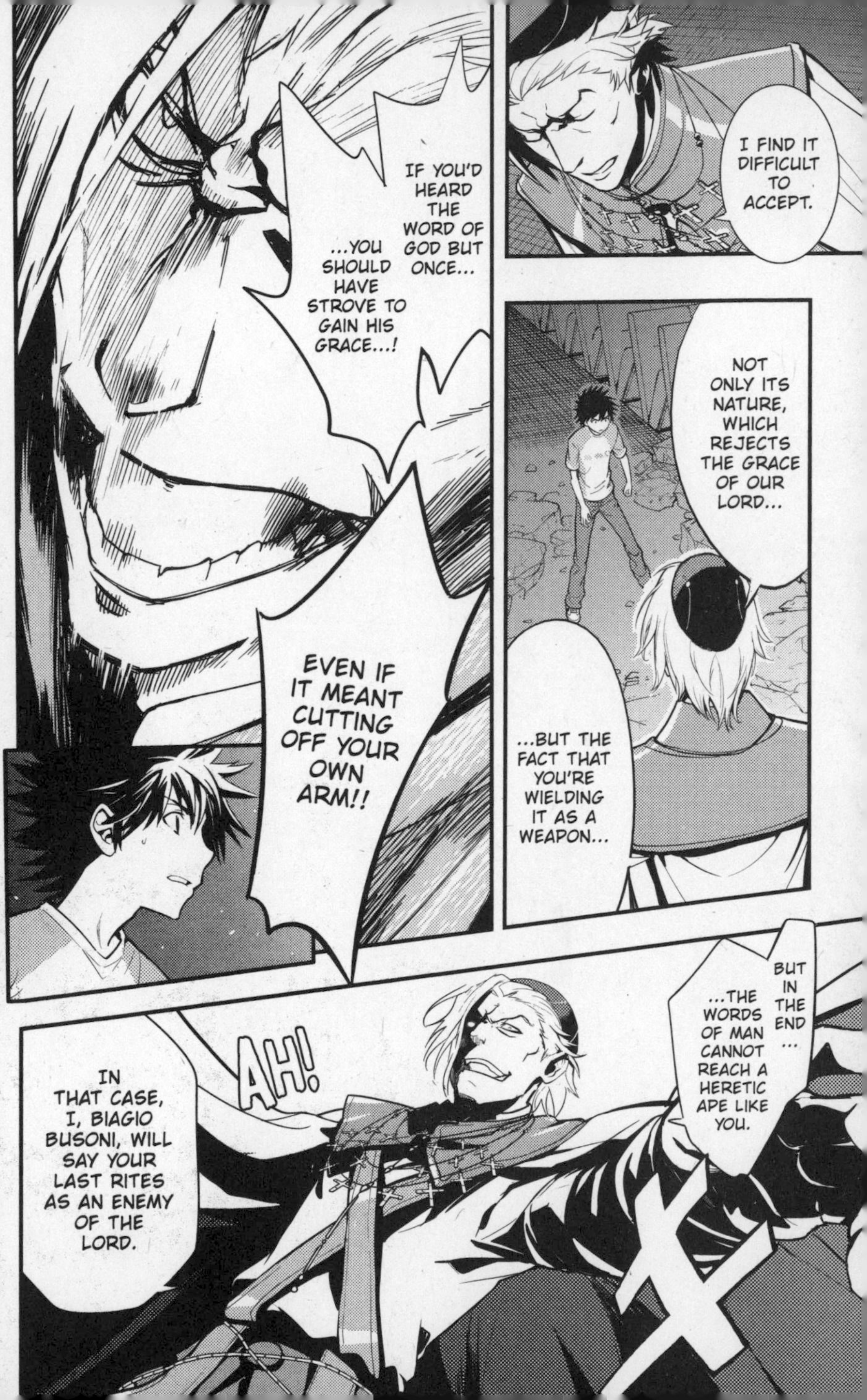
I FIND IT DIFFICULT TO ACCEPT.
NOT ONLY ITS NATURE, WHICH REJECTS THE GRACE OF OUR LORD...
...BUT THE FACT THAT YOU'RE WIELDING IT AS A WEAPON...
IF YOU'D HEARD THE WORD OF GOD BUT ONCE...
...YOU SHOULD HAVE STROVE TO GAIN HIS GRACE...!
EVEN IF IT MEANT CUTTING OFF YOUR OWN ARM!!
BUT IN THE END...
...THE WORDS OF MAN CANNOT REACH A HERETIC APE LIKE YOU.
AH!
IN THAT CASE, I, BIAGIO BUSONI, WILL SAY YOUR LAST RITES AS AN ENEMY OF THE LORD.

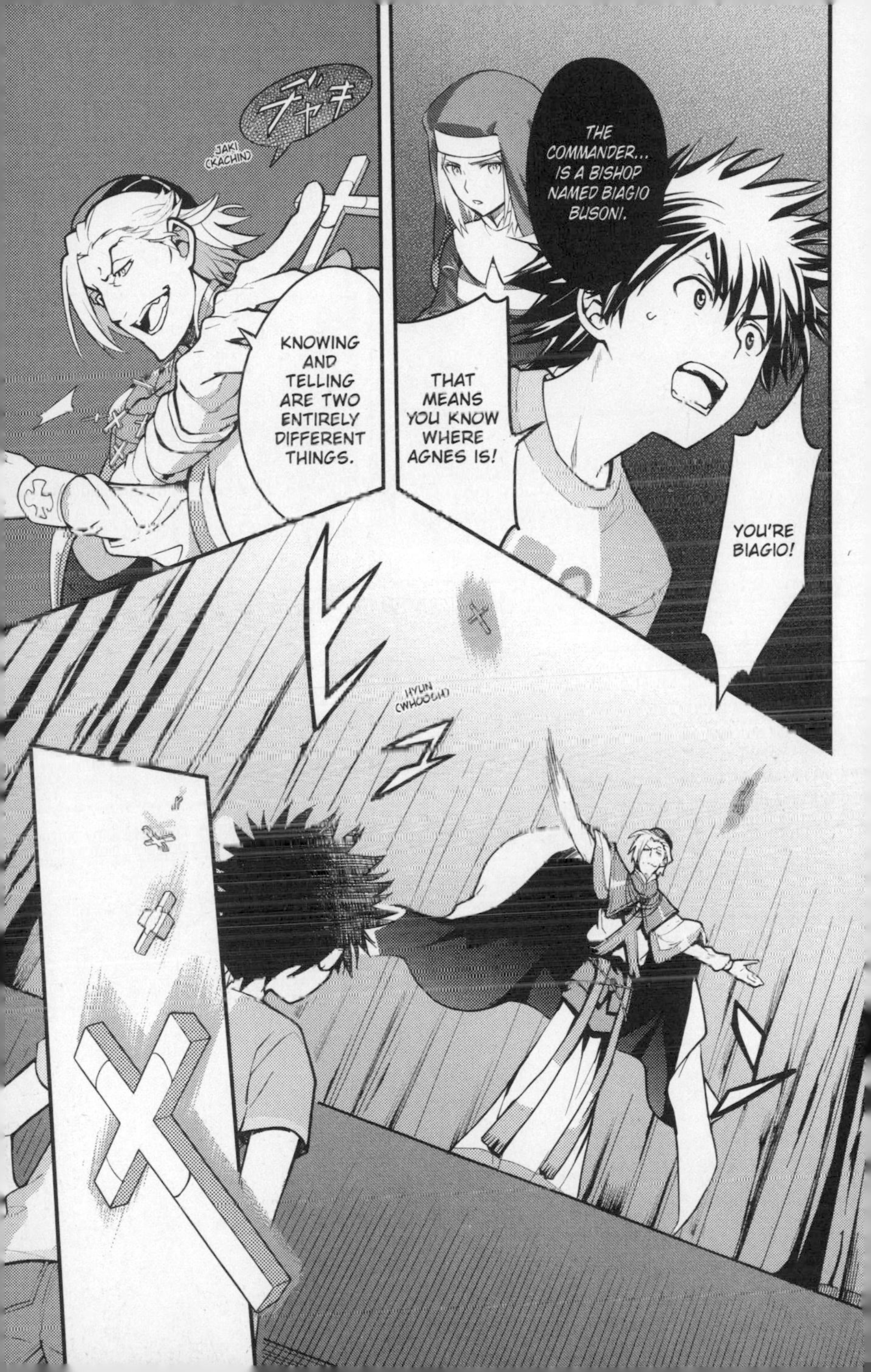
THE COMMANDER... IS A BISHOP NAMED BIAGIO BUSONI.
YOU'RE BIAGIO!
THAT MEANS YOU KNOW WHERE AGNES IS!
ジャキ
JAKI (KACHIN)
KNOWING AND TELLING ARE TWO ENTIRELY DIFFERENT THINGS.
HYUN (WHOOSH)

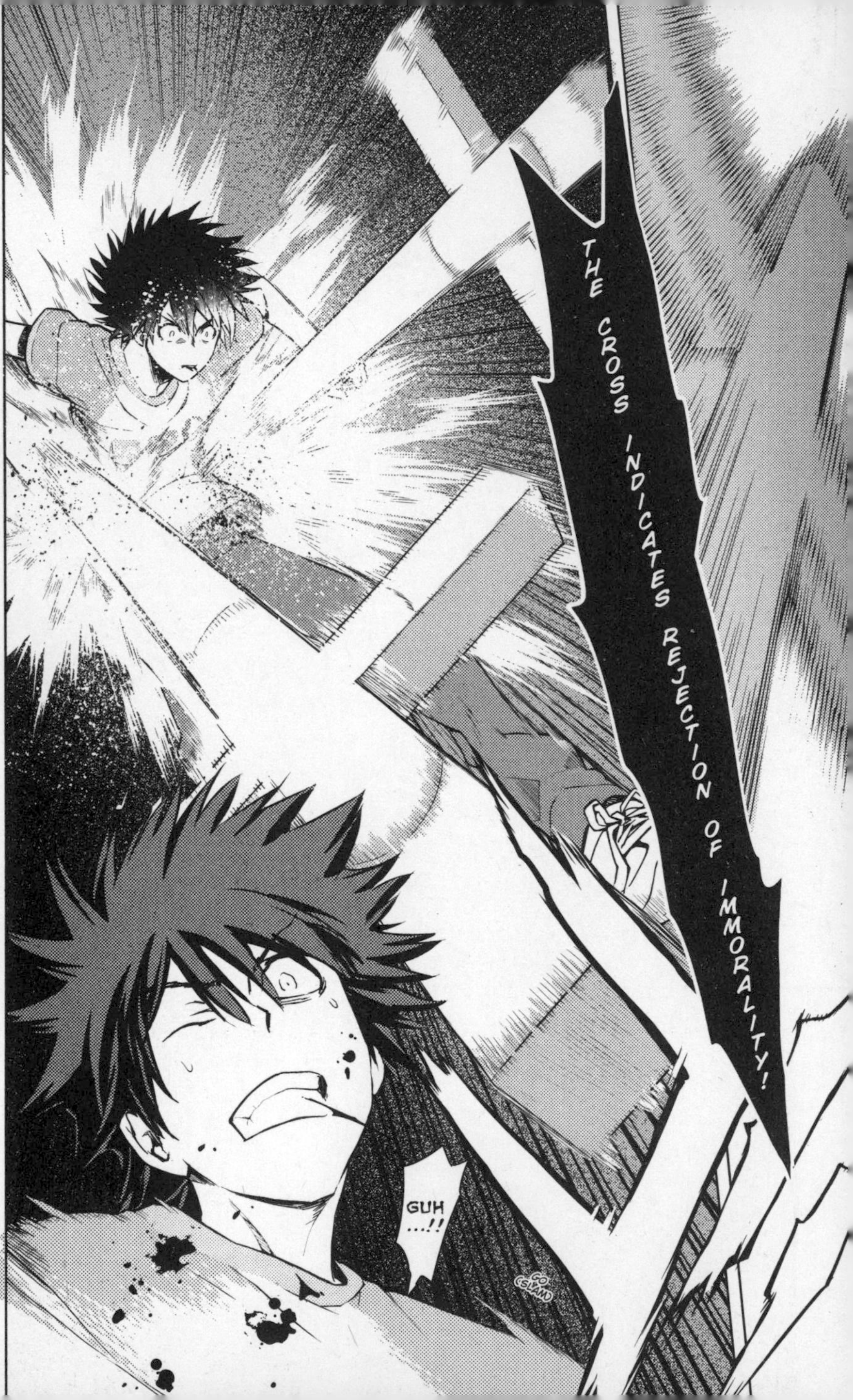
THE CROSS INDICATES REJECTION OF IMMORALITY!
GUH ...!!
GO (SLAM)

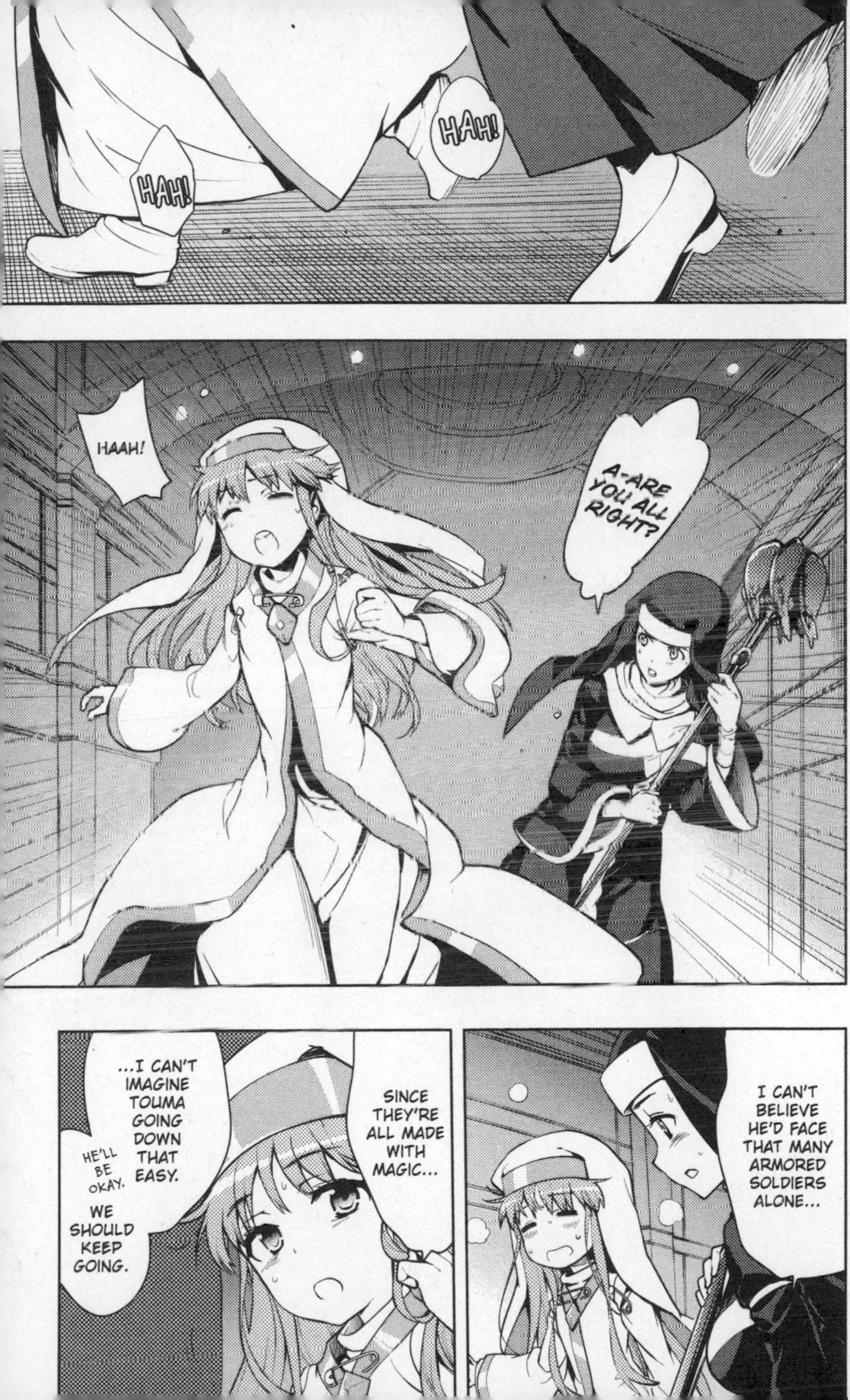
HAH!
HAH!
A-ARE YOU ALL RIGHT?
HAAH!
I CAN'T BELIEVE HE'D FACE THAT MANY ARMORED SOLDIERS ALONE...
SINCE THEY'RE ALL MADE WITH MAGIC...
...I CAN'T IMAGINE TOUMA GOING DOWN THAT EASY.
HE'LL BE OKAY.
WE SHOULD KEEP GOING.

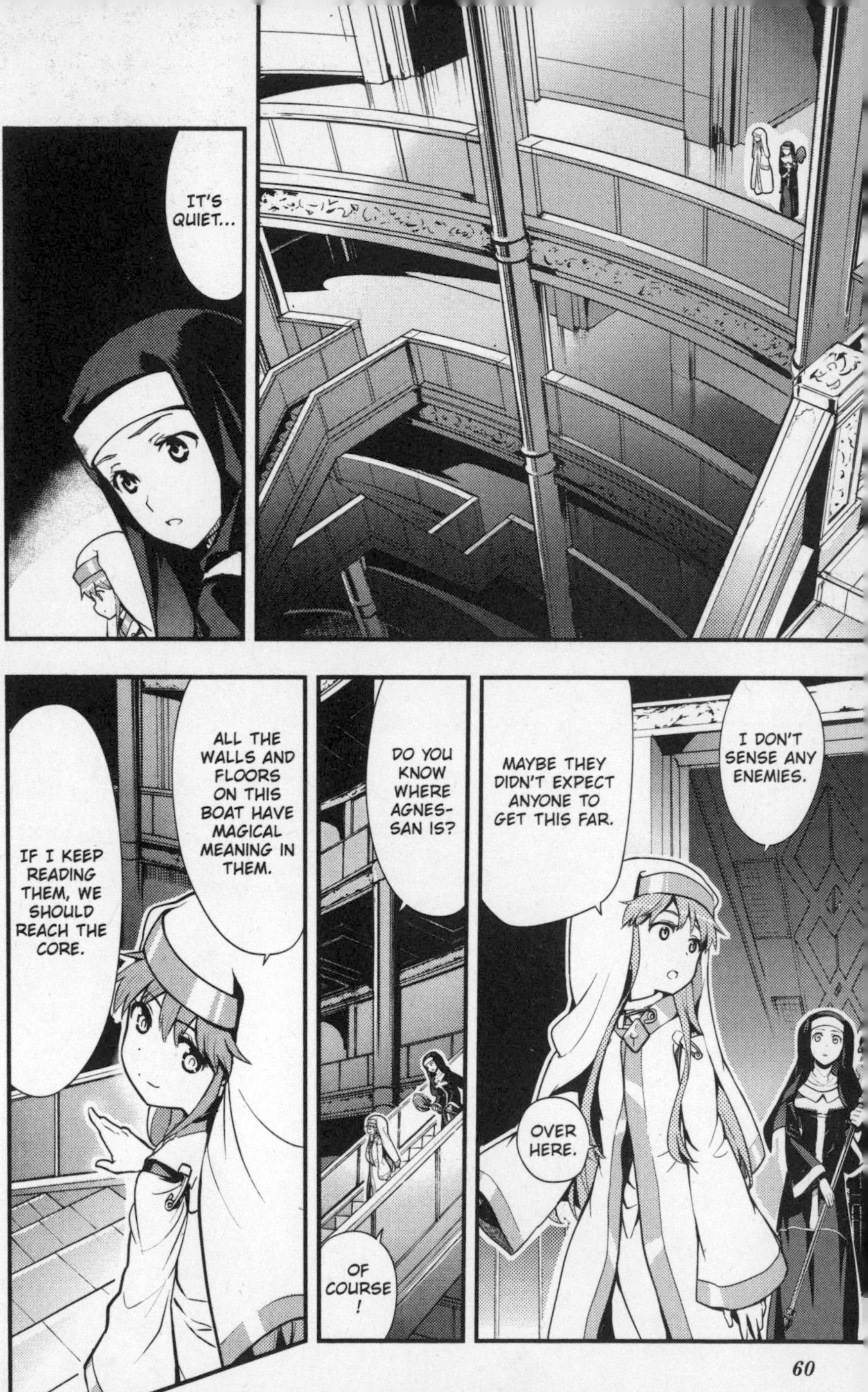
IT'S QUIET...
I DON'T SENSE ANY ENEMIES.
MAYBE THEY DIDN'T EXPECT ANYONE TO GET THIS FAR.
OVER HERE.
DO YOU KNOW WHERE AGNES-SAN IS?
OF COURSE!
ALL THE WALLS AND FLOORS ON THIS BOAT HAVE MAGICAL MEANING IN THEM.
IF I KEEP READING THEM, WE SHOULD REACH THE CORE.

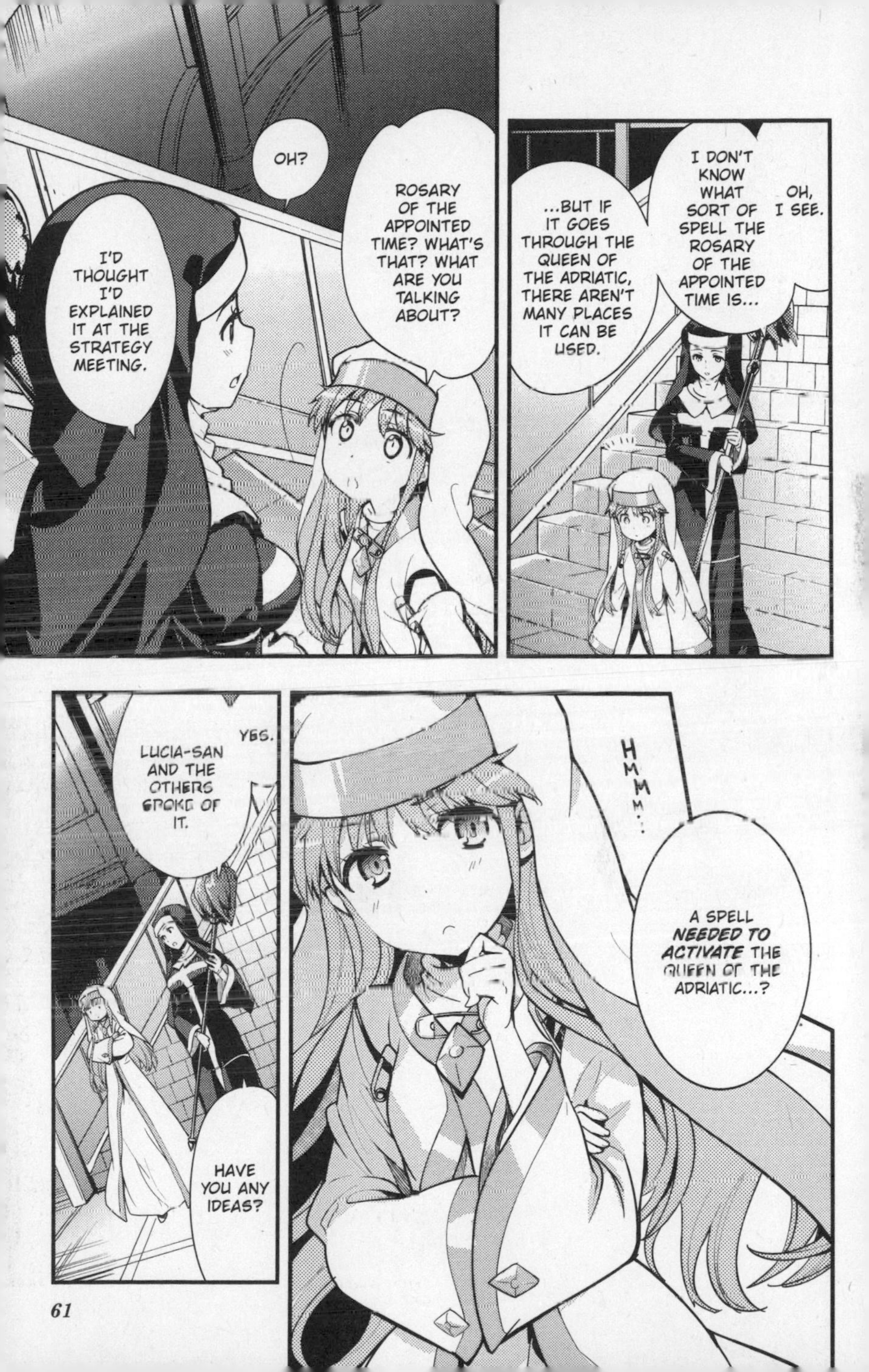

ROSARY OF THE APPOINTED TIME? WHAT'S THAT? WHAT ARE YOU TALKING ABOUT?
OH?
I'D THOUGHT I'D EXPLAINED IT AT THE STRATEGY MEETING.
OH, I SEE.
I DON'T KNOW WHAT SORT OF SPELL THE ROSARY OF THE APPOINTED TIME IS...
...BUT IF IT GOES THROUGH THE QUEEN OF THE ADRIATIC, THERE AREN'T MANY PLACES IT CAN BE USED.
YES.
LUCIA-SAN AND THE OTHERS SPOKE OF IT.
HAVE YOU ANY IDEAS?
HMMM...
A SPELL ***NEEDED TO ACTIVATE*** THE QUEEN OF THE ADRIATIC...?

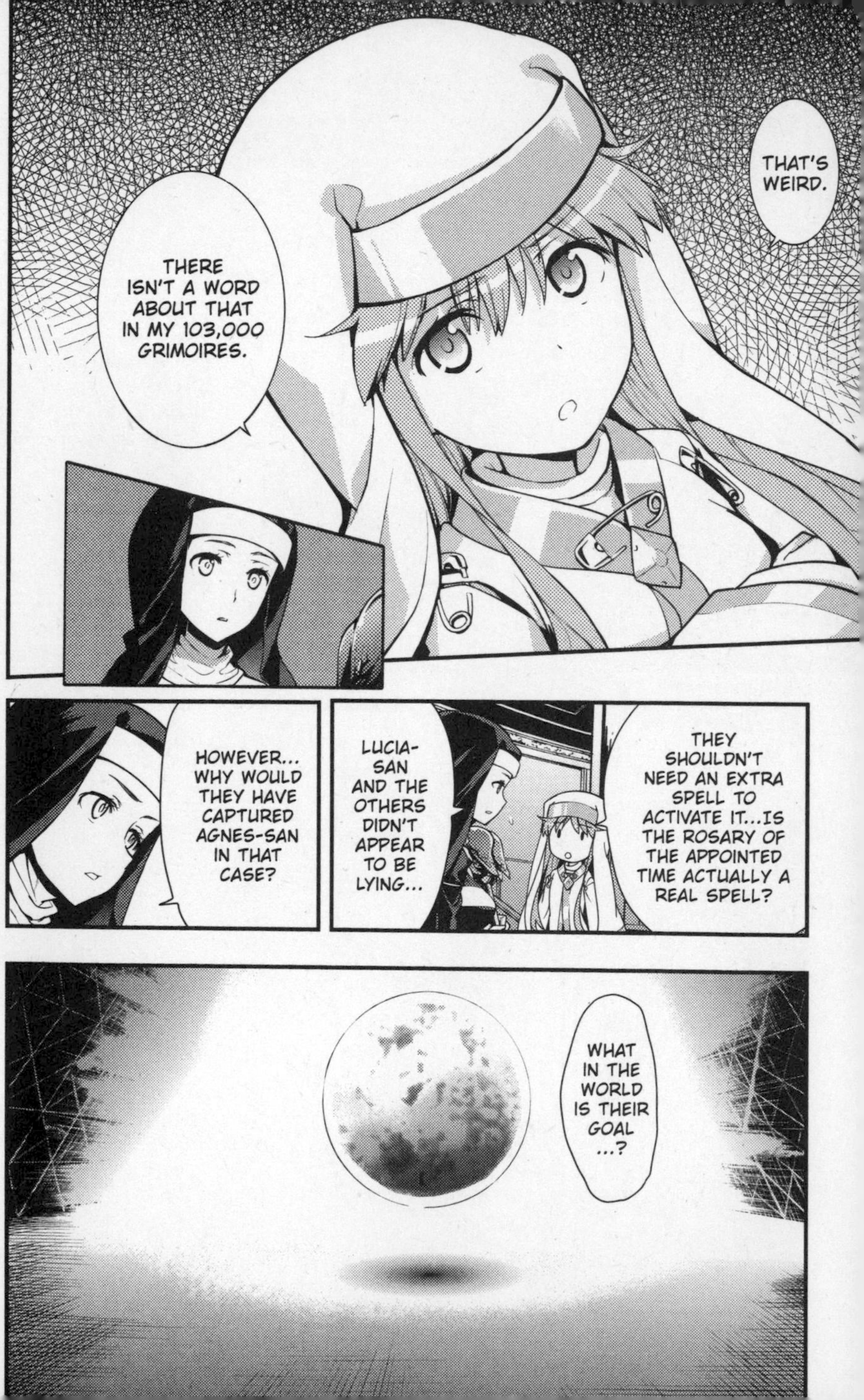
THAT'S WEIRD.
THERE ISN'T A WORD ABOUT THAT IN MY 103,000 GRIMOIRES.
THEY SHOULDN'T NEED AN EXTRA SPELL TO ACTIVATE IT...IS THE ROSARY OF THE APPOINTED TIME ACTUALLY A REAL SPELL?
LUCIA-SAN AND THE OTHERS DIDN'T APPEAR TO BE LYING...
HOWEVER... WHY WOULD THEY HAVE CAPTURED AGNES-SAN IN THAT CASE?
WHAT IN THE WORLD IS THEIR GOAL ...?

#94 ROSARY OF THE APPOINTED TIME ②

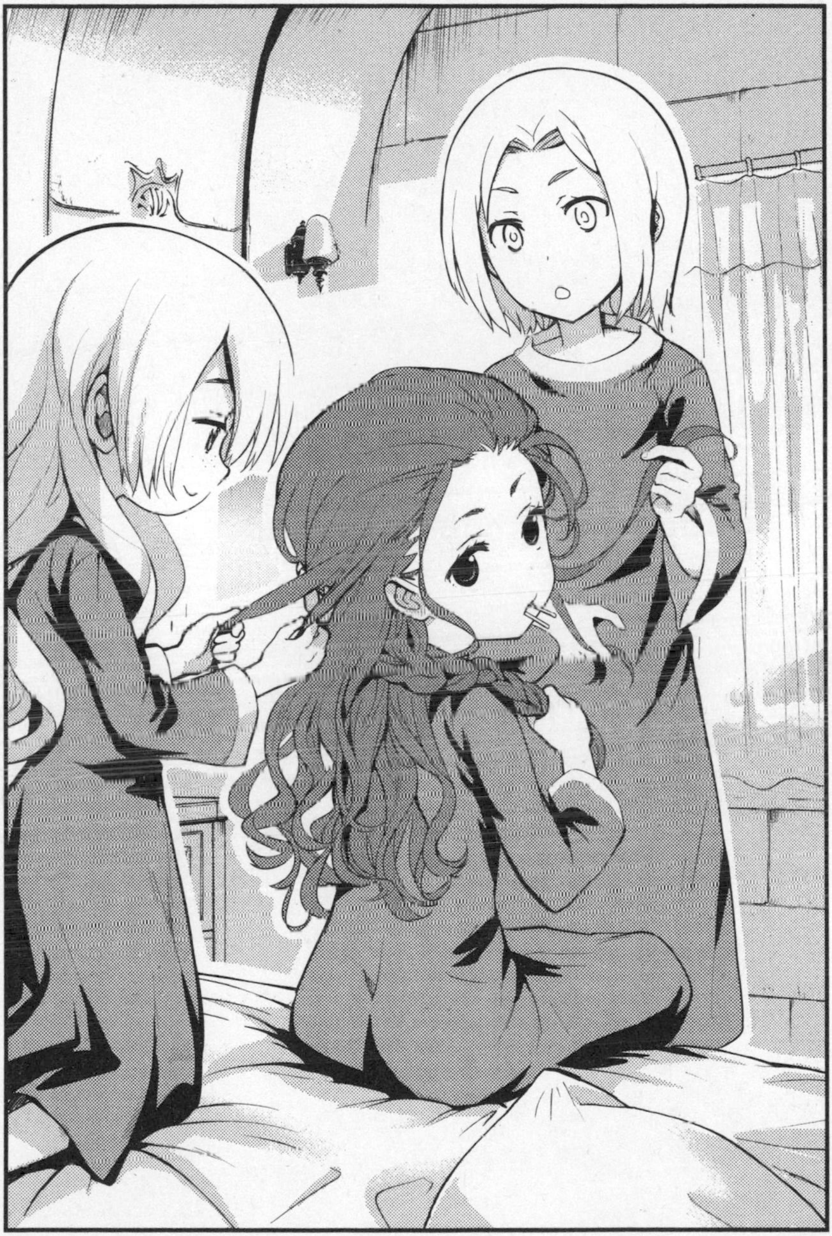

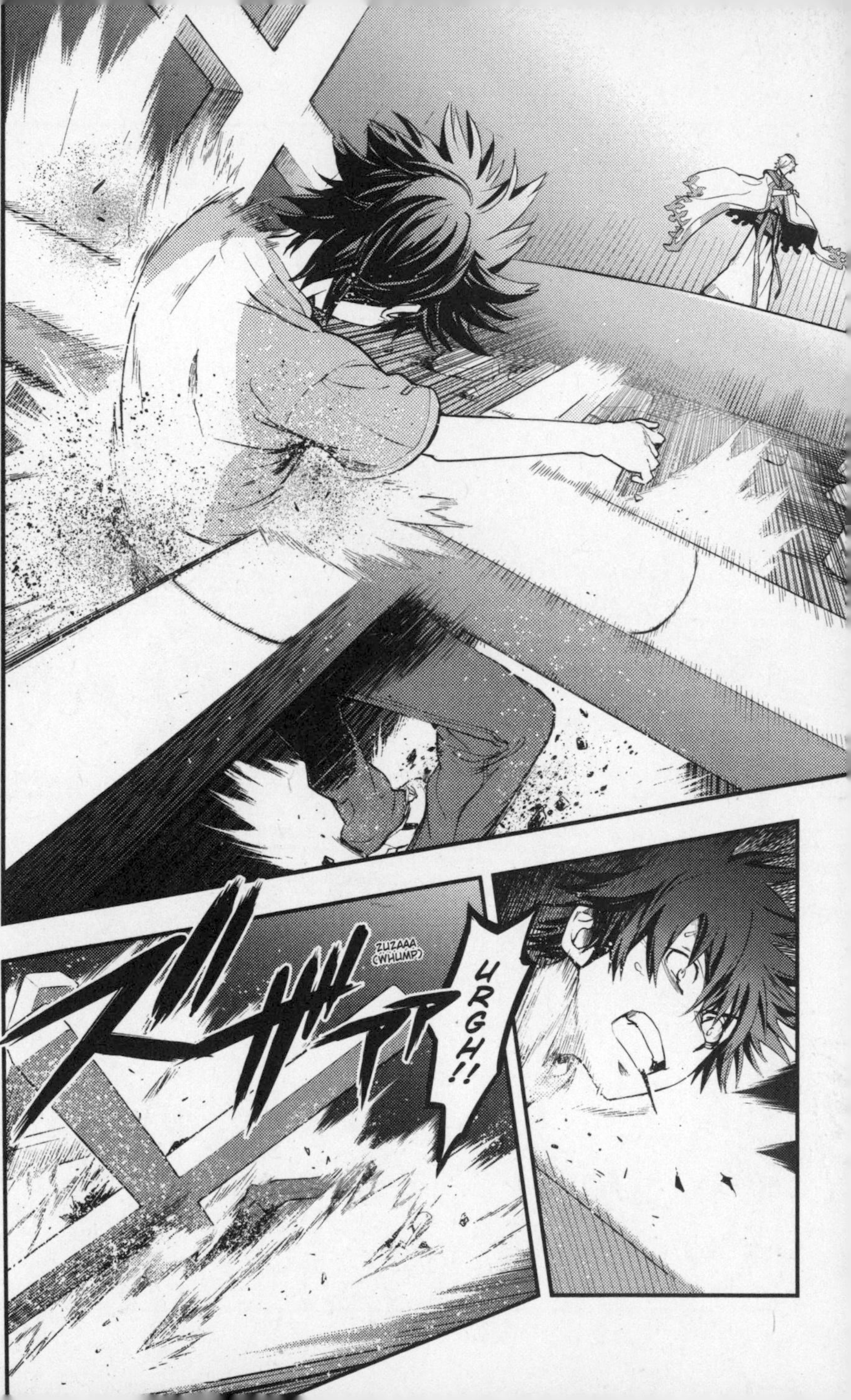
URGH!!
ZUZAAA (WHUMP)

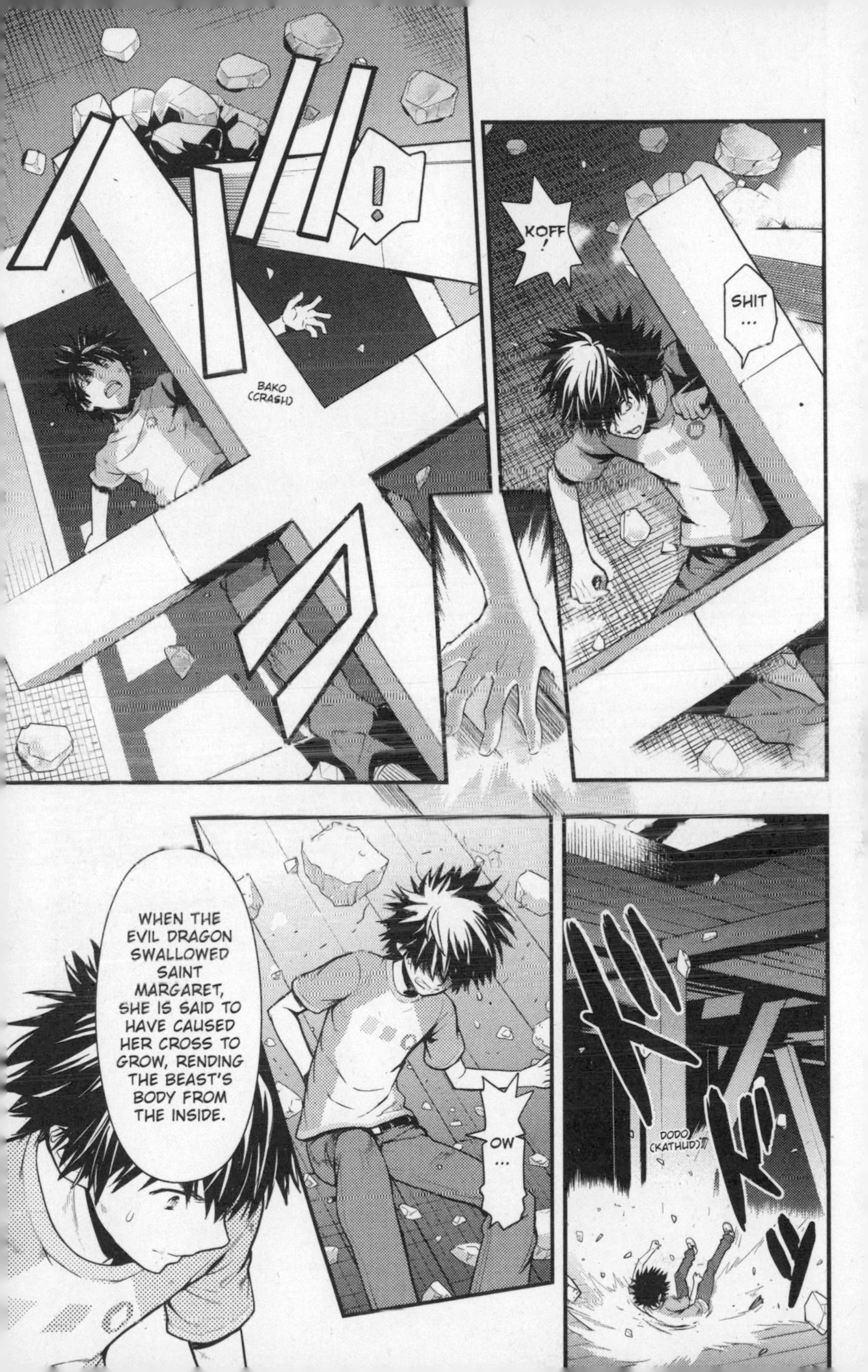
KOFF!
SHIT...
!
BAKO (CRASH)
DODO (KATHUD)
OW...
WHEN THE EVIL DRAGON SWALLOWED SAINT MARGARET, SHE IS SAID TO HAVE CAUSED HER CROSS TO GROW, RENDING THE BEAST'S BODY FROM THE INSIDE.

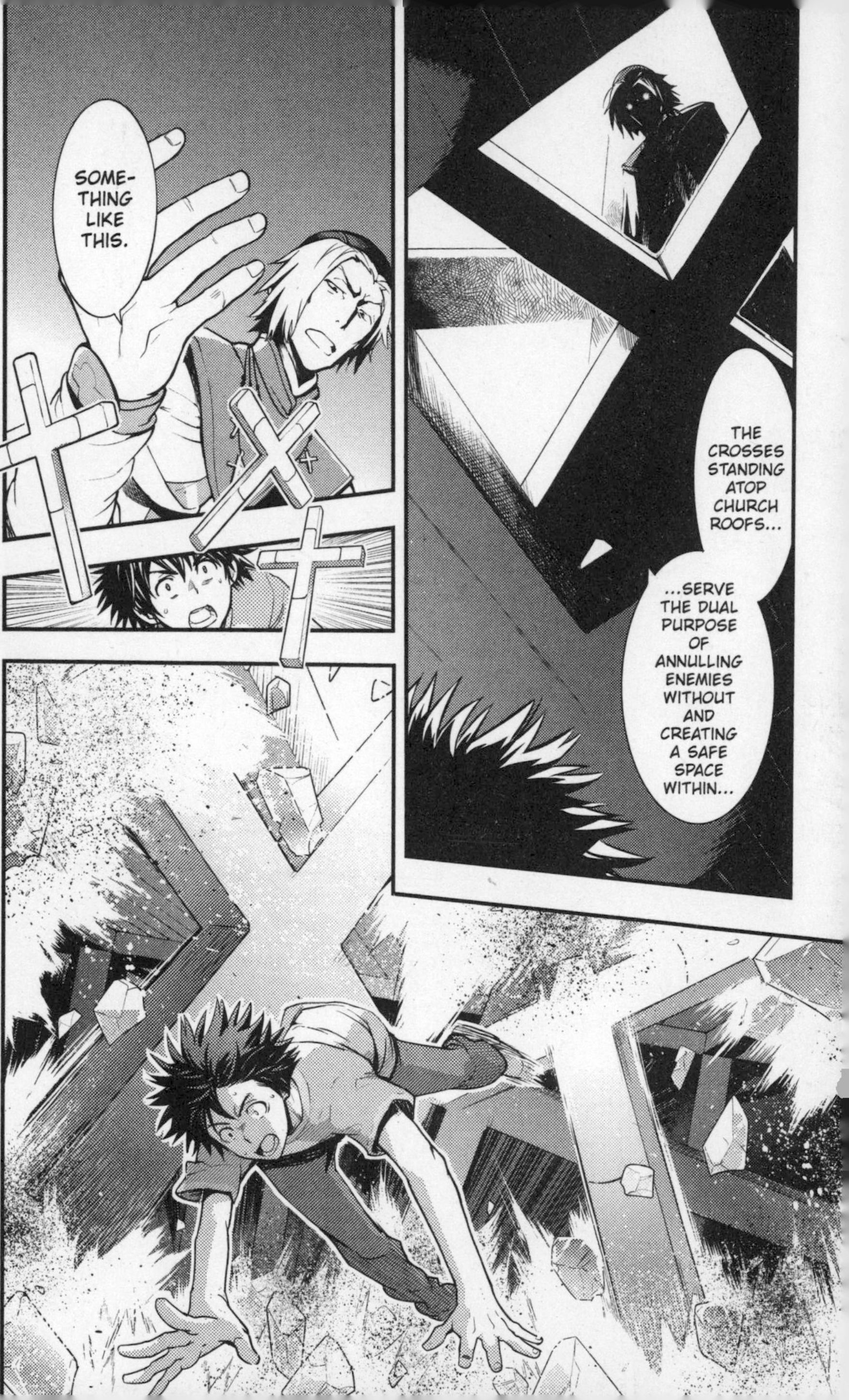
THE CROSSES STANDING ATOP CHURCH ROOFS...
...SERVE THE DUAL PURPOSE OF ANNULLING ENEMIES WITHOUT AND CREATING A SAFE SPACE WITHIN...
SOME-THING LIKE THIS.

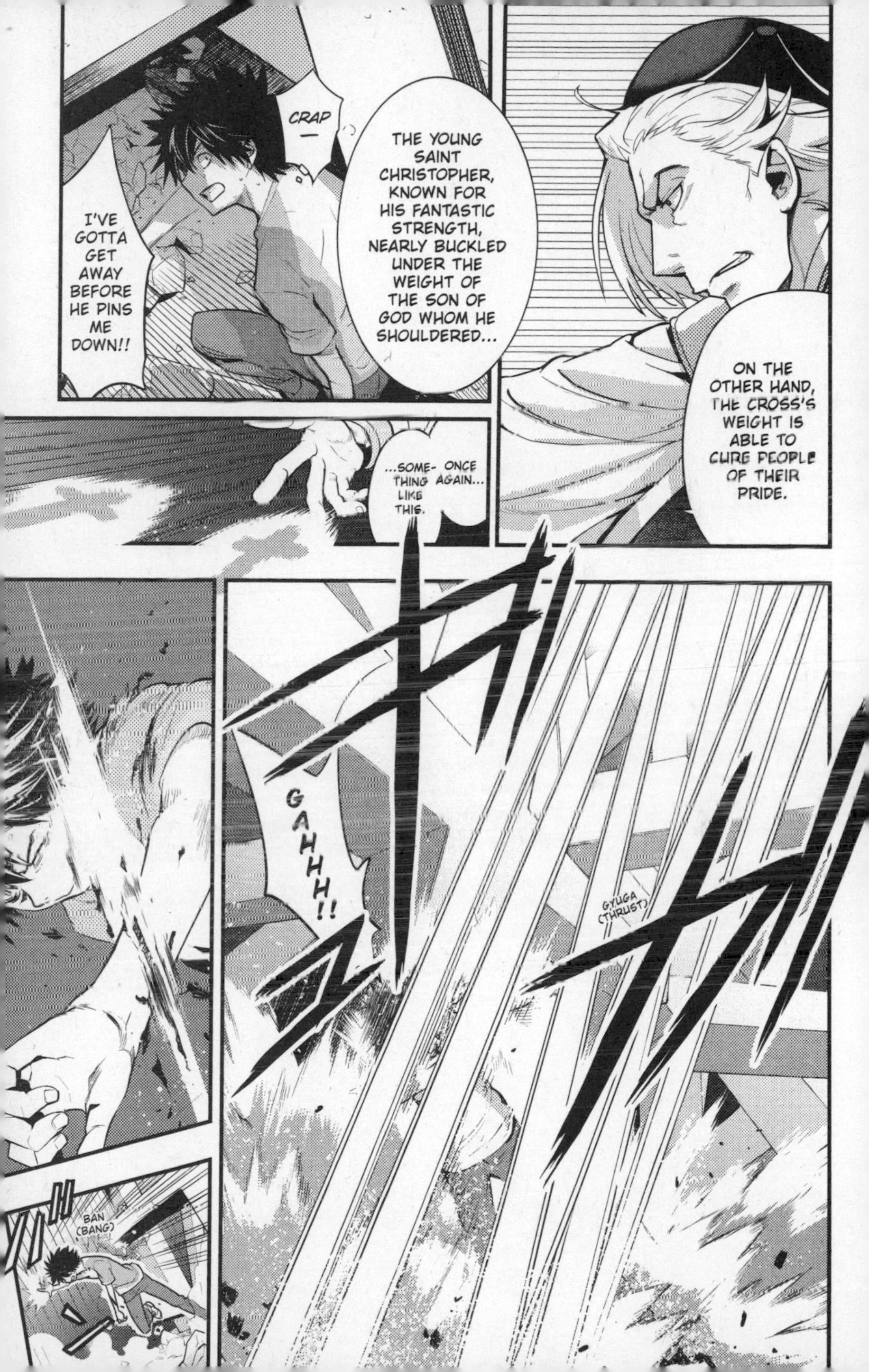
THE YOUNG SAINT CHRISTOPHER, KNOWN FOR HIS FANTASTIC STRENGTH, NEARLY BUCKLED UNDER THE WEIGHT OF THE SON OF GOD WHOM HE SHOULDERED...
ON THE OTHER HAND, THE CROSS'S WEIGHT IS ABLE TO CURE PEOPLE OF THEIR PRIDE.
CRAP —
I'VE GOTTA GET AWAY BEFORE HE PINS ME DOWN!!
ONCE AGAIN... ...SOME-THING LIKE THIS.
GYUGA (THRUST)
GAHHH!!
BAN (BANG)

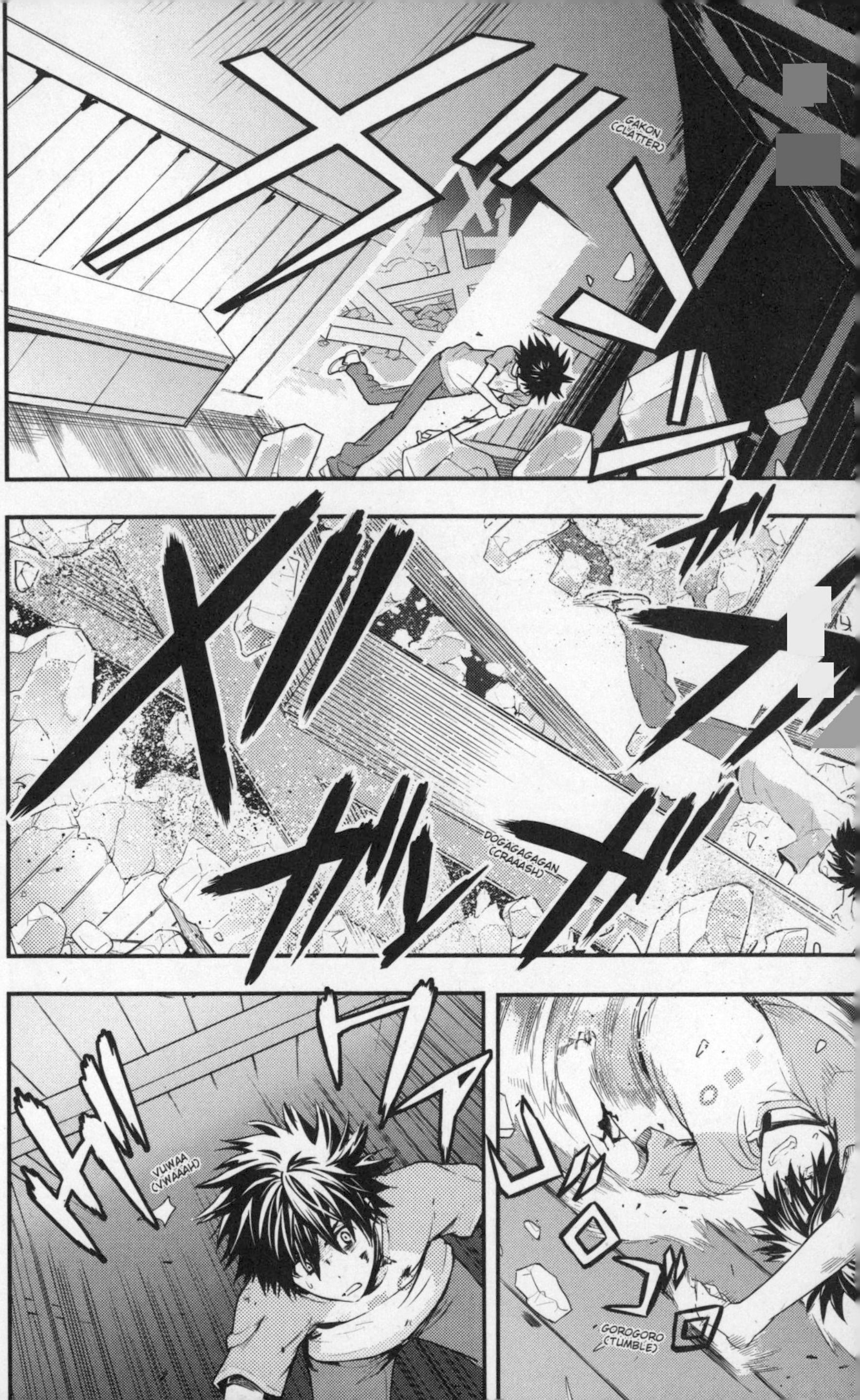
GAKON
(CLATTER)
DOGAGAGAGAN
(CRAAASH)
GOROGORO
(TUMBLE)
VUWAA
(VWAAAH)

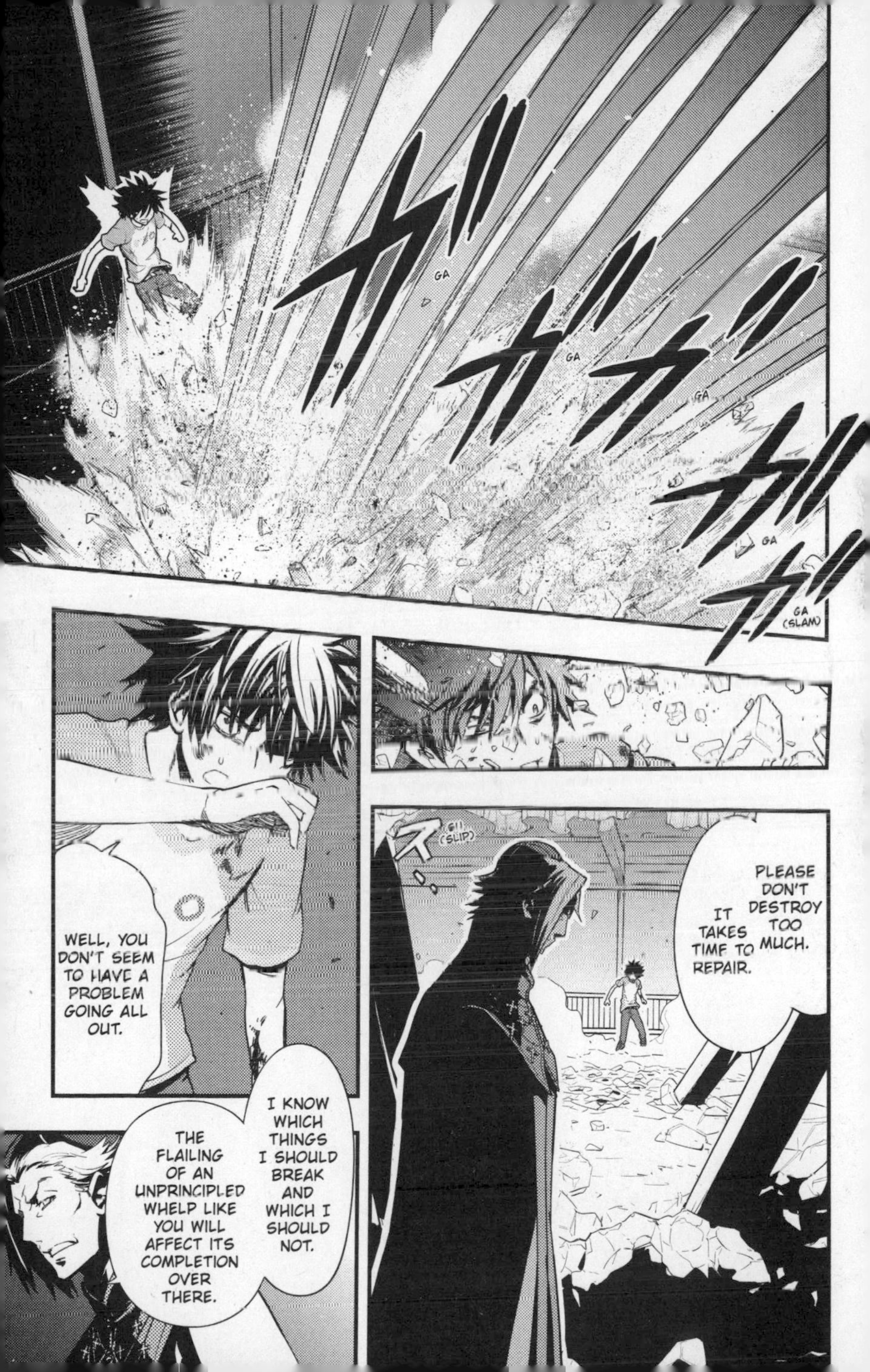
GA
GA
GA
GA
GA (SLAM)
WELL, YOU DON'T SEEM TO HAVE A PROBLEM GOING ALL OUT.
GI (SLIP)
PLEASE DON'T DESTROY TOO MUCH.
IT TAKES TIME TO REPAIR.
I KNOW WHICH THINGS I SHOULD BREAK AND WHICH I SHOULD NOT.
THE FLAILING OF AN UNPRINCIPLED WHELP LIKE YOU WILL AFFECT ITS COMPLETION OVER THERE.

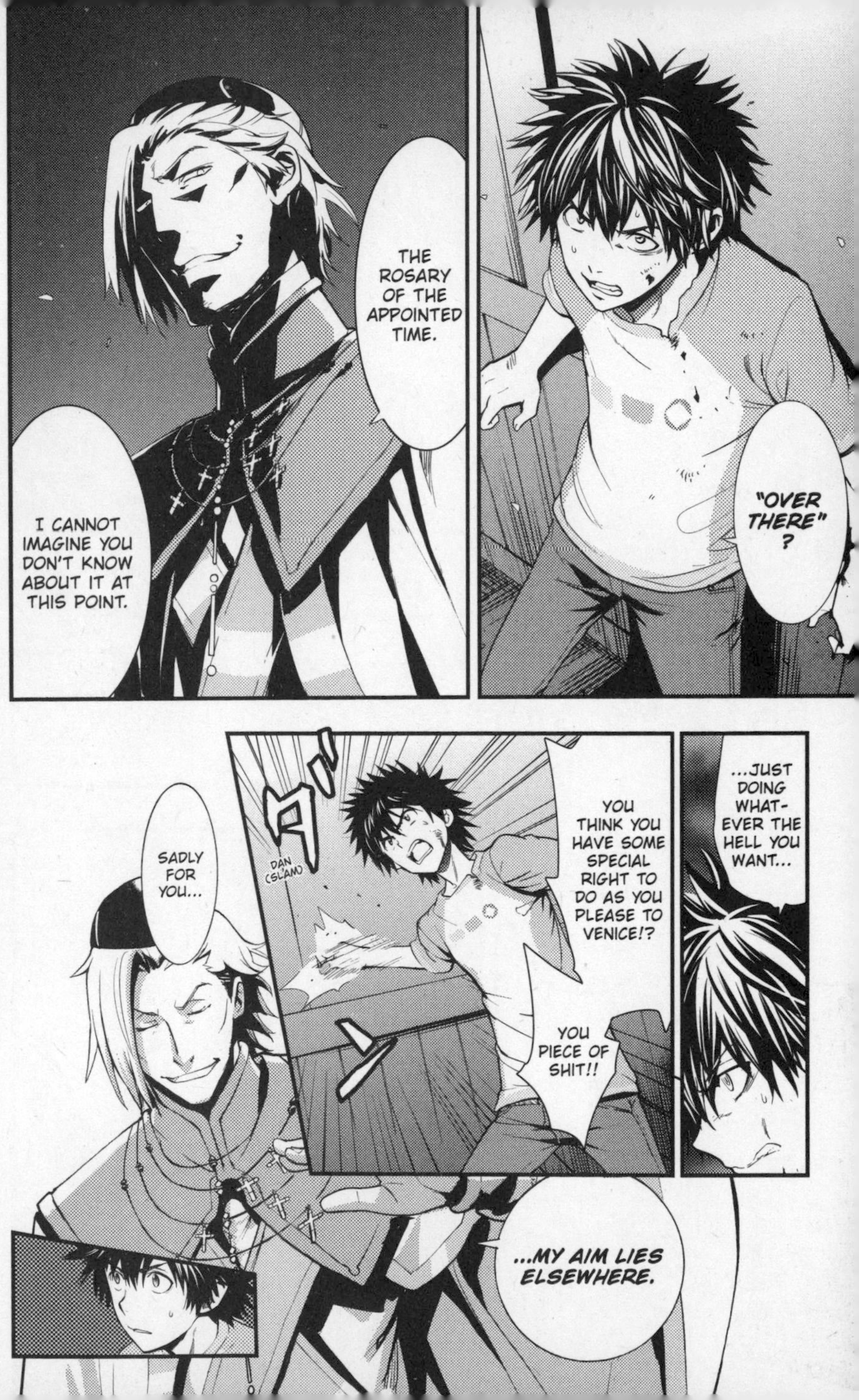
"OVER THERE"?
THE ROSARY OF THE APPOINTED TIME.
I CANNOT IMAGINE YOU DON'T KNOW ABOUT IT AT THIS POINT.
...JUST DOING WHAT-EVER THE HELL YOU WANT...
YOU THINK YOU HAVE SOME SPECIAL RIGHT TO DO AS YOU PLEASE TO VENICE!?
DAN (SLAM)
YOU PIECE OF SHIT!!
SADLY FOR YOU...
...MY AIM LIES ELSEWHERE.

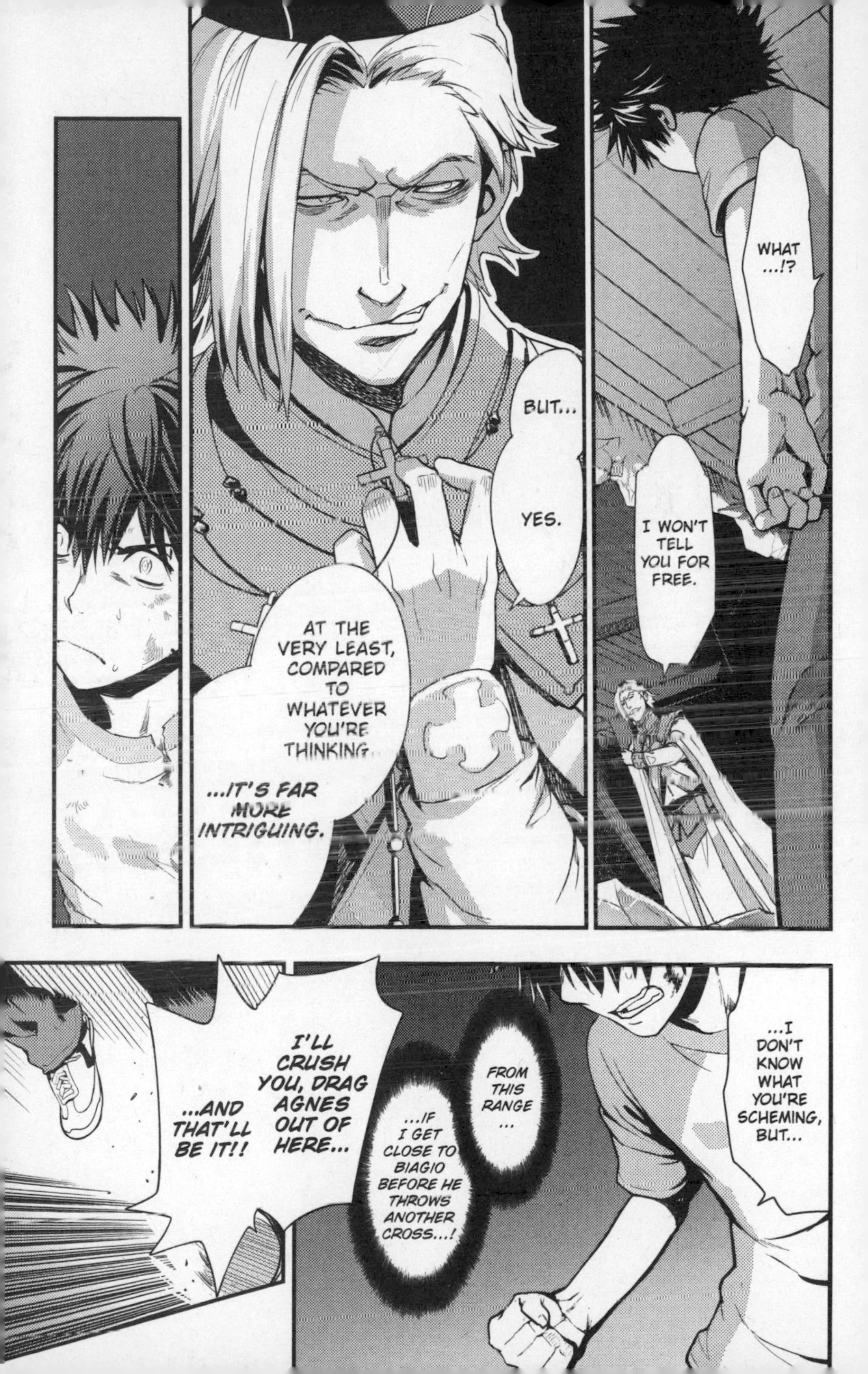
WHAT ...!?
I WON'T TELL YOU FOR FREE.
BUT...
YES.
AT THE VERY LEAST, COMPARED TO WHATEVER YOU'RE THINKING...
...IT'S FAR MORE INTRIGUING.
...I DON'T KNOW WHAT YOU'RE SCHEMING, BUT...
FROM THIS RANGE...
...IF I GET CLOSE TO BIAGIO BEFORE HE THROWS ANOTHER CROSS...!
I'LL CRUSH YOU, DRAG AGNES OUT OF HERE...
...AND THAT'LL BE IT!!

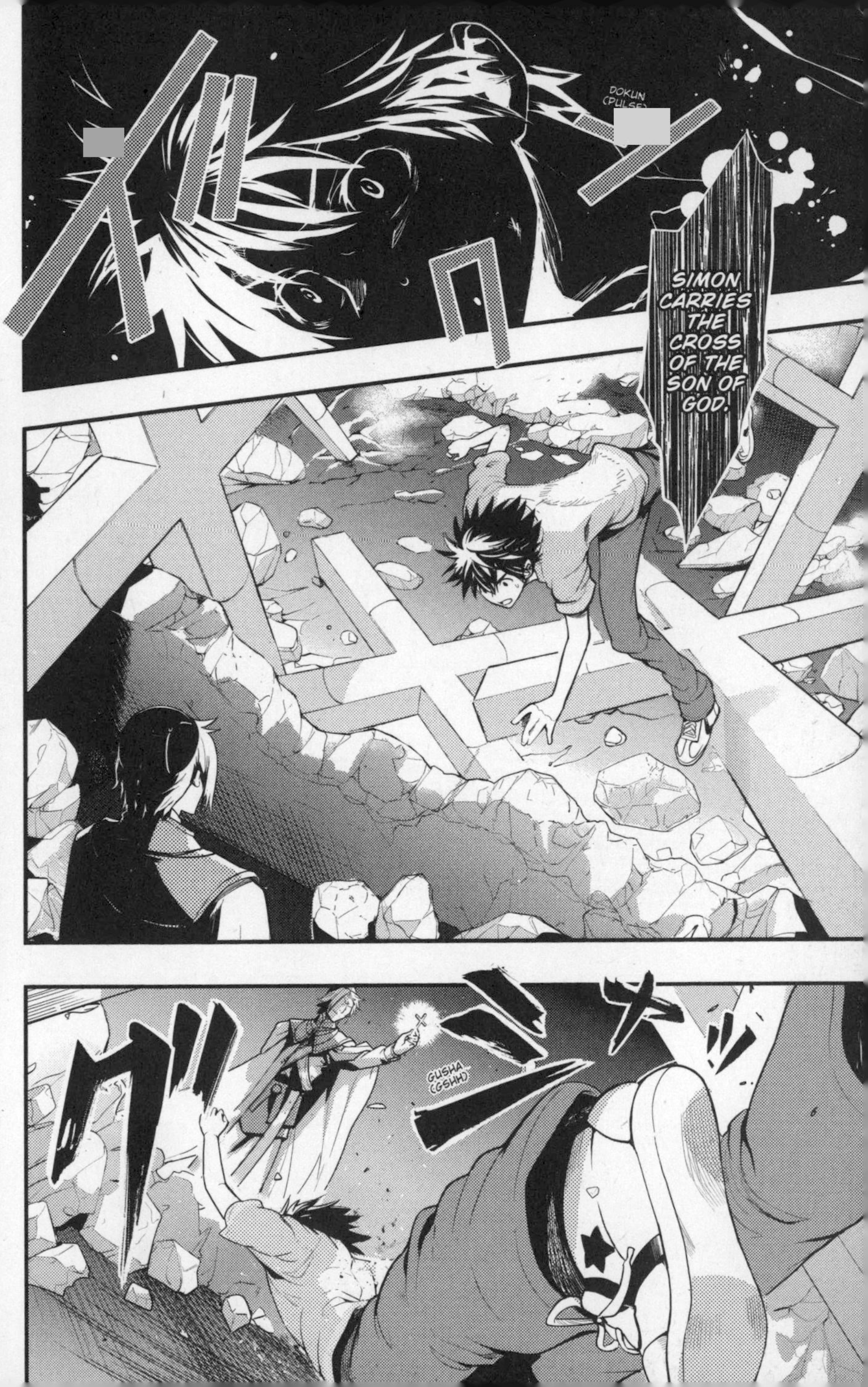
DOKUN (PULSE)
SIMON CARRIES THE CROSS OF THE SON OF GOD.
GUSHA (GSHH)

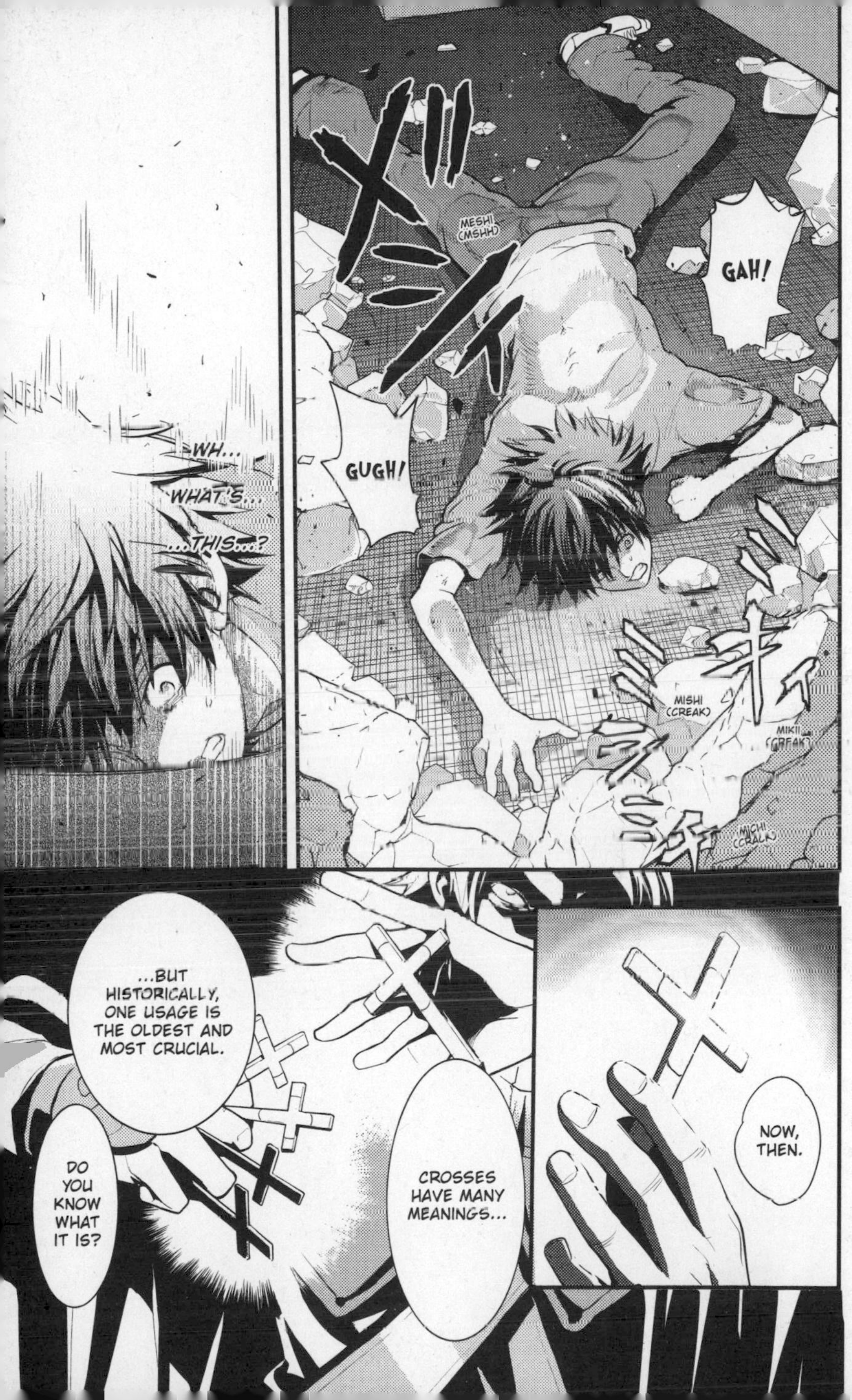
GAH!
MESHI (MSHH)
GUGH!
MIKII (CREAK)
MISHI (CREAK)
MICHI (CRALK)
WH... WHAT'S... ...THIS...?
NOW, THEN.
CROSSES HAVE MANY MEANINGS...
...BUT HISTORICALLY, ONE USAGE IS THE OLDEST AND MOST CRUCIAL.
DO YOU KNOW WHAT IT IS?

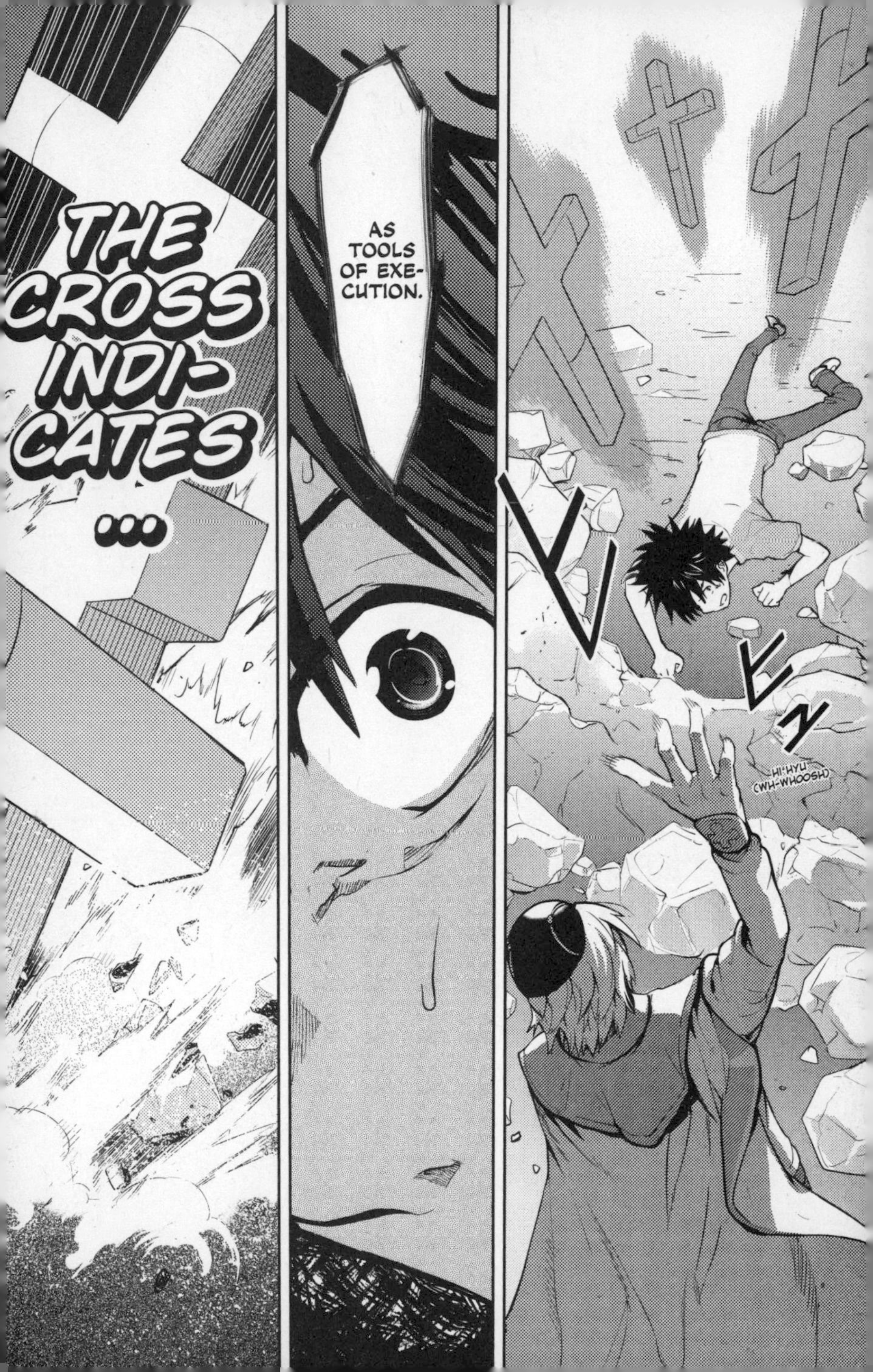

HI-HYU
(WH-WHOOSH)
AS TOOLS OF EXE-CUTION.
THE CROSS INDI-CATES ...

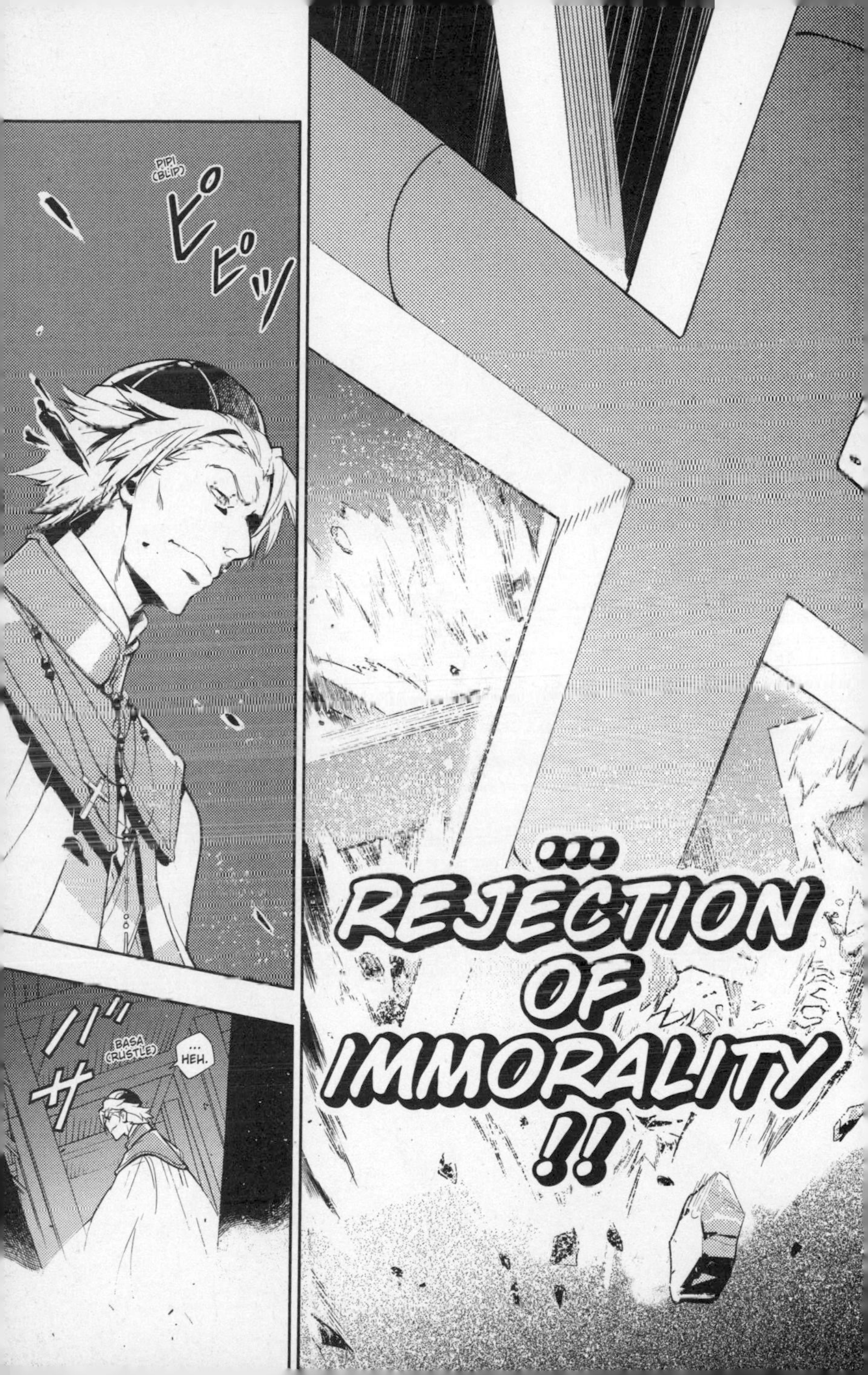
...REJECTION OF IMMORALITY!!
PIPI (BLIP)
ピピッ
BASA (RUSTLE)
バサ
...HEH.

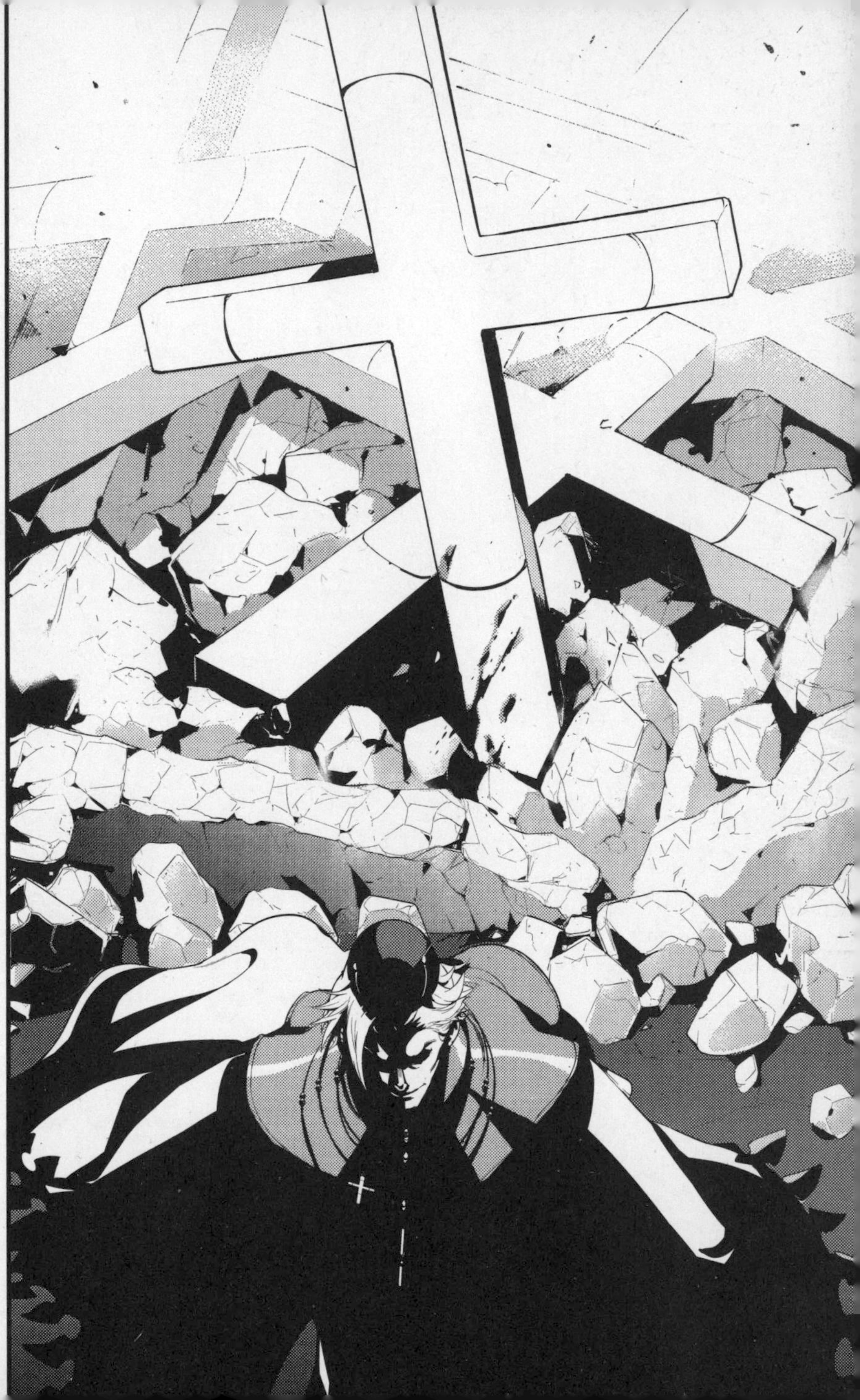

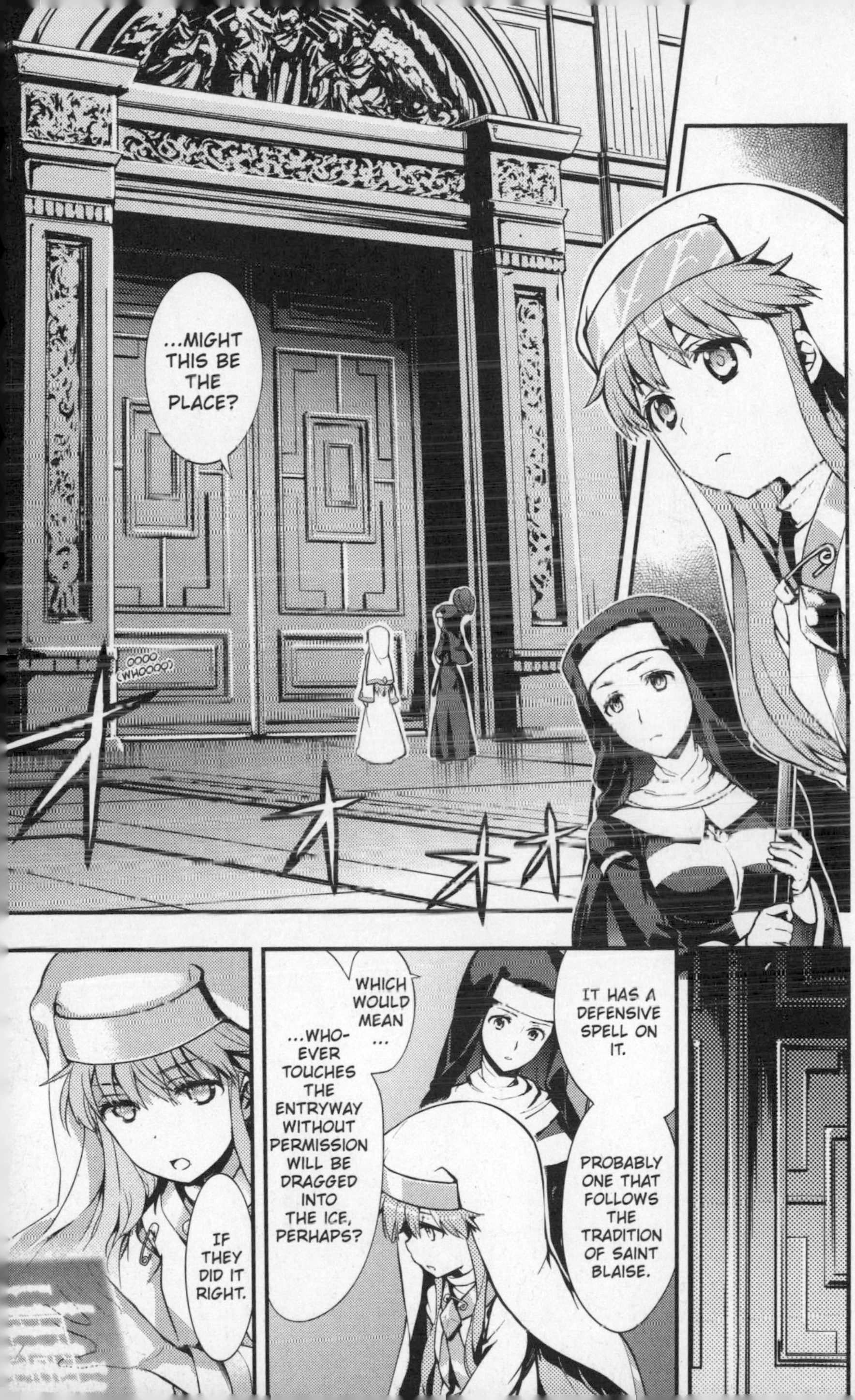
...MIGHT THIS BE THE PLACE?
OOOO (WHOOOO)
IT HAS A DEFENSIVE SPELL ON IT.
PROBABLY ONE THAT FOLLOWS THE TRADITION OF SAINT BLAISE.
WHICH WOULD MEAN ...
...WHO-EVER TOUCHES THE ENTRYWAY WITHOUT PERMISSION WILL BE DRAGGED INTO THE ICE, PERHAPS?
IF THEY DID IT RIGHT.

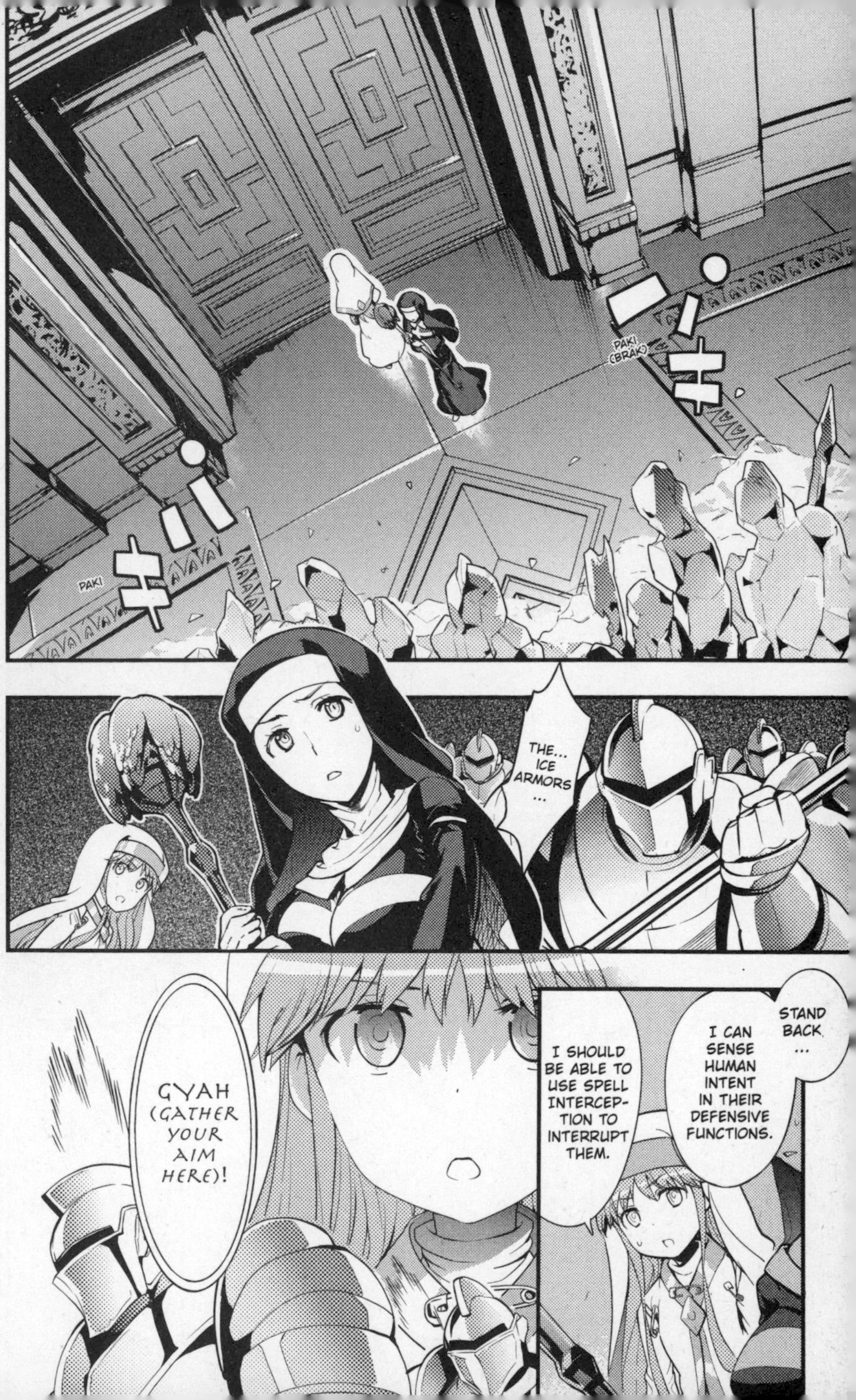
PAKI (BRAK)
PAKI
THE... ICE ARMORS ...
STAND BACK ...
I CAN SENSE HUMAN INTENT IN THEIR DEFENSIVE FUNCTIONS.
I SHOULD BE ABLE TO USE SPELL INTERCEPTION TO INTERRUPT THEM.
GYAH (GATHER YOUR AIM HERE)!

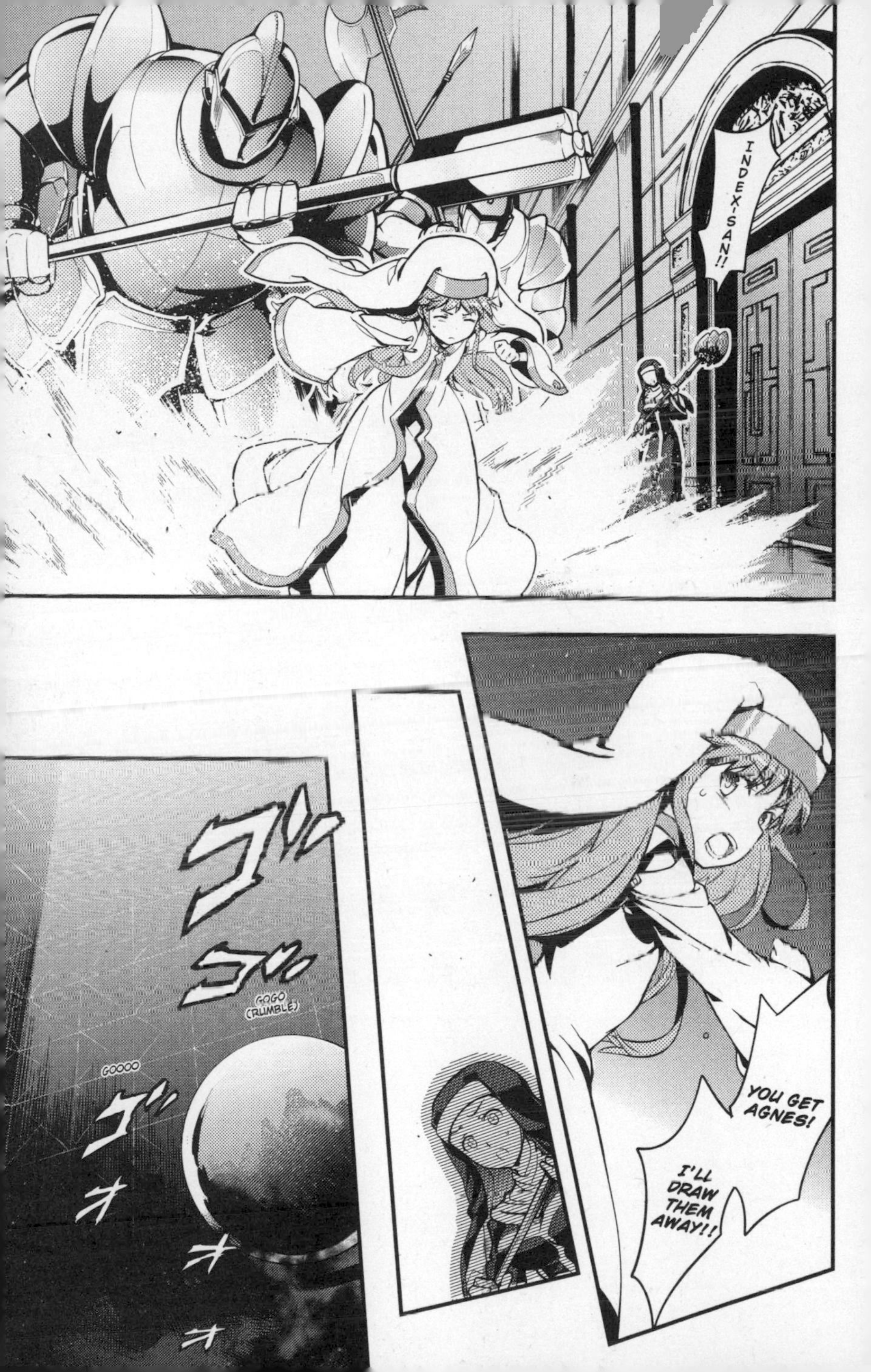
INDEXISAN!!
YOU GET AGNES!
I'LL DRAW THEM AWAY!!
GOGO (RUMBLE)
GOOOO

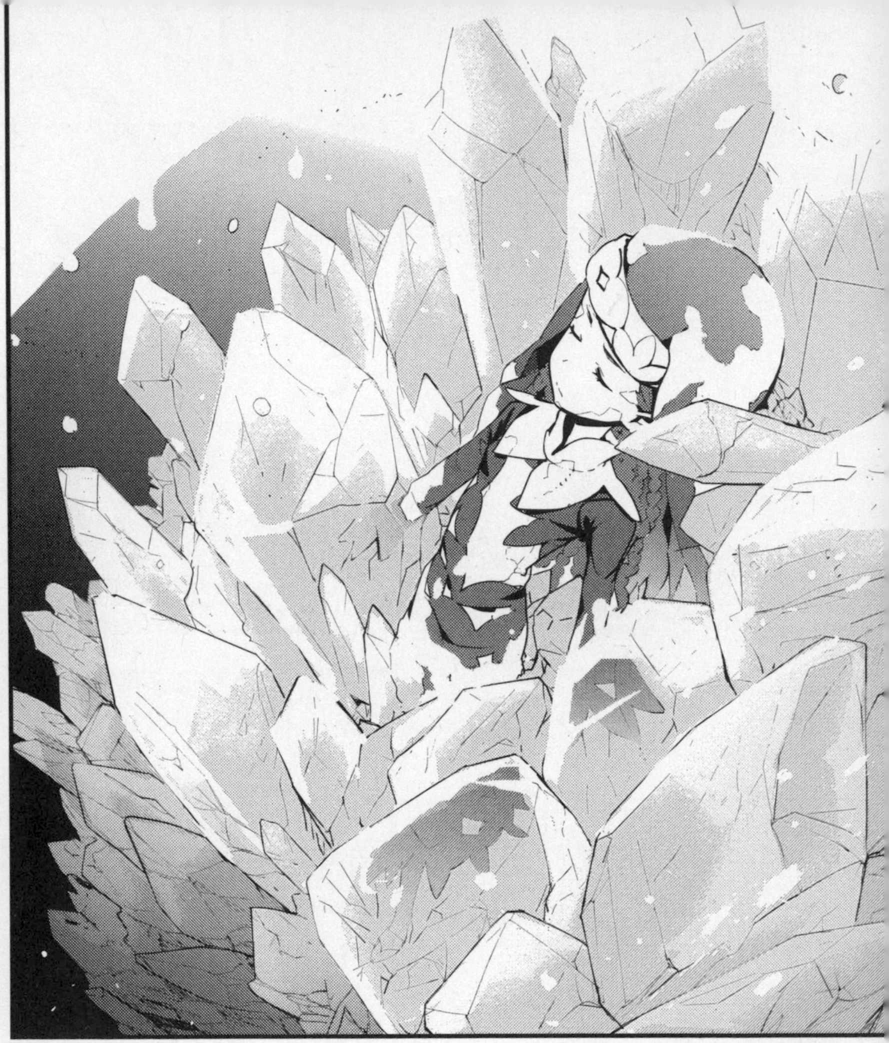

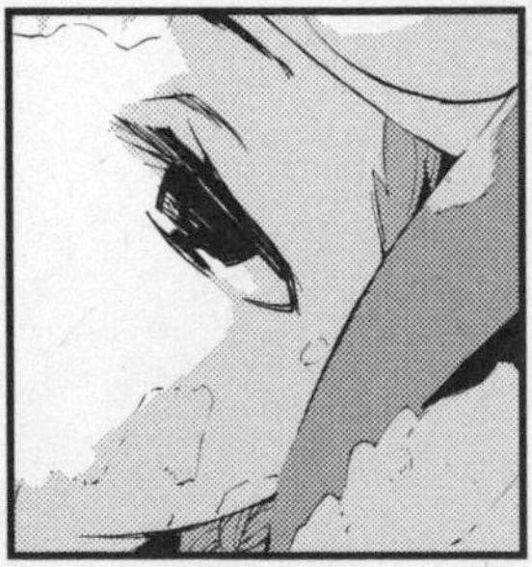

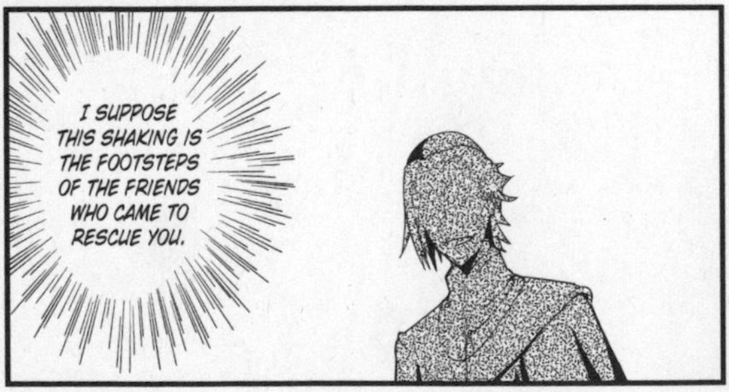
I SUPPOSE THIS SHAKING IS THE FOOTSTEPS OF THE FRIENDS WHO CAME TO RESCUE YOU.

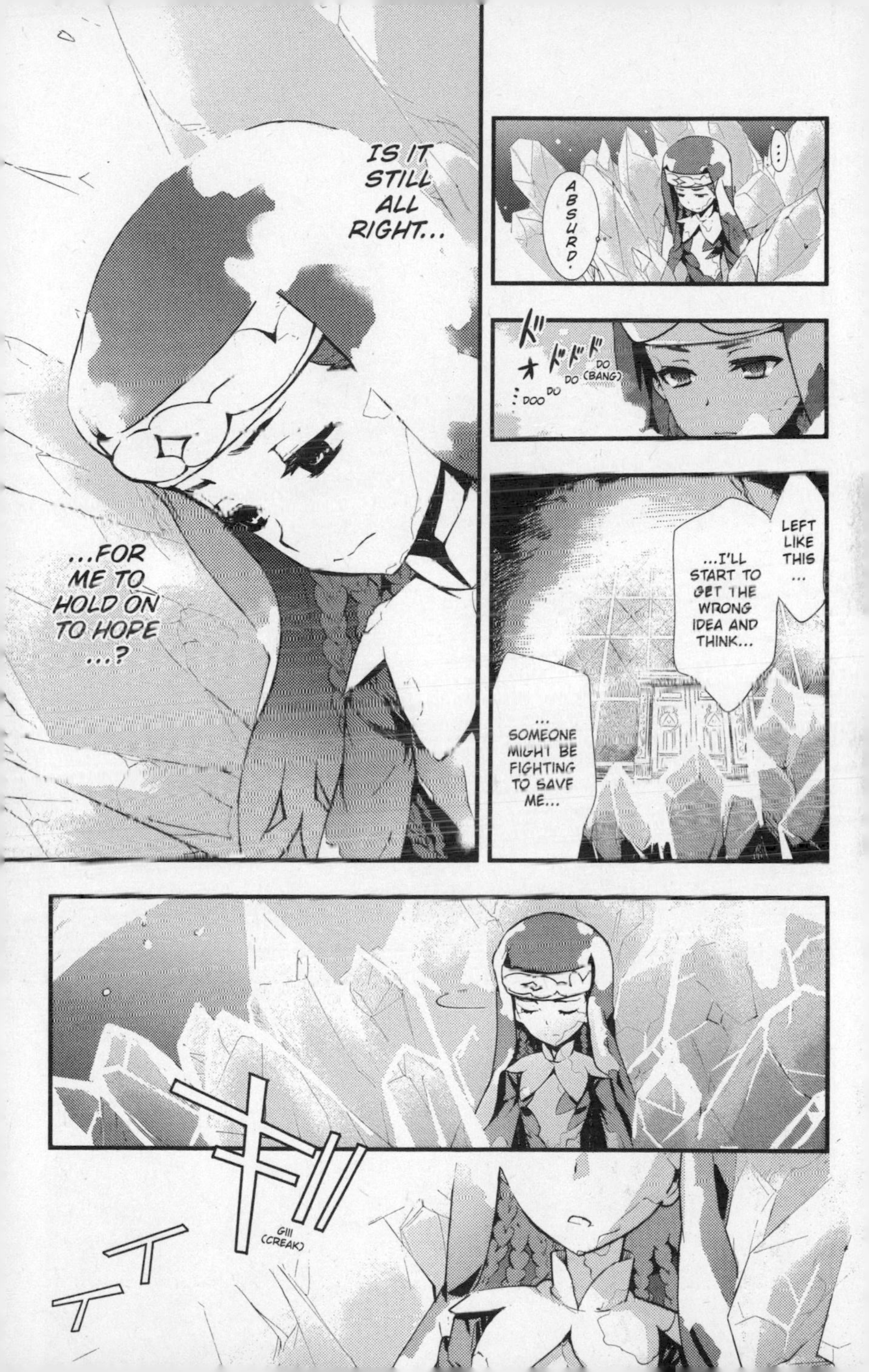
…
ABSURD.
DO DO DO (BANG) …DOO
LEFT LIKE THIS…
…I'LL START TO GET THE WRONG IDEA AND THINK…
…SOMEONE MIGHT BE FIGHTING TO SAVE ME…
IS IT STILL ALL RIGHT…
…FOR ME TO HOLD ON TO HOPE…?
GIII (CREAK)

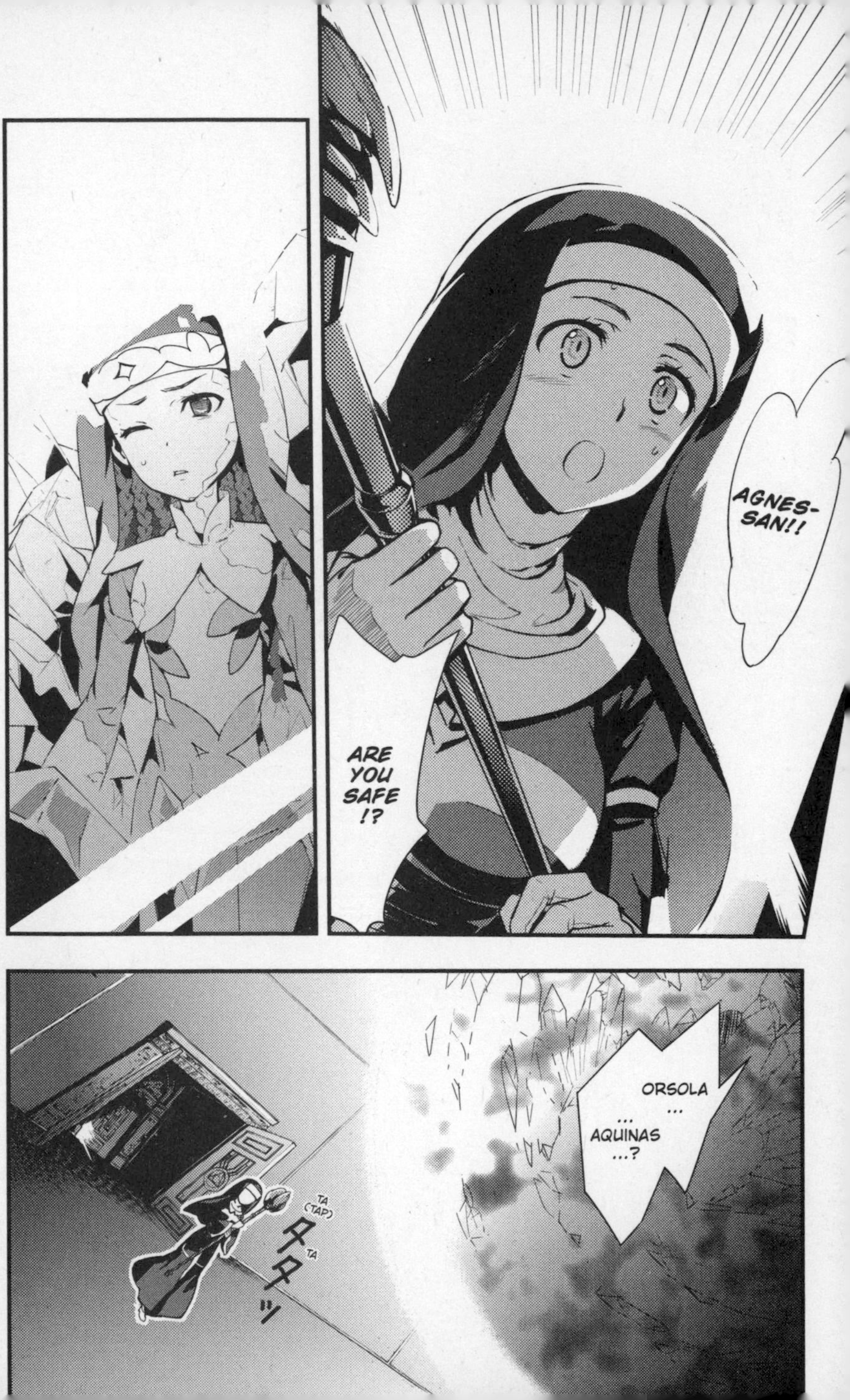
AGNES-SAN!!
ARE YOU SAFE!?
ORSOLA ... AQUINAS ...?
タタッ
TA (TAP) TA

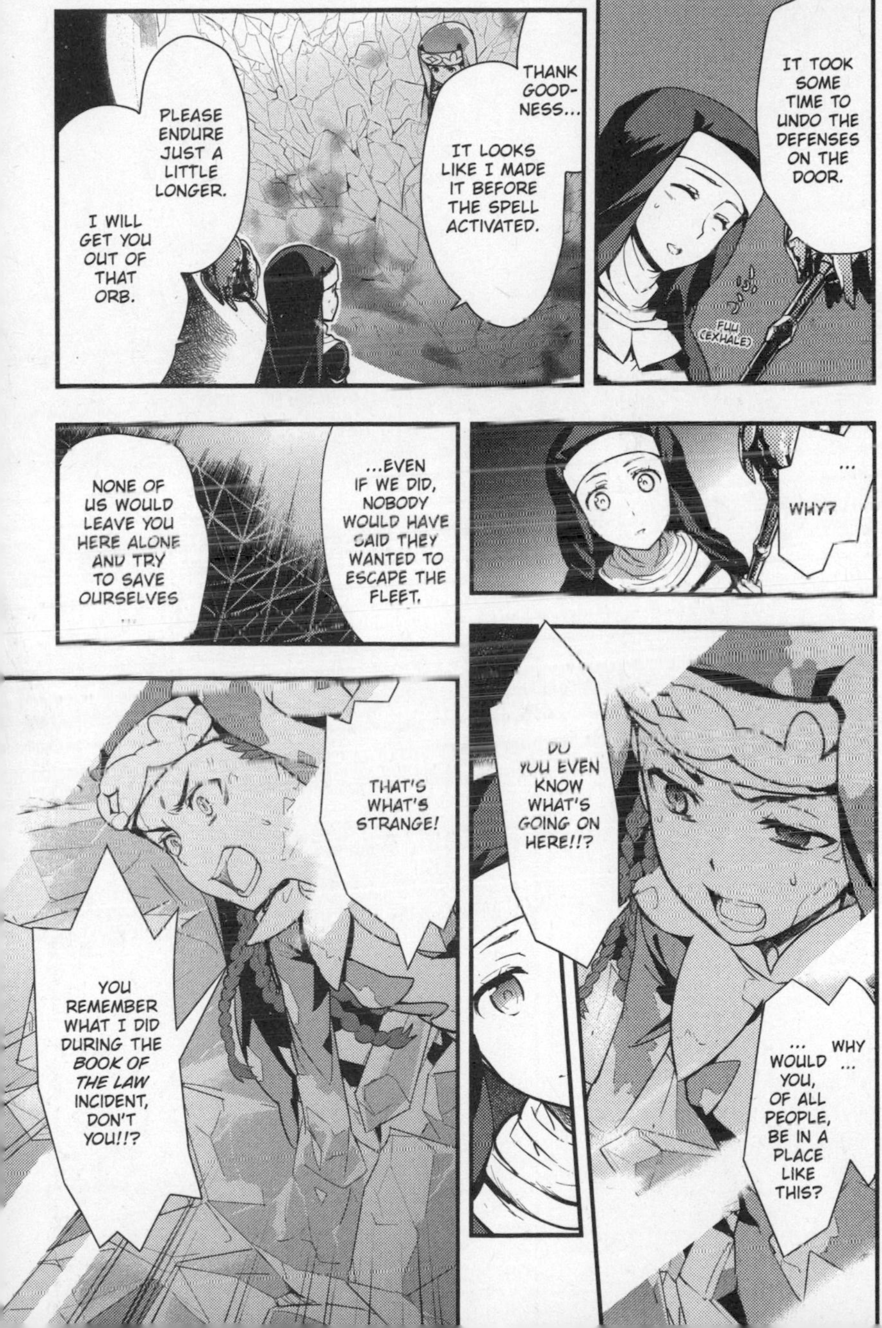
IT TOOK SOME TIME TO UNDO THE DEFENSES ON THE DOOR.
FUU (EXHALE)
THANK GOODNESS...
IT LOOKS LIKE I MADE IT BEFORE THE SPELL ACTIVATED.
PLEASE ENDURE JUST A LITTLE LONGER.
I WILL GET YOU OUT OF THAT ORB.
... WHY?
...EVEN IF WE DID, NOBODY WOULD HAVE SAID THEY WANTED TO ESCAPE THE FLEET.
NONE OF US WOULD LEAVE YOU HERE ALONE AND TRY TO SAVE OURSELVES
DO YOU EVEN KNOW WHAT'S GOING ON HERE!!?
... WHY ... WOULD YOU, OF ALL PEOPLE, BE IN A PLACE LIKE THIS?
THAT'S WHAT'S STRANGE!
YOU REMEMBER WHAT I DID DURING THE *BOOK OF THE LAW* INCIDENT, DON'T YOU!!?

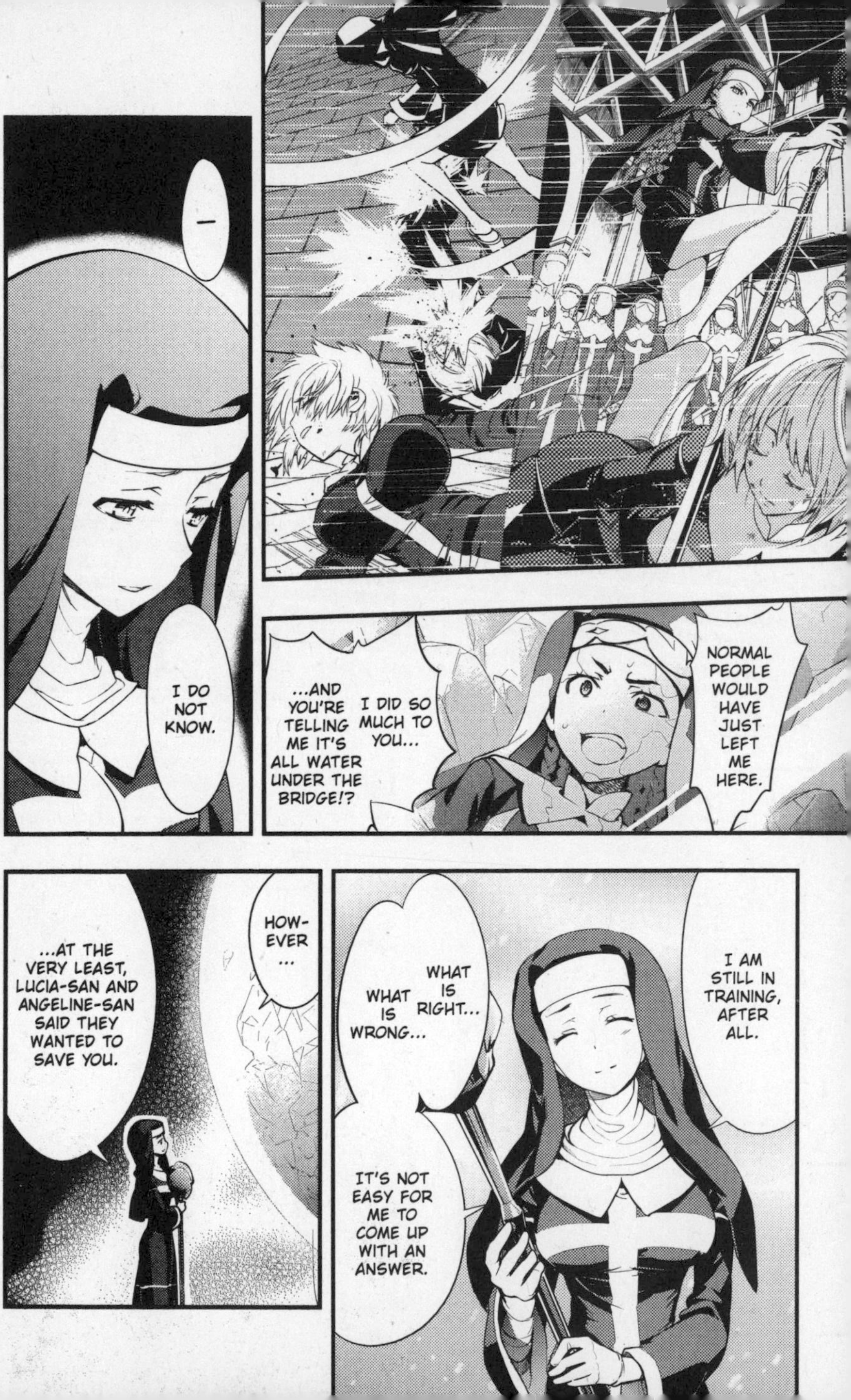
NORMAL PEOPLE WOULD HAVE JUST LEFT ME HERE.
I DID SO MUCH TO YOU...
...AND YOU'RE TELLING ME IT'S ALL WATER UNDER THE BRIDGE!?
—
I DO NOT KNOW.
I AM STILL IN TRAINING, AFTER ALL.
WHAT IS RIGHT...
WHAT IS WRONG...
IT'S NOT EASY FOR ME TO COME UP WITH AN ANSWER.
HOW-EVER...
...AT THE VERY LEAST, LUCIA-SAN AND ANGELINE-SAN SAID THEY WANTED TO SAVE YOU.

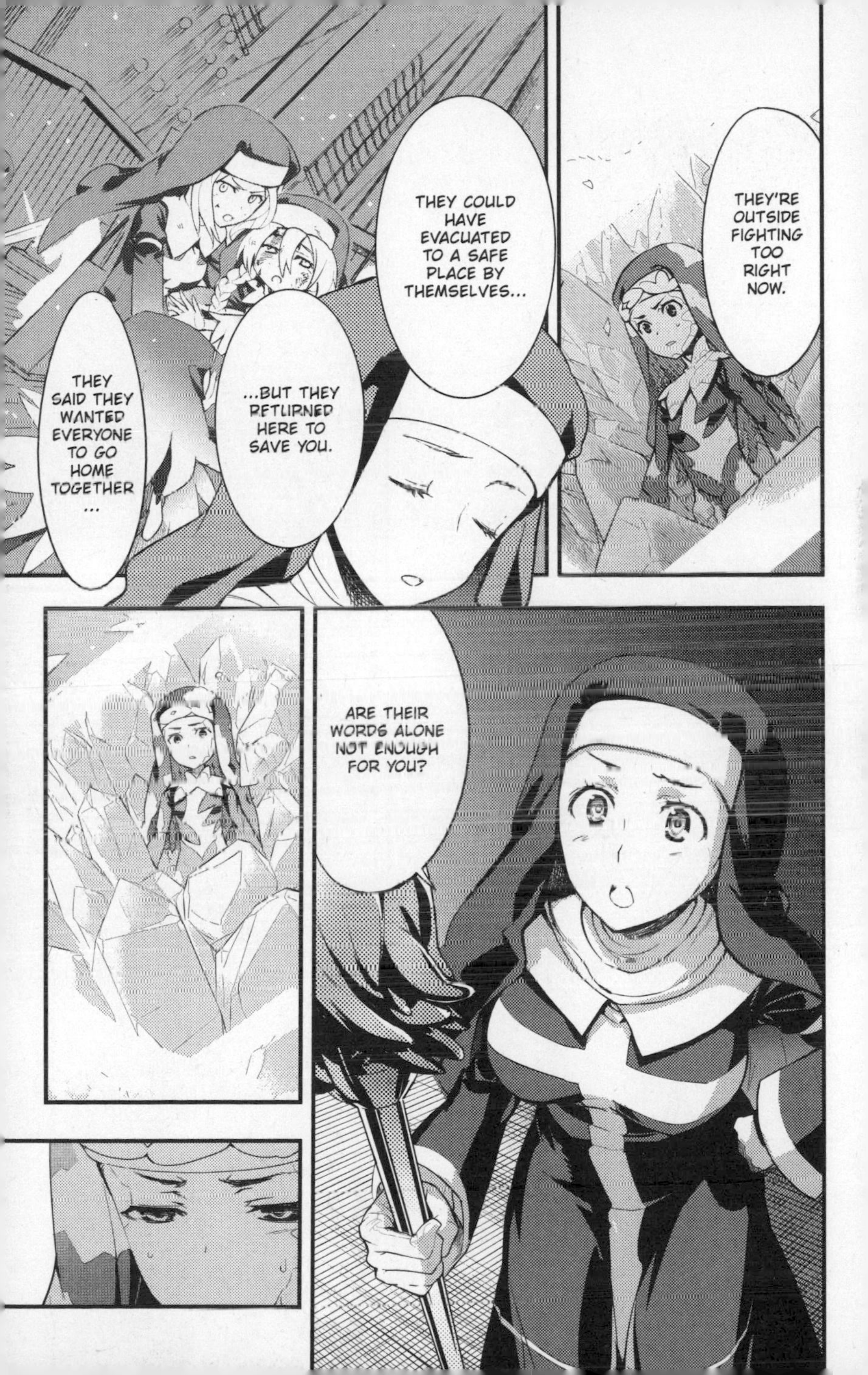
THEY'RE OUTSIDE FIGHTING TOO RIGHT NOW.
THEY COULD HAVE EVACUATED TO A SAFE PLACE BY THEMSELVES...
...BUT THEY RETURNED HERE TO SAVE YOU.
THEY SAID THEY WANTED EVERYONE TO GO HOME TOGETHER...
ARE THEIR WORDS ALONE NOT ENOUGH FOR YOU?

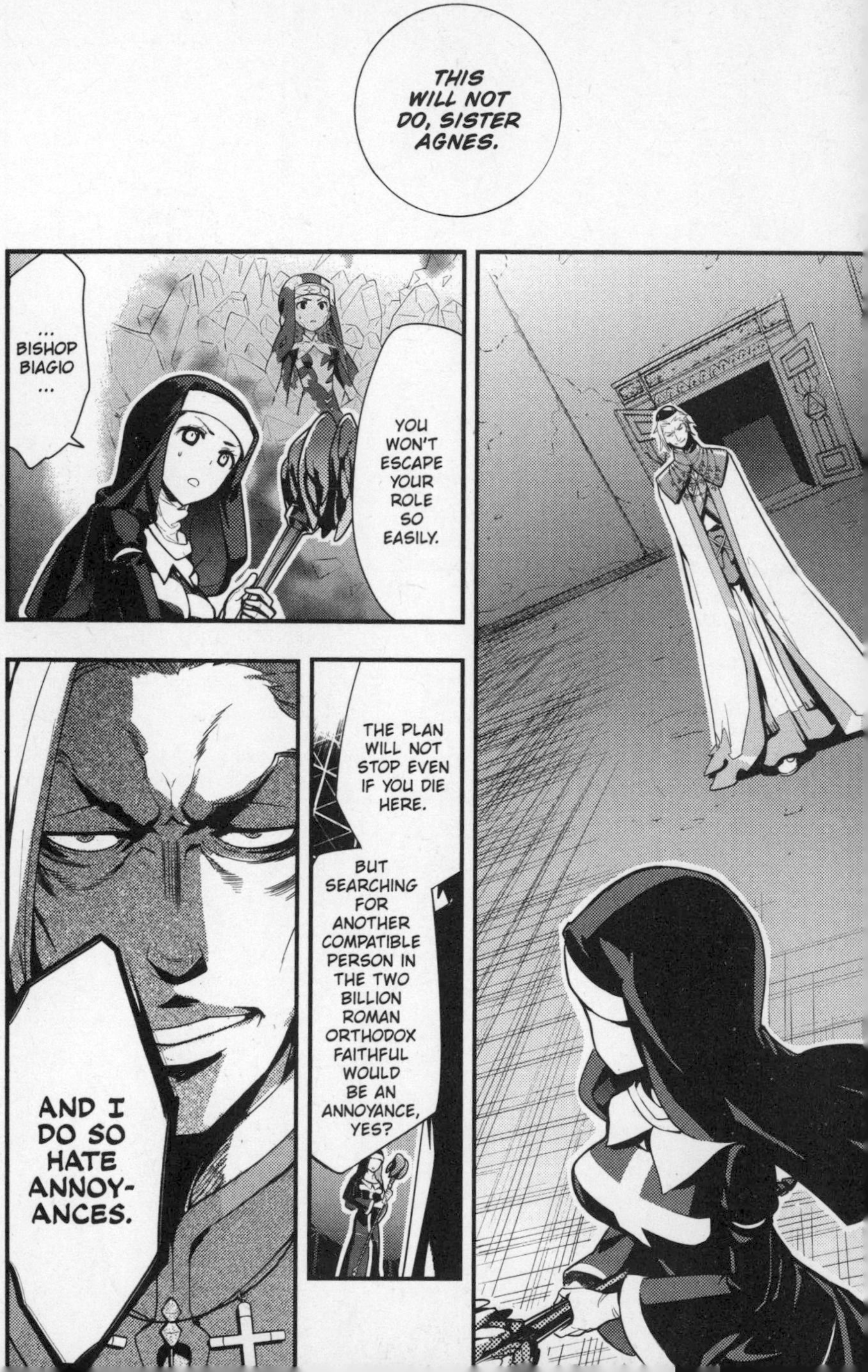
THIS WILL NOT DO, SISTER AGNES.
YOU WON'T ESCAPE YOUR ROLE SO EASILY.
... BISHOP BIAGIO ...
THE PLAN WILL NOT STOP EVEN IF YOU DIE HERE.
BUT SEARCHING FOR ANOTHER COMPATIBLE PERSON IN THE TWO BILLION ROMAN ORTHODOX FAITHFUL WOULD BE AN ANNOYANCE, YES?
AND I DO SO HATE ANNOY-ANCES.

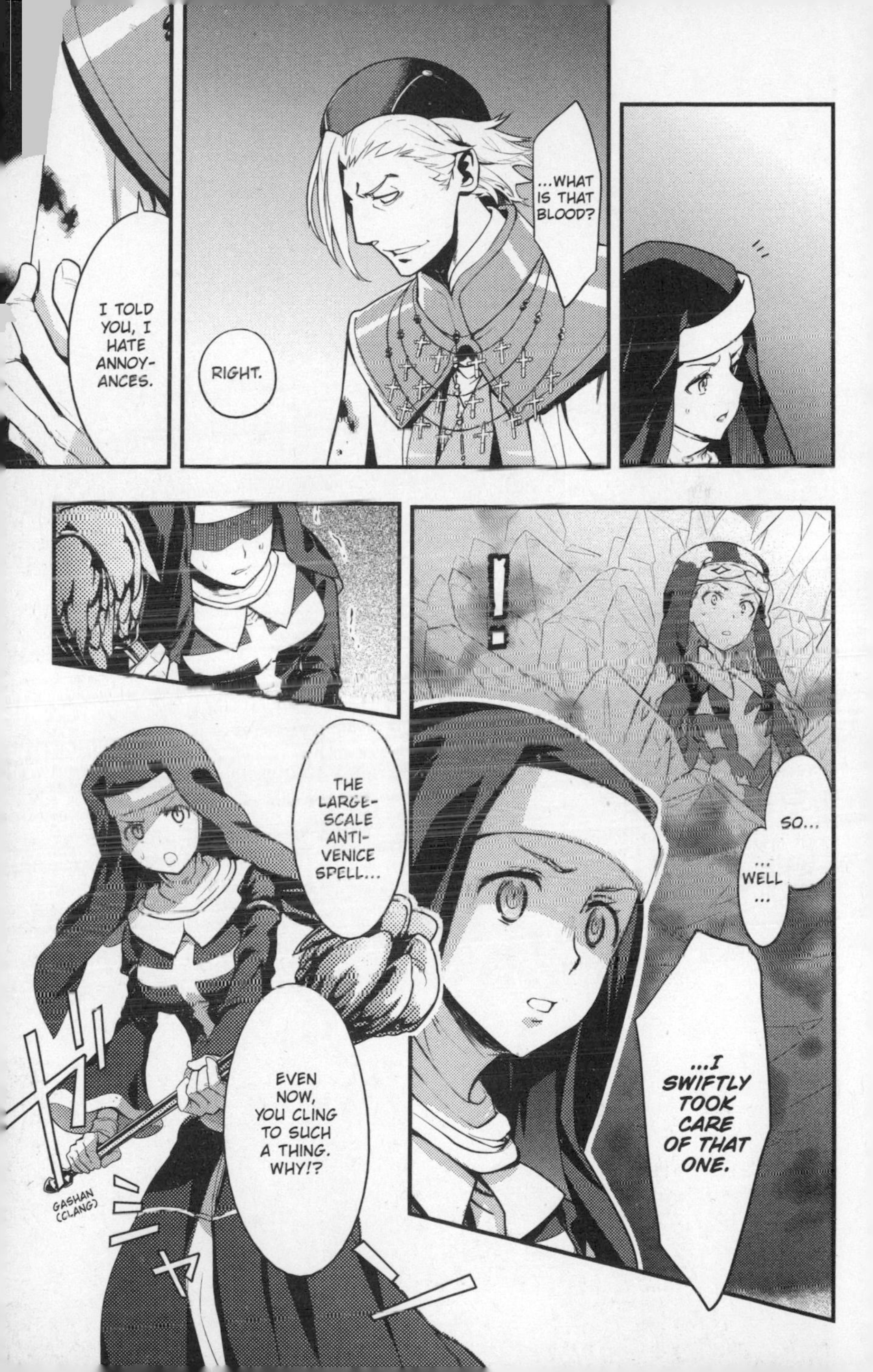
...WHAT IS THAT BLOOD?
RIGHT.
I TOLD YOU, I HATE ANNOY-ANCES.
SO... ...WELL...
...I SWIFTLY TOOK CARE OF THAT ONE.
THE LARGE-SCALE ANTI-VENICE SPELL...
EVEN NOW, YOU CLING TO SUCH A THING. WHY!?
GASHAN (CLANG)

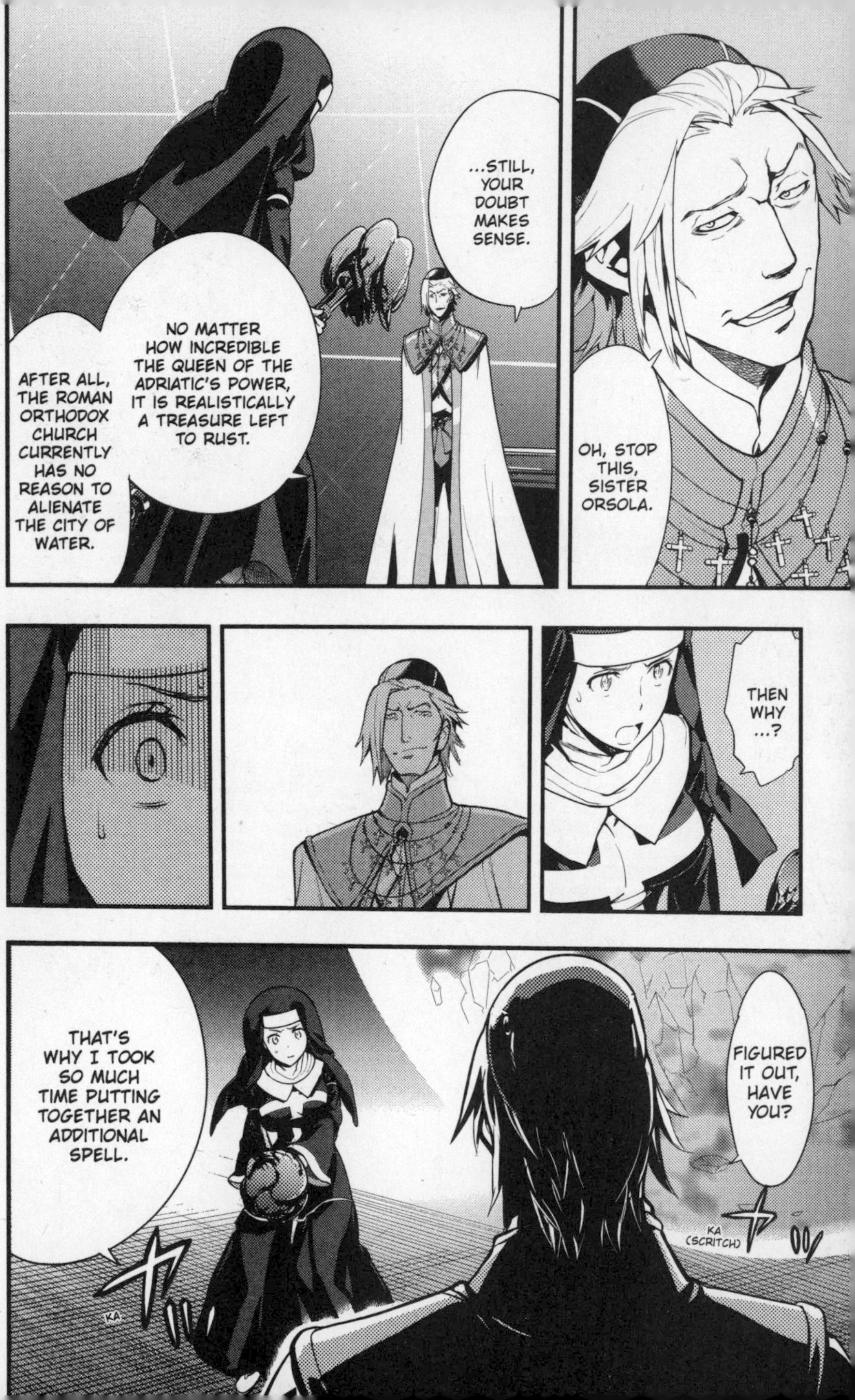
OH, STOP THIS, SISTER ORSOLA.
...STILL, YOUR DOUBT MAKES SENSE.
NO MATTER HOW INCREDIBLE THE QUEEN OF THE ADRIATIC'S POWER, IT IS REALISTICALLY A TREASURE LEFT TO RUST.
AFTER ALL, THE ROMAN ORTHODOX CHURCH CURRENTLY HAS NO REASON TO ALIENATE THE CITY OF WATER.
THEN WHY ...?
FIGURED IT OUT, HAVE YOU?
KA (SCRITCH)
THAT'S WHY I TOOK SO MUCH TIME PUTTING TOGETHER AN ADDITIONAL SPELL.
KA

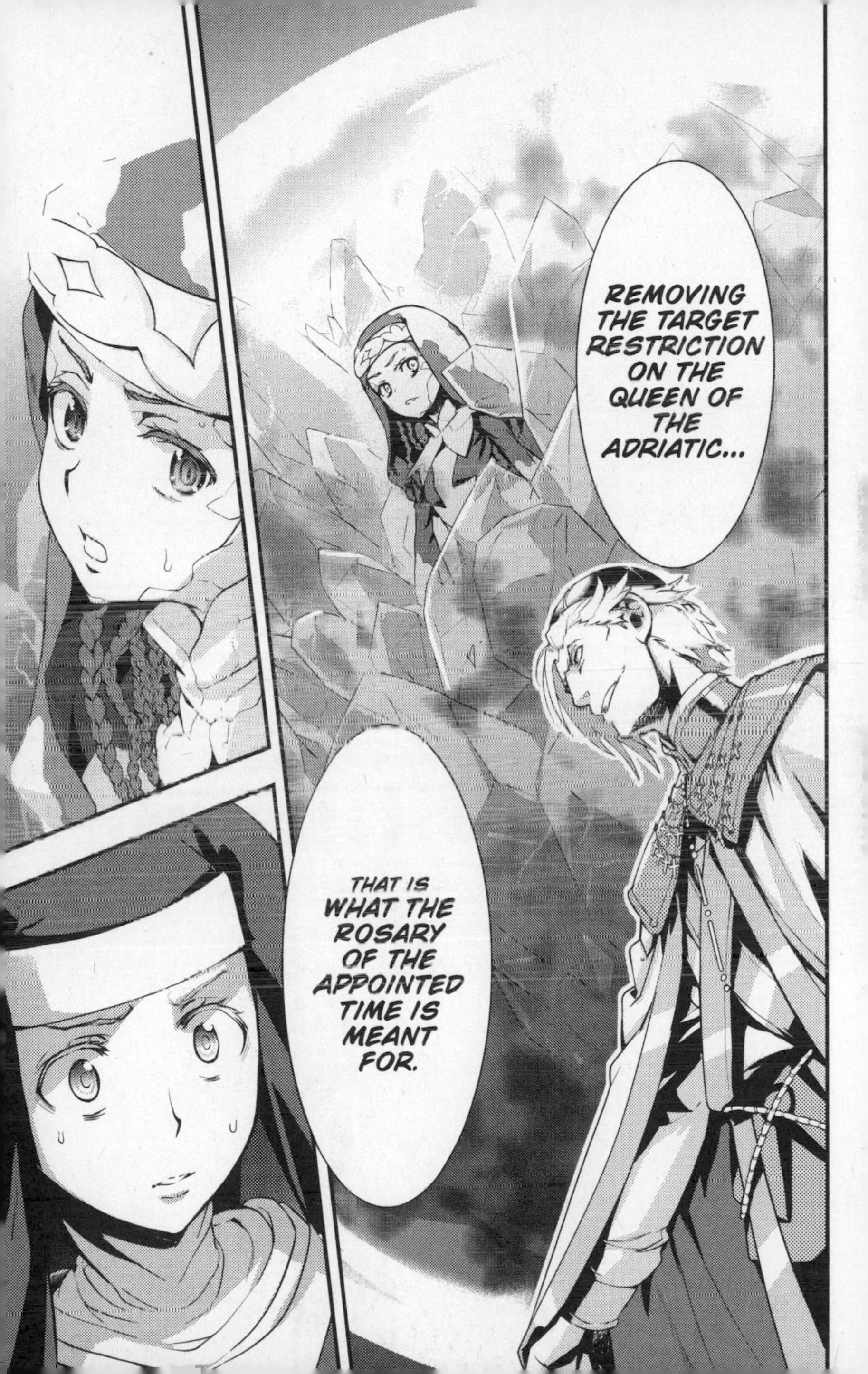
REMOVING THE TARGET RESTRICTION ON THE QUEEN OF THE ADRIATIC...
THAT IS WHAT THE ROSARY OF THE APPOINTED TIME IS MEANT FOR.

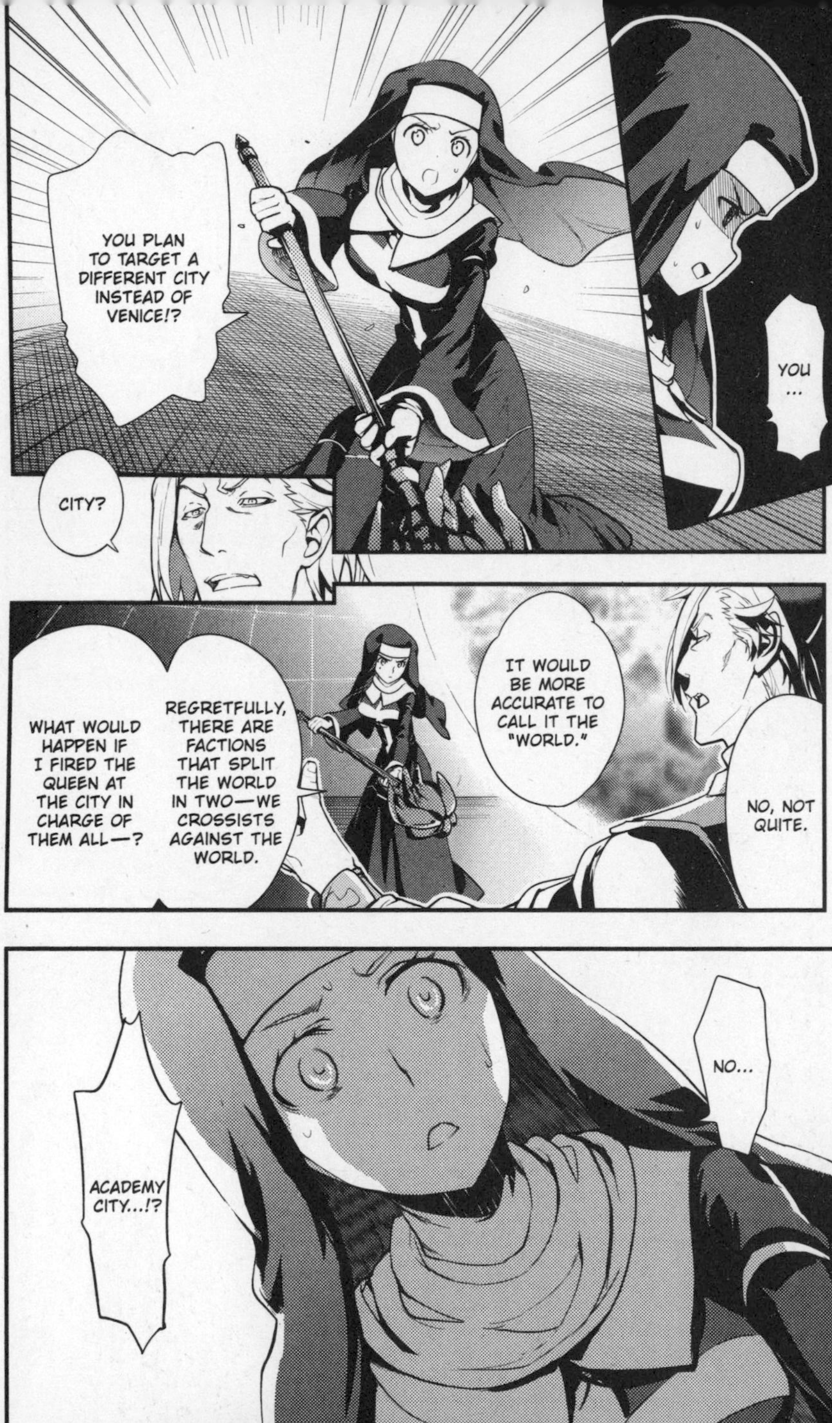
YOU ...
YOU PLAN TO TARGET A DIFFERENT CITY INSTEAD OF VENICE!?
CITY?
NO, NOT QUITE.
IT WOULD BE MORE ACCURATE TO CALL IT THE "WORLD."
REGRETFULLY, THERE ARE FACTIONS THAT SPLIT THE WORLD IN TWO—WE CROSSISTS AGAINST THE WORLD.
WHAT WOULD HAPPEN IF I FIRED THE QUEEN AT THE CITY IN CHARGE OF THEM ALL—?
NO...
ACADEMY CITY...!?

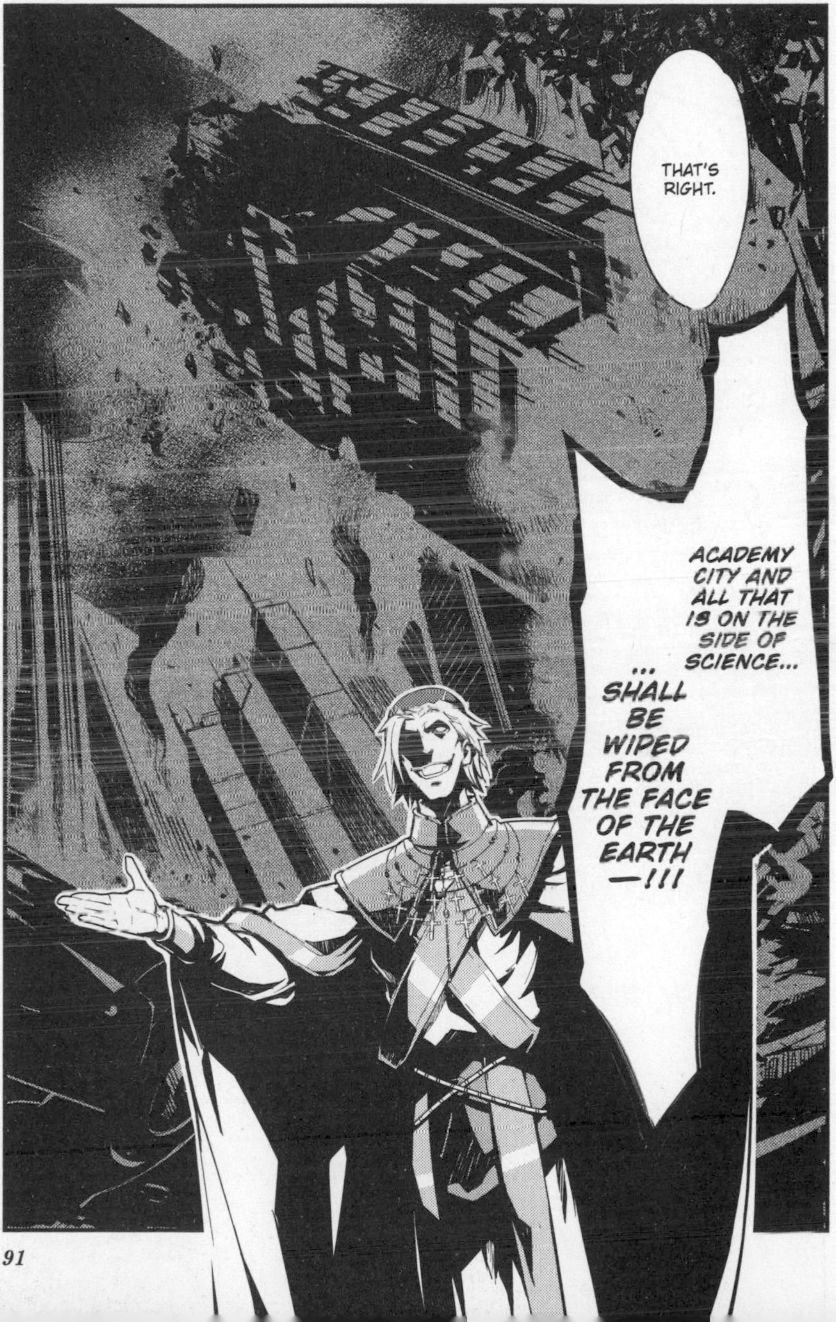
THAT'S RIGHT.
ACADEMY CITY AND ALL THAT IS ON THE SIDE OF SCIENCE...
...SHALL BE WIPED FROM THE FACE OF THE EARTH—!!!

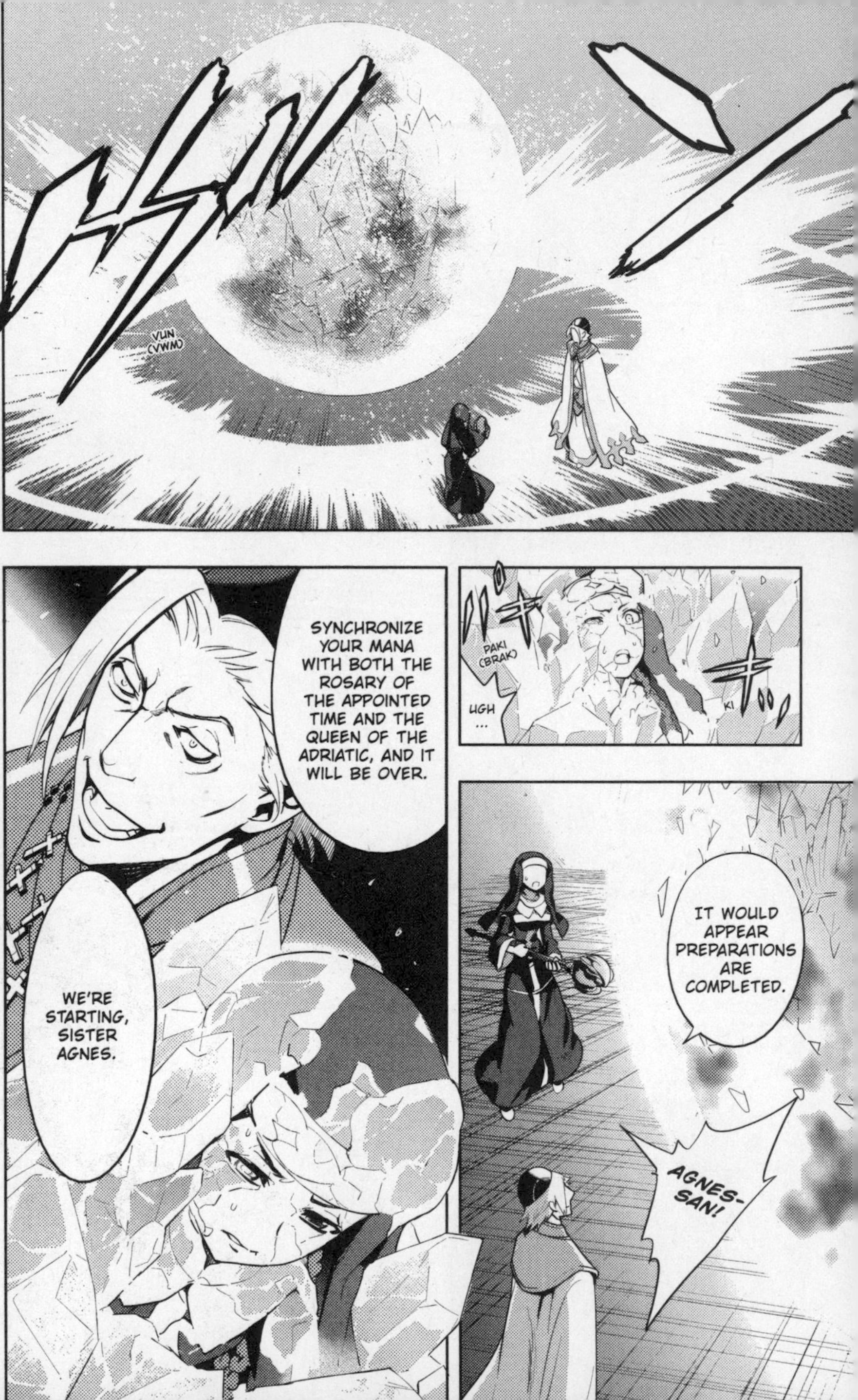
VUN (VWM)
PAKI (BRAK)
UGH ...
KI
IT WOULD APPEAR PREPARATIONS ARE COMPLETED.
AGNES-SAN!
SYNCHRONIZE YOUR MANA WITH BOTH THE ROSARY OF THE APPOINTED TIME AND THE QUEEN OF THE ADRIATIC, AND IT WILL BE OVER.
WE'RE STARTING, SISTER AGNES.

#95 ROSARY OF THE APPOINTED TIME ③

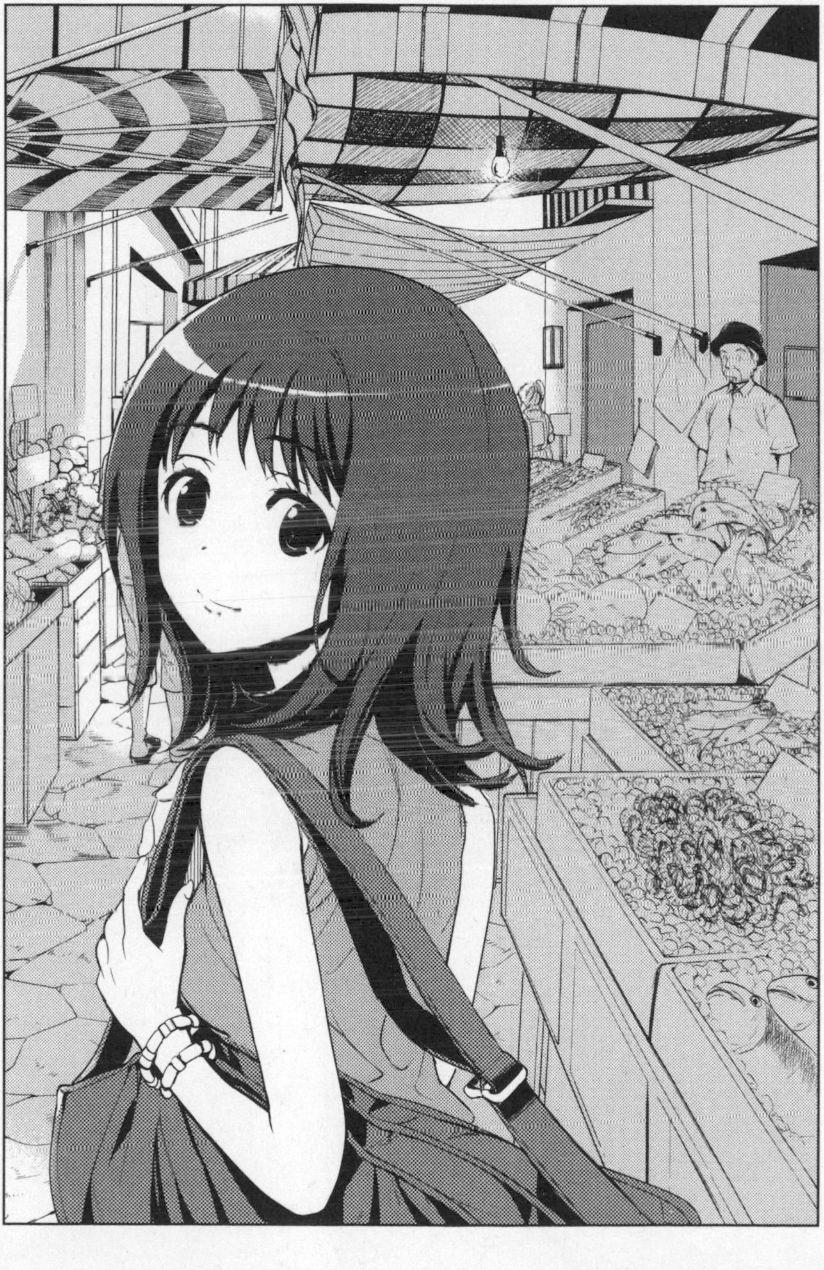

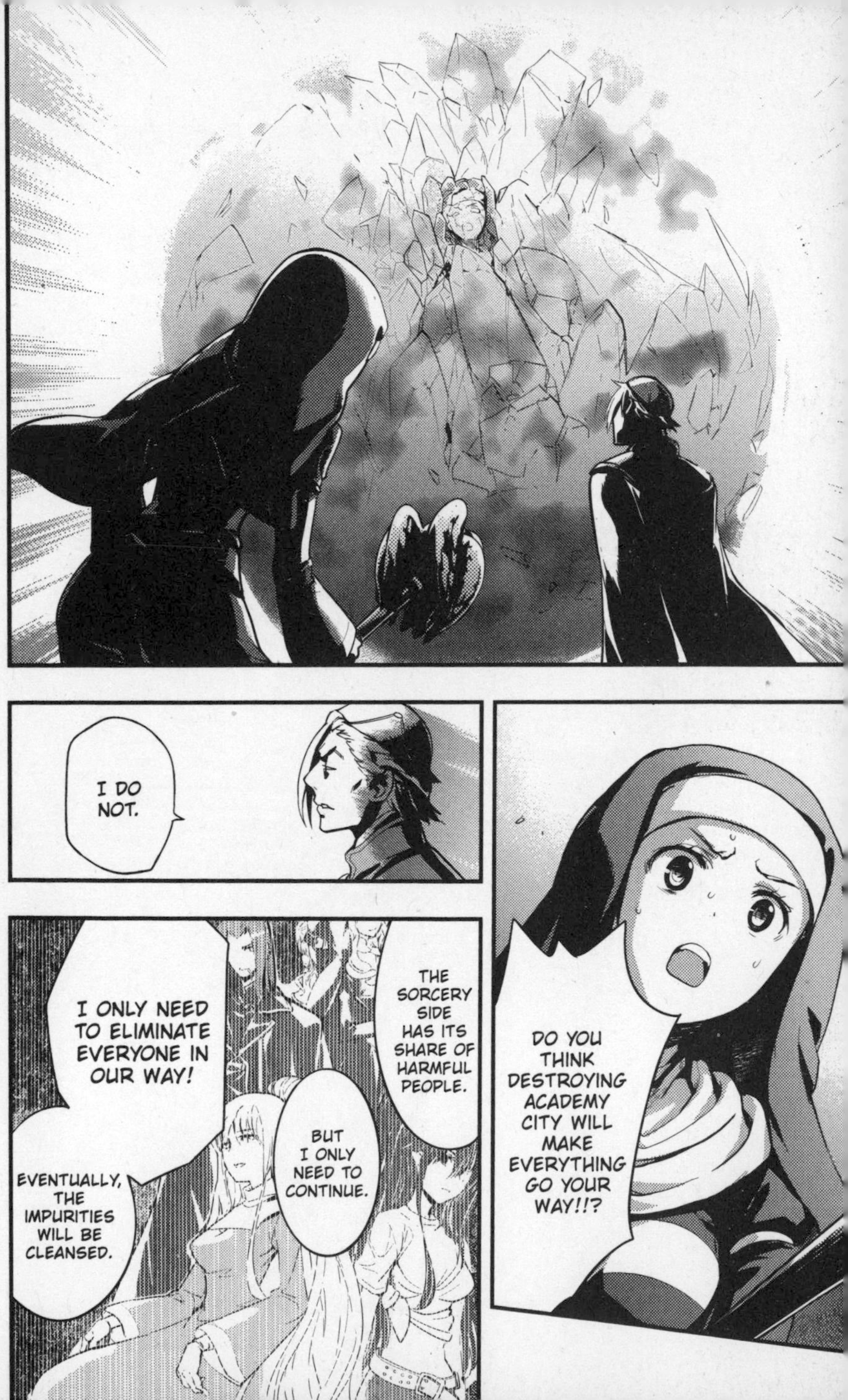

DO YOU THINK DESTROYING ACADEMY CITY WILL MAKE EVERYTHING GO YOUR WAY!!?
I DO NOT.
THE SORCERY SIDE HAS ITS SHARE OF HARMFUL PEOPLE.
I ONLY NEED TO ELIMINATE EVERYONE IN OUR WAY!
BUT I ONLY NEED TO CONTINUE.
EVENTUALLY, THE IMPURITIES WILL BE CLEANSED.

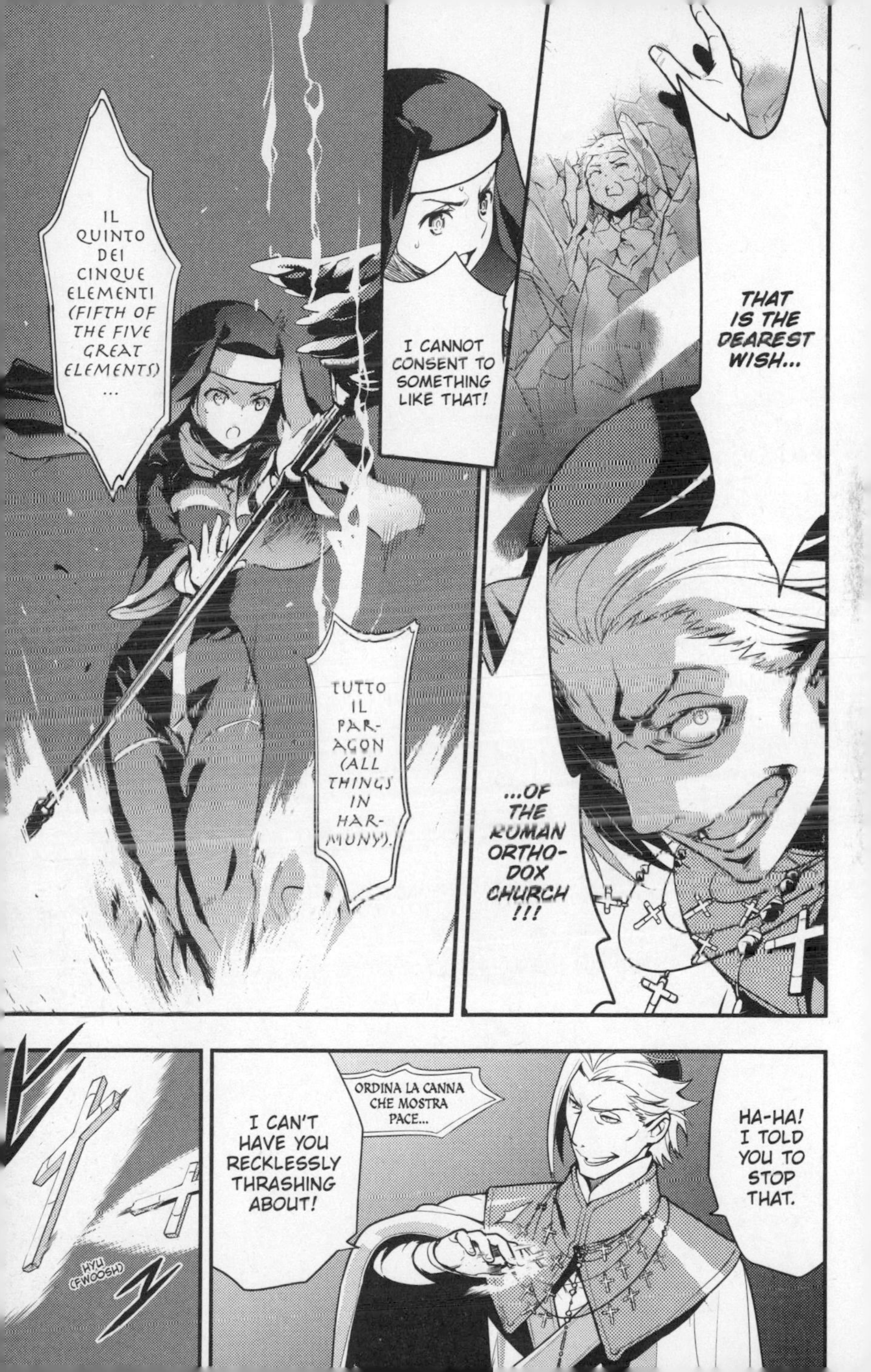
THAT IS THE DEAREST WISH...
...OF THE ROMAN ORTHODOX CHURCH!!!
I CANNOT CONSENT TO SOMETHING LIKE THAT!
IL QUINTO DEI CINQUE ELEMENTI (FIFTH OF THE FIVE GREAT ELEMENTS)...
TUTTO IL PARAGON (ALL THINGS IN HARMONY).
HA-HA! I TOLD YOU TO STOP THAT.
ORDINA LA CANNA CHE MOSTRA PACE...
I CAN'T HAVE YOU RECKLESSLY THRASHING ABOUT!
HYU (FWOOSH)

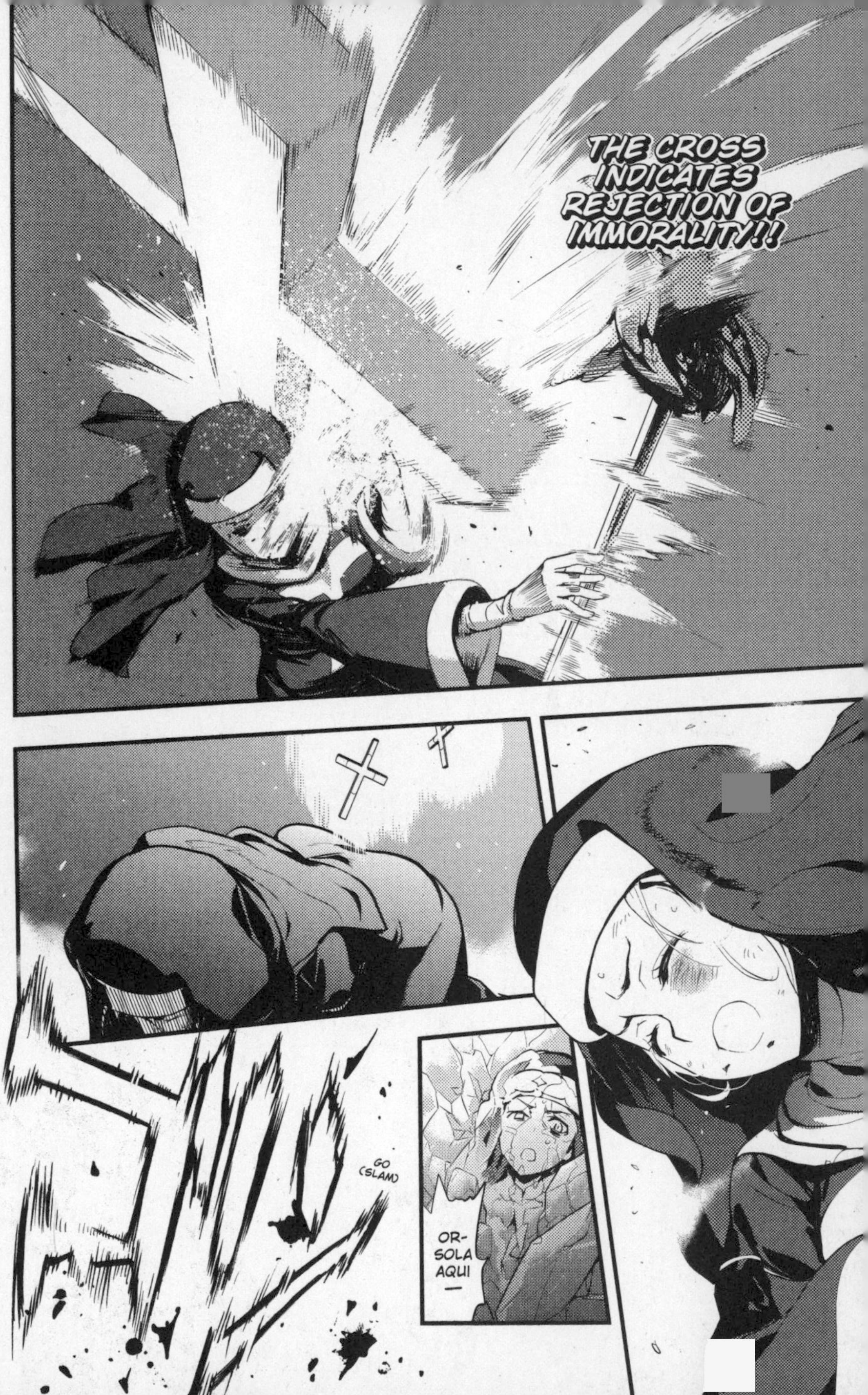
THE CROSS INDICATES REJECTION OF IMMORALITY!!
OR-SOLA AQUI —
GO (SLAM)

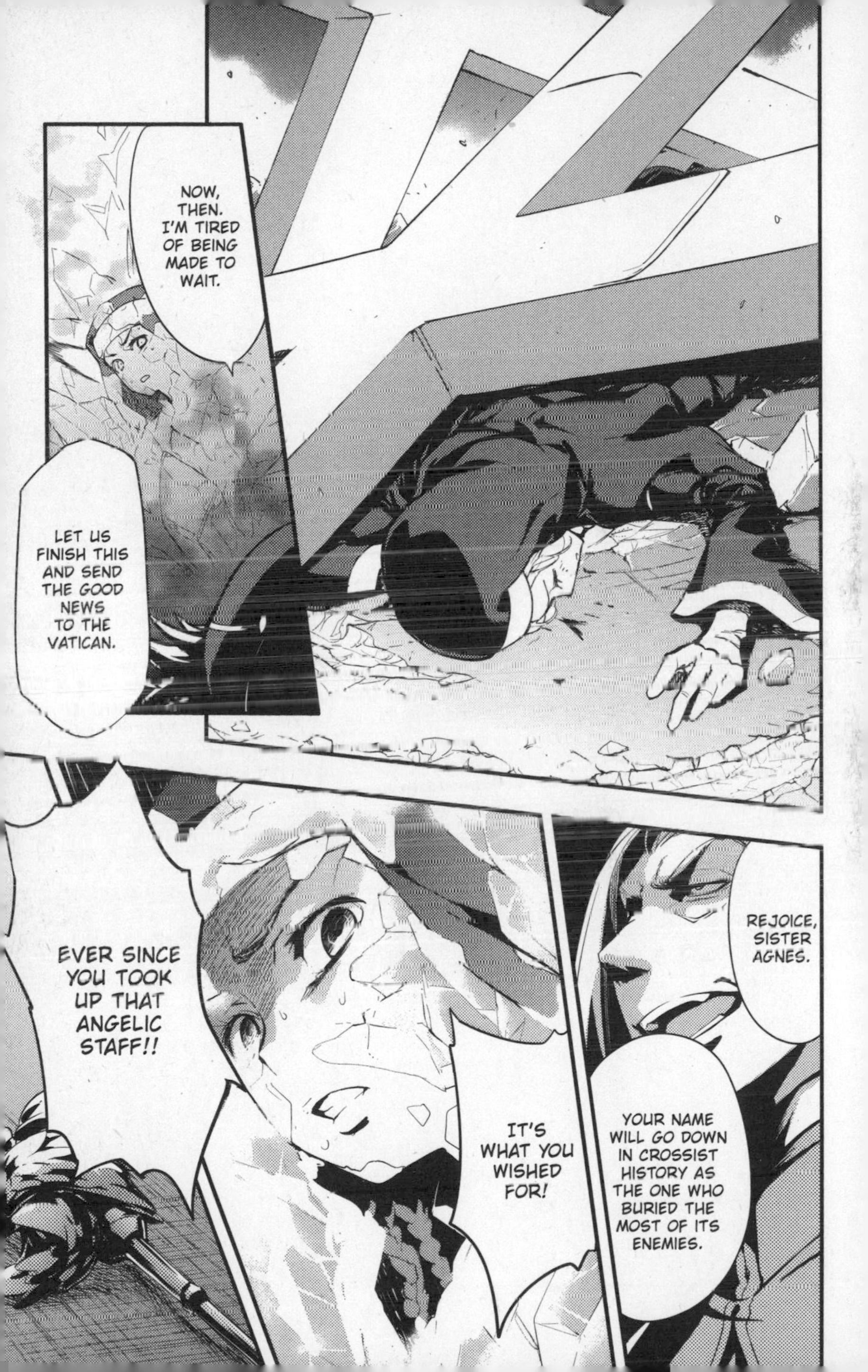
NOW, THEN. I'M TIRED OF BEING MADE TO WAIT.
LET US FINISH THIS AND SEND THE GOOD NEWS TO THE VATICAN.
REJOICE, SISTER AGNES.
YOUR NAME WILL GO DOWN IN CROSSIST HISTORY AS THE ONE WHO BURIED THE MOST OF ITS ENEMIES.
IT'S WHAT YOU WISHED FOR!
EVER SINCE YOU TOOK UP THAT ANGELIC STAFF!!

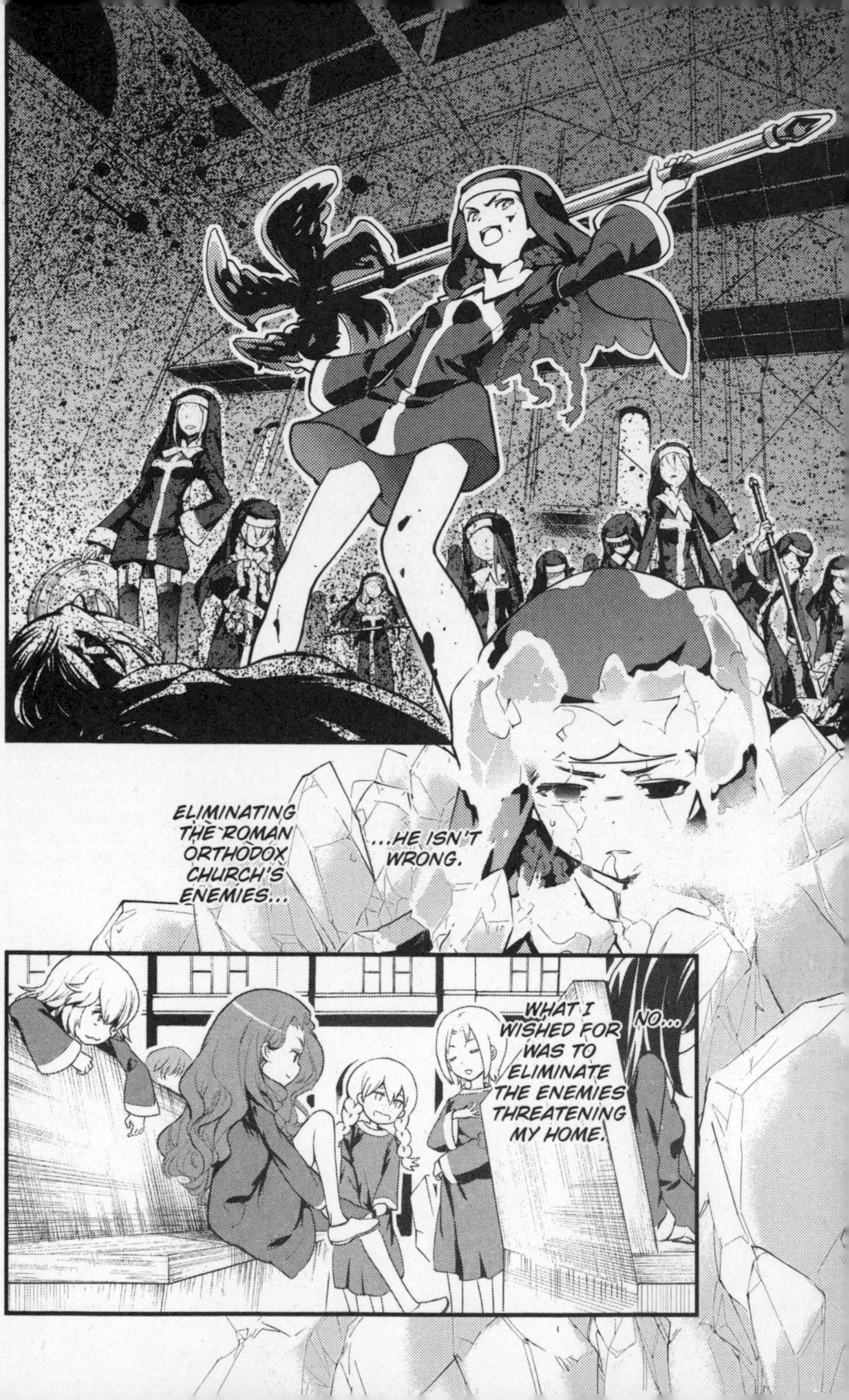
...HE ISN'T WRONG.
ELIMINATING THE ROMAN ORTHODOX CHURCH'S ENEMIES...
NO...
WHAT I WISHED FOR WAS TO ELIMINATE THE ENEMIES THREATENING MY HOME.

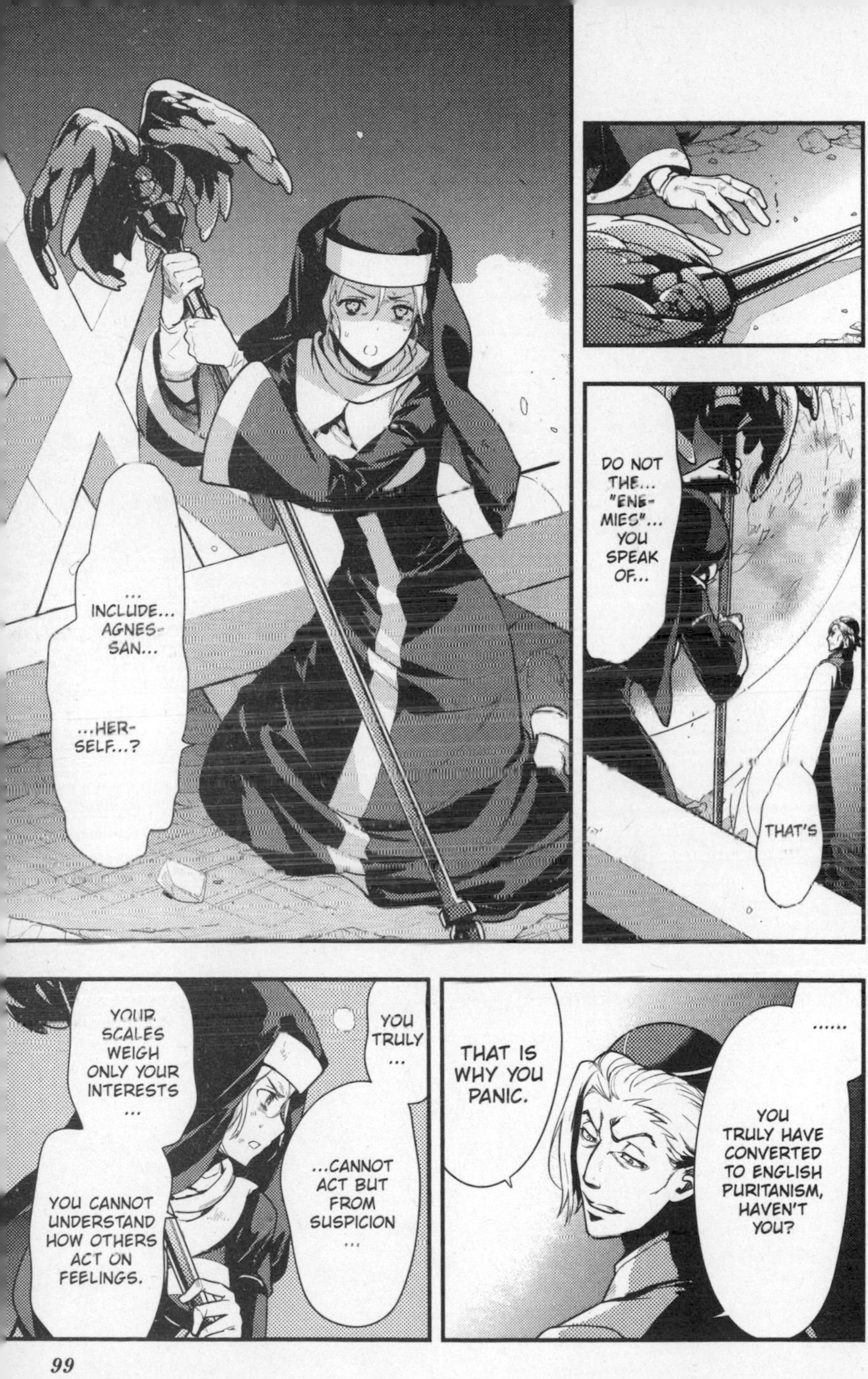
DO NOT THE... "ENEMIES"... YOU SPEAK OF...
THAT'S
... INCLUDE... AGNES-SAN...
...HER-SELF...?
......
YOU TRULY HAVE CONVERTED TO ENGLISH PURITANISM, HAVEN'T YOU?
THAT IS WHY YOU PANIC.
YOU TRULY ...
...CANNOT ACT BUT FROM SUSPICION ...
YOUR SCALES WEIGH ONLY YOUR INTERESTS ...
YOU CANNOT UNDERSTAND HOW OTHERS ACT ON FEELINGS.

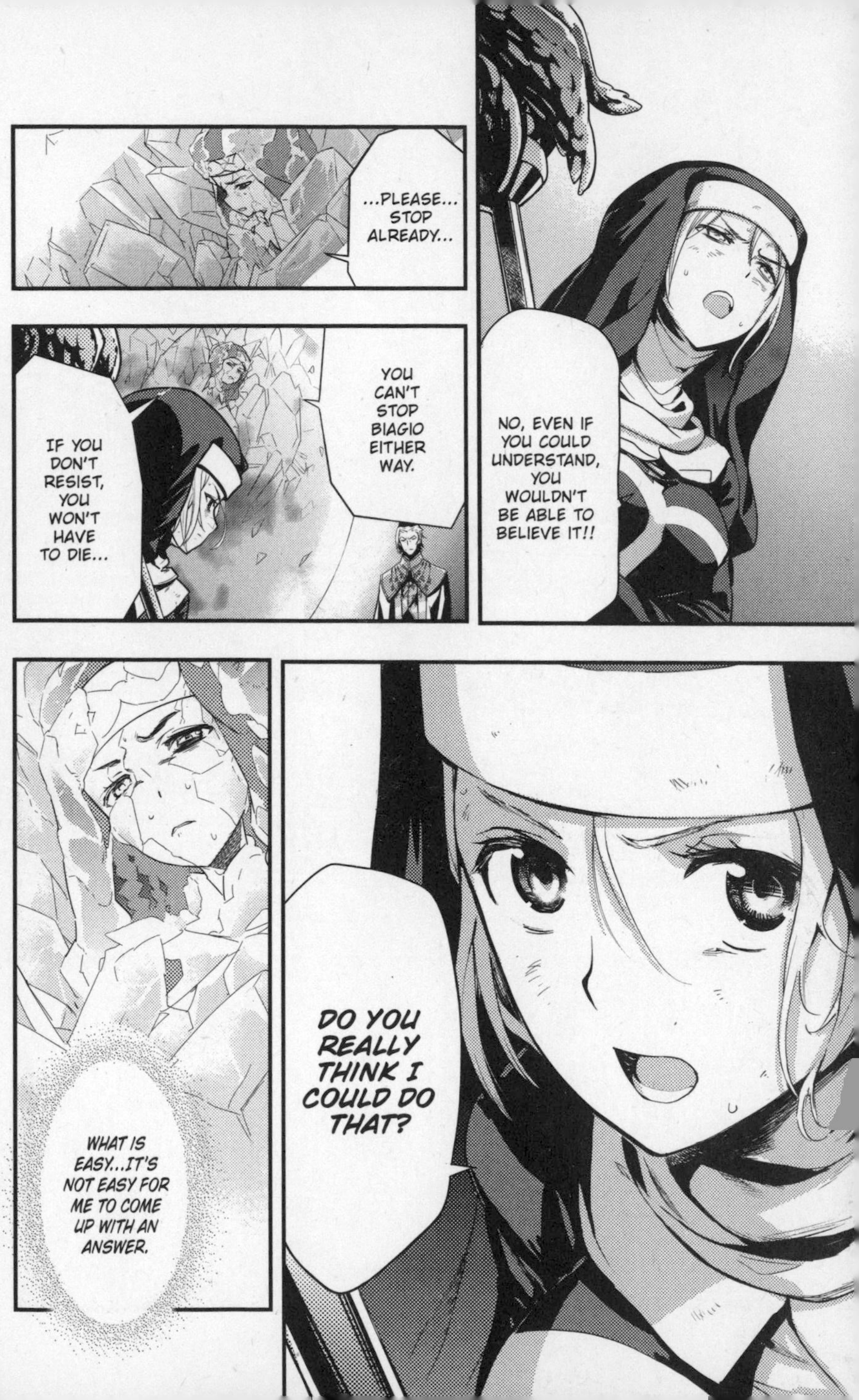
NO, EVEN IF YOU COULD UNDERSTAND, YOU WOULDN'T BE ABLE TO BELIEVE IT!!
...PLEASE... STOP ALREADY...
YOU CAN'T STOP BIAGIO EITHER WAY.
IF YOU DON'T RESIST, YOU WON'T HAVE TO DIE...
DO YOU REALLY THINK I COULD DO THAT?
WHAT IS EASY...IT'S NOT EASY FOR ME TO COME UP WITH AN ANSWER.

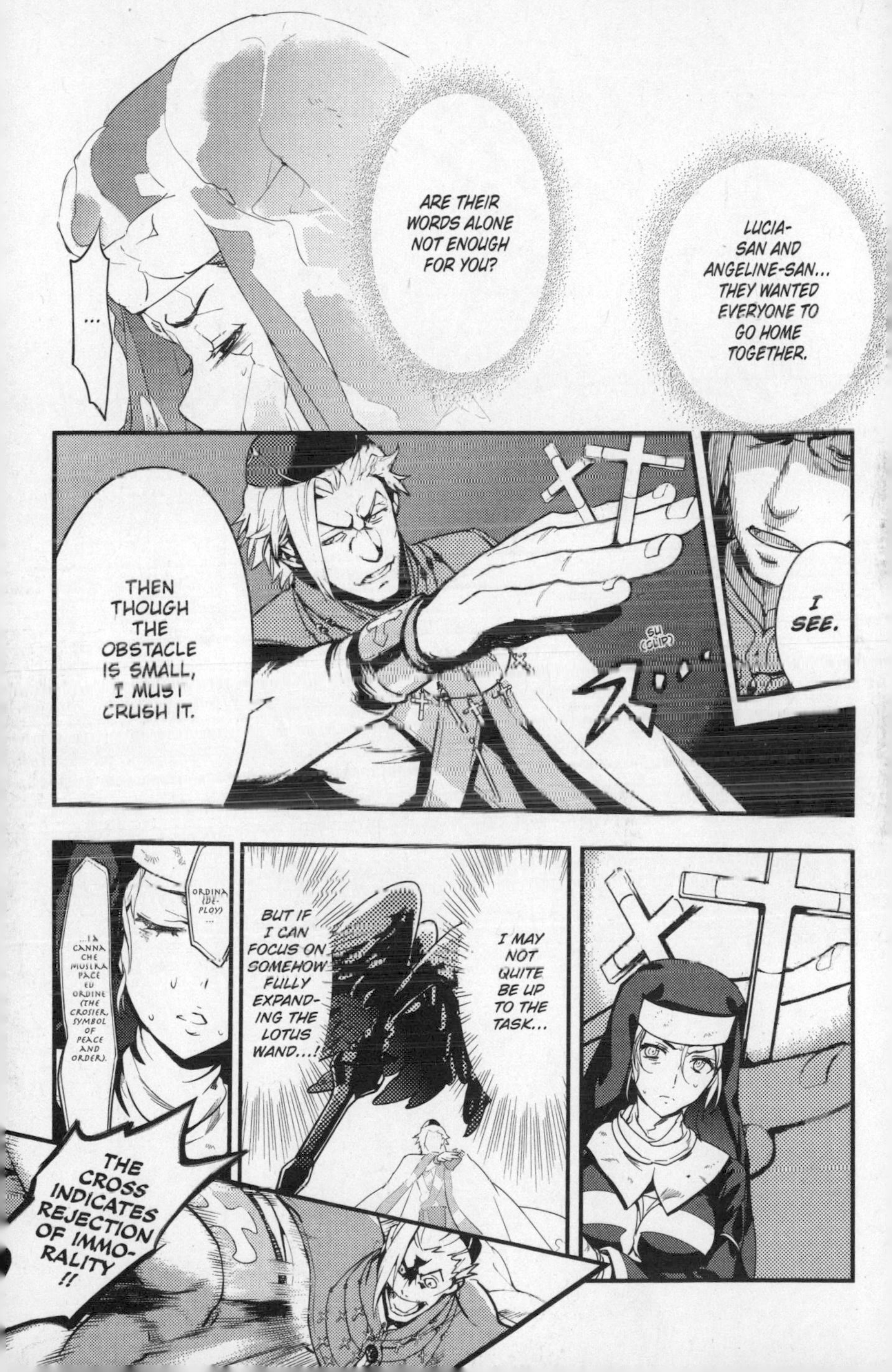
LUCIA-SAN AND ANGELINE-SAN... THEY WANTED EVERYONE TO GO HOME TOGETHER.
ARE THEIR WORDS ALONE NOT ENOUGH FOR YOU?
...
I SEE.
SU (CLIP)
THEN THOUGH THE OBSTACLE IS SMALL, I MUST CRUSH IT.
I MAY NOT QUITE BE UP TO THE TASK...
BUT IF I CAN FOCUS ON SOMEHOW FULLY EXPANDING THE LOTUS WAND...!
ORDINA (DEPLOY) ...
...LA CANNA CHE MOSTRA PACE EU ORDINE (THE CROSIER, SYMBOL OF PEACE AND ORDER).
THE CROSS INDICATES REJECTION OF IMMORALITY!!

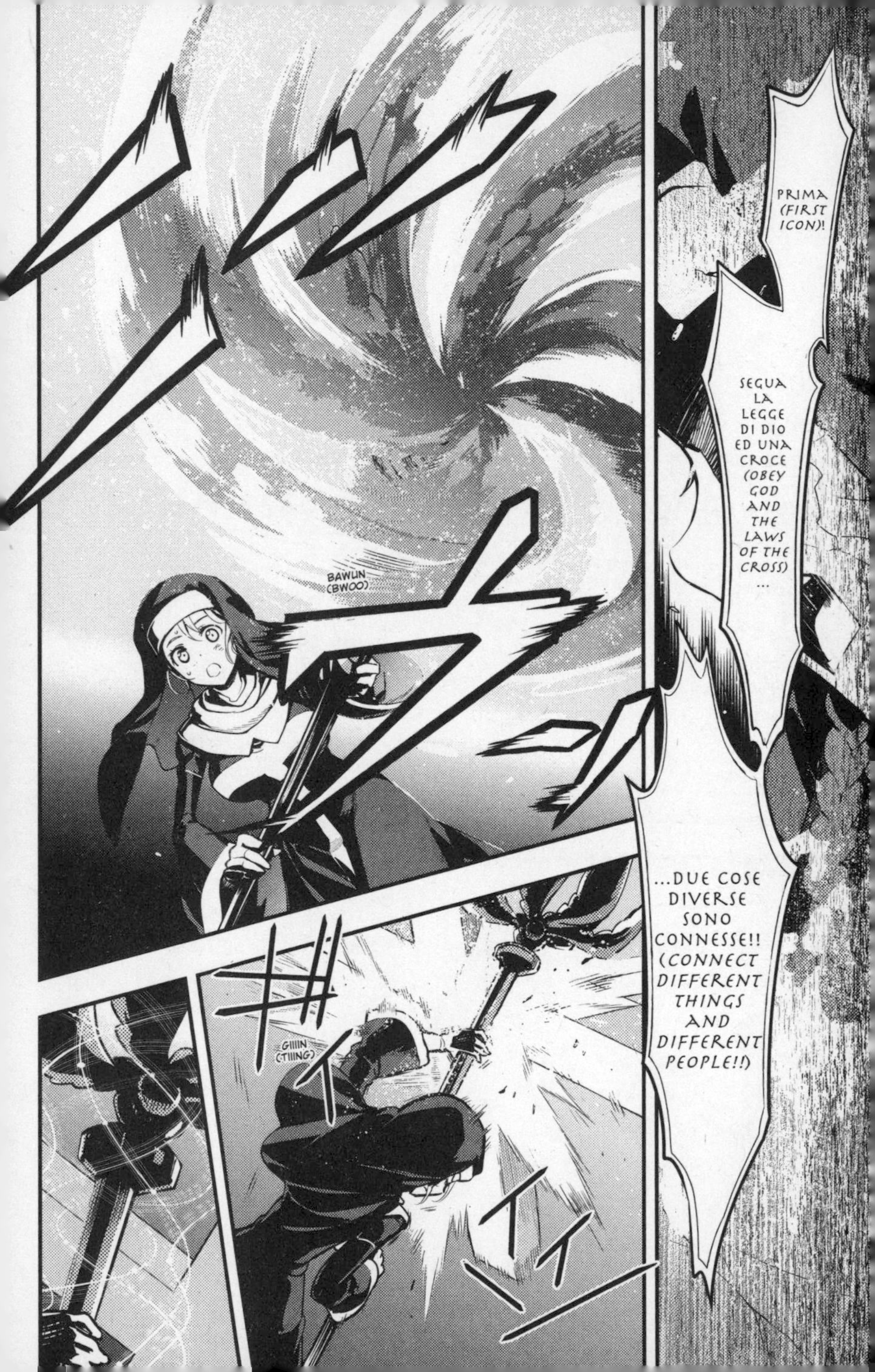
PRIMA (FIRST ICON)!
SEGUA LA LEGGE DI DIO ED UNA CROCE (OBEY GOD AND THE LAWS OF THE CROSS)...
...DUE COSE DIVERSE SONO CONNESSE!! (CONNECT DIFFERENT THINGS AND DIFFERENT PEOPLE!!)
BAWUN (BWOO)
GIIIN (TIIING)

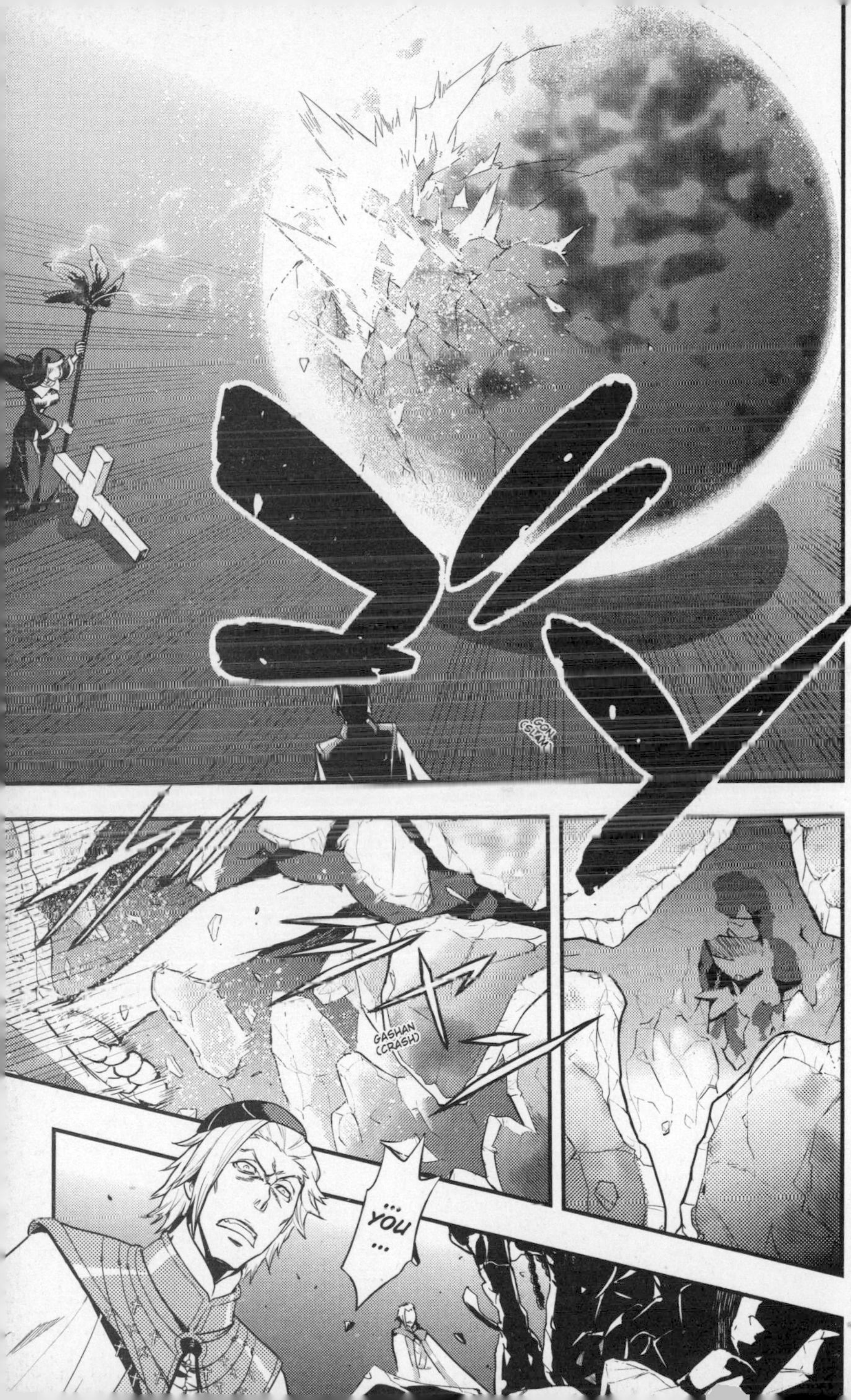
GON (SLAM)
GASHAN (CRASH)
...YOU...

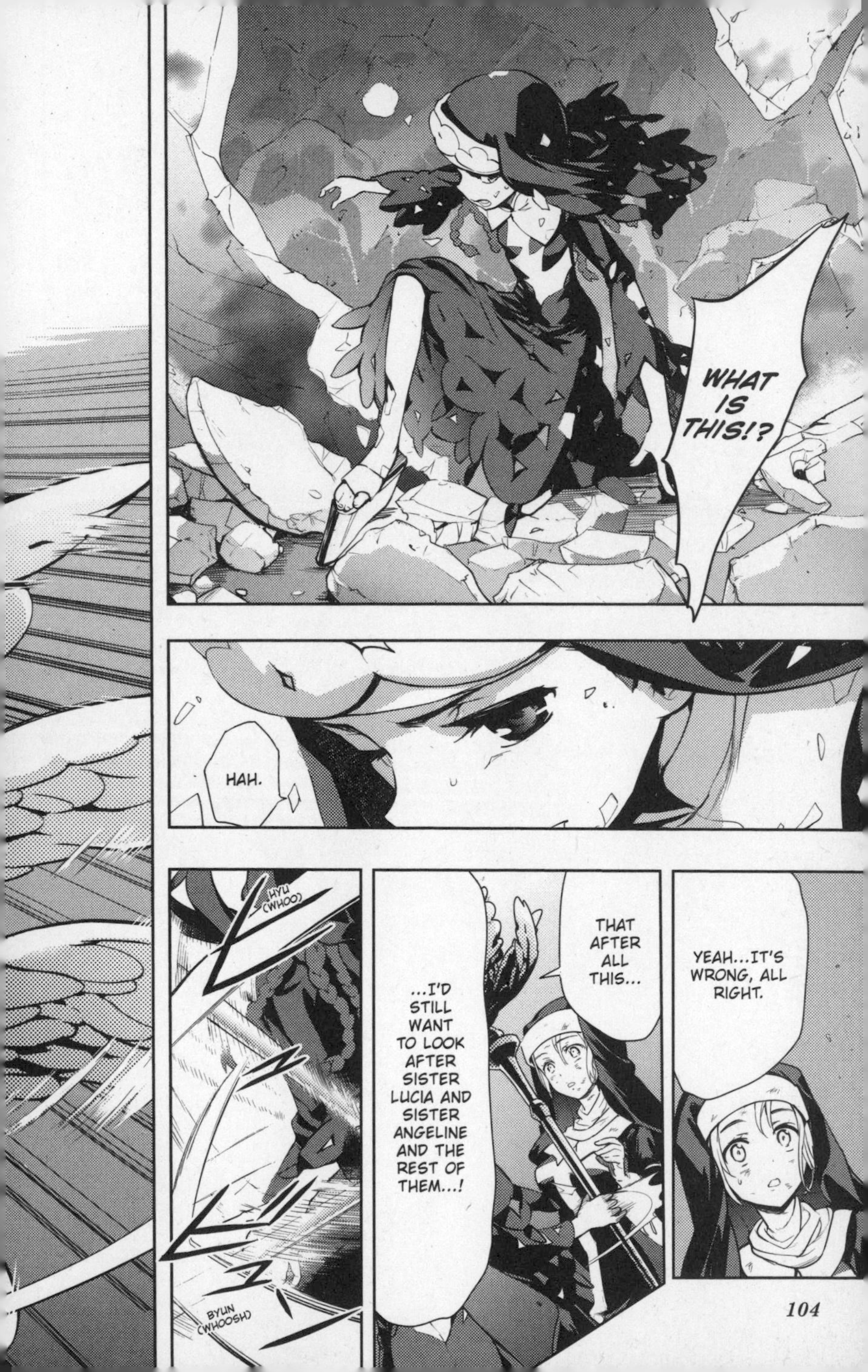
WHAT IS THIS!?
HAH.
YEAH...IT'S WRONG, ALL RIGHT.
THAT AFTER ALL THIS...
...I'D STILL WANT TO LOOK AFTER SISTER LUCIA AND SISTER ANGELINE AND THE REST OF THEM...!
HYU (WHOO)
BYUN (WHOOSH)

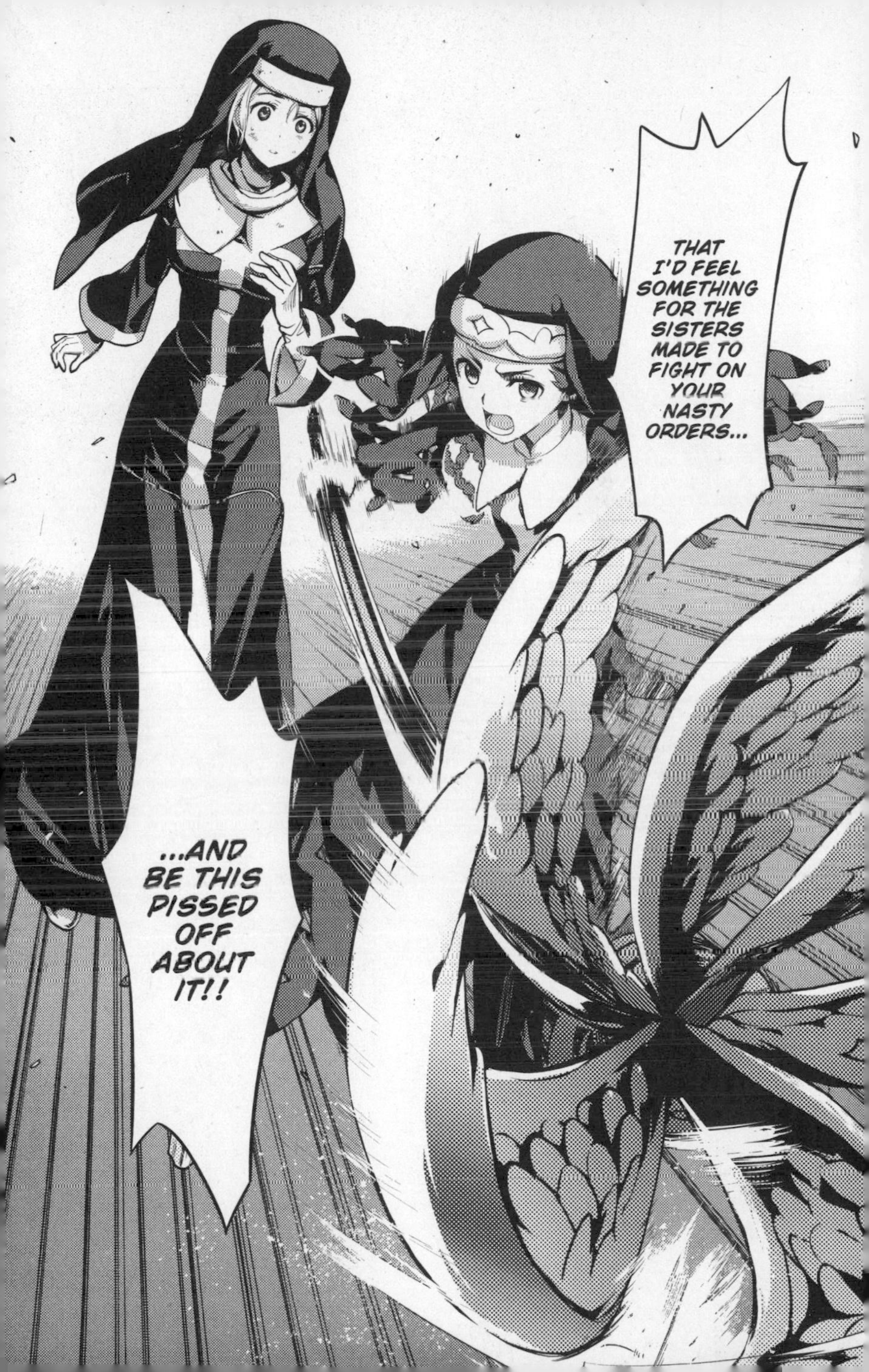
THAT I'D FEEL SOMETHING FOR THE SISTERS MADE TO FIGHT ON YOUR NASTY ORDERS...
...AND BE THIS PISSED OFF ABOUT IT!!

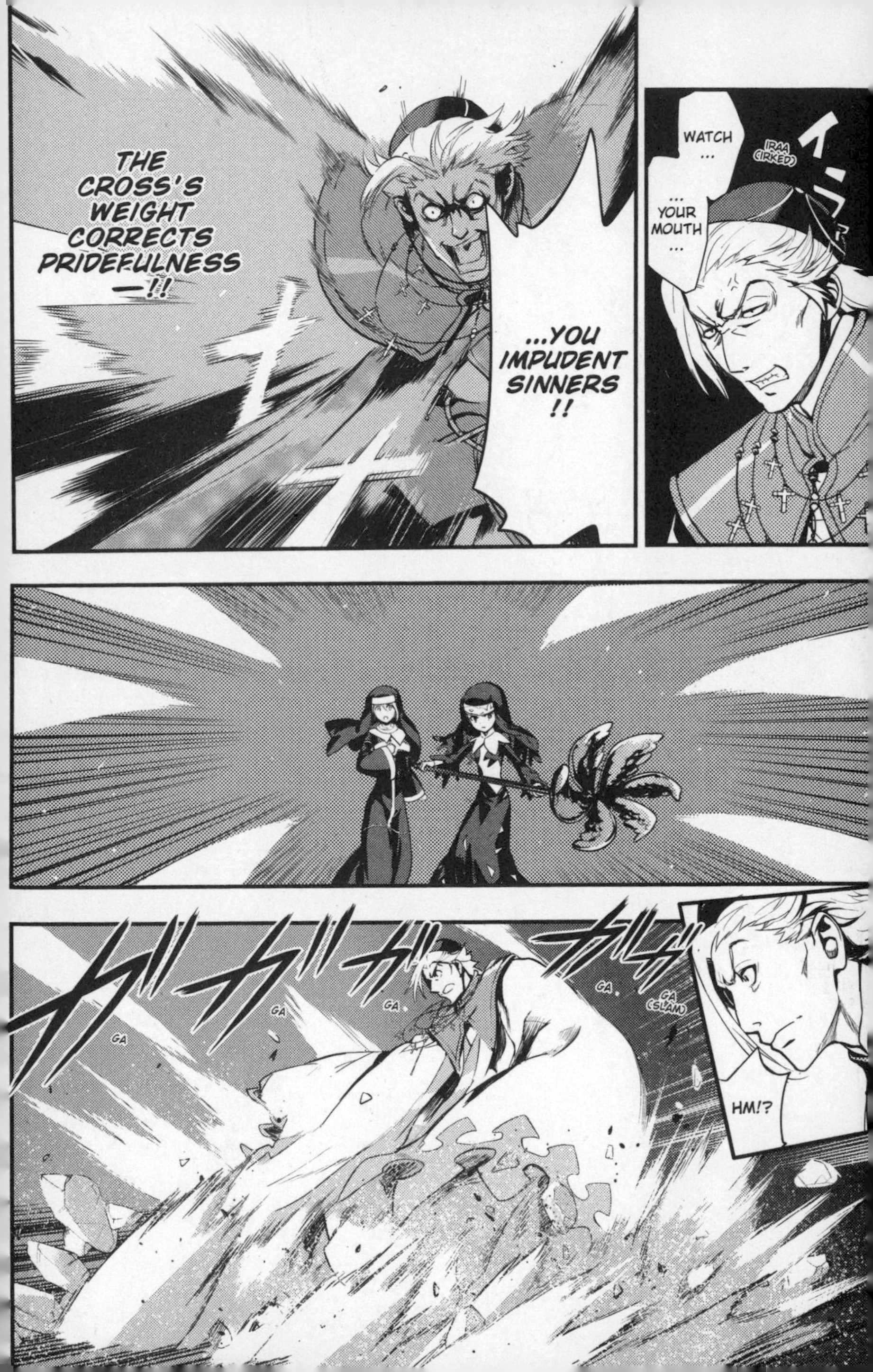
IRAA (IRKED)
WATCH ... ... YOUR MOUTH ...
...YOU IMPUDENT SINNERS !!
THE CROSS'S WEIGHT CORRECTS PRIDEFULNESS —!!
HM!?
GA (SLAM)
GA
GA
GA
GA

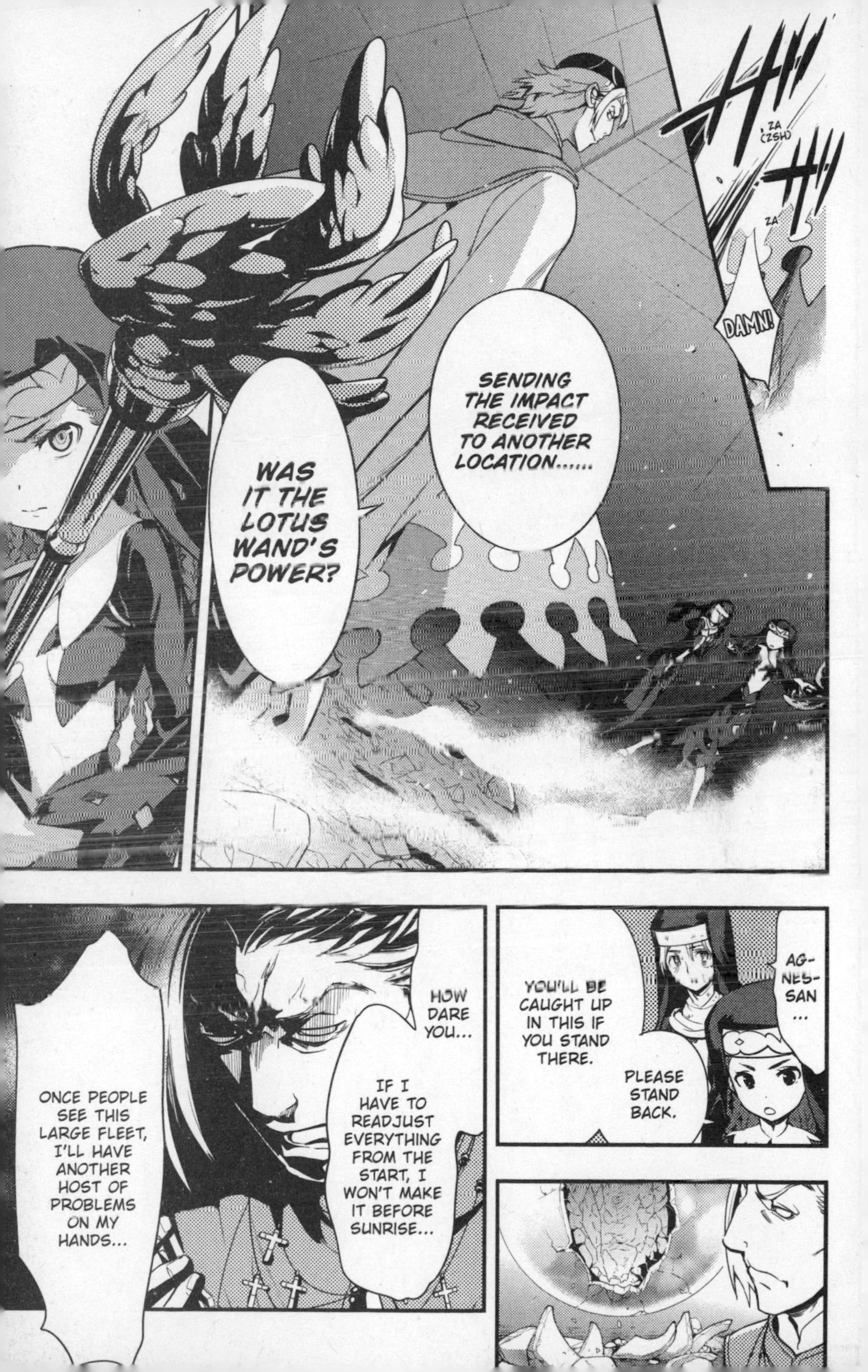
ZA (ZSH)
ZA
DAMN!
SENDING THE IMPACT RECEIVED TO ANOTHER LOCATION......
WAS IT THE LOTUS WAND'S POWER?
AG-NES-SAN...
YOU'LL BE CAUGHT UP IN THIS IF YOU STAND THERE.
PLEASE STAND BACK.
HOW DARE YOU...
IF I HAVE TO READJUST EVERYTHING FROM THE START, I WON'T MAKE IT BEFORE SUNRISE...
ONCE PEOPLE SEE THIS LARGE FLEET, I'LL HAVE ANOTHER HOST OF PROBLEMS ON MY HANDS...

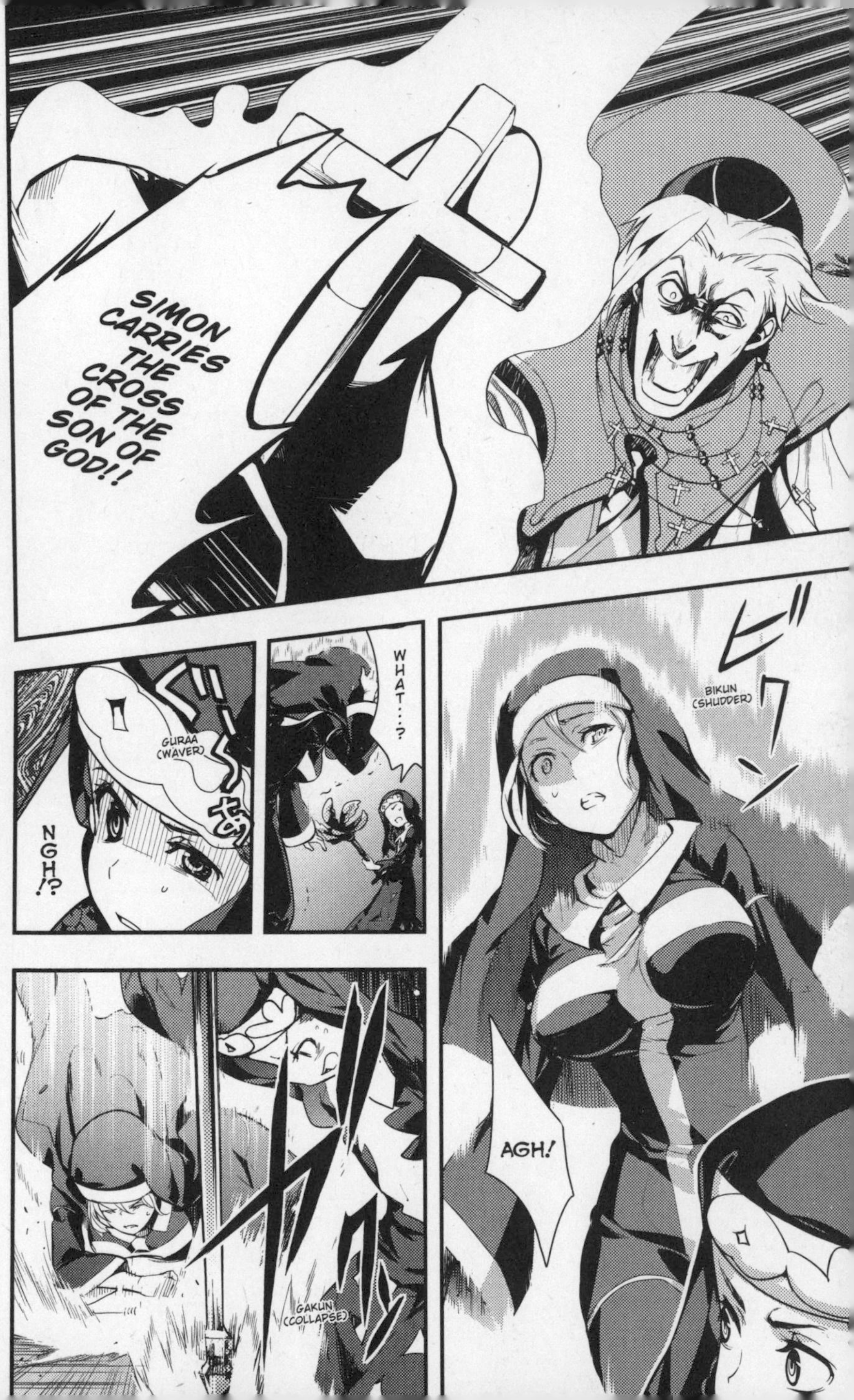
SIMON CARRIES THE CROSS OF THE SON OF GOD!!
BIKUN (SHUDDER)
AGH!
WHAT...?
GURAA (WAVER)
NGH!?
GAKUN (COLLAPSE)

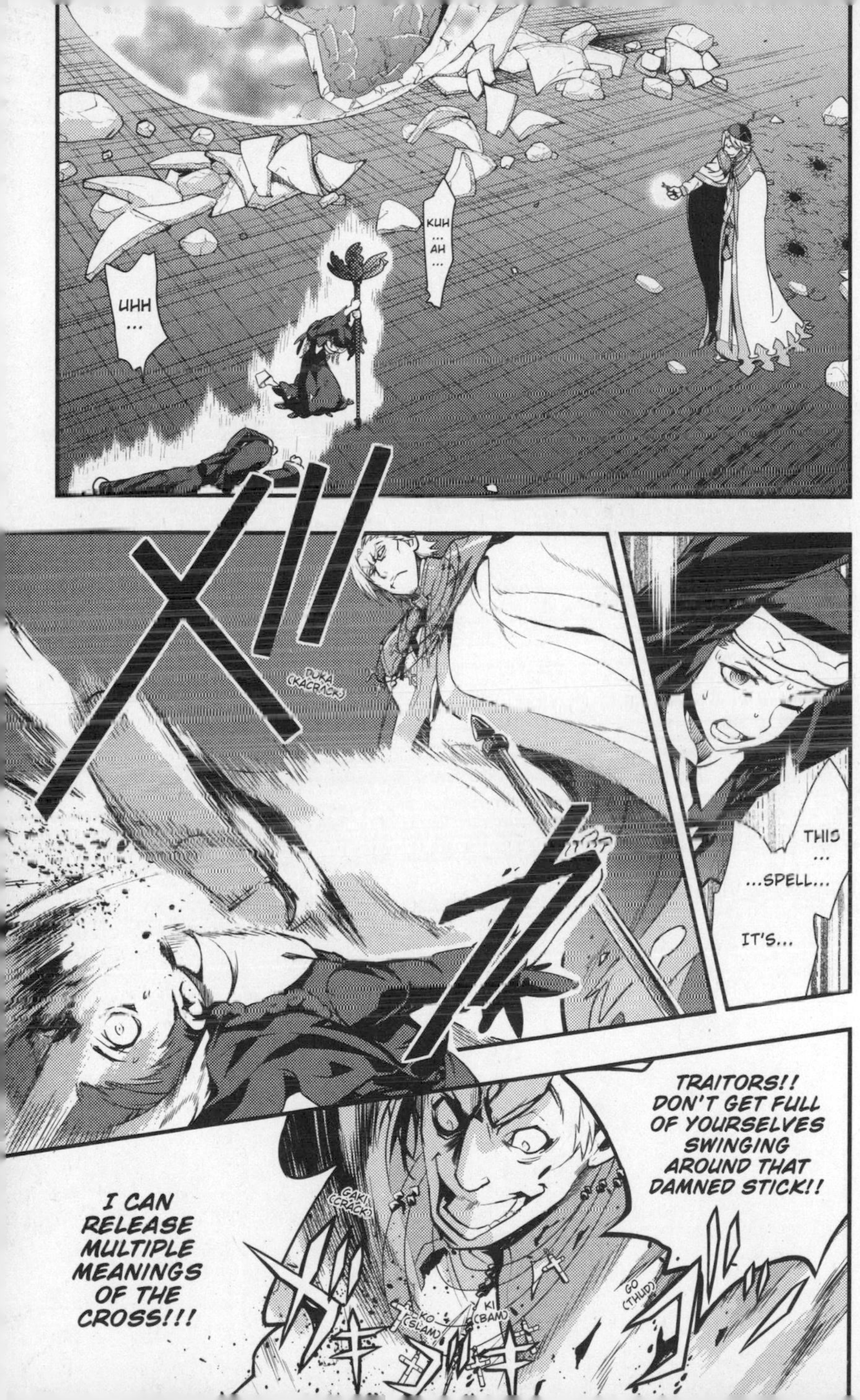
KUH... AH...
UHH...
THIS... ...SPELL... IT'S...
DUKA (KACRACK)
TRAITORS!! DON'T GET FULL OF YOURSELVES SWINGING AROUND THAT DAMNED STICK!!
GO (THUD)
GAKI (CRACK)
KI (BAM)
KO (SLAM)
I CAN RELEASE MULTIPLE MEANINGS OF THE CROSS!!!

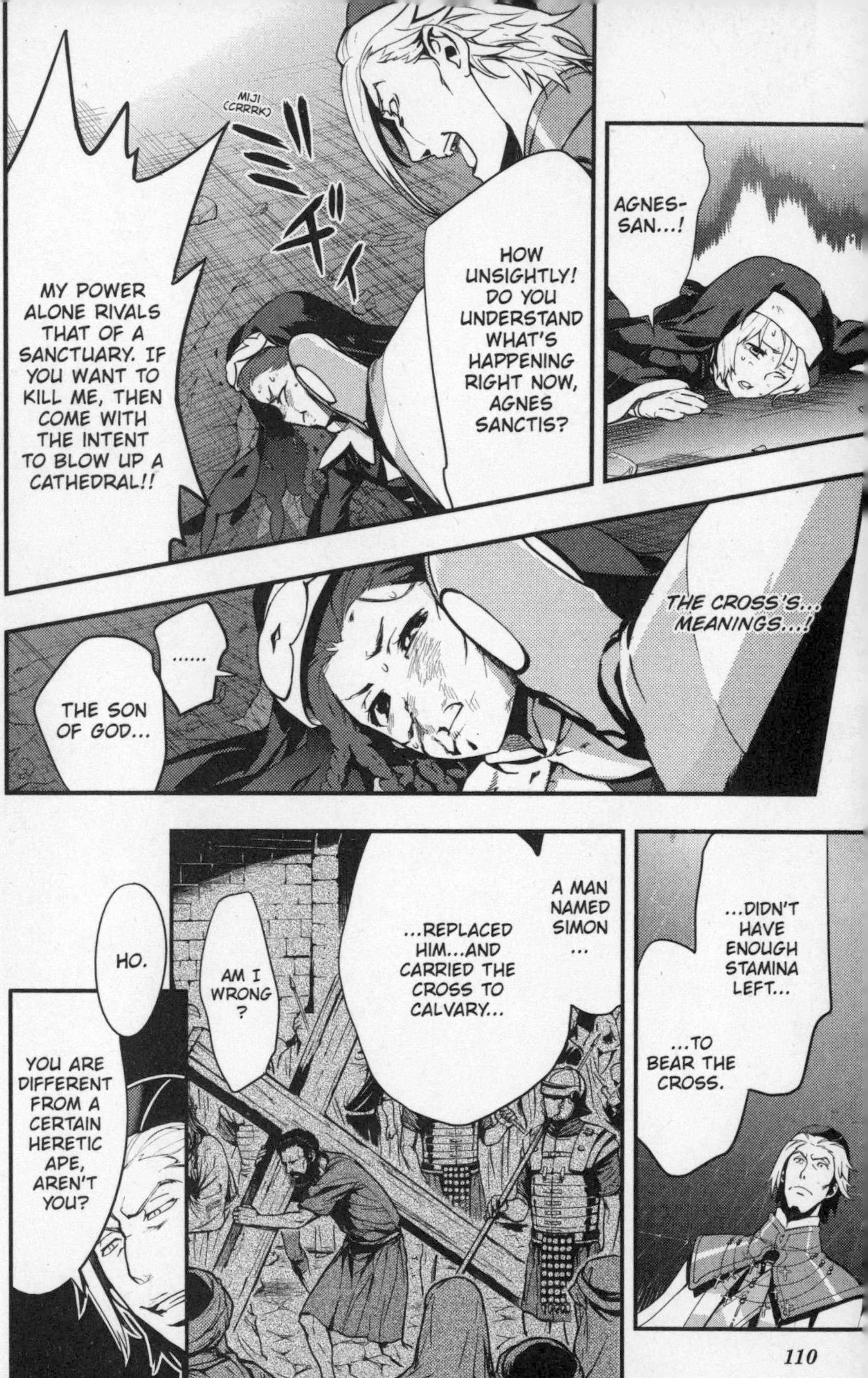
AGNES-SAN...!
HOW UNSIGHTLY! DO YOU UNDERSTAND WHAT'S HAPPENING RIGHT NOW, AGNES SANCTIS?
MIJI (CRRRK)
MY POWER ALONE RIVALS THAT OF A SANCTUARY. IF YOU WANT TO KILL ME, THEN COME WITH THE INTENT TO BLOW UP A CATHEDRAL!!
THE CROSS'S... MEANINGS...!
......
THE SON OF GOD...
...DIDN'T HAVE ENOUGH STAMINA LEFT...
...TO BEAR THE CROSS.
A MAN NAMED SIMON ...
...REPLACED HIM...AND CARRIED THE CROSS TO CALVARY...
AM I WRONG ?
HO.
YOU ARE DIFFERENT FROM A CERTAIN HERETIC APE, AREN'T YOU?

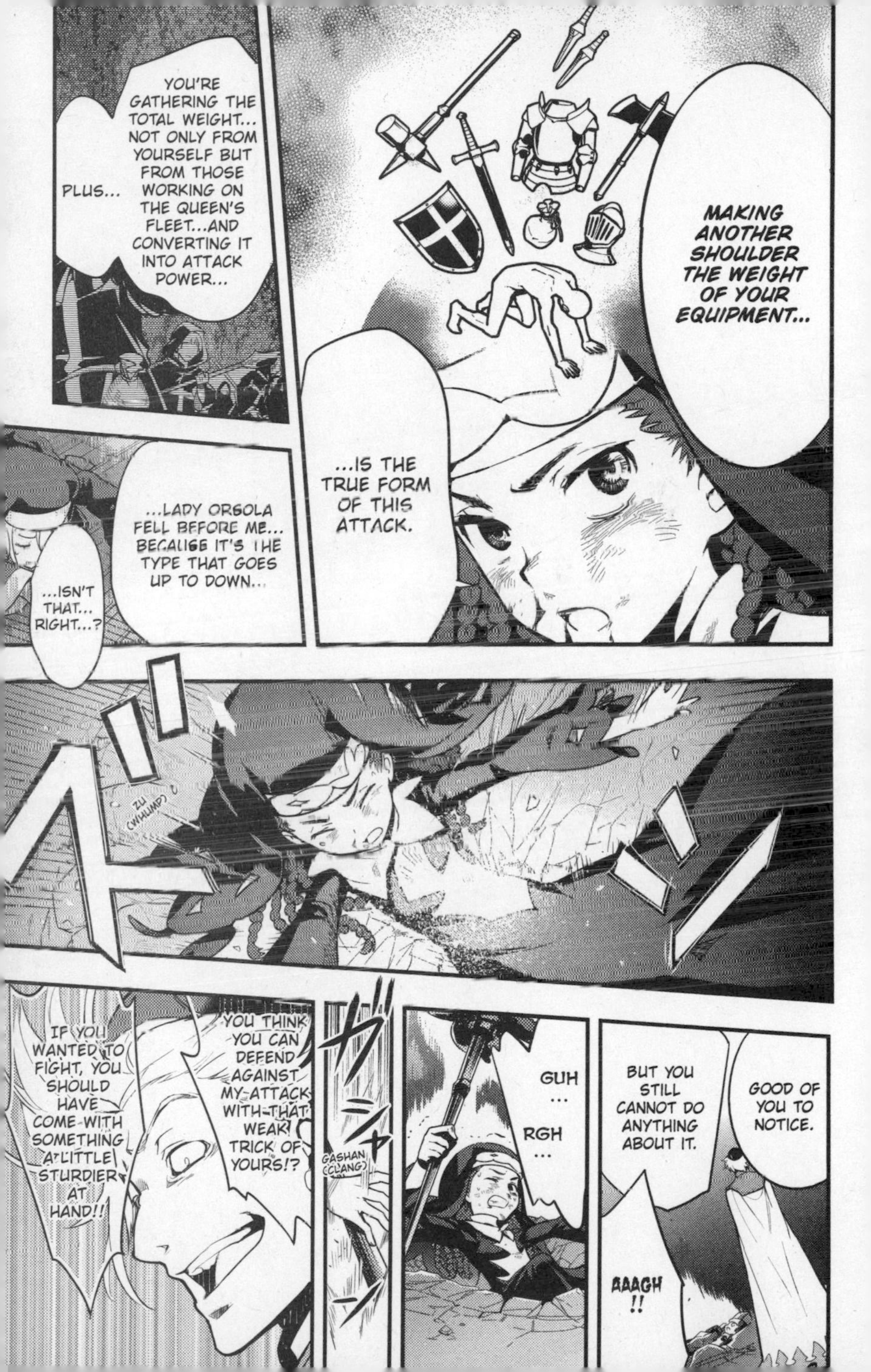
YOU'RE GATHERING THE TOTAL WEIGHT... NOT ONLY FROM YOURSELF BUT FROM THOSE WORKING ON THE QUEEN'S FLEET...AND CONVERTING IT INTO ATTACK POWER...
PLUS...
MAKING ANOTHER SHOULDER THE WEIGHT OF YOUR EQUIPMENT...
...IS THE TRUE FORM OF THIS ATTACK.
...LADY ORSOLA FELL BEFORE ME... BECAUSE IT'S THE TYPE THAT GOES UP TO DOWN...
...ISN'T THAT... RIGHT...?
ZU (WHUMP)
GOOD OF YOU TO NOTICE.
BUT YOU STILL CANNOT DO ANYTHING ABOUT IT.
AAAGH !!
GUH ...
RGH ...
GASHAN (CLANG)
YOU THINK YOU CAN DEFEND AGAINST MY ATTACK WITH THAT WEAK TRICK OF YOURS!?
IF YOU WANTED TO FIGHT, YOU SHOULD HAVE COME WITH SOMETHING A LITTLE STURDIER AT HAND!!

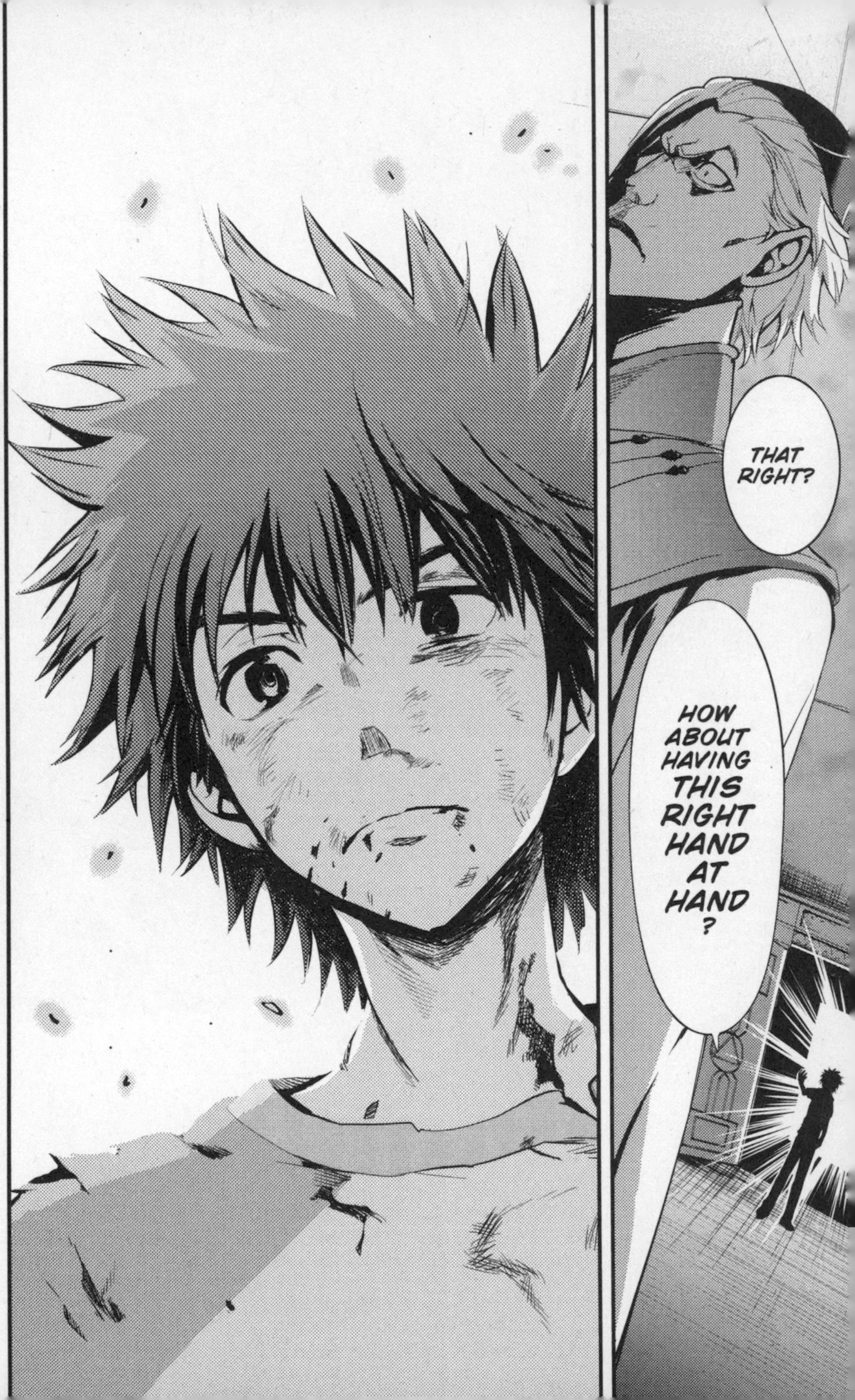
THAT RIGHT?
HOW ABOUT HAVING THIS RIGHT HAND AT HAND ?

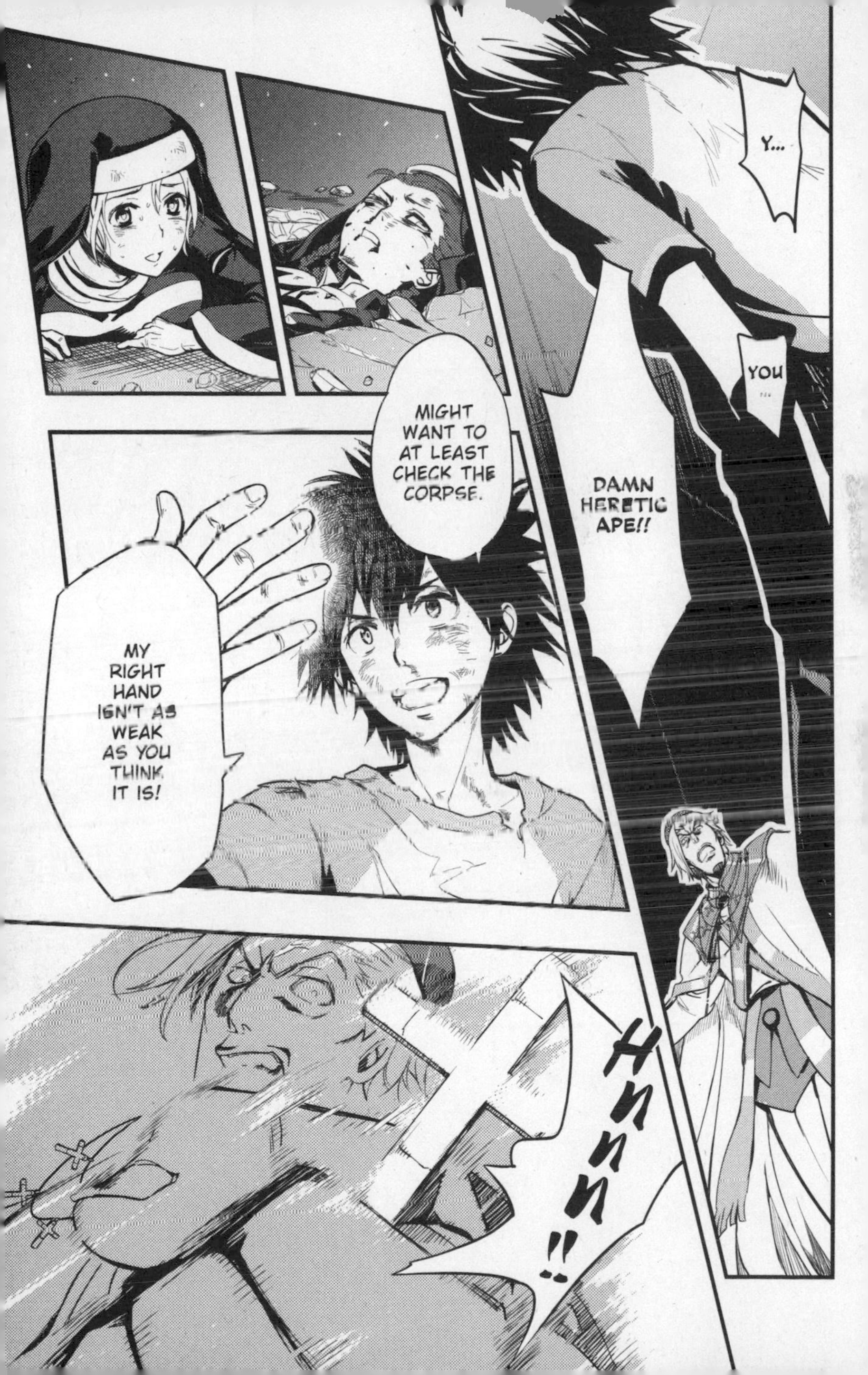
Y...
YOU...
DAMN HERETIC APE!!
MIGHT WANT TO AT LEAST CHECK THE CORPSE.
MY RIGHT HAND ISN'T AS WEAK AS YOU THINK IT IS!
HNNNN!!

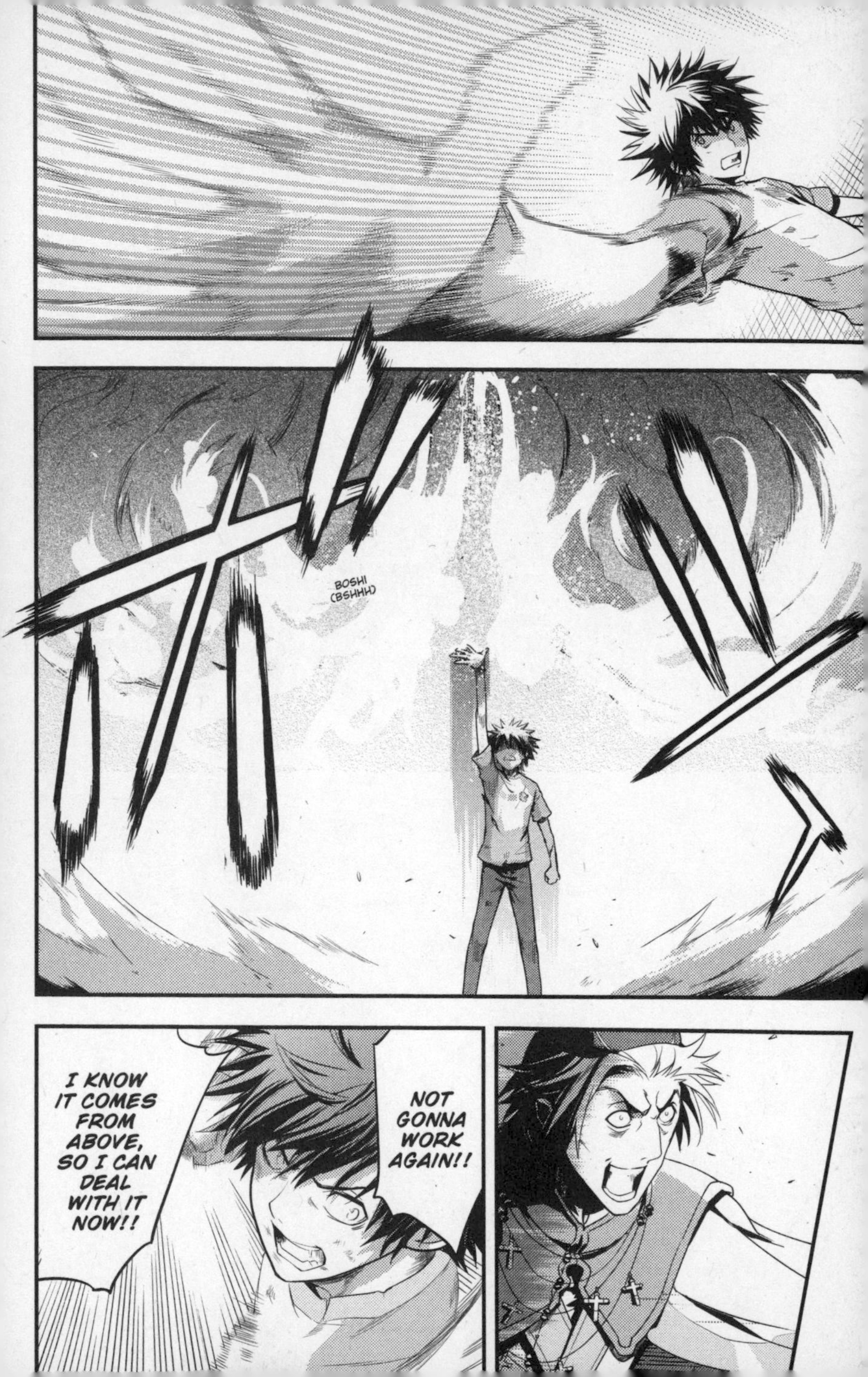
BOSHI
(BSHHH)
NOT GONNA WORK AGAIN!!
I KNOW IT COMES FROM ABOVE, SO I CAN DEAL WITH IT NOW!!

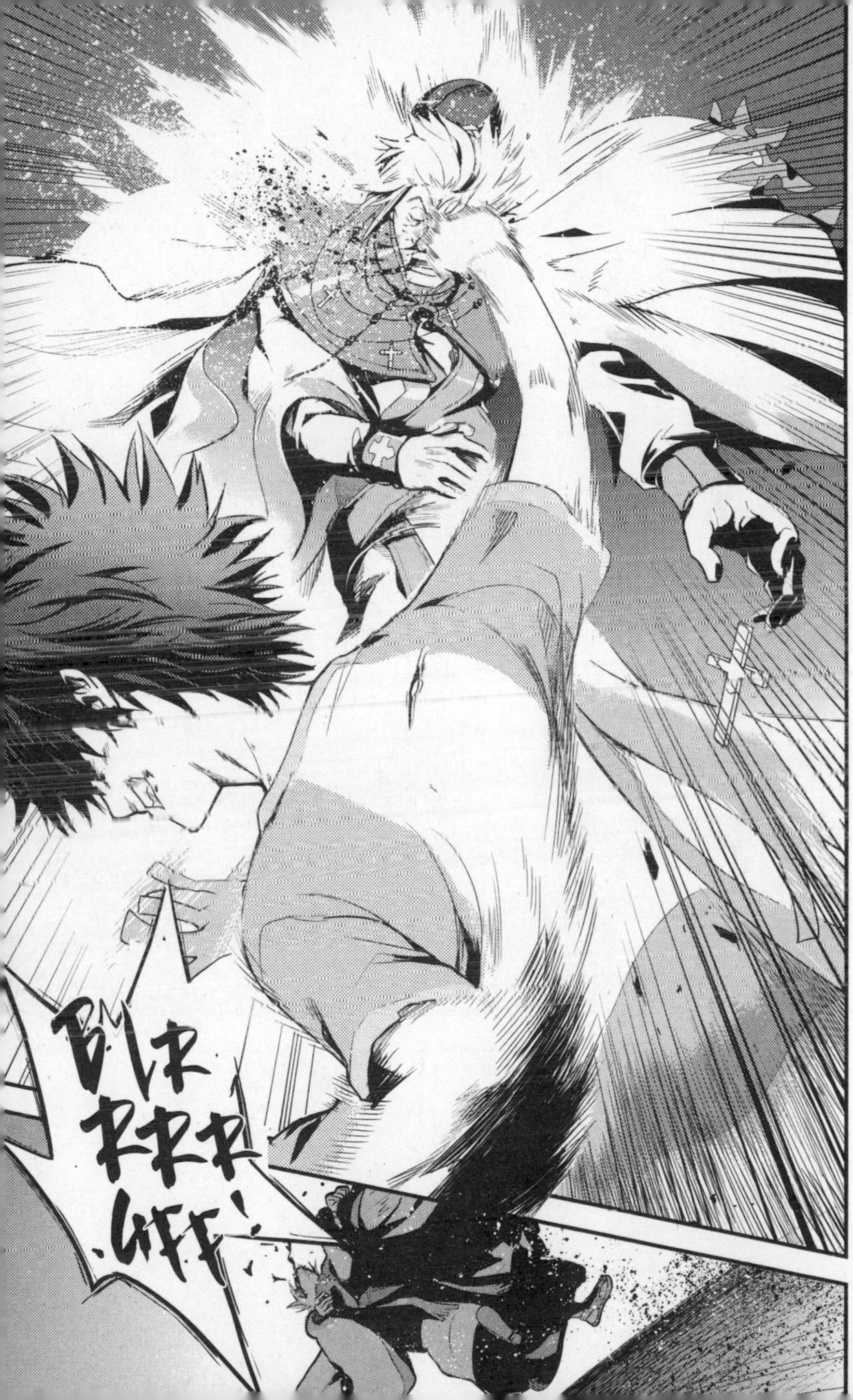
BLRRRRGFF!

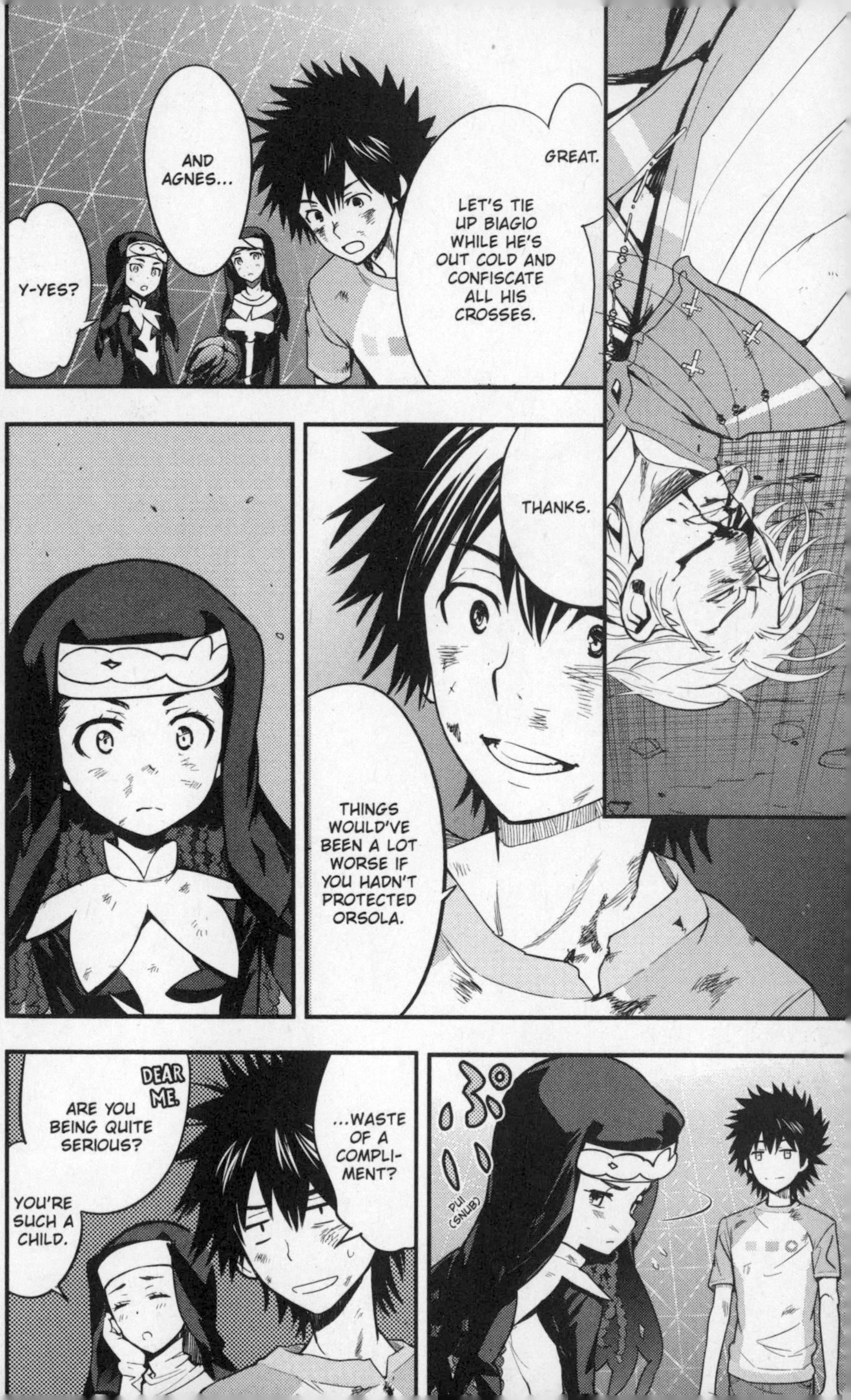
GREAT.
LET'S TIE UP BIAGIO WHILE HE'S OUT COLD AND CONFISCATE ALL HIS CROSSES.
AND AGNES...
Y-YES?
THANKS.
THINGS WOULD'VE BEEN A LOT WORSE IF YOU HADN'T PROTECTED ORSOLA.
PUI (SNUB)
...WASTE OF A COMPLI- MENT?
DEAR ME.
ARE YOU BEING QUITE SERIOUS?
YOU'RE SUCH A CHILD.

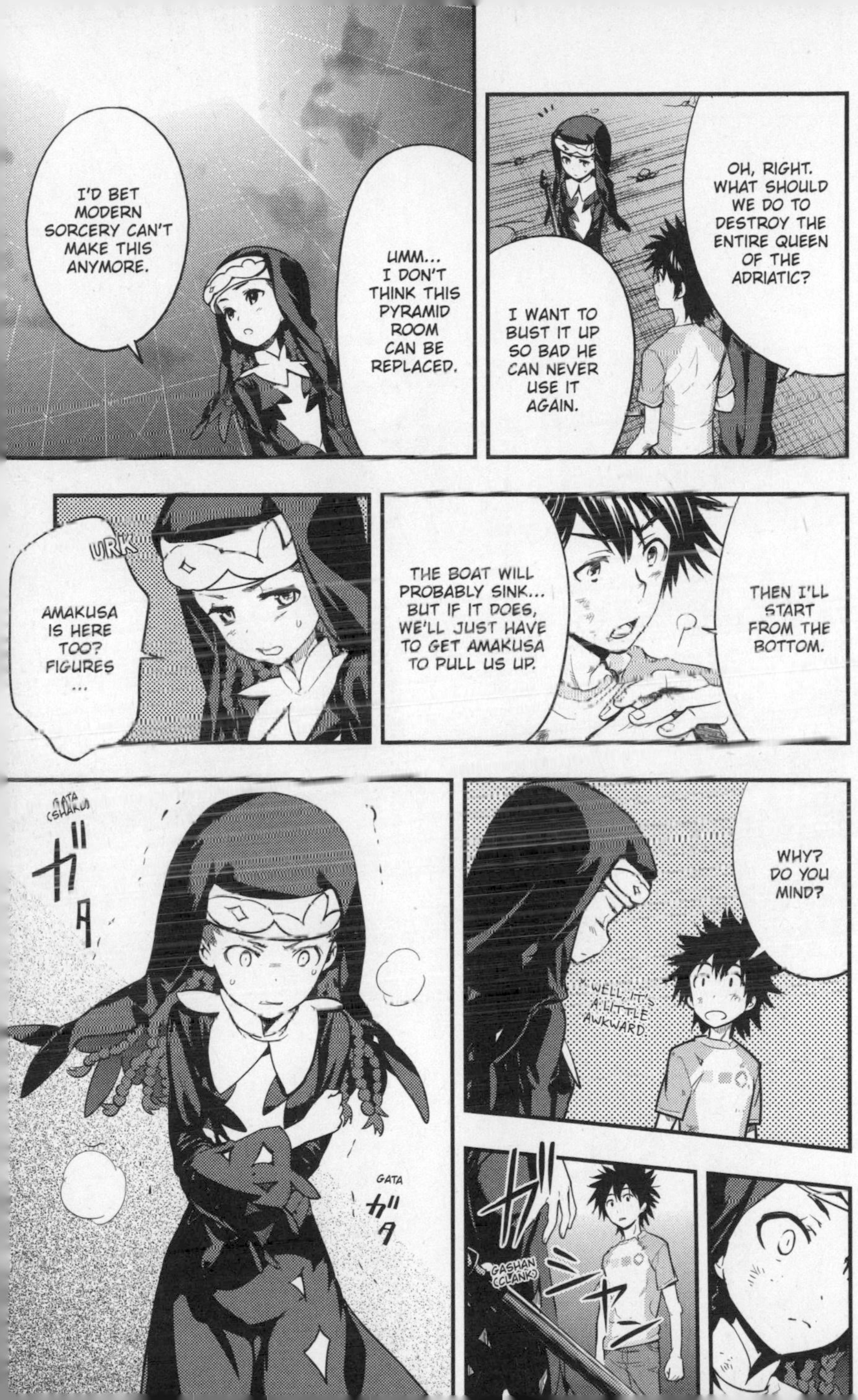
OH, RIGHT. WHAT SHOULD WE DO TO DESTROY THE ENTIRE QUEEN OF THE ADRIATIC?
I WANT TO BUST IT UP SO BAD HE CAN NEVER USE IT AGAIN.
UMM... I DON'T THINK THIS PYRAMID ROOM CAN BE REPLACED.
I'D BET MODERN SORCERY CAN'T MAKE THIS ANYMORE.
THEN I'LL START FROM THE BOTTOM.
THE BOAT WILL PROBABLY SINK... BUT IF IT DOES, WE'LL JUST HAVE TO GET AMAKUSA TO PULL US UP.
URK
AMAKUSA IS HERE TOO? FIGURES ...
WHY? DO YOU MIND?
WELL, IT'S A LITTLE AWKWARD.
GASHAN (CLANK)
GATA (SHAKU)
GATA

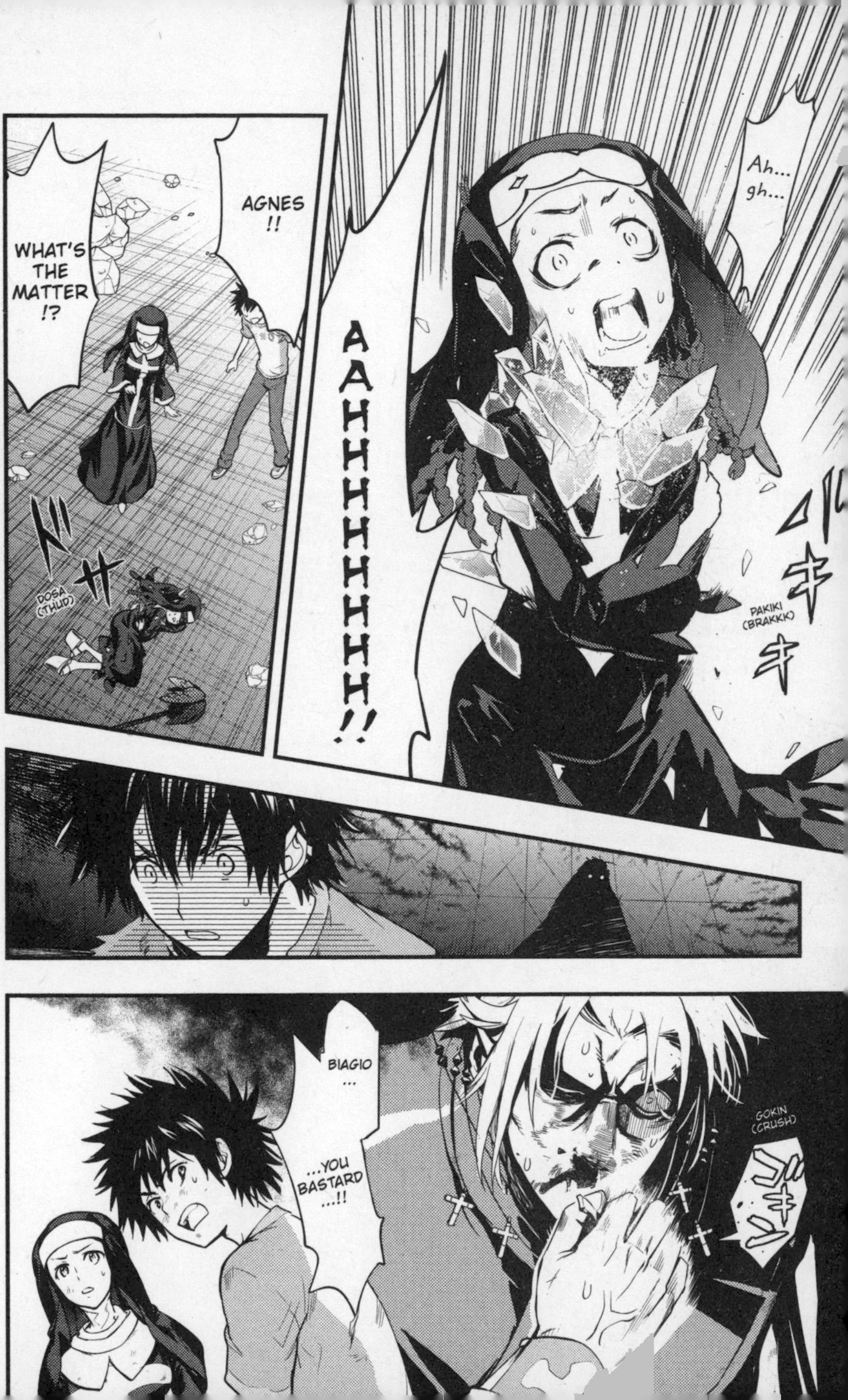
Ah... gh...
AAHHHHHHHH!!
PAKIKI (BRAKKK)
AGNES!!
WHAT'S THE MATTER!?
DOSA (THUD)
GOKIN (CRUSH)
BIAGIO...
...YOU BASTARD...!!

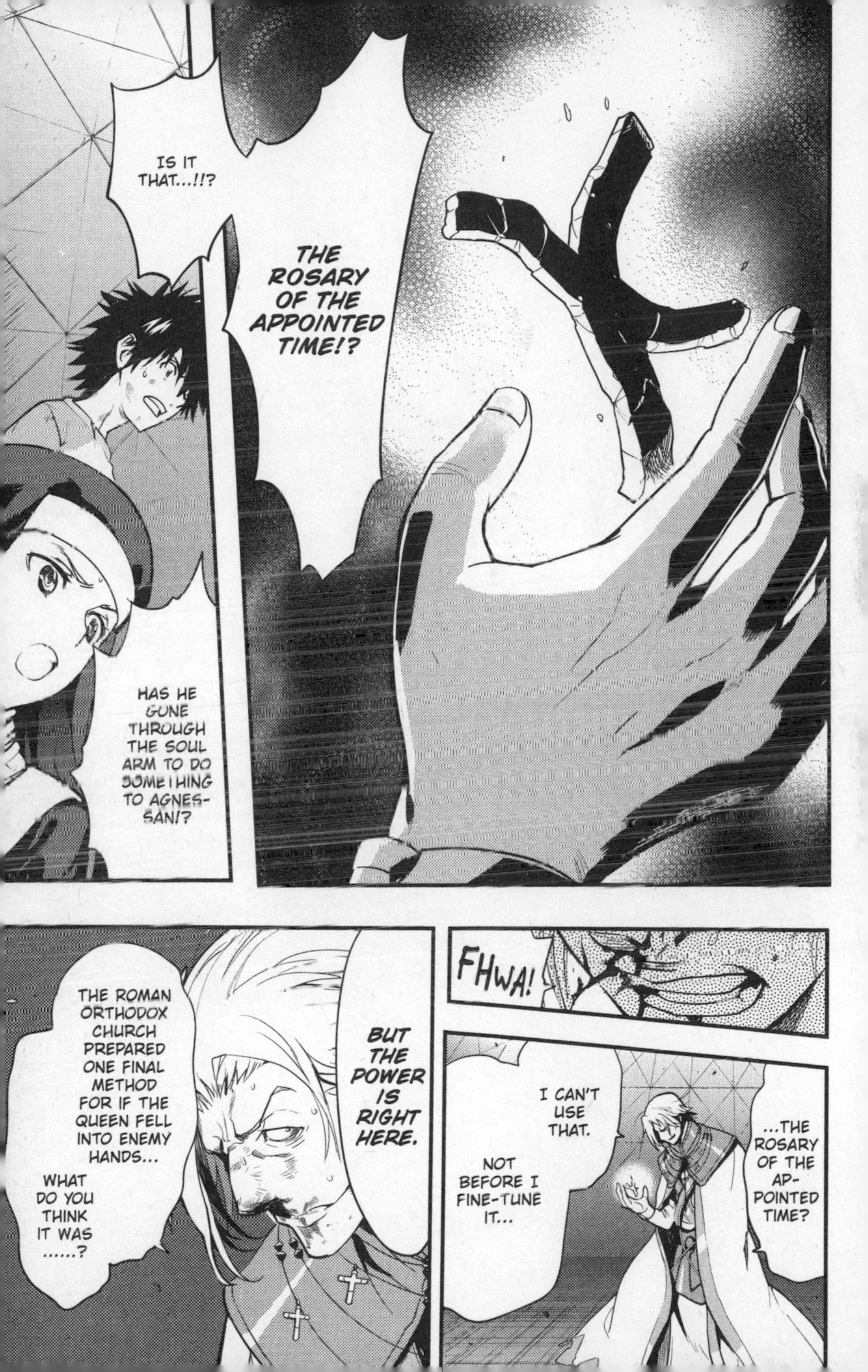
IS IT THAT...!!?
THE ROSARY OF THE APPOINTED TIME!?
HAS HE GONE THROUGH THE SOUL ARM TO DO SOMETHING TO AGNES-SAN!?
FHWA!
...THE ROSARY OF THE AP-POINTED TIME?
I CAN'T USE THAT.
NOT BEFORE I FINE-TUNE IT...
BUT THE POWER IS RIGHT HERE.
THE ROMAN ORTHODOX CHURCH PREPARED ONE FINAL METHOD FOR IF THE QUEEN FELL INTO ENEMY HANDS...
WHAT DO YOU THINK IT WAS ......?

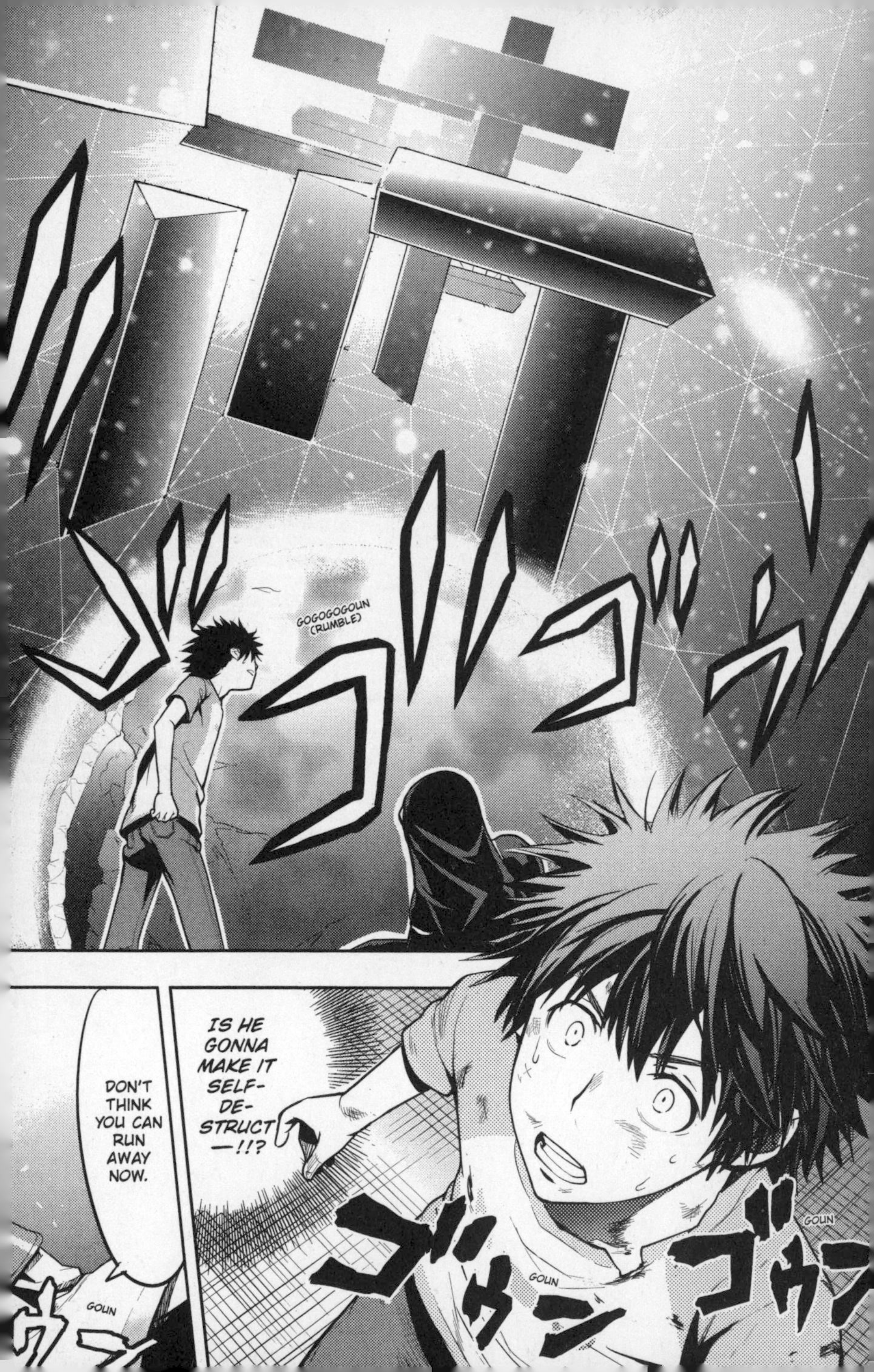
GOGOGOGOUN (RUMBLE)
IS HE GONNA MAKE IT SELF-DESTRUCT—!!?
GOUN
GOUN
DON'T THINK YOU CAN RUN AWAY NOW.
GOUN

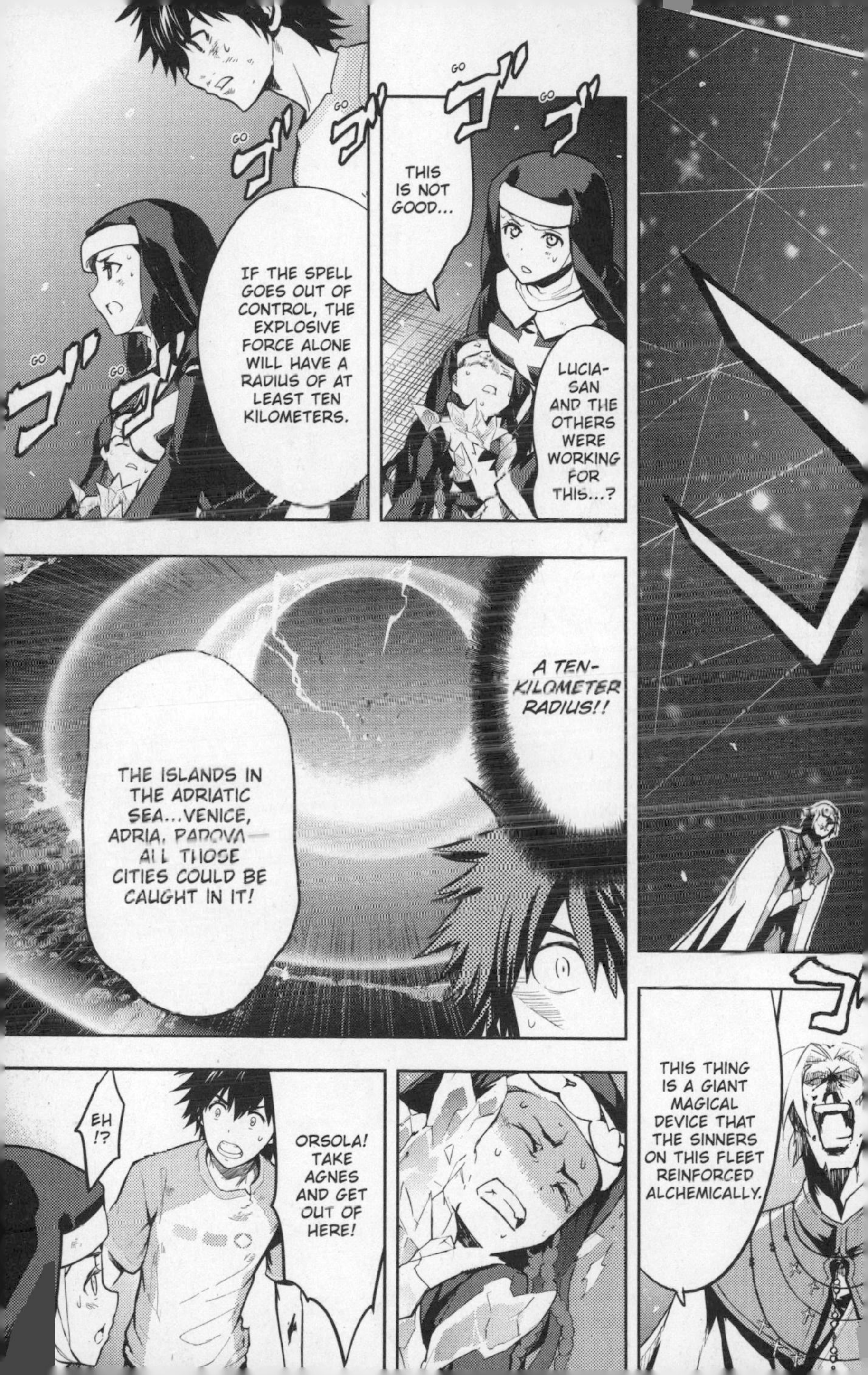
GO
GO
THIS IS NOT GOOD...
LUCIA-SAN AND THE OTHERS WERE WORKING FOR THIS...?
GO
GO
GO
GO
IF THE SPELL GOES OUT OF CONTROL, THE EXPLOSIVE FORCE ALONE WILL HAVE A RADIUS OF AT LEAST TEN KILOMETERS.
A TEN-KILOMETER RADIUS!!
THE ISLANDS IN THE ADRIATIC SEA...VENICE, ADRIA, PADOVA—ALL THOSE CITIES COULD BE CAUGHT IN IT!
THIS THING IS A GIANT MAGICAL DEVICE THAT THE SINNERS ON THIS FLEET REINFORCED ALCHEMICALLY.
ORSOLA! TAKE AGNES AND GET OUT OF HERE!
EH!?

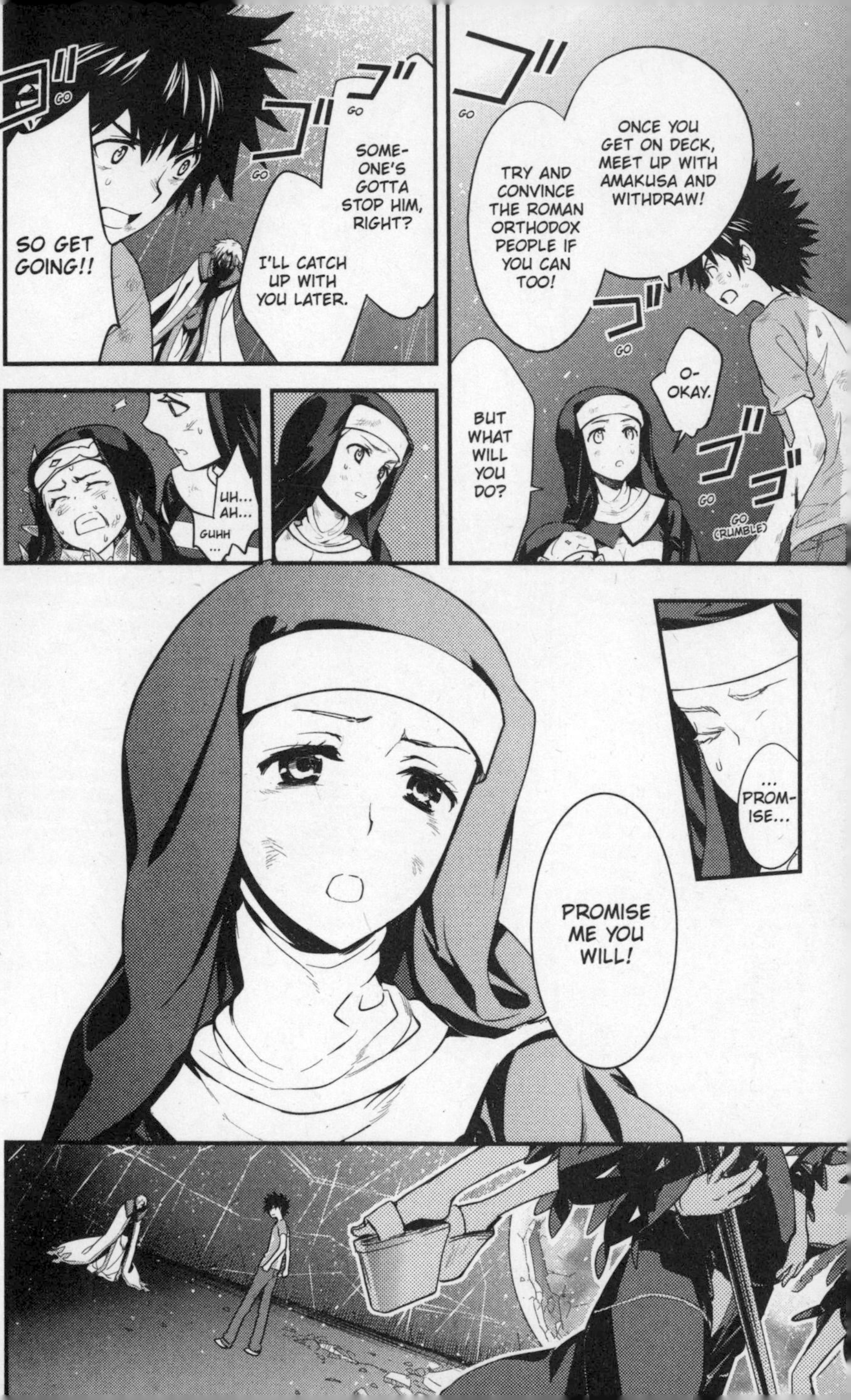
GO
ONCE YOU GET ON DECK, MEET UP WITH AMAKUSA AND WITHDRAW!
TRY AND CONVINCE THE ROMAN ORTHODOX PEOPLE IF YOU CAN TOO!
GO
O-OKAY.
BUT WHAT WILL YOU DO?
GO
GO (RUMBLE)
GO
GO
GO
SOME-ONE'S GOTTA STOP HIM, RIGHT?
I'LL CATCH UP WITH YOU LATER.
SO GET GOING!!
UH... AH...
GUHH ...
... PROMISE...
PROMISE ME YOU WILL!

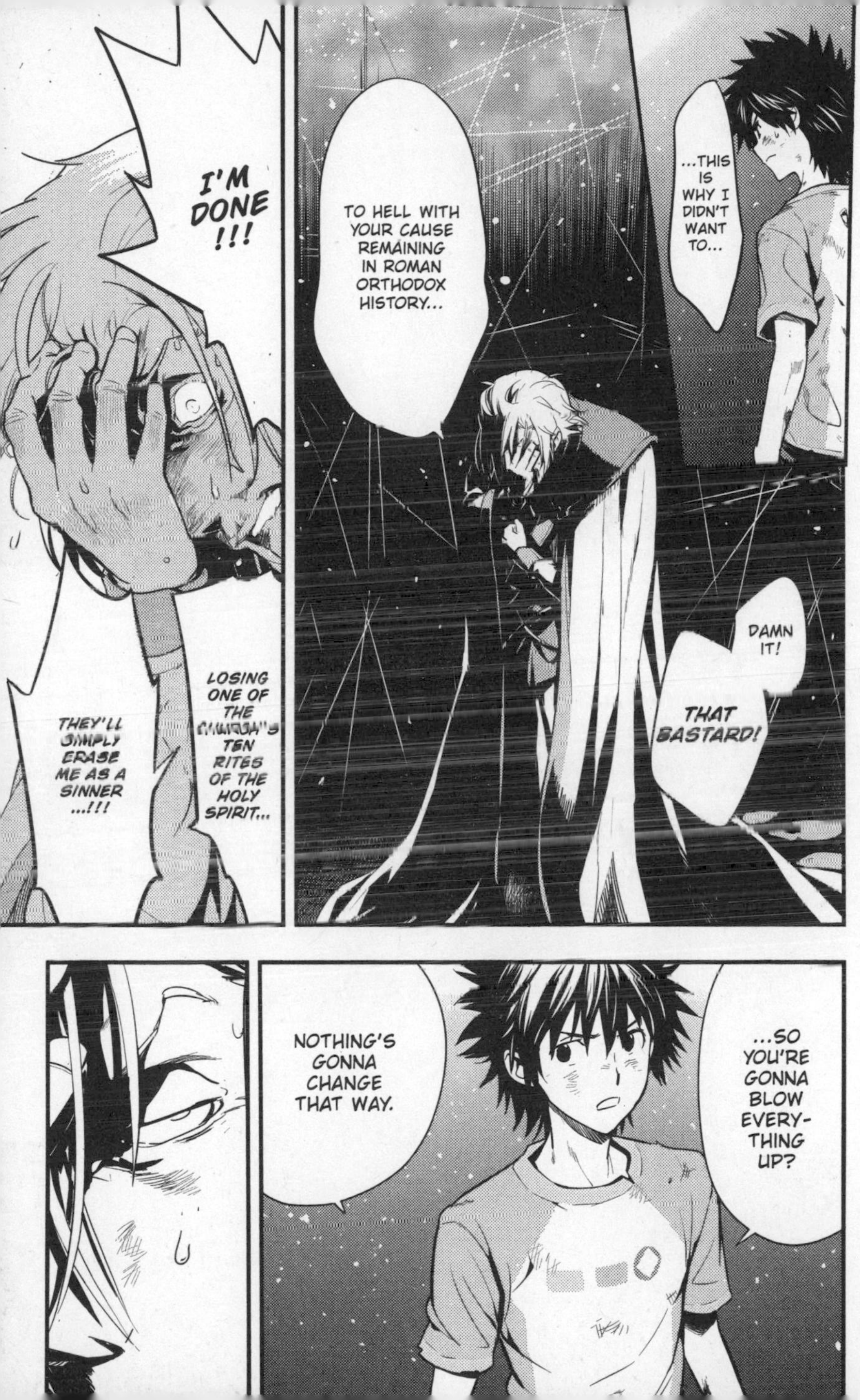
...THIS IS WHY I DIDN'T WANT TO...
TO HELL WITH YOUR CAUSE REMAINING IN ROMAN ORTHODOX HISTORY...
DAMN IT!
THAT BASTARD!
I'M DONE!!!
LOSING ONE OF THE CHURCH'S TEN RITES OF THE HOLY SPIRIT...
THEY'LL SIMPLY ERASE ME AS A SINNER...!!!
...SO YOU'RE GONNA BLOW EVERY-THING UP?
NOTHING'S GONNA CHANGE THAT WAY.

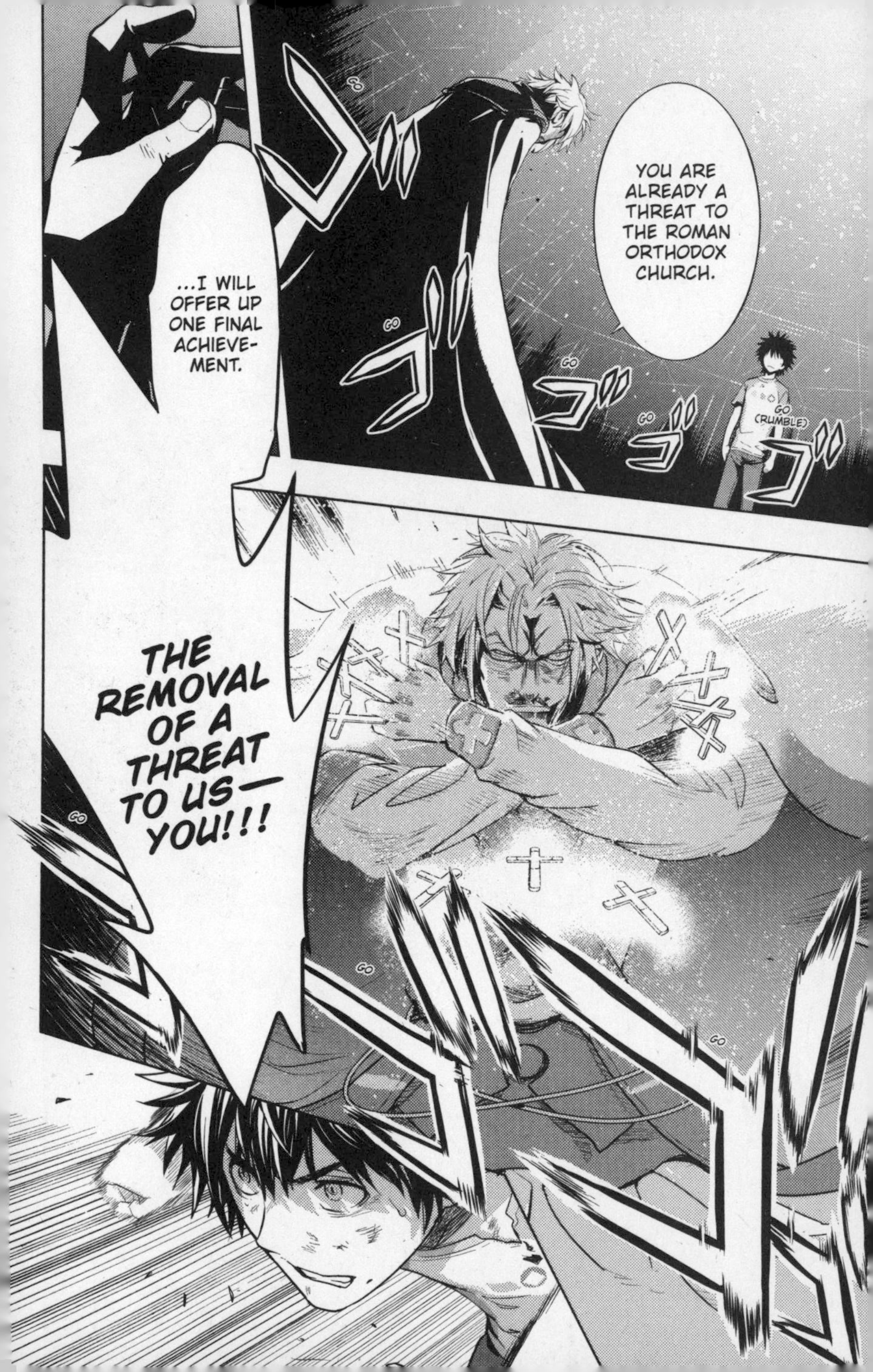
YOU ARE ALREADY A THREAT TO THE ROMAN ORTHODOX CHURCH.
GO (RUMBLE)
GO
GO
GO
GO
...I WILL OFFER UP ONE FINAL ACHIEVEMENT.
GO
GO
GO
THE REMOVAL OF A THREAT TO US—YOU!!!

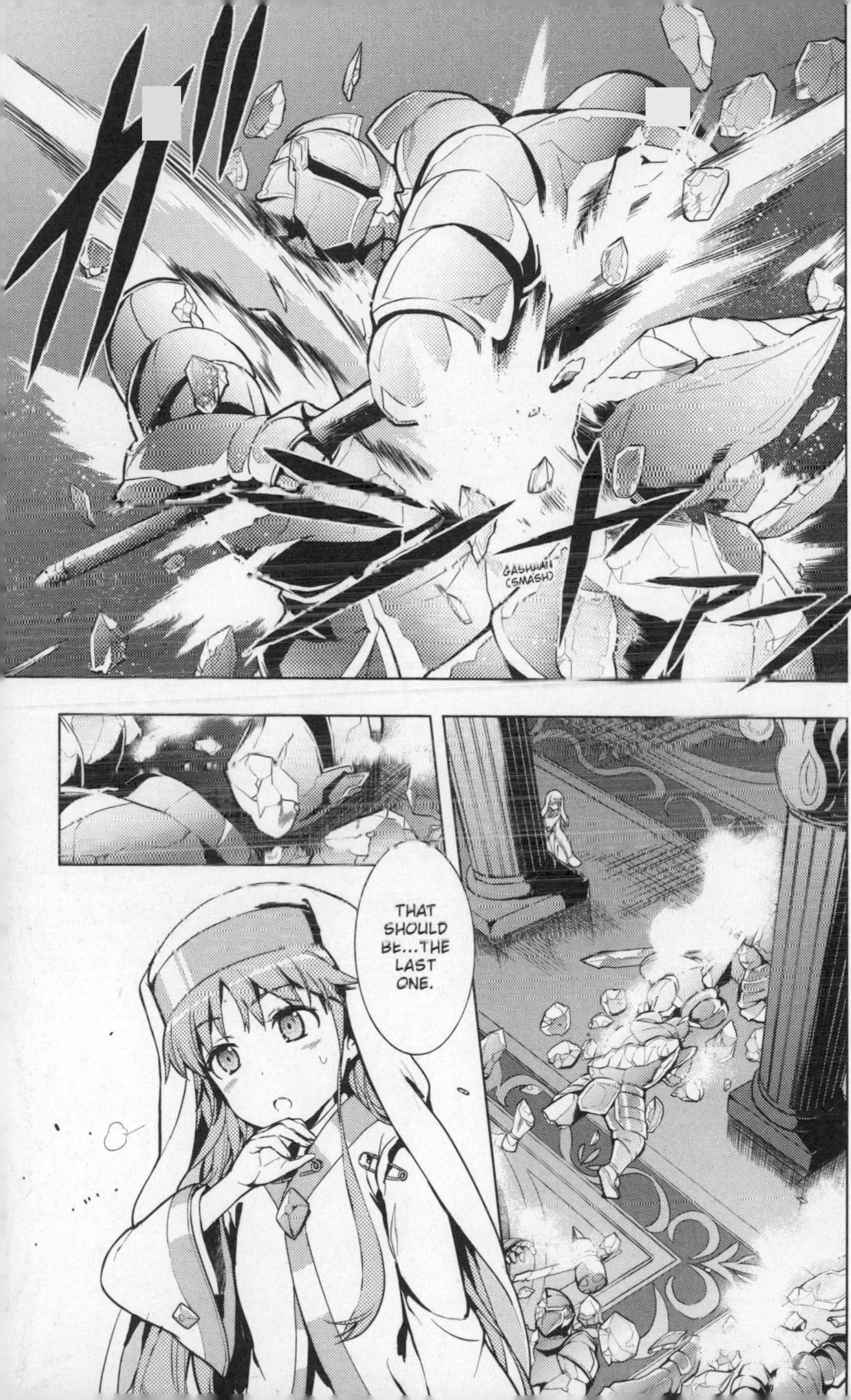
GASHAAN (SMASH)
THAT SHOULD BE...THE LAST ONE.

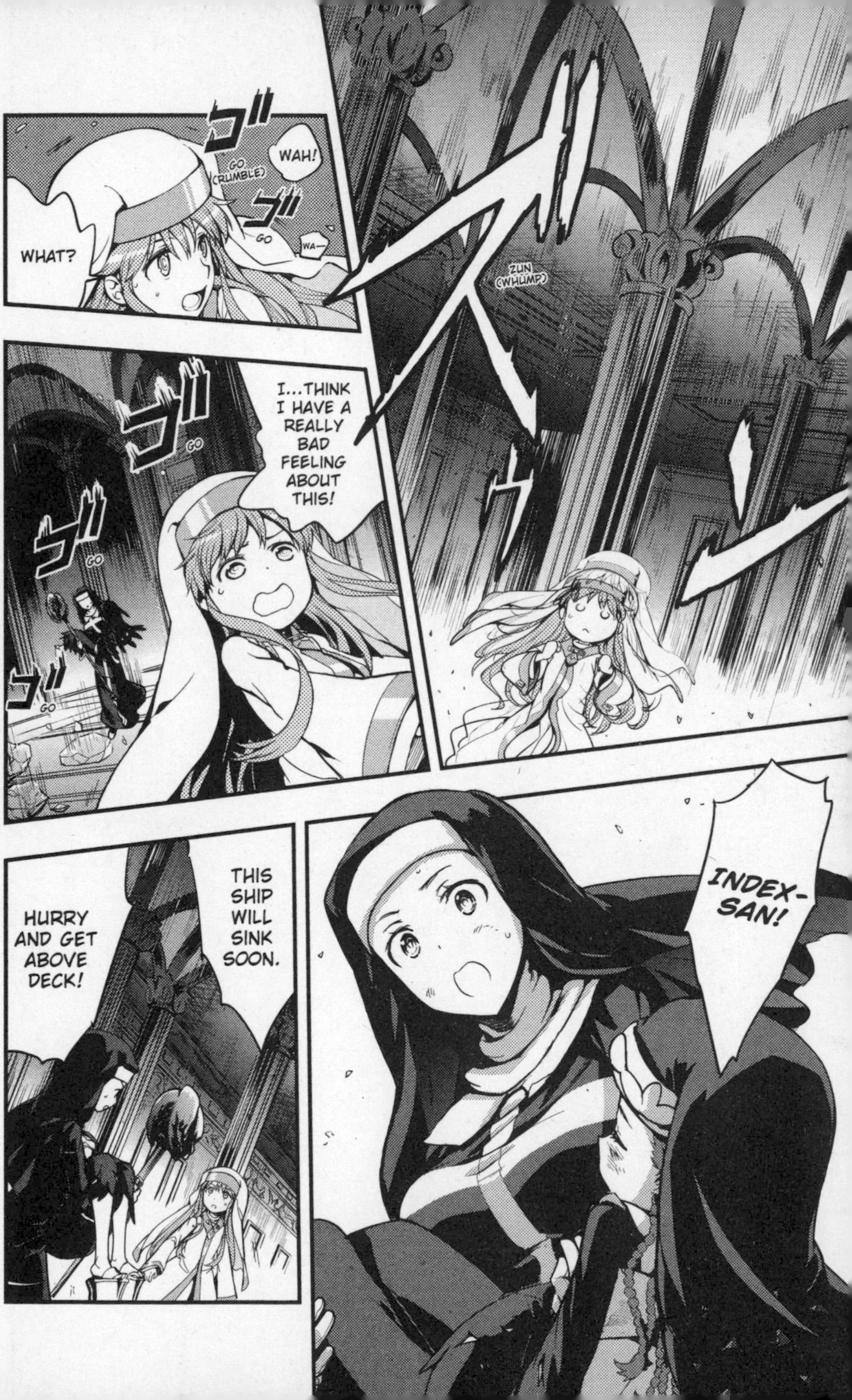
ZUN (WHUMP)
GO (CRUMBLE)
WAH!
GO
WA—
WHAT?
I...THINK I HAVE A REALLY BAD FEELING ABOUT THIS!
GO
GO
GO
INDEX-SAN!
THIS SHIP WILL SINK SOON.
HURRY AND GET ABOVE DECK!

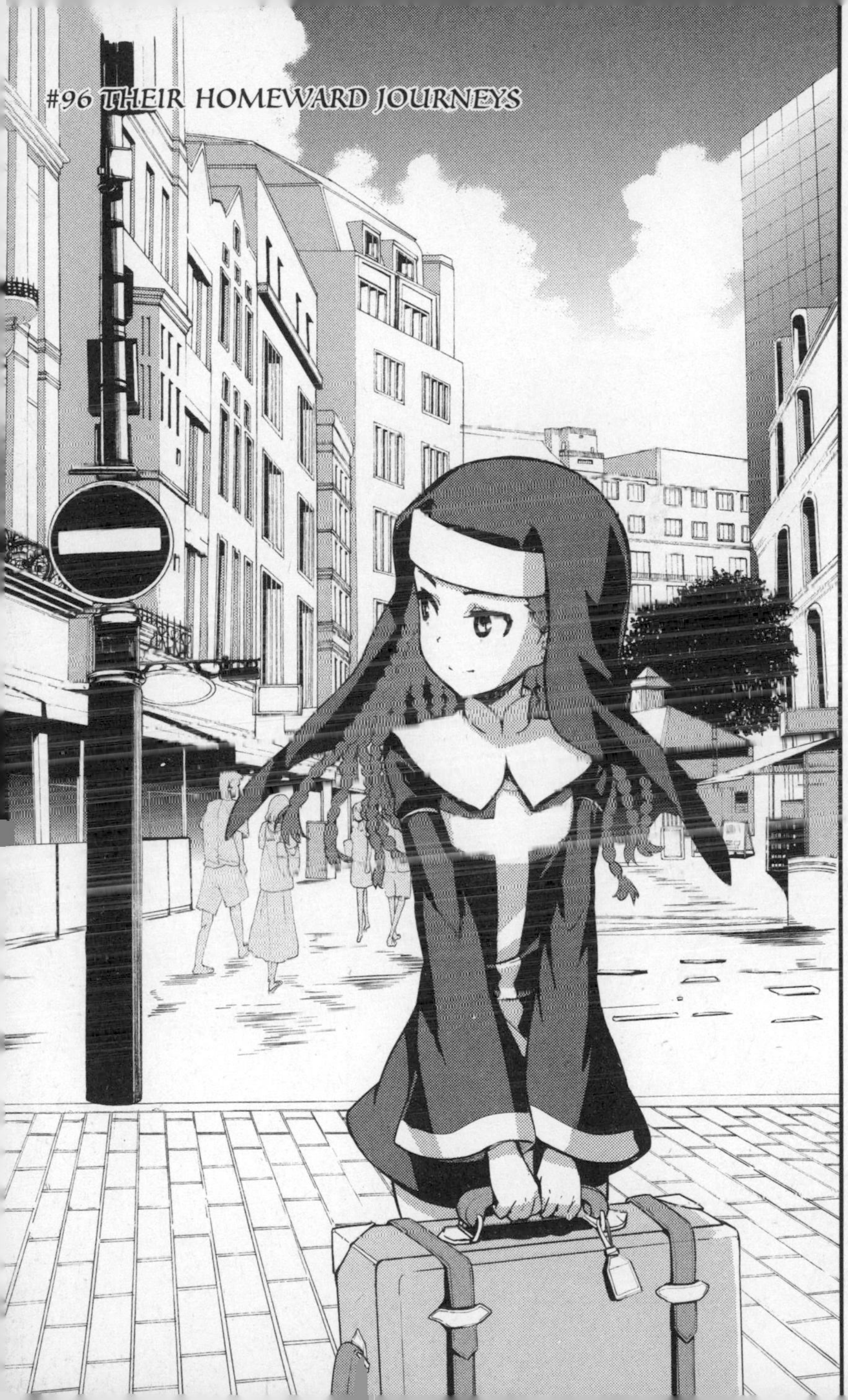
#96 THEIR HOMEWARD JOURNEYS

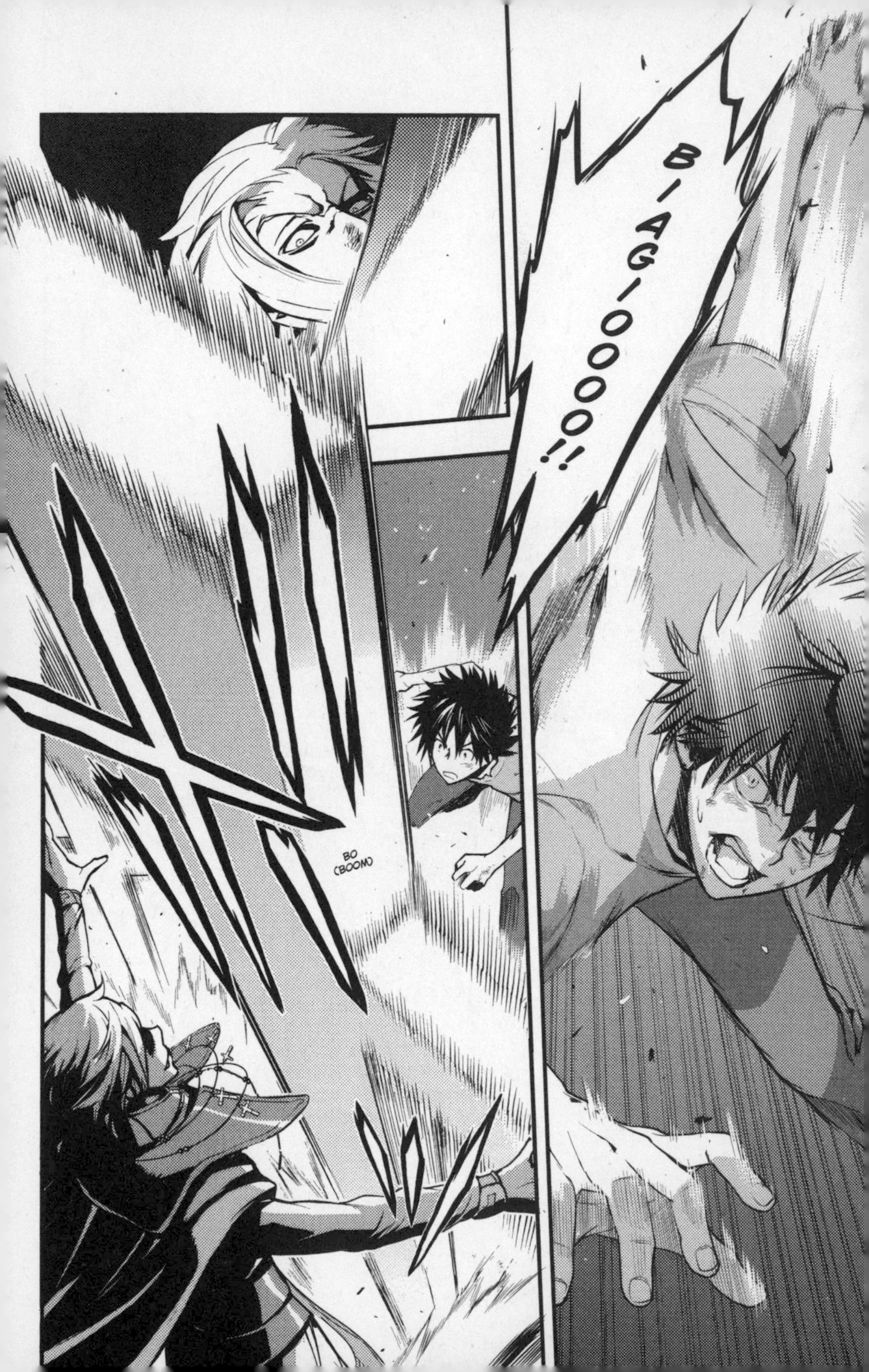
B-AG-OOOOO!!
BO (BOOM)

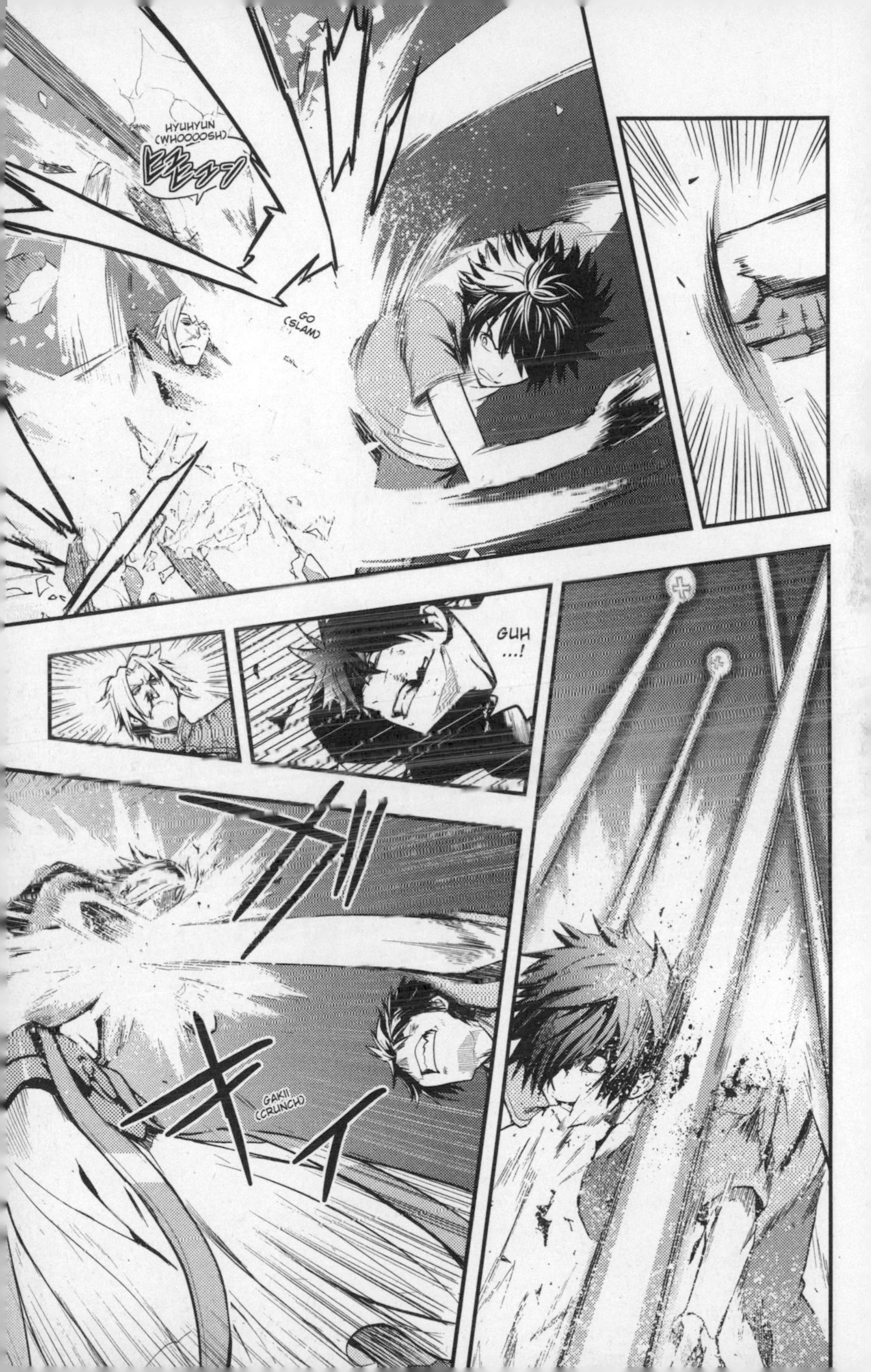
HYUHYUN (WHOOOOSH)
GO (SLAM)
GUH ...!
GAKII (CRUNCH)

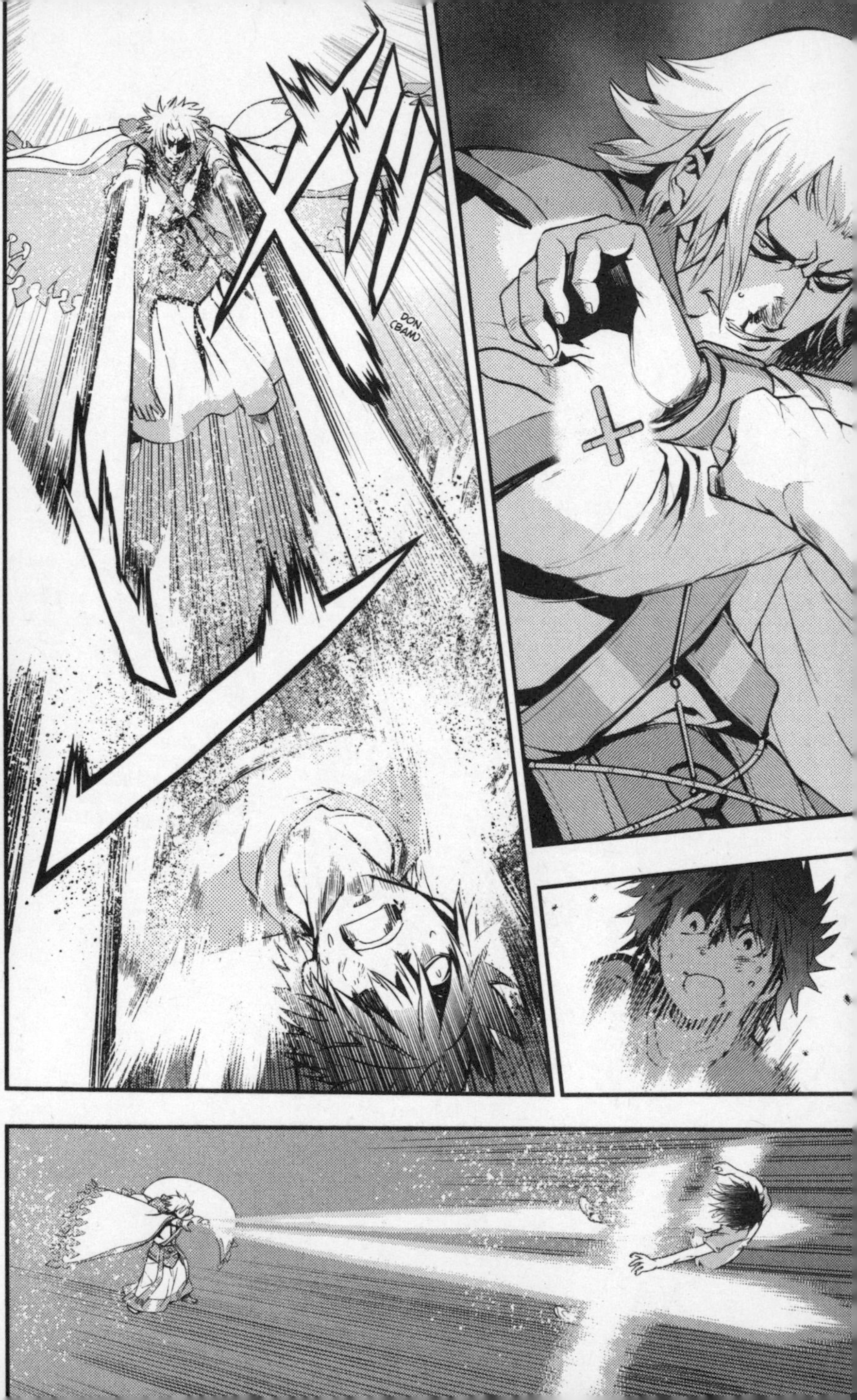
DON
(BAM)

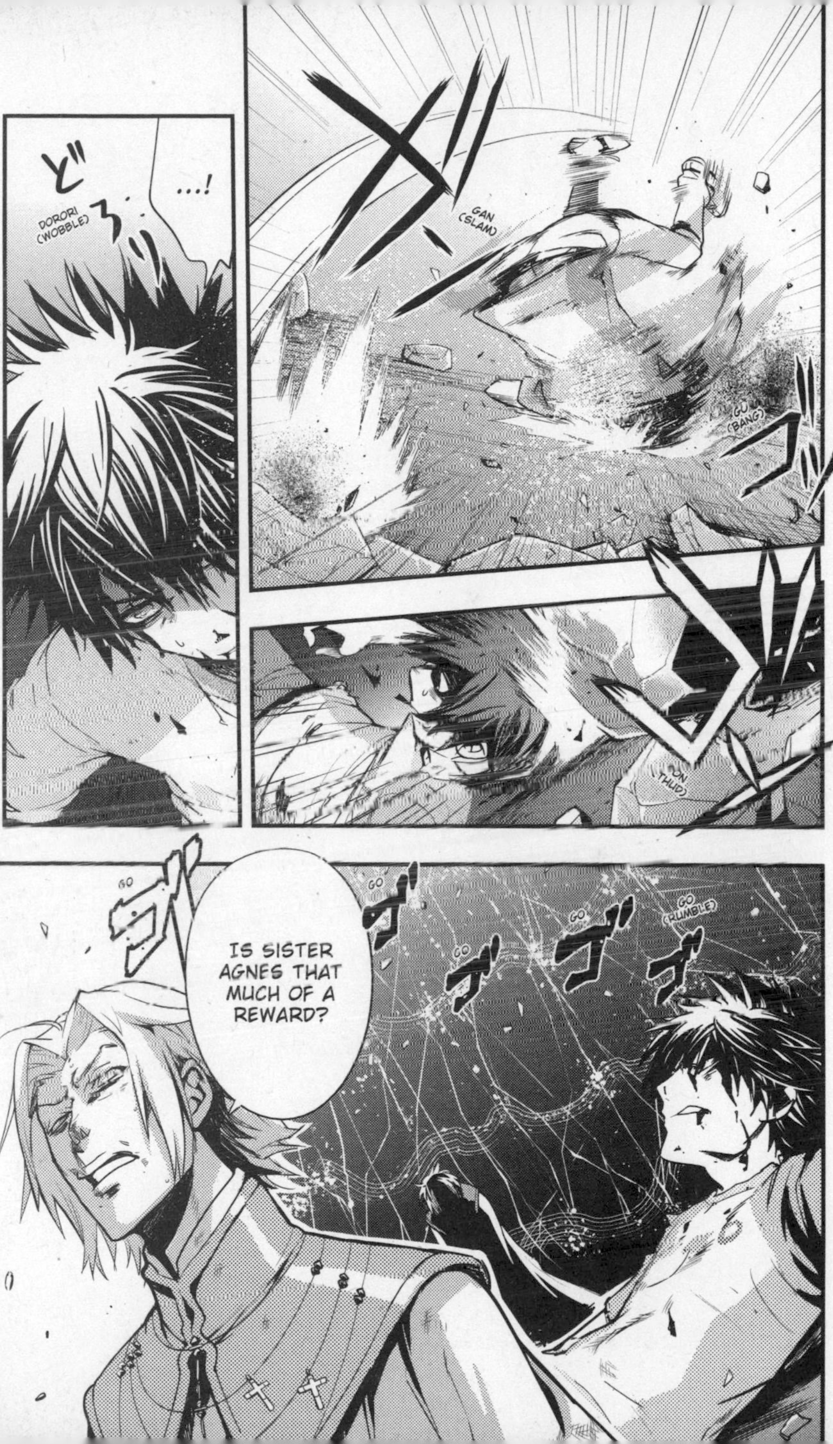
GAN (SLAM)
GU (BANG)
ON
(THUD)
DORORI (WOBBLE)
...!
GO (RUMBLE)
GO
GO
GO
IS SISTER AGNES THAT MUCH OF A REWARD?
GO

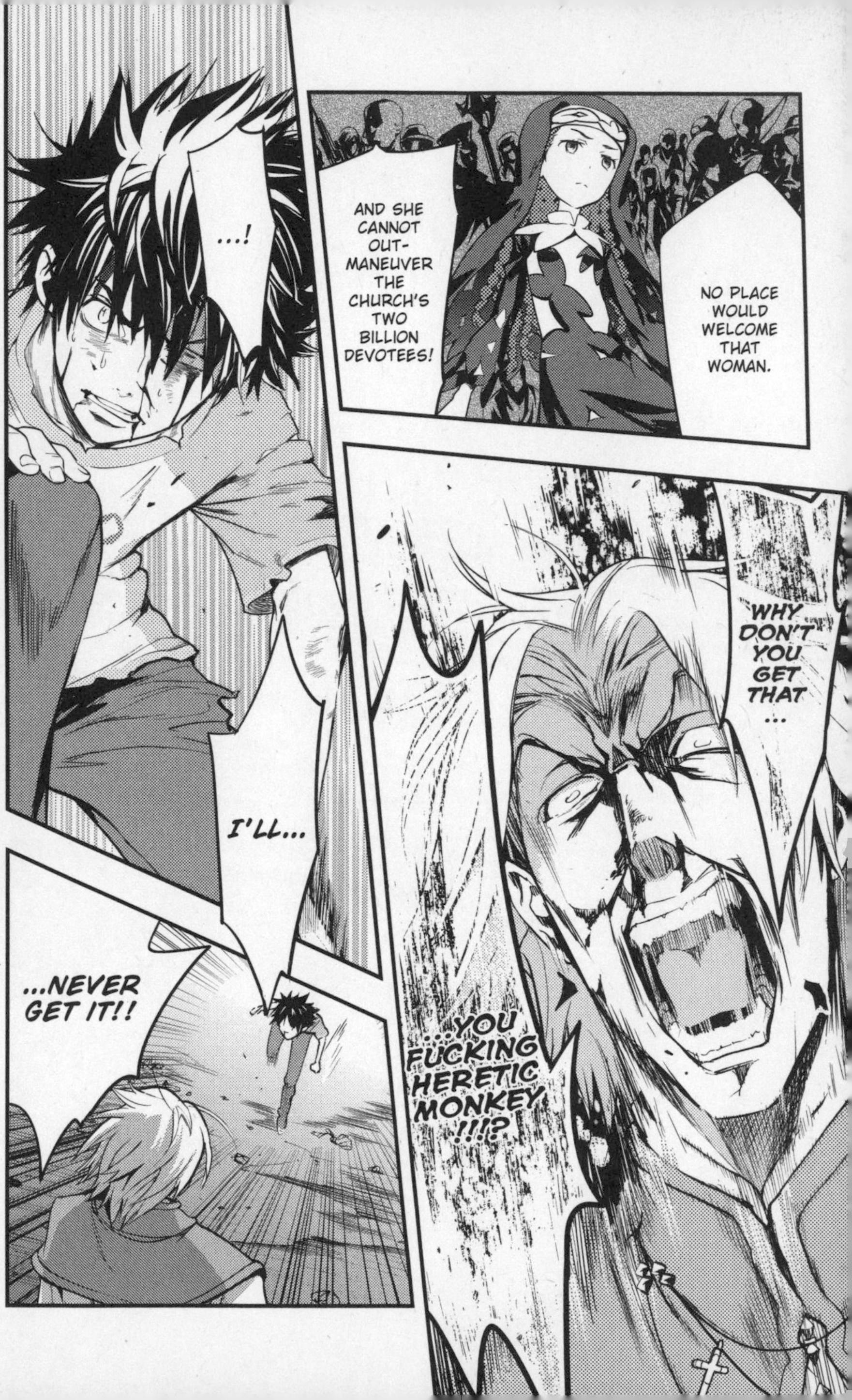
NO PLACE WOULD WELCOME THAT WOMAN.
AND SHE CANNOT OUT-MANEUVER THE CHURCH'S TWO BILLION DEVOTEES!
WHY DON'T YOU GET THAT ...
...YOU FUCKING HERETIC MONKEY!!!?
...!
I'LL...
...NEVER GET IT!!

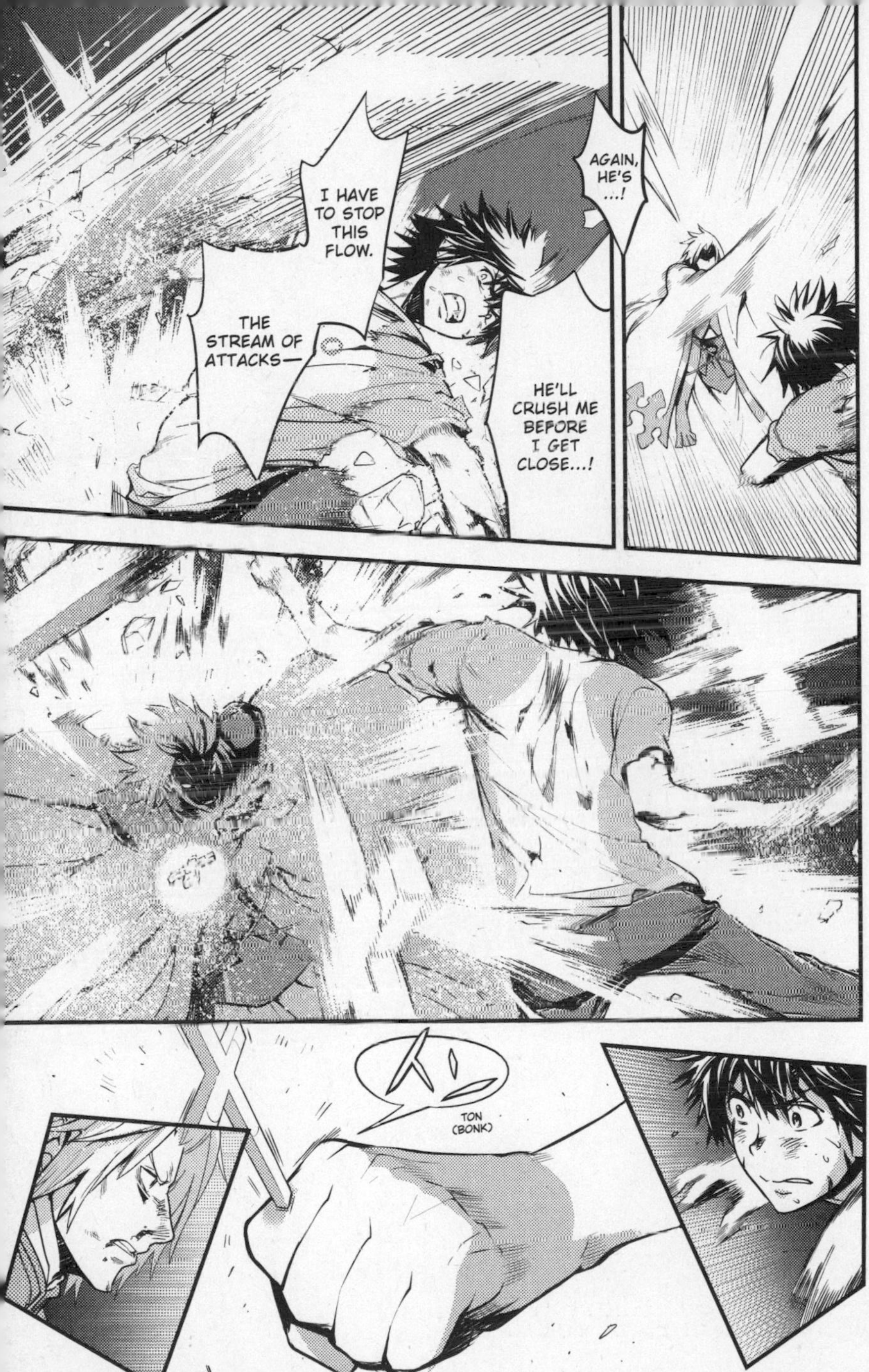
AGAIN, HE'S ...!
I HAVE TO STOP THIS FLOW.
THE STREAM OF ATTACKS—
HE'LL CRUSH ME BEFORE I GET CLOSE...!
TON (BONK)

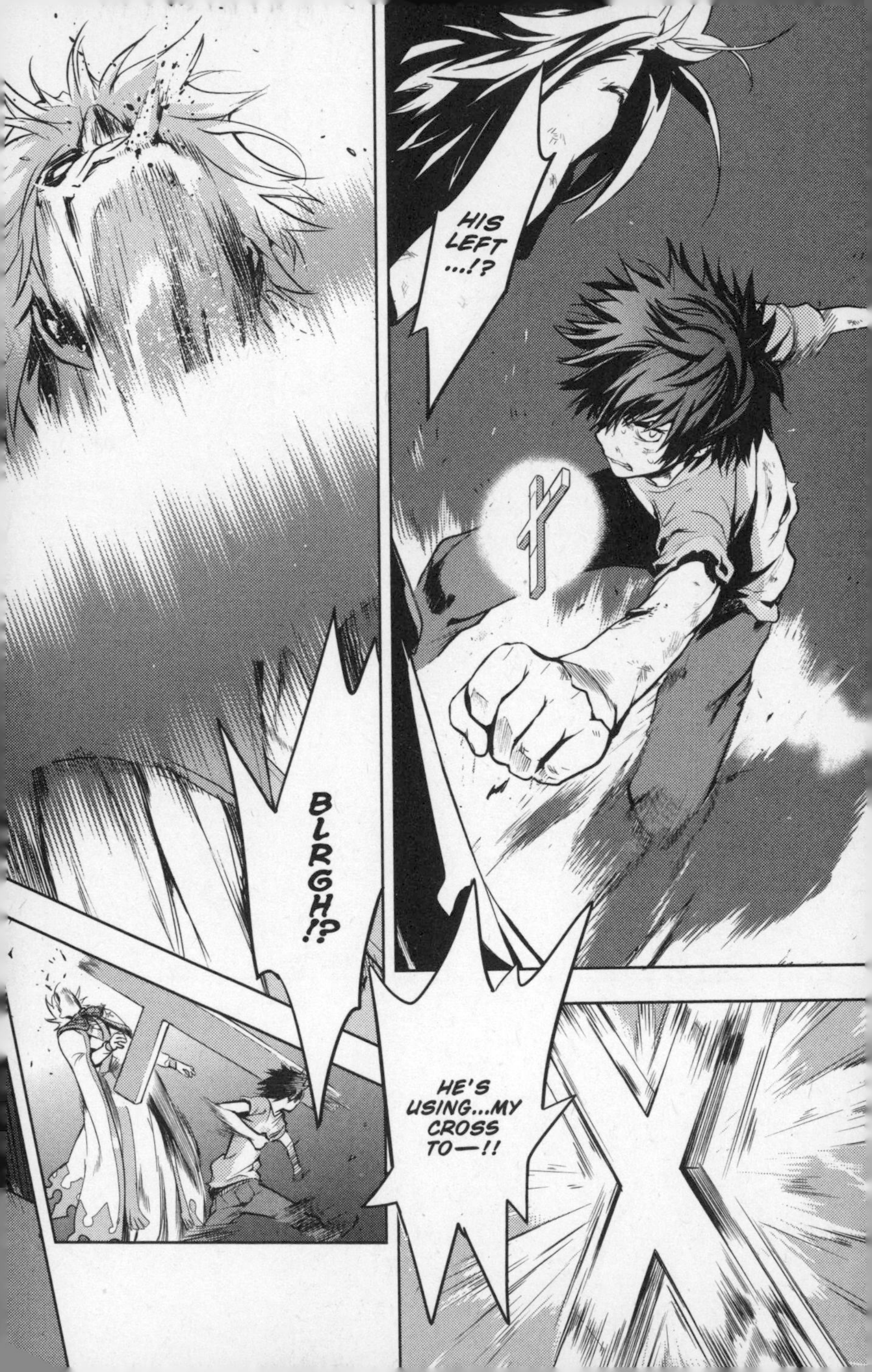
HIS LEFT ...!?
BLRGH!?
HE'S USING...MY CROSS TO—!!

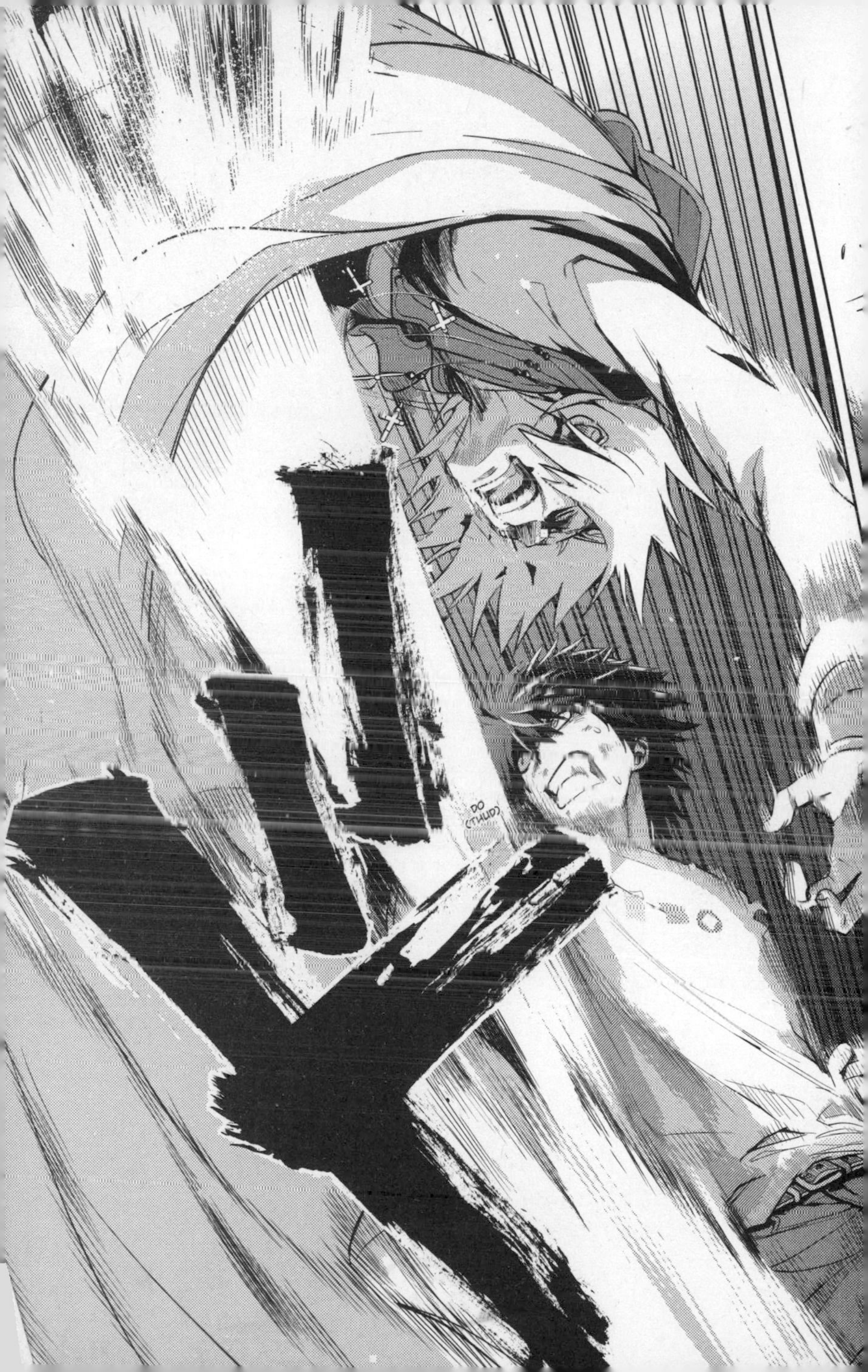
DO
(THUD)

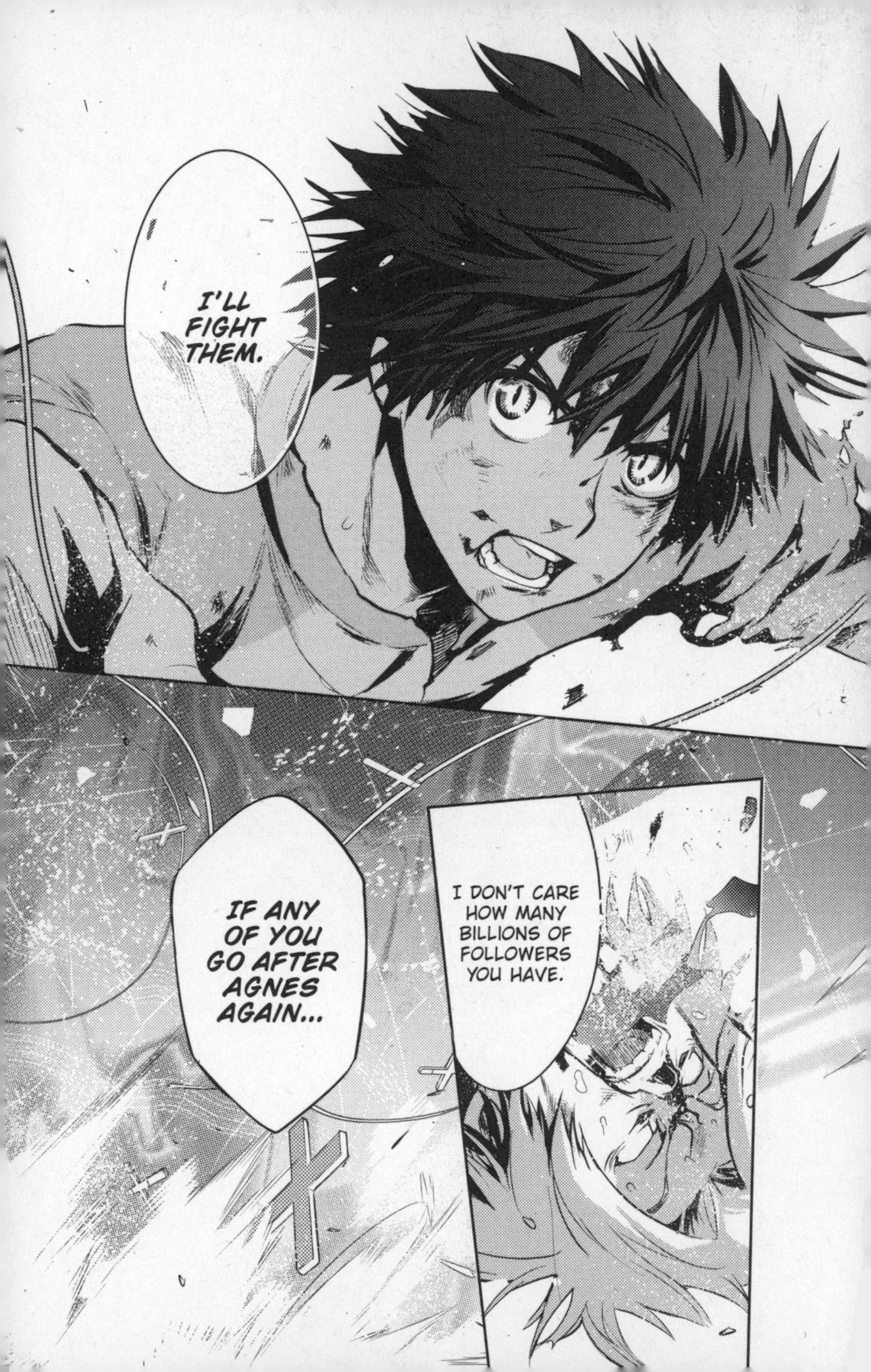
I'LL FIGHT THEM.
I DON'T CARE HOW MANY BILLIONS OF FOLLOWERS YOU HAVE.
IF ANY OF YOU GO AFTER AGNES AGAIN...

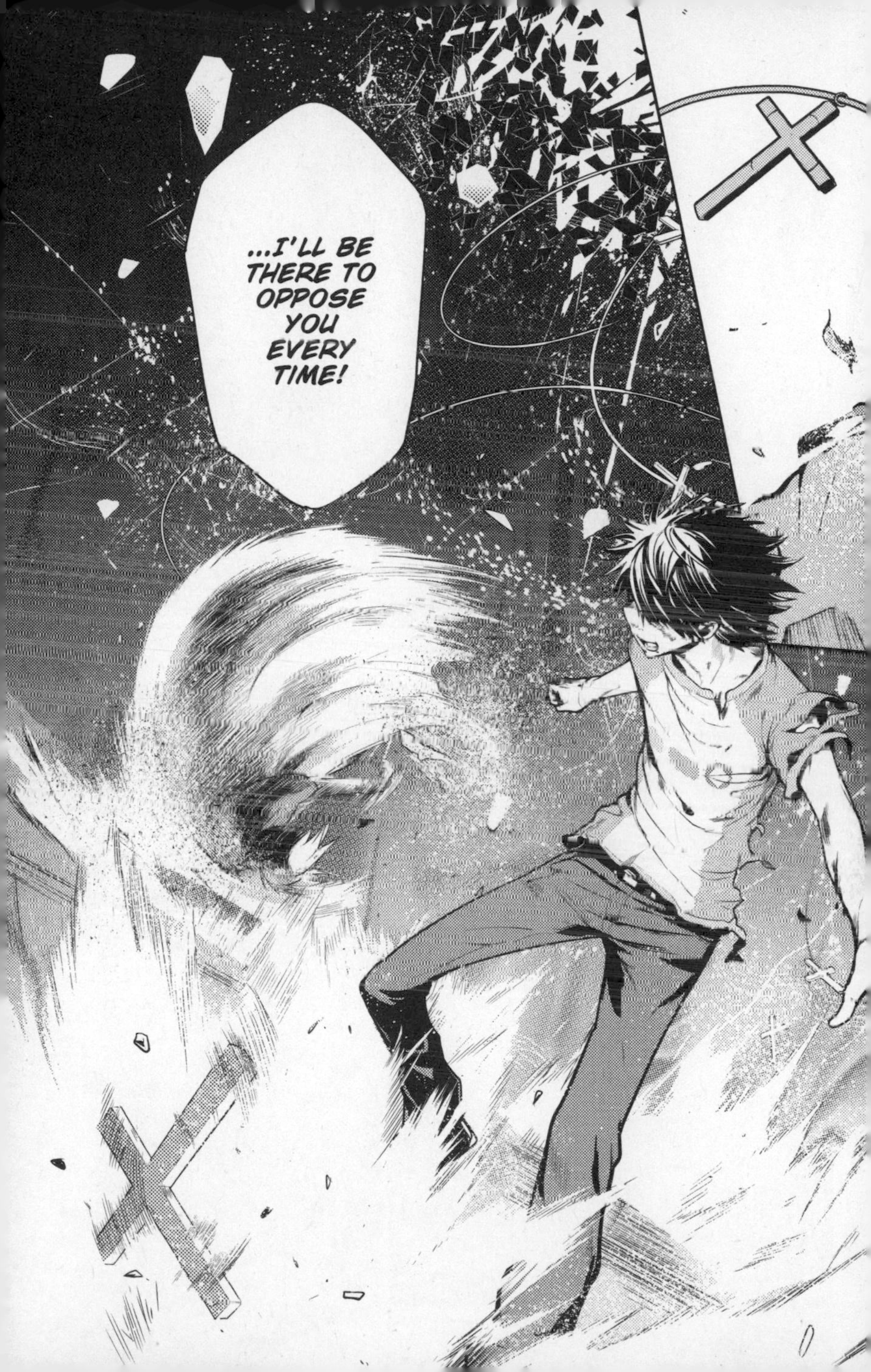
...I'LL BE THERE TO OPPOSE YOU EVERY TIME!

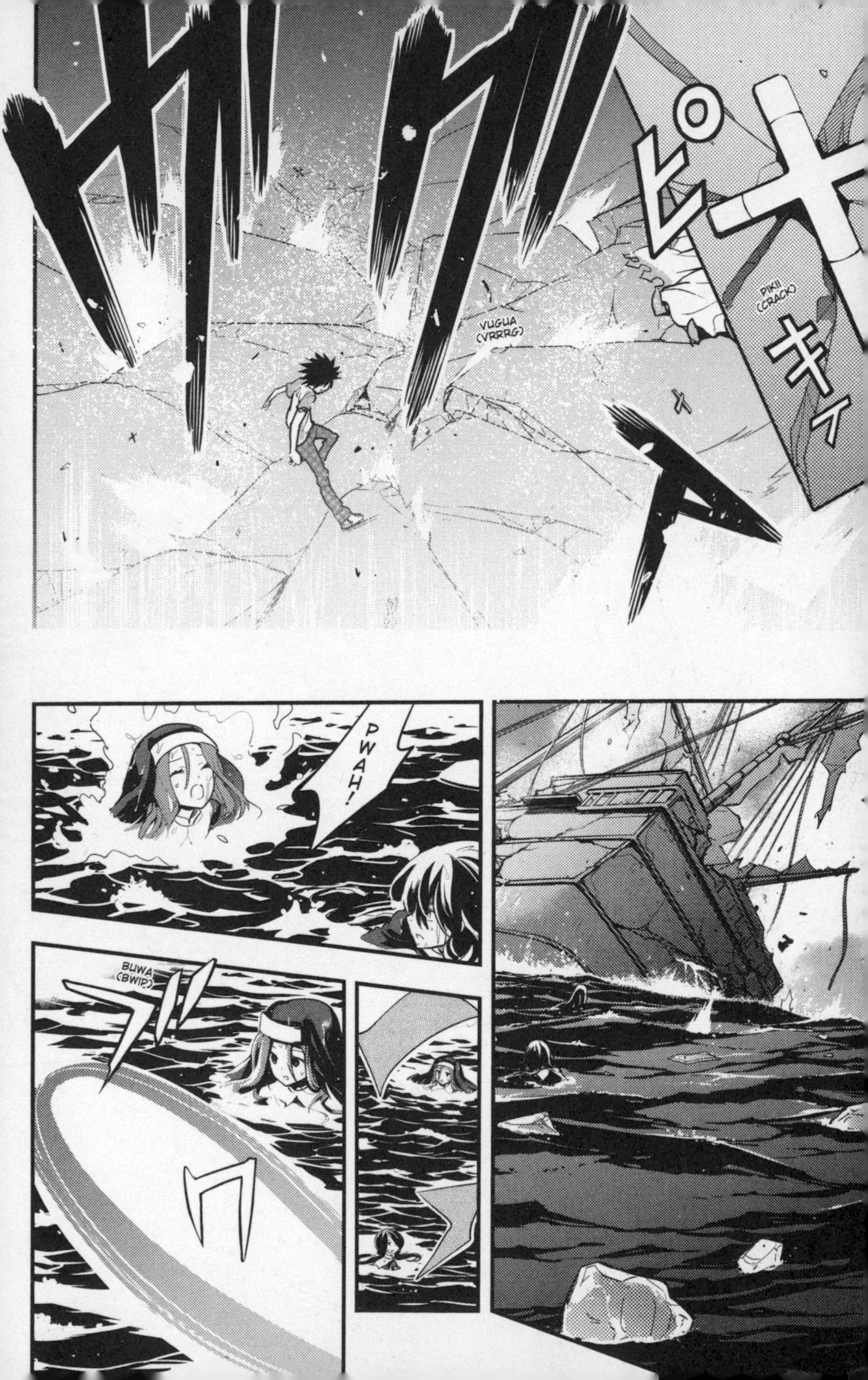
PIKII
(CRACK)
VUGUA
(VRRRG)
PWAH!
BUWA
(BWIP)

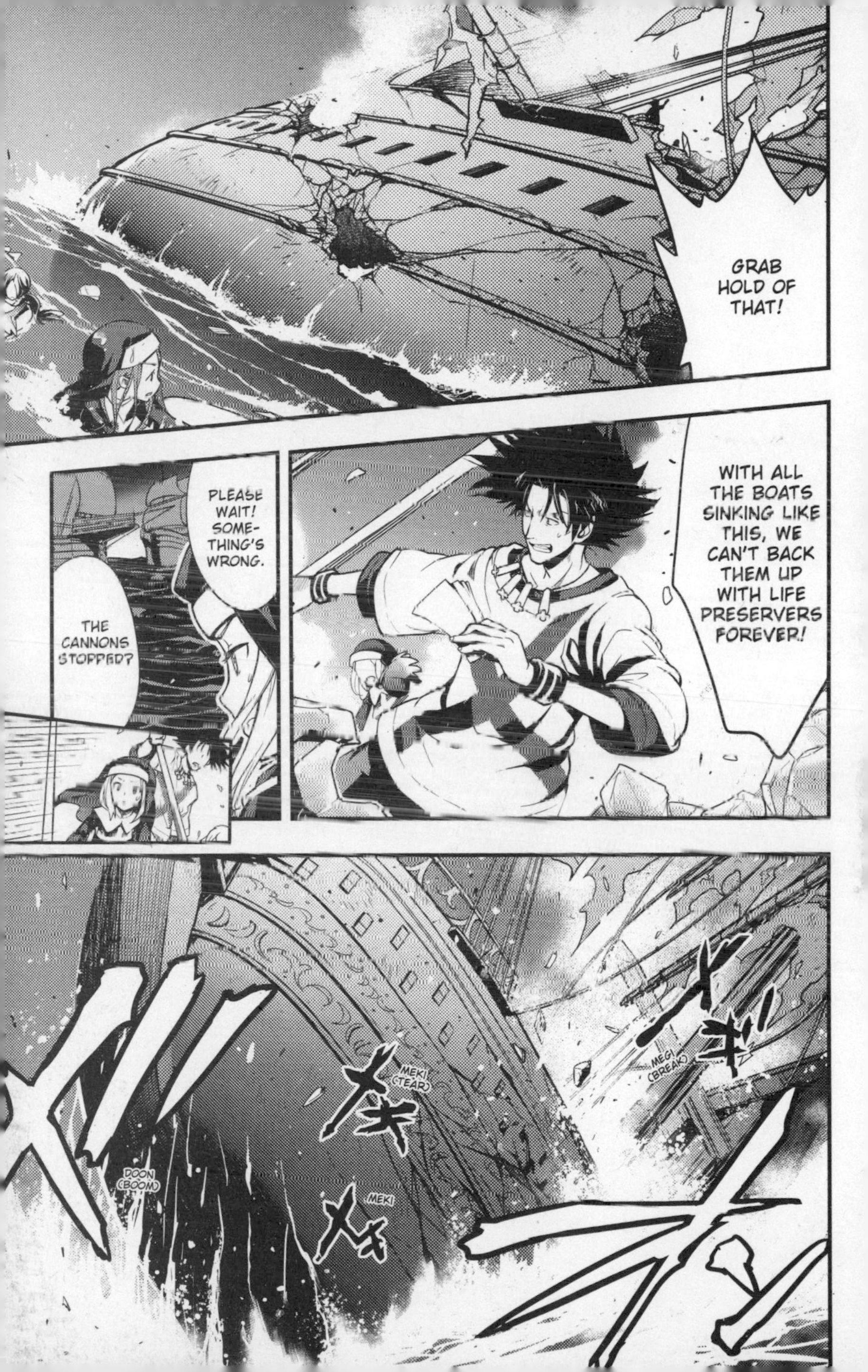
GRAB HOLD OF THAT!
WITH ALL THE BOATS SINKING LIKE THIS, WE CAN'T BACK THEM UP WITH LIFE PRESERVERS FOREVER!
PLEASE WAIT! SOMETHING'S WRONG.
THE CANNONS STOPPED?
MEGI (BREAK)
MEKI (TEAR)
MEKI
DOON (BOOM)

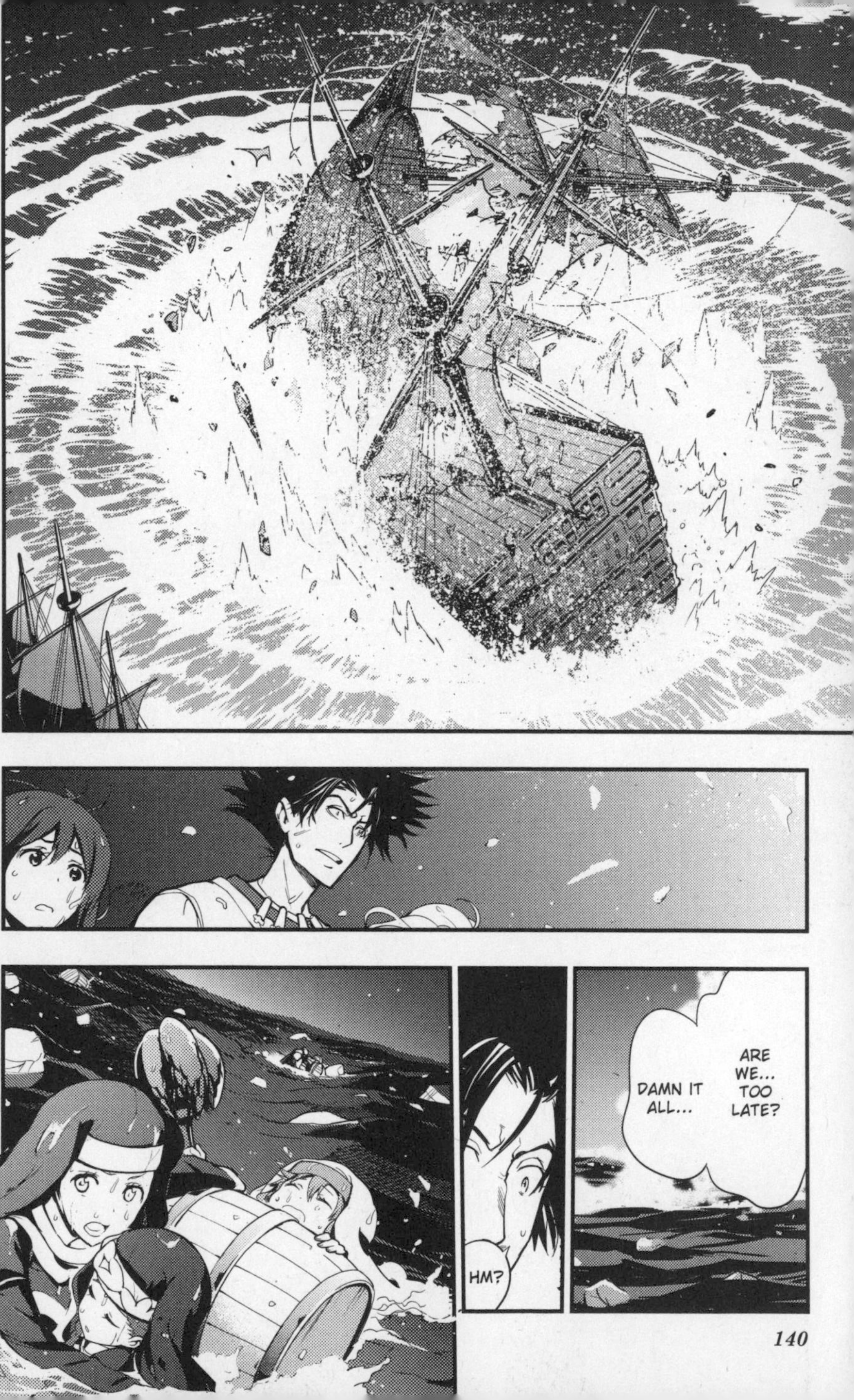
ARE WE... TOO LATE?
DAMN IT ALL...
HM?

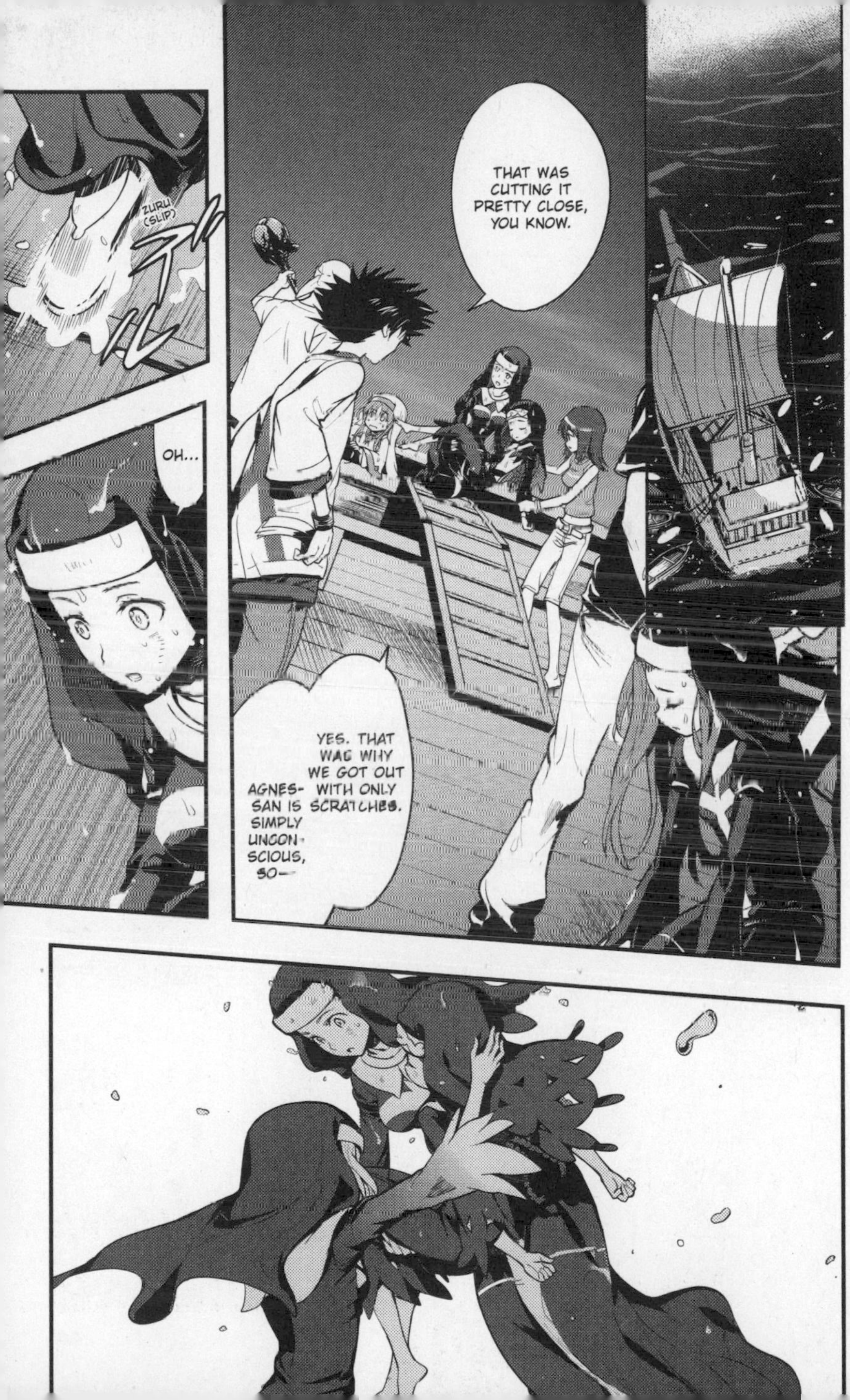
THAT WAS CUTTING IT PRETTY CLOSE, YOU KNOW.
YES. THAT WAS WHY WE GOT OUT WITH ONLY SCRATCHES.
AGNES-SAN IS SIMPLY UNCONSCIOUS, SO—
ZURU (SLIP)
OH...

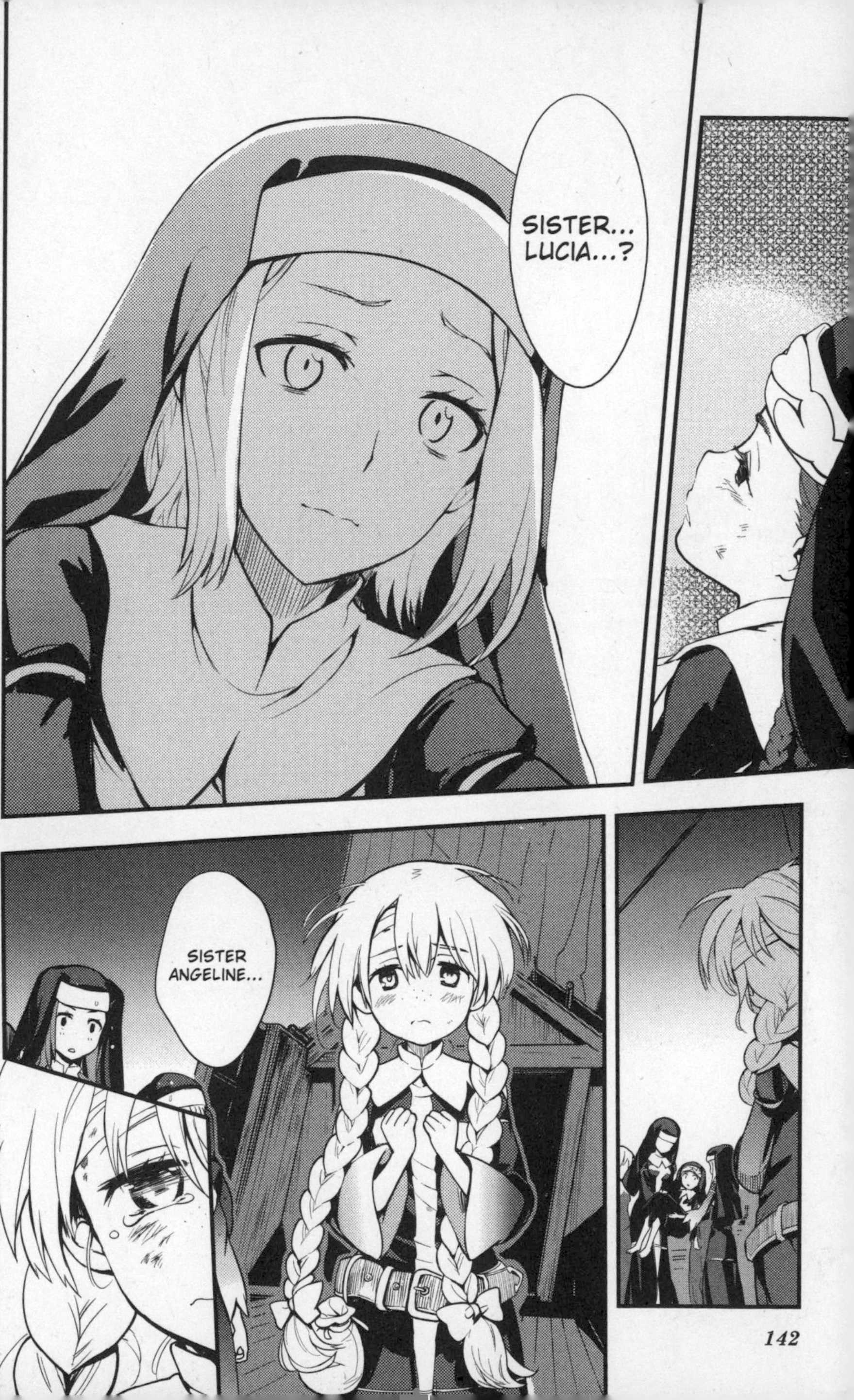
SISTER... LUCIA...?
SISTER ANGELINE...

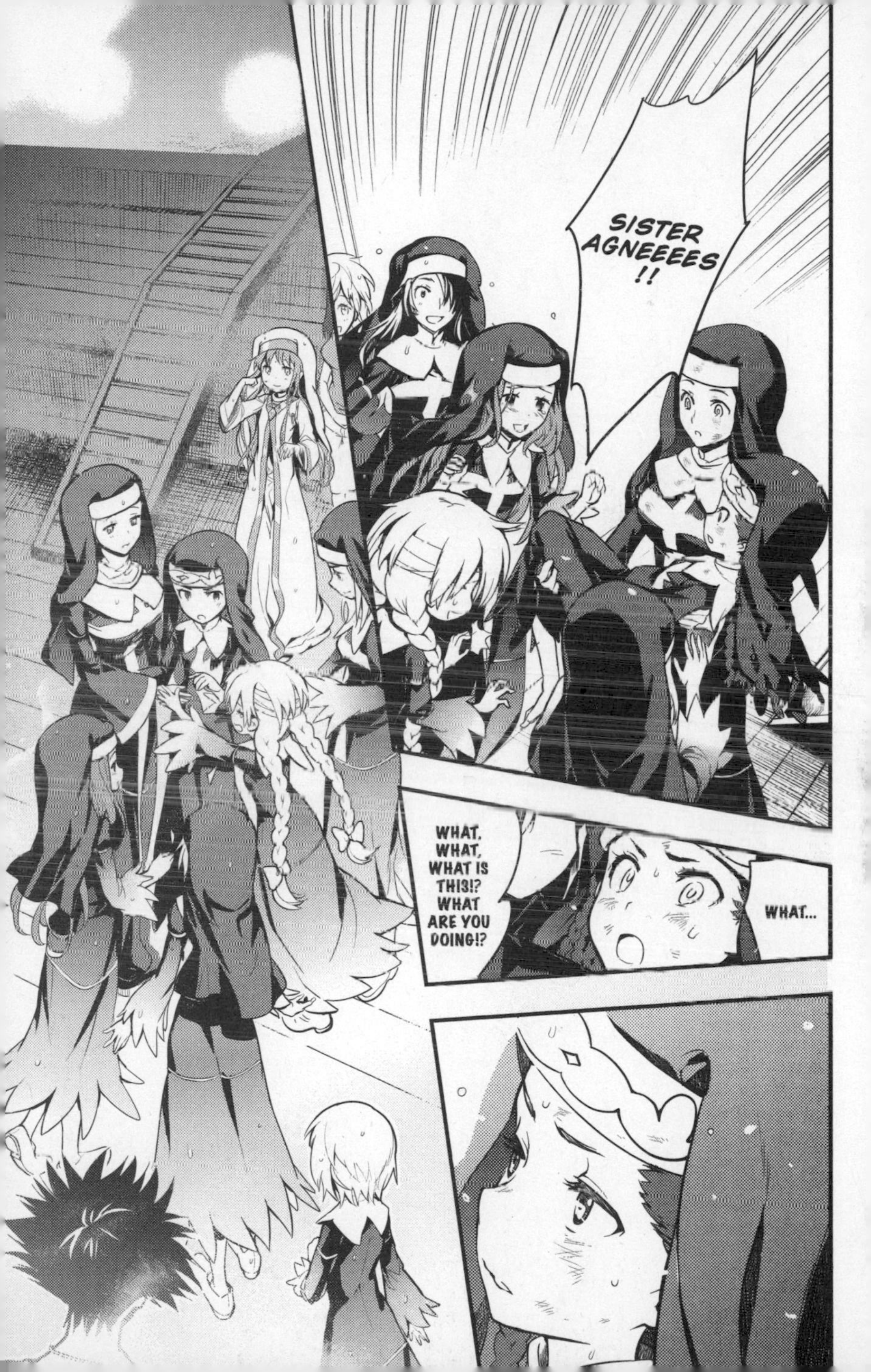
SISTER AGNEEEES!!
WHAT...
WHAT, WHAT, WHAT IS THIS!? WHAT ARE YOU DOING!?

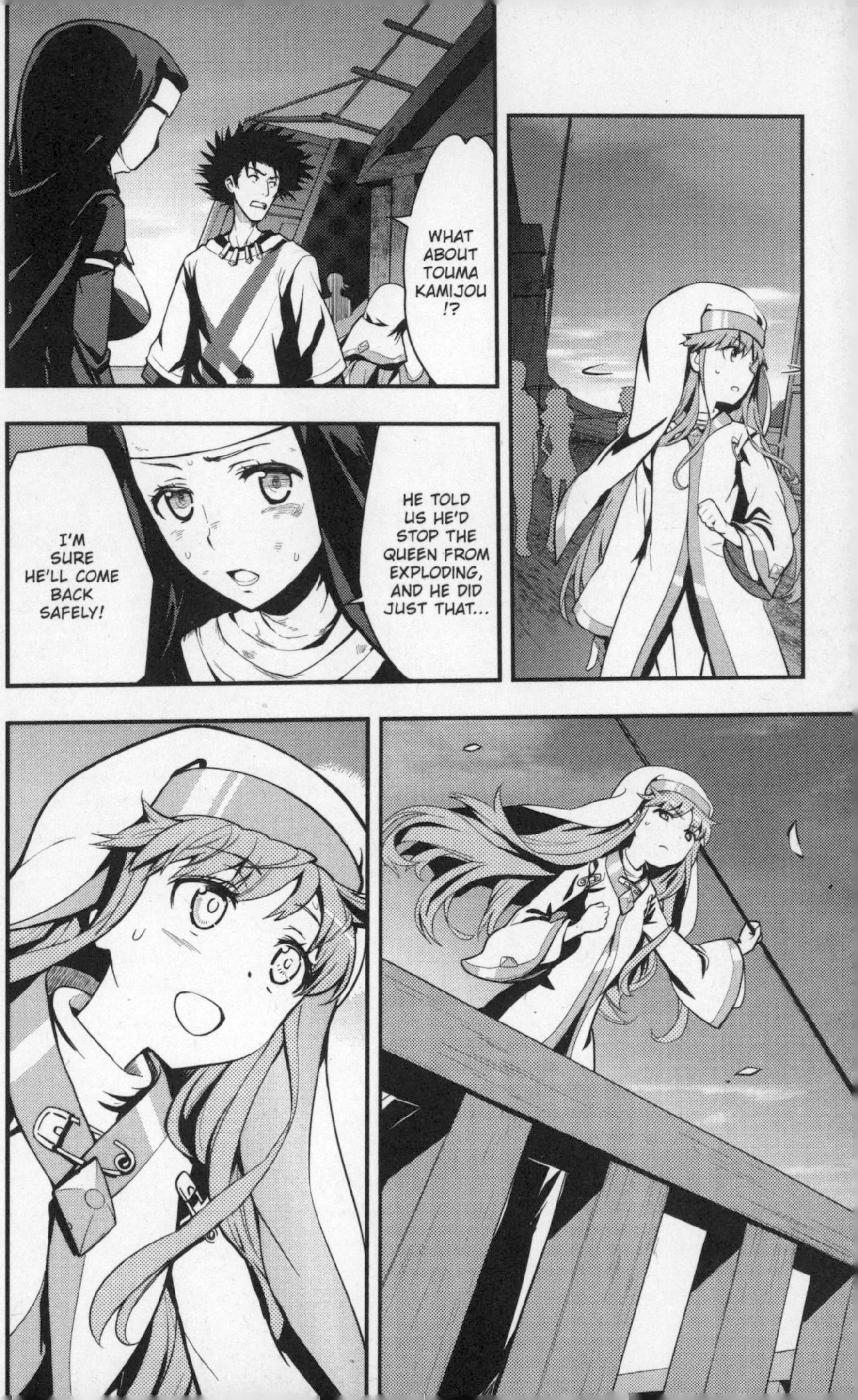
WHAT ABOUT TOUMA KAMIJOU!?
HE TOLD US HE'D STOP THE QUEEN FROM EXPLODING, AND HE DID JUST THAT...
I'M SURE HE'LL COME BACK SAFELY!

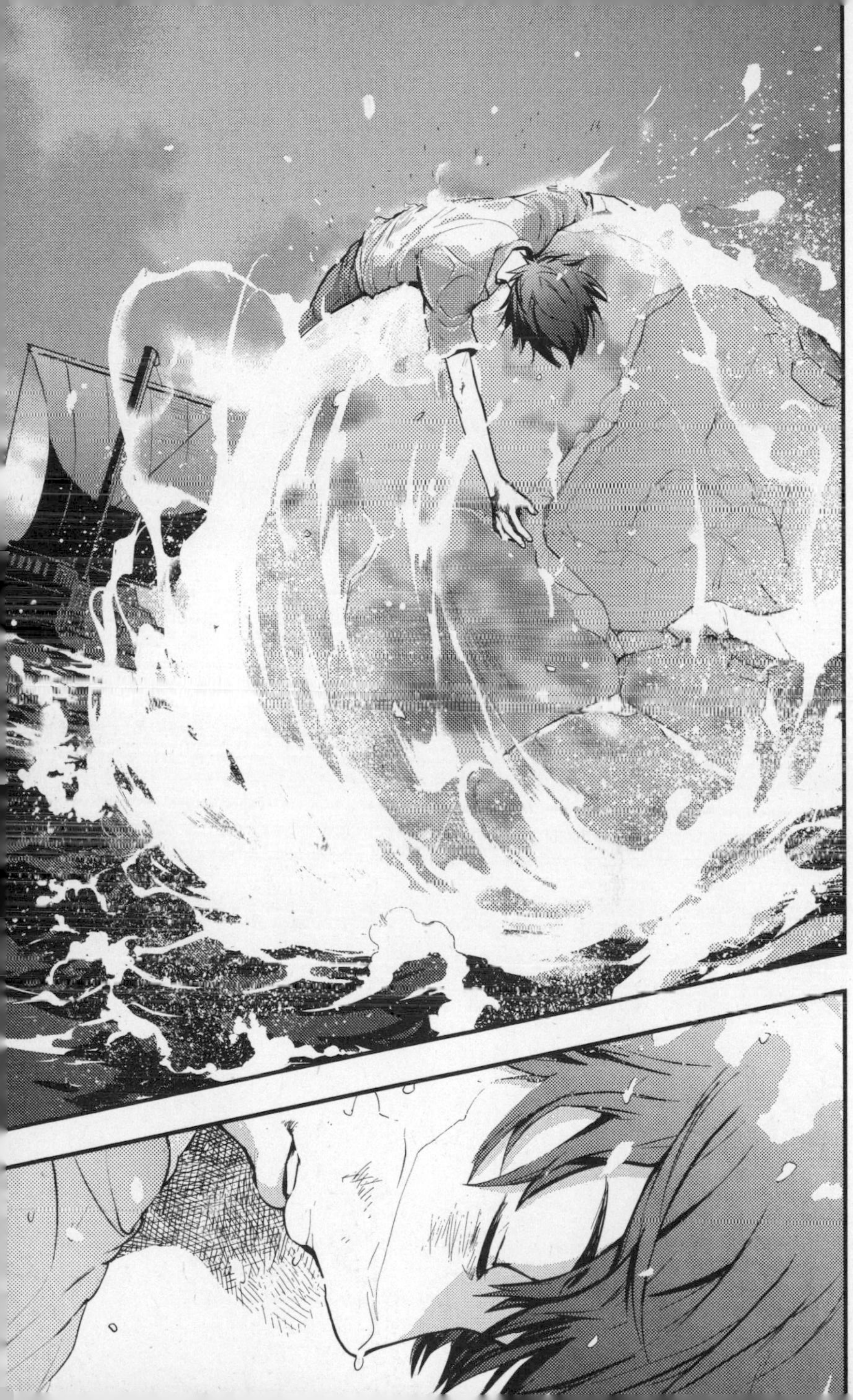

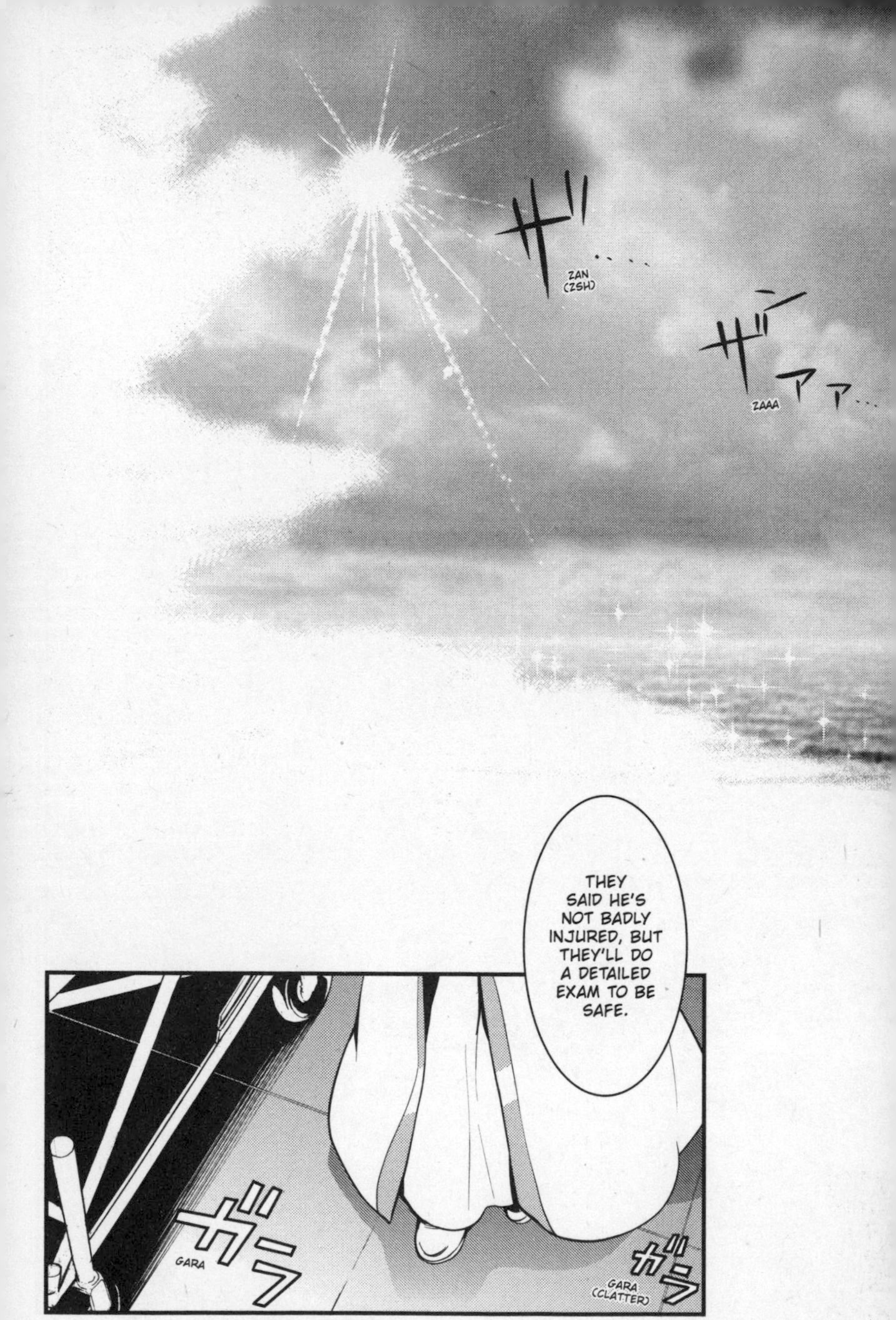
ザン
ZAN (ZSH)
ザアア
ZAAA
THEY SAID HE'S NOT BADLY INJURED, BUT THEY'LL DO A DETAILED EXAM TO BE SAFE.
ガラ
GARA (CLATTER)
ガラ
GARA

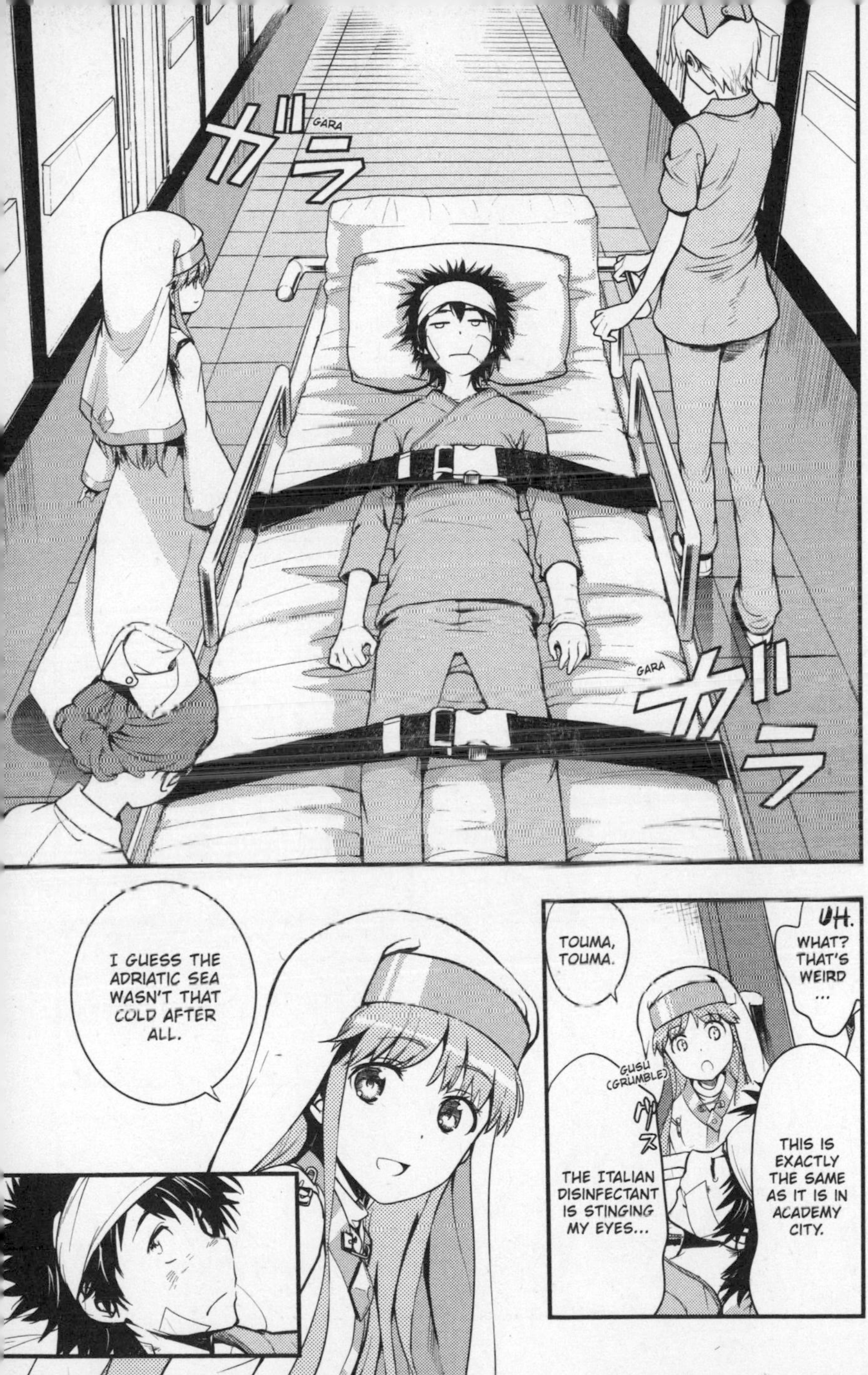
GARA
GARA
UH. WHAT? THAT'S WEIRD...
TOUMA, TOUMA.
THIS IS EXACTLY THE SAME AS IT IS IN ACADEMY CITY.
GUSU (GRUMBLE)
THE ITALIAN DISINFECTANT IS STINGING MY EYES...
I GUESS THE ADRIATIC SEA WASN'T THAT COLD AFTER ALL.

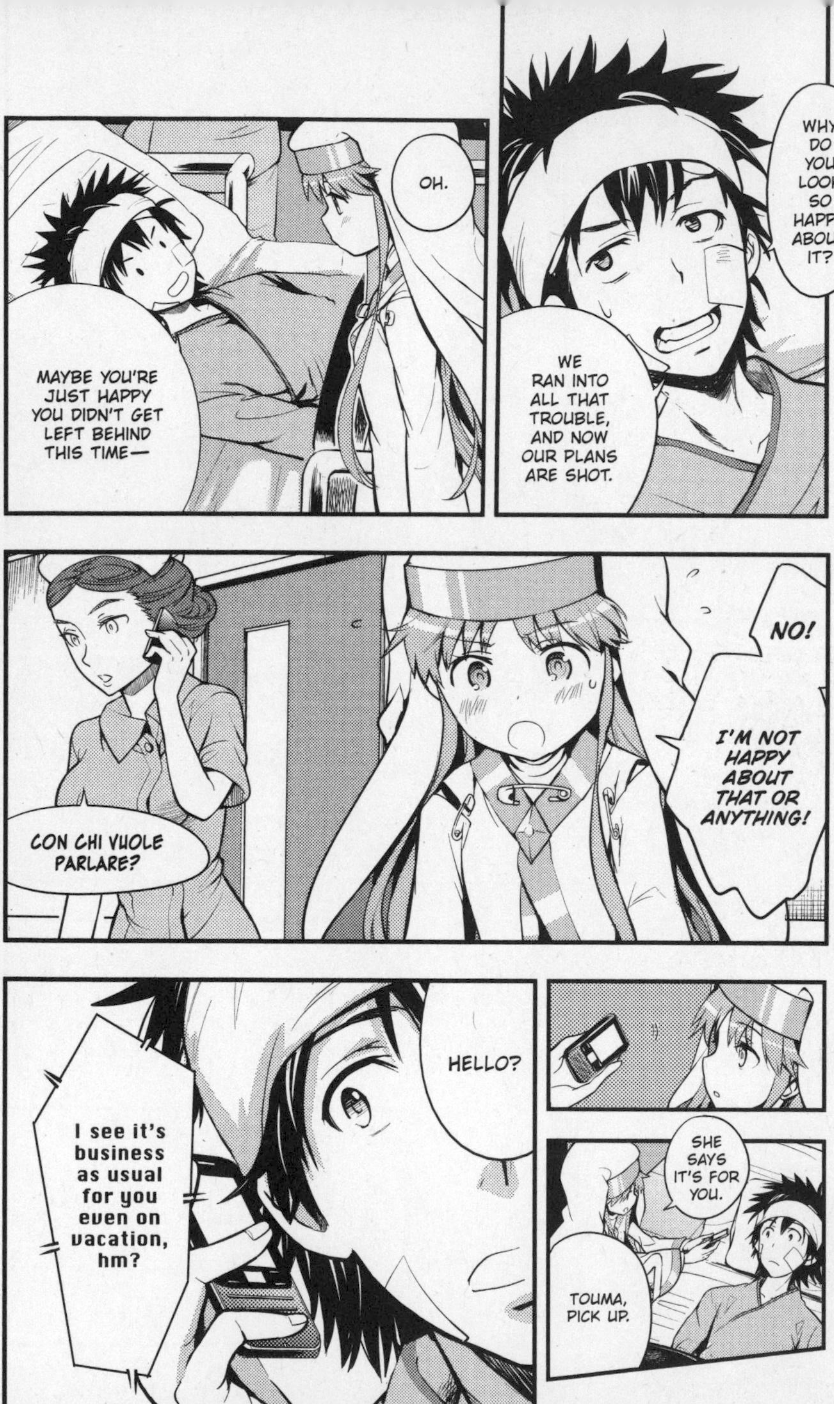
WHY DO YOU LOOK SO HAPPY ABOUT IT?
WE RAN INTO ALL THAT TROUBLE, AND NOW OUR PLANS ARE SHOT.
OH.
MAYBE YOU'RE JUST HAPPY YOU DIDN'T GET LEFT BEHIND THIS TIME—
NO!
I'M NOT HAPPY ABOUT THAT OR ANYTHING!
CON CHI VUOLE PARLARE?
SHE SAYS IT'S FOR YOU.
TOUMA, PICK UP.
HELLO?
I see it's business as usual for you even on vacation, hm?

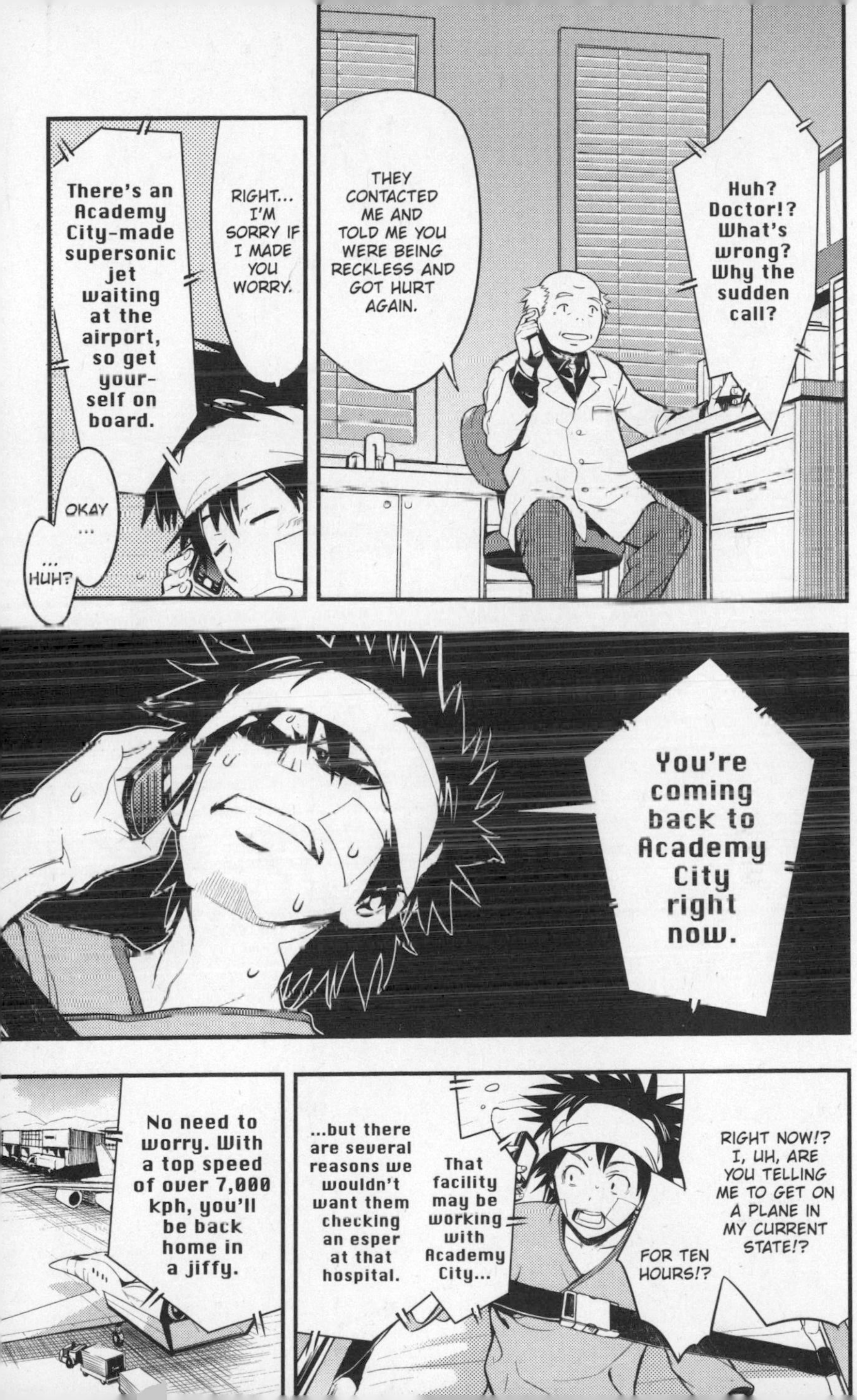
Huh? Doctor!? What's wrong? Why the sudden call?
THEY CONTACTED ME AND TOLD ME YOU WERE BEING RECKLESS AND GOT HURT AGAIN.
RIGHT... I'M SORRY IF I MADE YOU WORRY.
There's an Academy City-made supersonic jet waiting at the airport, so get your-self on board.
OKAY ... ... HUH?
You're coming back to Academy City right now.
RIGHT NOW!? I, UH, ARE YOU TELLING ME TO GET ON A PLANE IN MY CURRENT STATE!?
FOR TEN HOURS!?
That facility may be working with Academy City...
...but there are several reasons we wouldn't want them checking an esper at that hospital.
No need to worry. With a top speed of over 7,000 kph, you'll be back home in a jiffy.

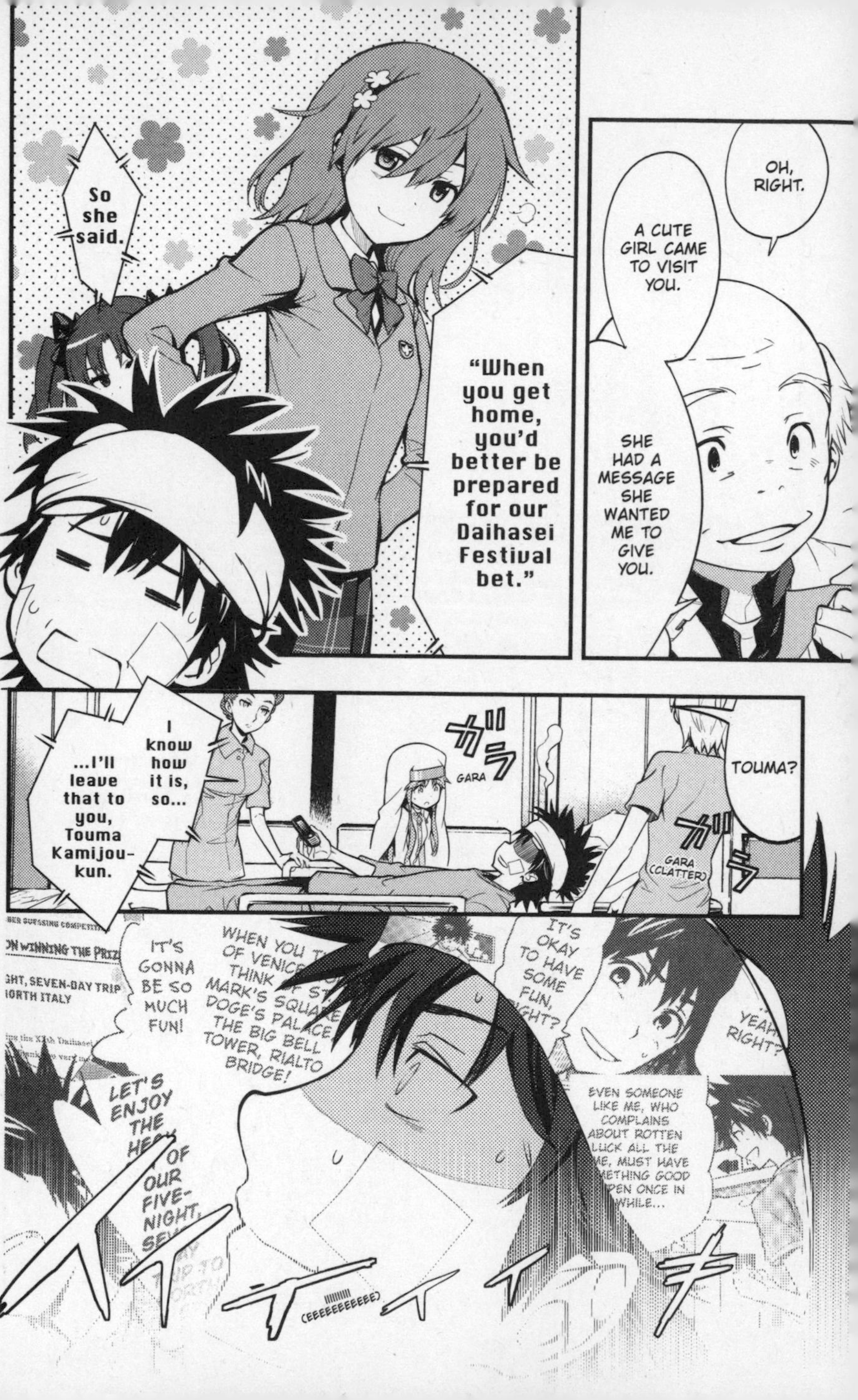
OH, RIGHT.
A CUTE GIRL CAME TO VISIT YOU.
SHE HAD A MESSAGE SHE WANTED ME TO GIVE YOU.
"When you get home, you'd better be prepared for our Daihasei Festival bet."
So she said.
TOUMA?
GARA (CLATTER)
GARA
I know how it is, so...
...I'll leave that to you, Touma Kamijou-kun.
YEAH, RIGHT?
IT'S OKAY TO HAVE SOME FUN, RIGHT?
EVEN SOMEONE LIKE ME, WHO COMPLAINS ABOUT ROTTEN LUCK ALL THE ME, MUST HAVE METHING GOOD PEN ONCE IN WHILE...
WHEN YOU T OF VENIC THINK MARK'S SQUARE, DOGE'S PALACE, THE BIG BELL TOWER, RIALTO BRIDGE!
IT'S GONNA BE SO MUCH FUN!
ON WINNING THE PRIZ
GHT, SEVEN-DAY TRIP ORTH ITALY
LET'S ENJOY THE HE OF OUR FIVE-NIGHT, SEV TRIP TO ORTH
(EEEEEEEEEEE)

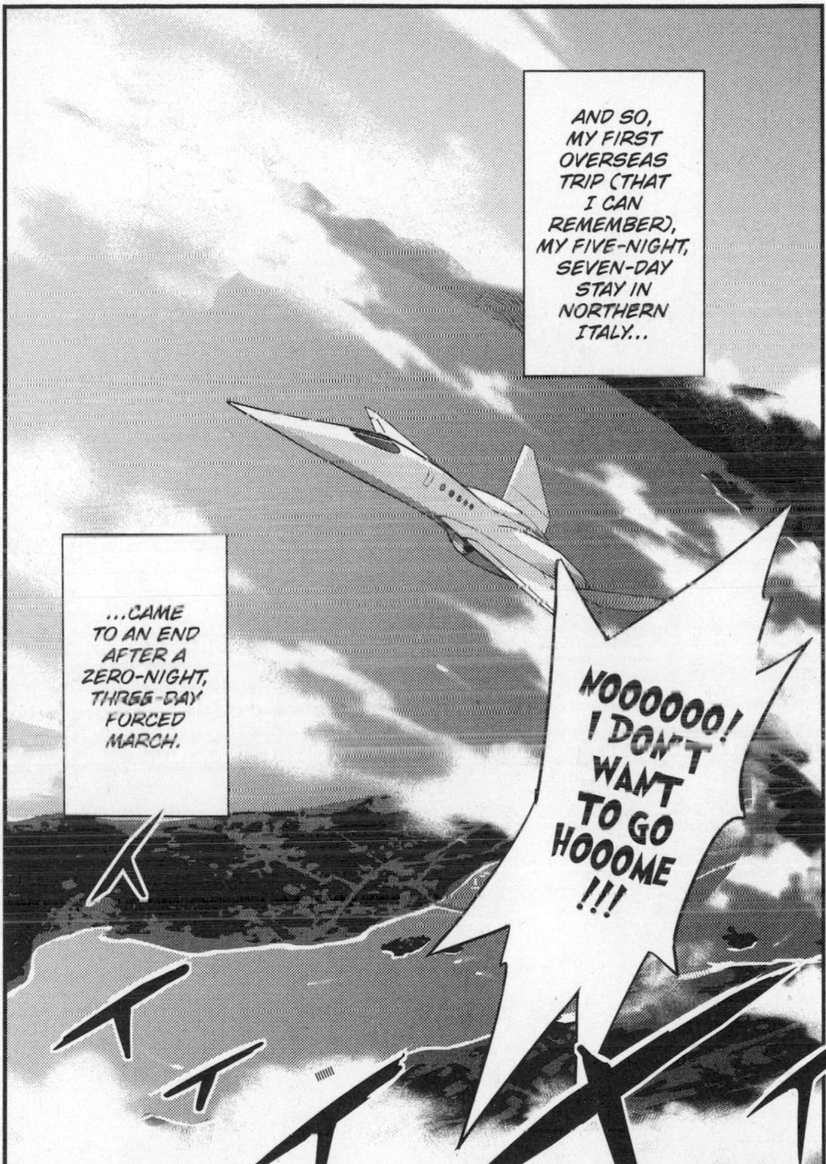
AND SO, MY FIRST OVERSEAS TRIP (THAT I CAN REMEMBER), MY FIVE-NIGHT, SEVEN-DAY STAY IN NORTHERN ITALY...
...CAME TO AN END AFTER A ZERO-NIGHT, THREE-DAY FORCED MARCH.
NOOOOOO! I DON'T WANT TO GO HOOOME!!!

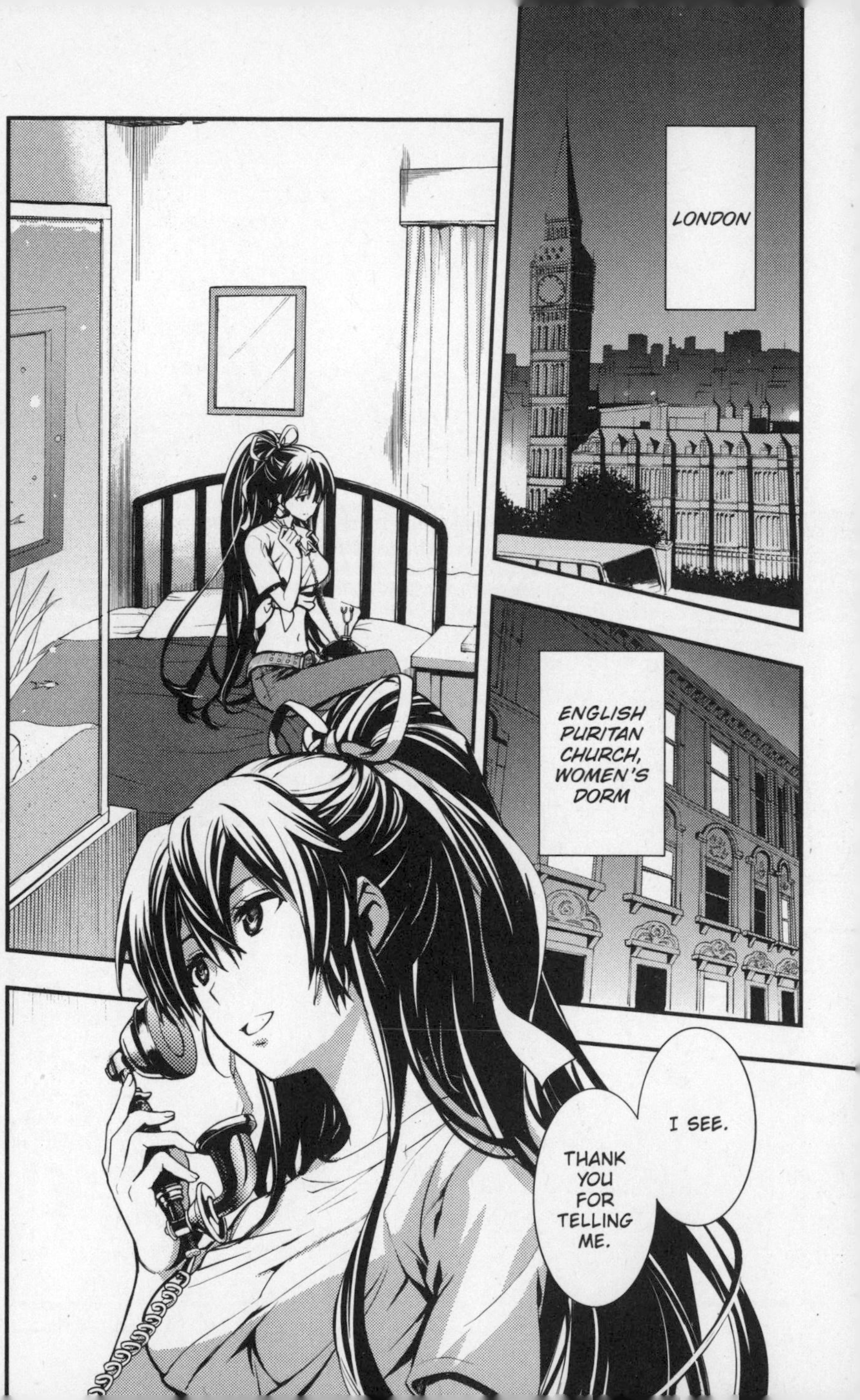
LONDON
ENGLISH PURITAN CHURCH, WOMEN'S DORM
I SEE.
THANK YOU FOR TELLING ME.

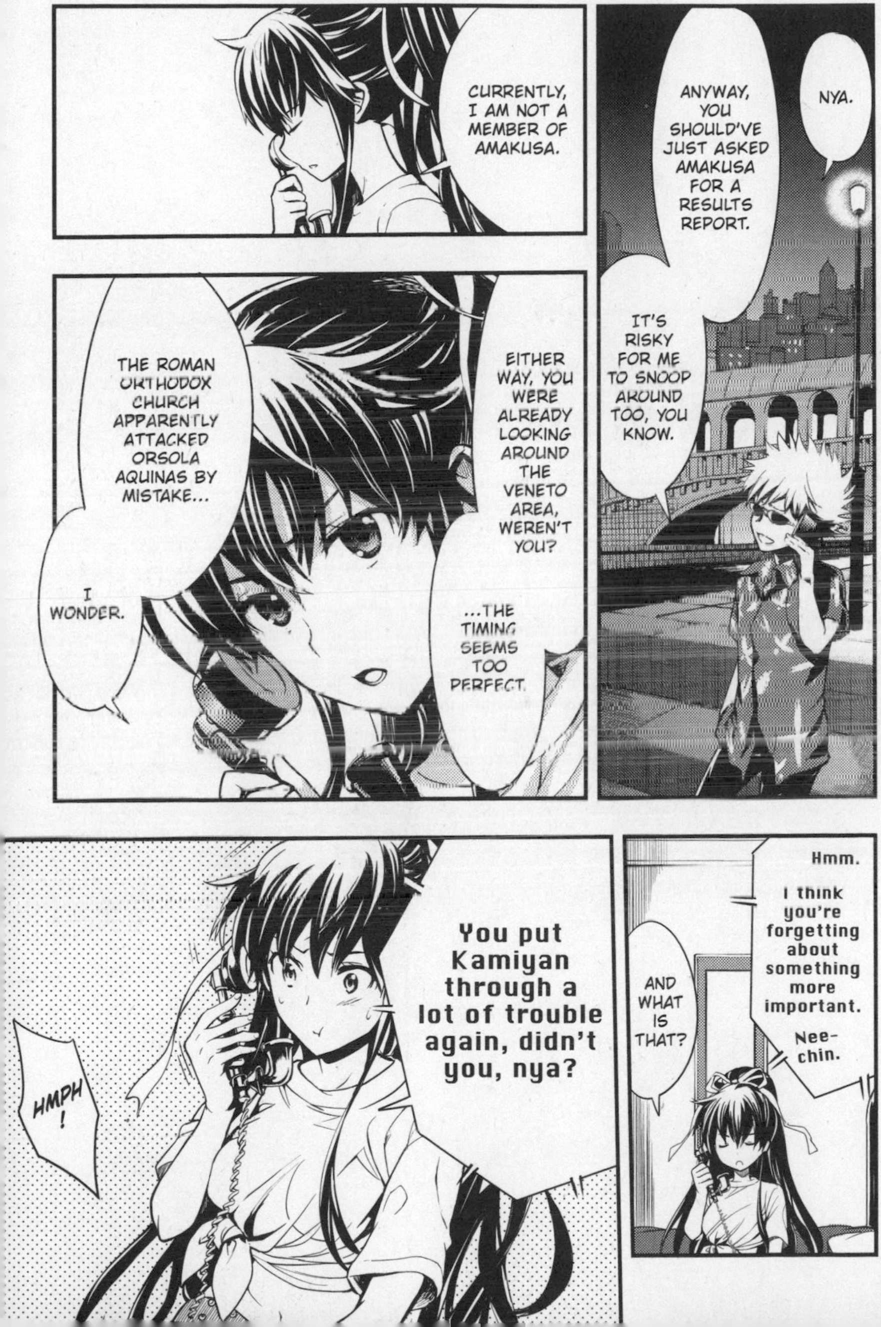
NYA.
ANYWAY, YOU SHOULD'VE JUST ASKED AMAKUSA FOR A RESULTS REPORT.
IT'S RISKY FOR ME TO SNOOP AROUND TOO, YOU KNOW.
CURRENTLY, I AM NOT A MEMBER OF AMAKUSA.
EITHER WAY, YOU WERE ALREADY LOOKING AROUND THE VENETO AREA, WEREN'T YOU?
...THE TIMING SEEMS TOO PERFECT.
THE ROMAN ORTHODOX CHURCH APPARENTLY ATTACKED ORSOLA AQUINAS BY MISTAKE...
I WONDER.
Hmm.
I think you're forgetting about something more important.
Nee-chin.
AND WHAT IS THAT?
You put Kamiyan through a lot of trouble again, didn't you, nya?
HMPH!

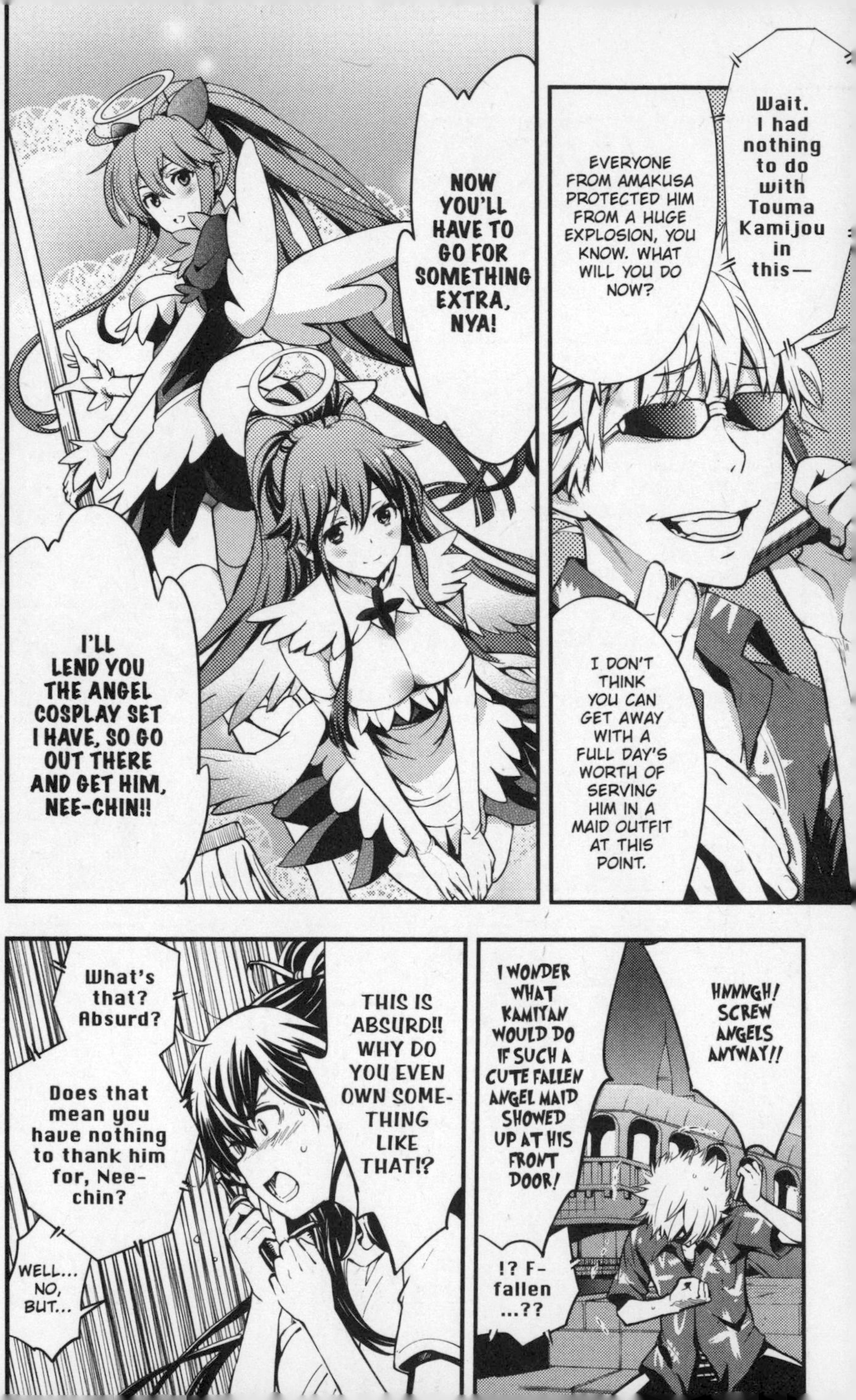
Wait. I had nothing to do with Touma Kamijou in this—
EVERYONE FROM AMAKUSA PROTECTED HIM FROM A HUGE EXPLOSION, YOU KNOW. WHAT WILL YOU DO NOW?
I DON'T THINK YOU CAN GET AWAY WITH A FULL DAY'S WORTH OF SERVING HIM IN A MAID OUTFIT AT THIS POINT.
NOW YOU'LL HAVE TO GO FOR SOMETHING EXTRA, NYA!
I'LL LEND YOU THE ANGEL COSPLAY SET I HAVE, SO GO OUT THERE AND GET HIM, NEE-CHIN!!
HNNNGH! SCREW ANGELS ANYWAY!!
I WONDER WHAT KAMIYAN WOULD DO IF SUCH A CUTE FALLEN ANGEL MAID SHOWED UP AT HIS FRONT DOOR!
!? F-fallen ...??
THIS IS ABSURD!! WHY DO YOU EVEN OWN SOME-THING LIKE THAT!?
What's that? Absurd?
Does that mean you have nothing to thank him for, Nee-chin?
WELL... NO, BUT...

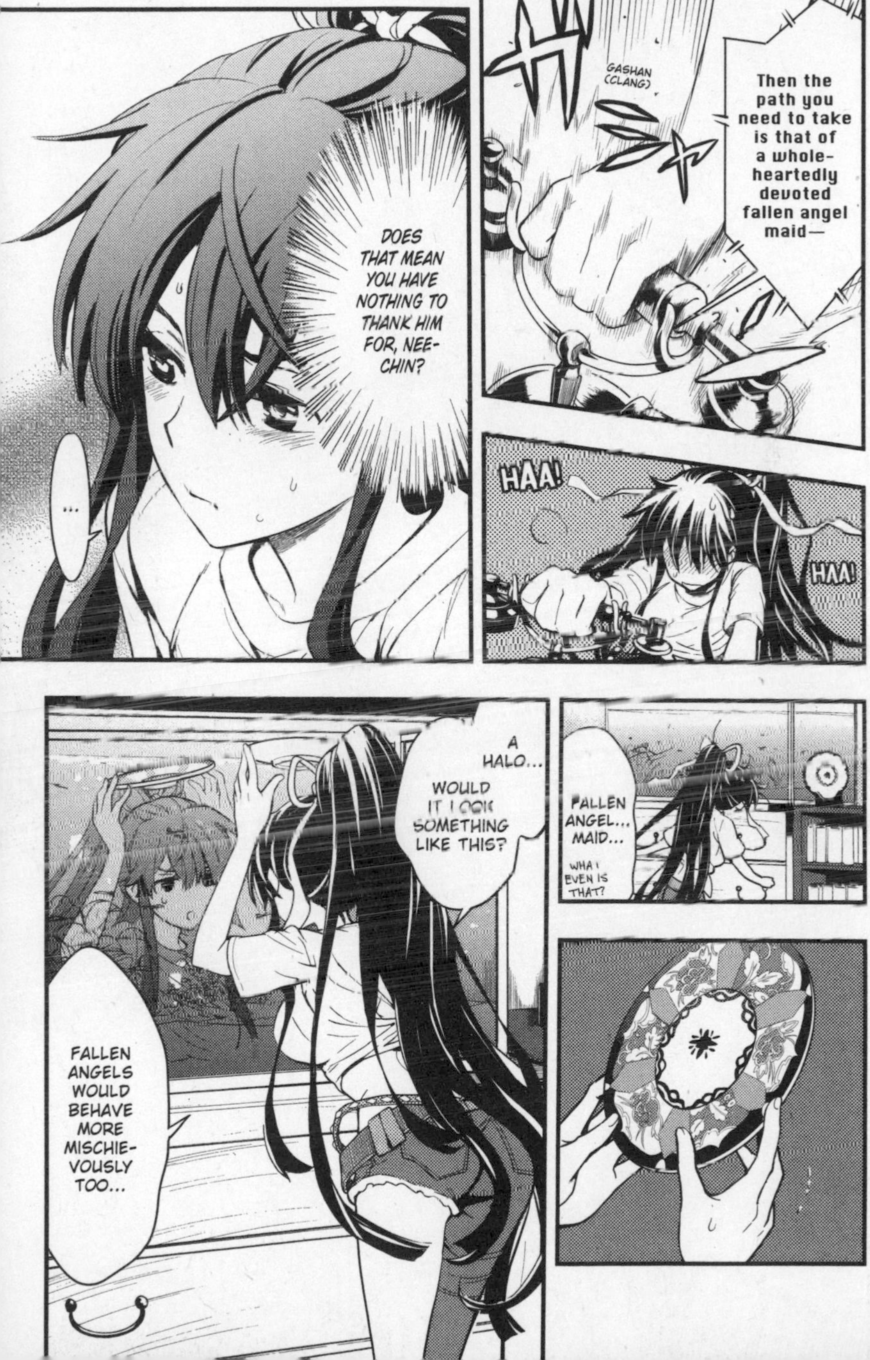

GASHAN (CLANG)
Then the path you need to take is that of a whole-heartedly devoted fallen angel maid—
HAA!
HAA!
DOES THAT MEAN YOU HAVE NOTHING TO THANK HIM FOR, NEE-CHIN?
...
FALLEN ANGEL... MAID...
WHAT EVEN IS THAT?
A HALO...
WOULD IT LOOK SOMETHING LIKE THIS?
FALLEN ANGELS WOULD BEHAVE MORE MISCHIEVOUSLY TOO...

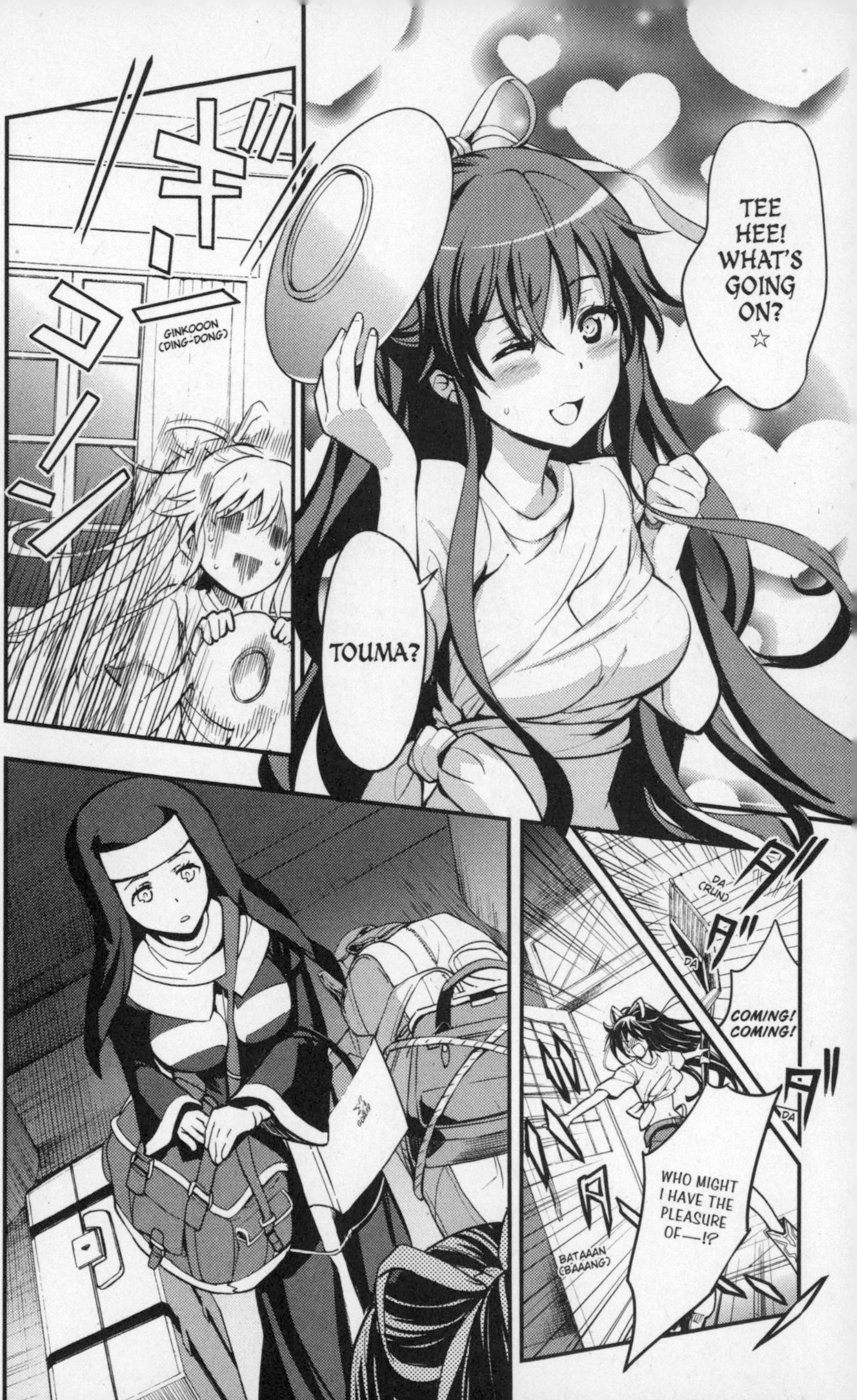
TEE HEE! WHAT'S GOING ON? ☆
TOUMA?
GINKOOON (DING-DONG)
DA (RUN)
DA
COMING! COMING!
DA
WHO MIGHT I HAVE THE PLEASURE OF—!?
BATAAAN (BAAANG)

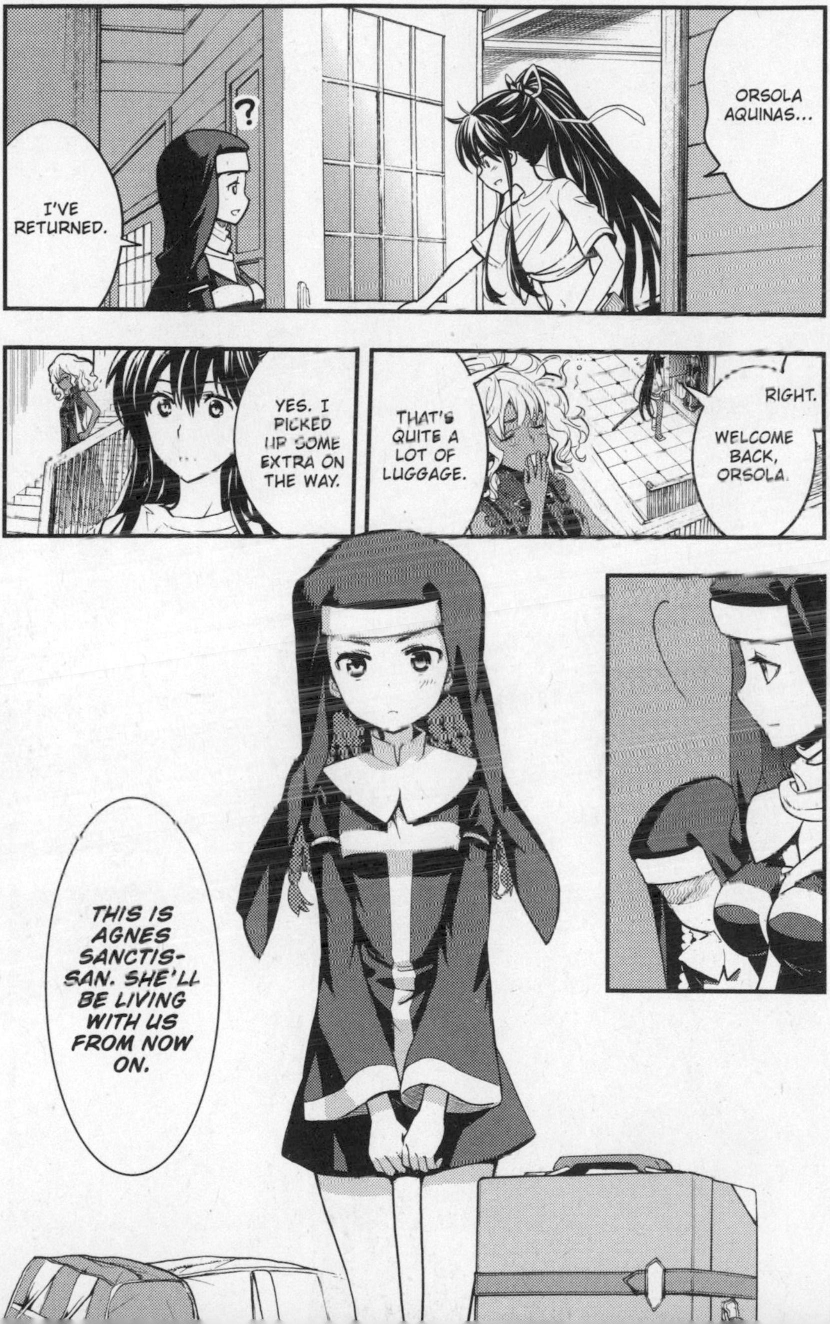
ORSOLA AQUINAS...
?
I'VE RETURNED.
RIGHT.
WELCOME BACK, ORSOLA.
THAT'S QUITE A LOT OF LUGGAGE.
YES. I PICKED UP SOME EXTRA ON THE WAY.
THIS IS AGNES SANCTIS-SAN. SHE'LL BE LIVING WITH US FROM NOW ON.

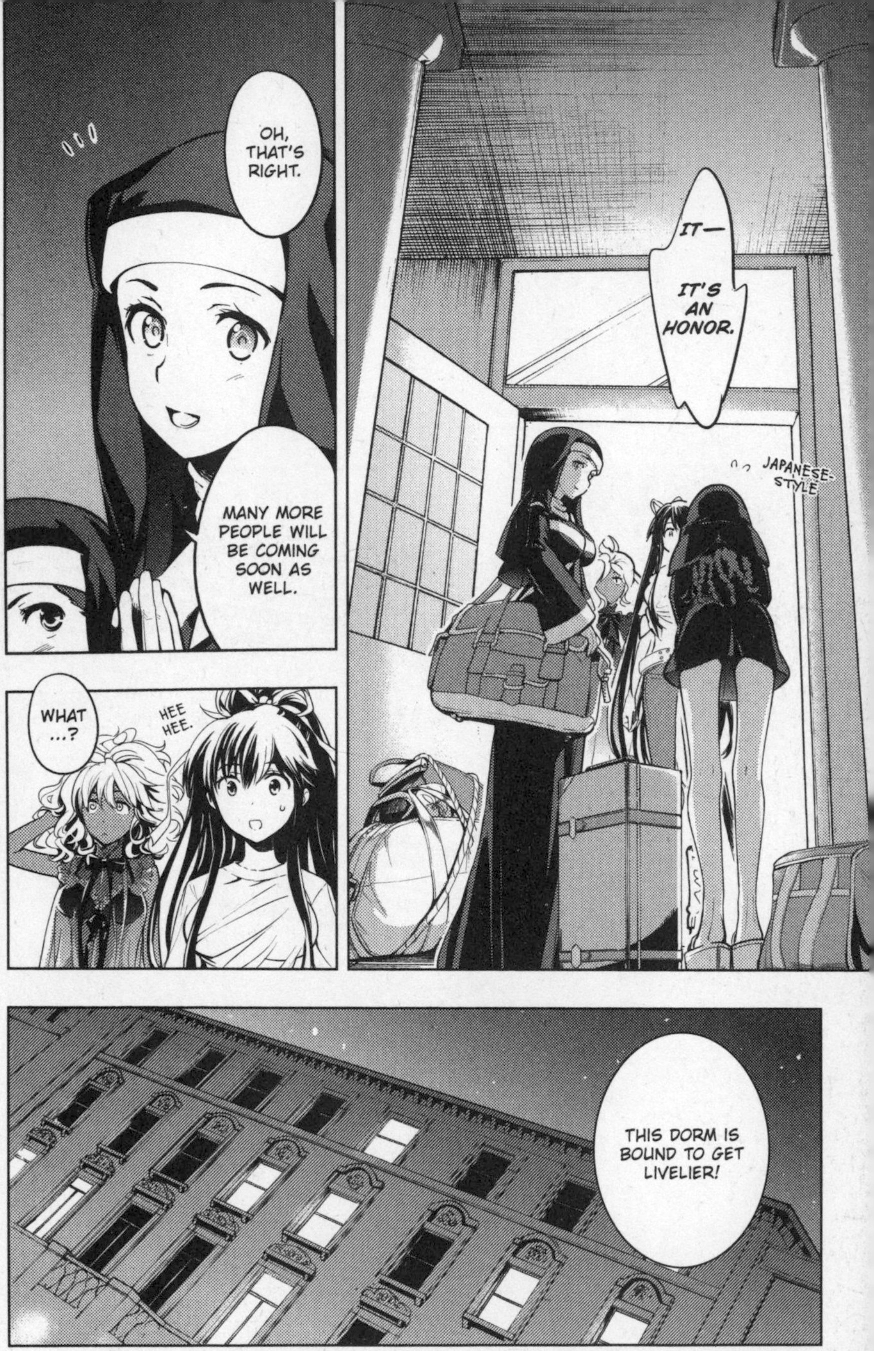
IT—
IT'S AN HONOR.
JAPANESE-STYLE
OH, THAT'S RIGHT.
MANY MORE PEOPLE WILL BE COMING SOON AS WELL.
HEE HEE.
WHAT ...?
THIS DORM IS BOUND TO GET LIVELIER!

A Certain Magical Index

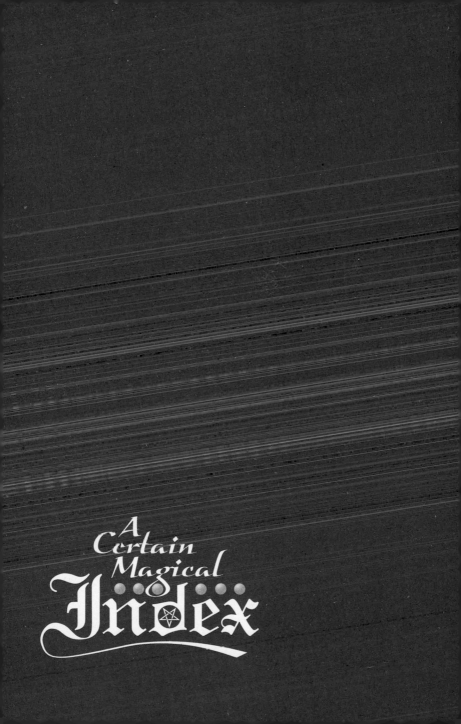

A Certain Magical Index

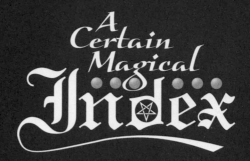

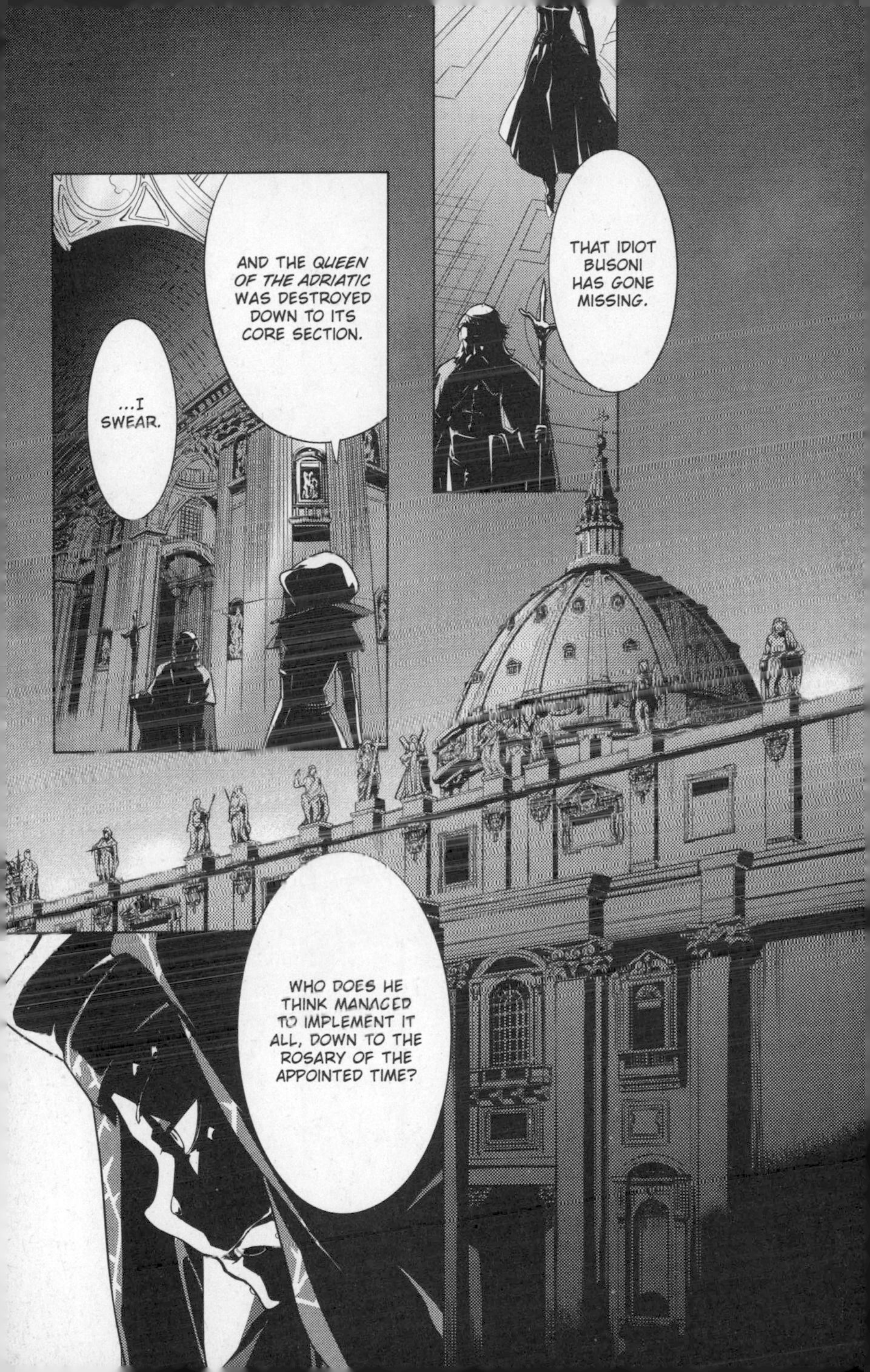
THAT IDIOT BUSONI HAS GONE MISSING.
AND THE *QUEEN OF THE ADRIATIC* WAS DESTROYED DOWN TO ITS CORE SECTION.
...I SWEAR.
WHO DOES HE THINK MANAGED TO IMPLEMENT IT ALL, DOWN TO THE ROSARY OF THE APPOINTED TIME?

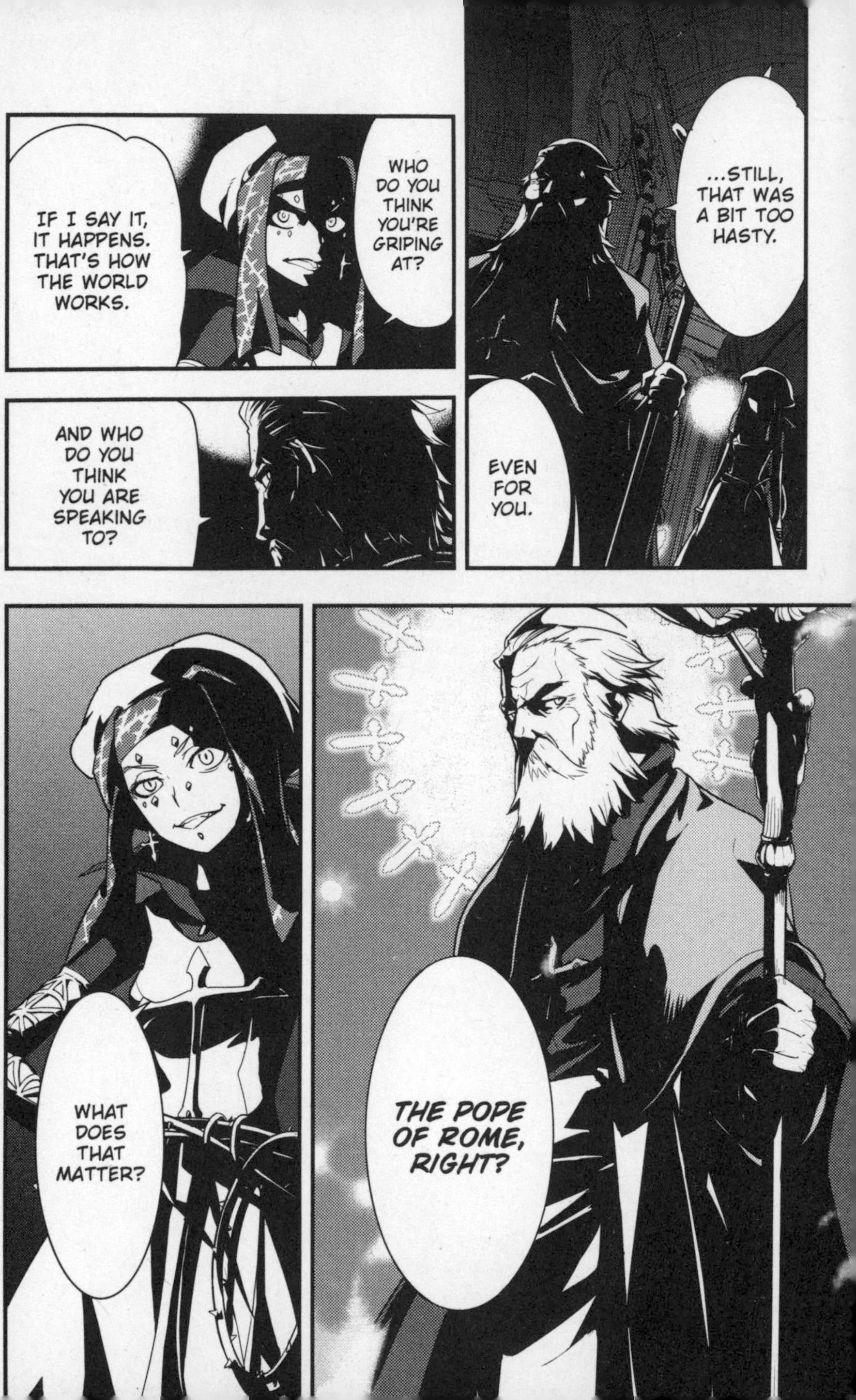
...STILL, THAT WAS A BIT TOO HASTY.
EVEN FOR YOU.
WHO DO YOU THINK YOU'RE GRIPING AT?
IF I SAY IT, IT HAPPENS. THAT'S HOW THE WORLD WORKS.
AND WHO DO YOU THINK YOU ARE SPEAKING TO?
THE POPE OF ROME, RIGHT?
WHAT DOES THAT MATTER?

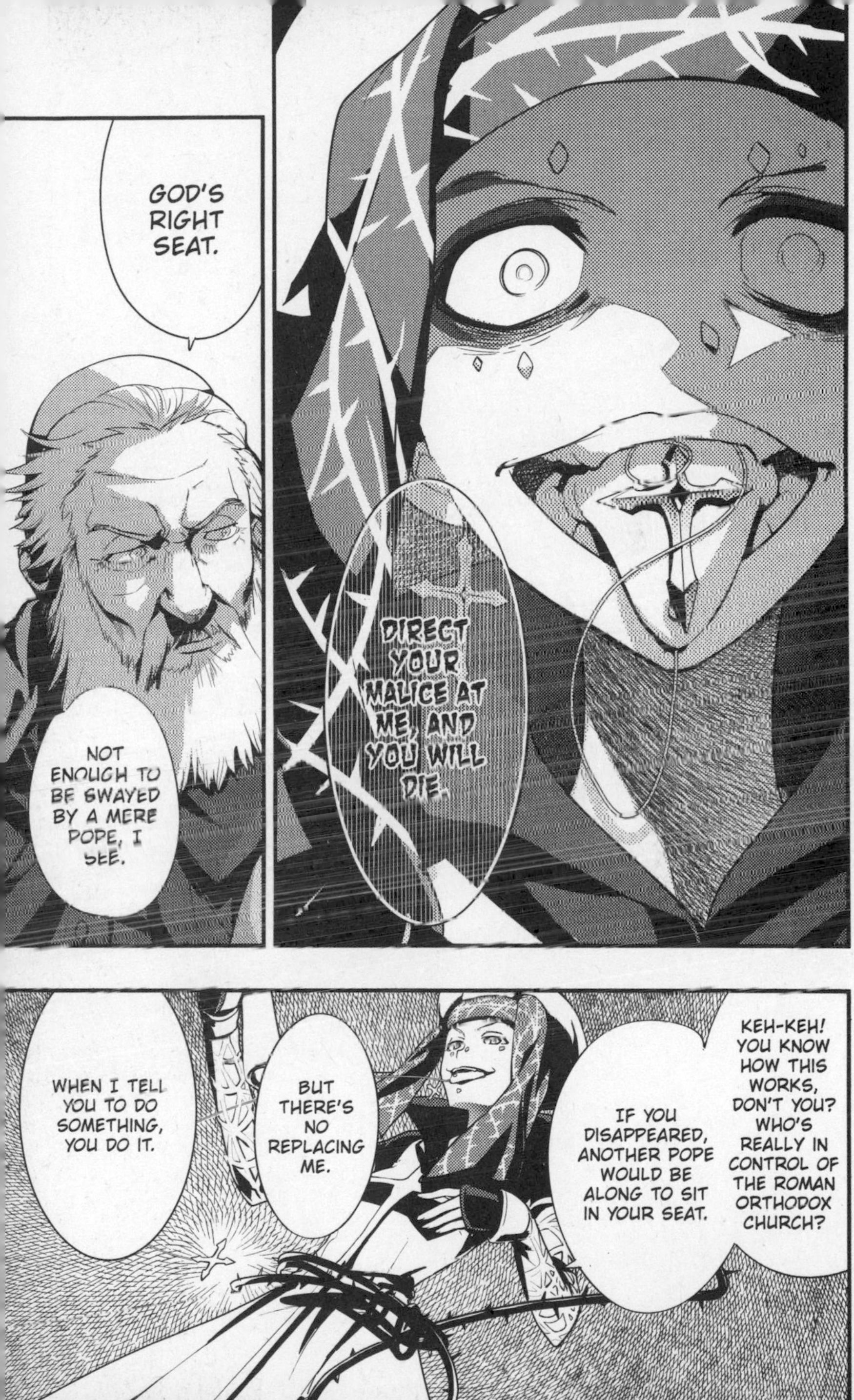
DIRECT YOUR MALICE AT ME, AND YOU WILL DIE.
GOD'S RIGHT SEAT.
NOT ENOUGH TO BE SWAYED BY A MERE POPE, I SEE.
KEH-KEH! YOU KNOW HOW THIS WORKS, DON'T YOU? WHO'S REALLY IN CONTROL OF THE ROMAN ORTHODOX CHURCH?
IF YOU DISAPPEARED, ANOTHER POPE WOULD BE ALONG TO SIT IN YOUR SEAT.
BUT THERE'S NO REPLACING ME.
WHEN I TELL YOU TO DO SOMETHING, YOU DO IT.

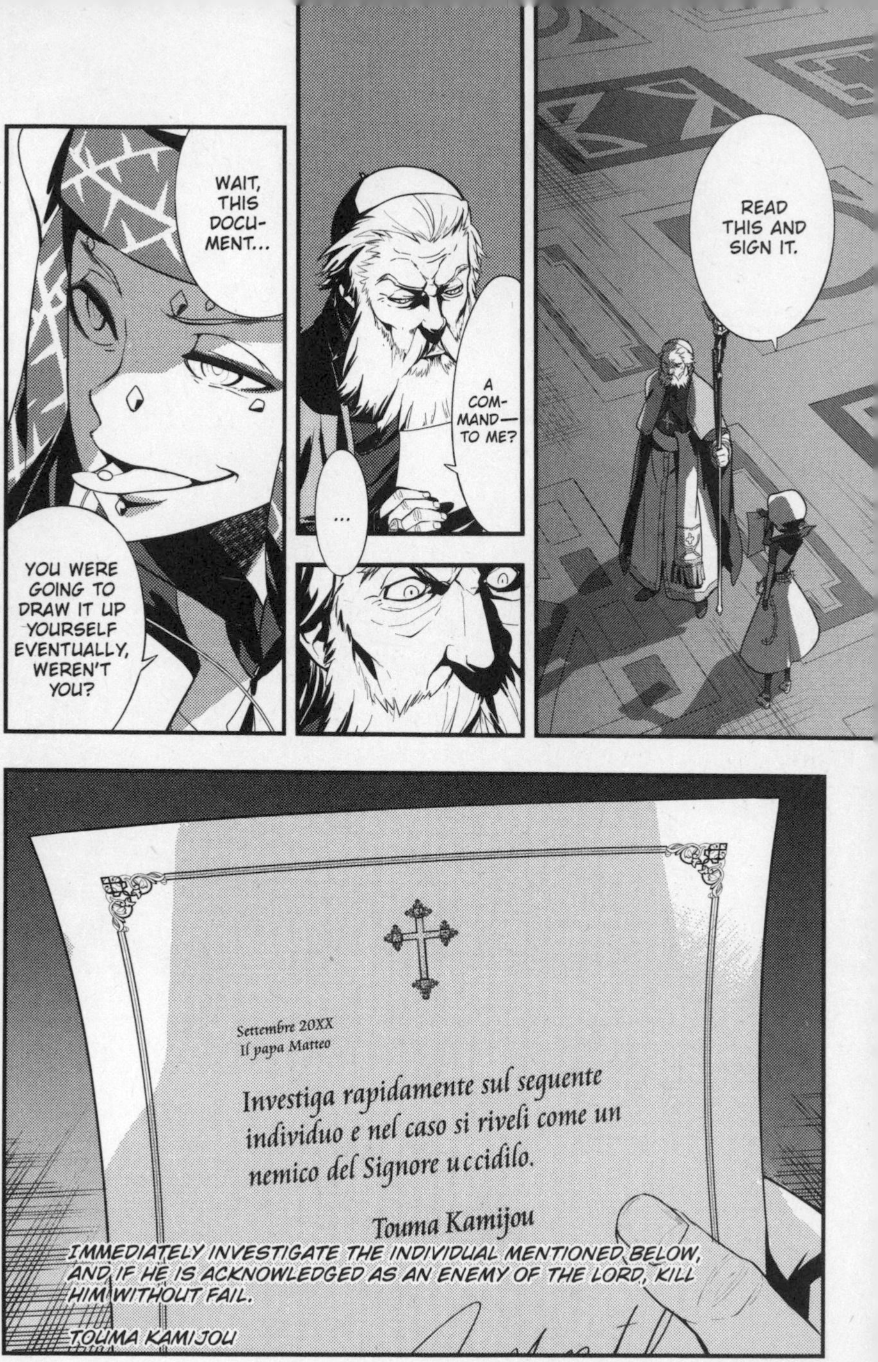
READ THIS AND SIGN IT.
A COMMAND—TO ME?
...
WAIT, THIS DOCUMENT...
YOU WERE GOING TO DRAW IT UP YOURSELF EVENTUALLY, WEREN'T YOU?
Settembre 20XX
Il papa Matteo
Investiga rapidamente sul seguente individuo e nel caso si riveli come un nemico del Signore uccidilo.
Touma Kamijou
IMMEDIATELY INVESTIGATE THE INDIVIDUAL MENTIONED BELOW, AND IF HE IS ACKNOWLEDGED AS AN ENEMY OF THE LORD, KILL HIM WITHOUT FAIL.
TOUMA KAMIJOU

#97 MIKOTO'S PUNISHMENT GAME

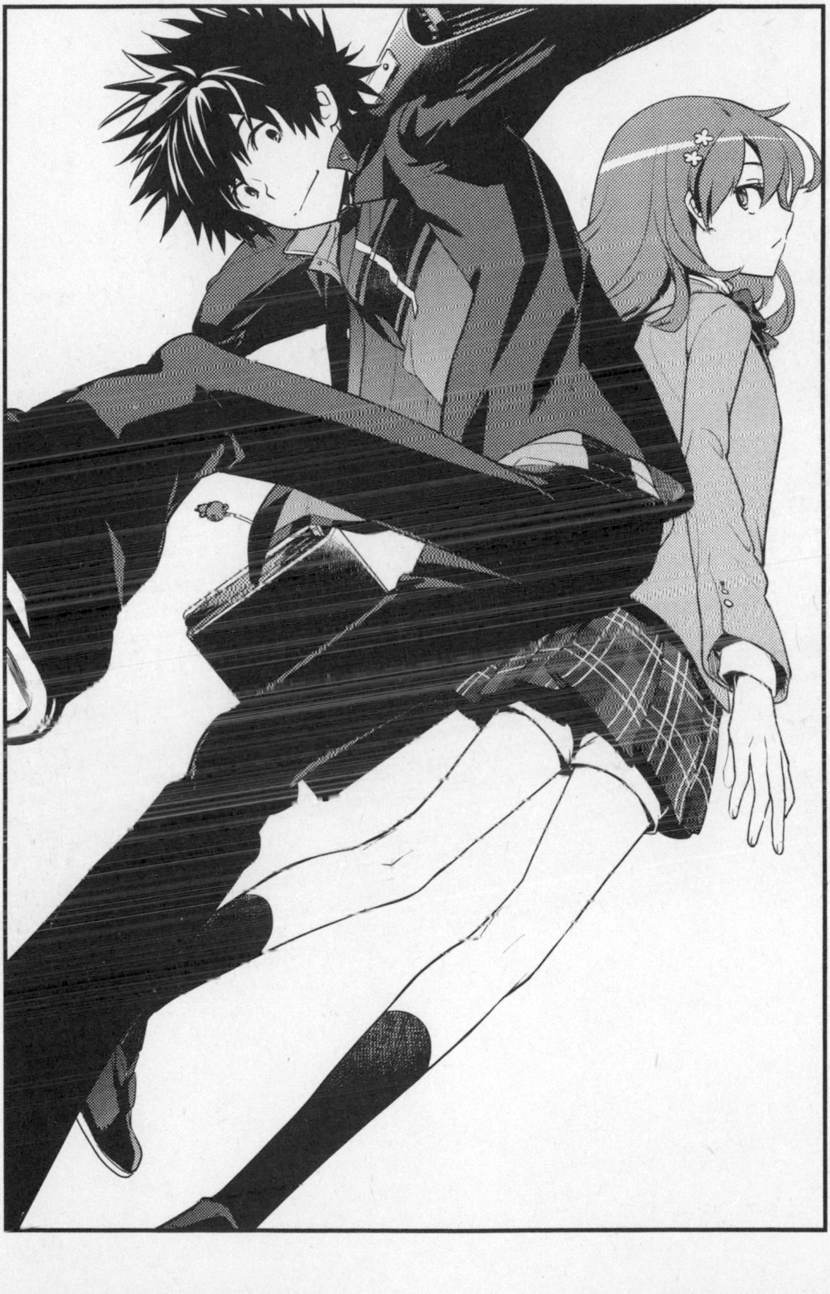

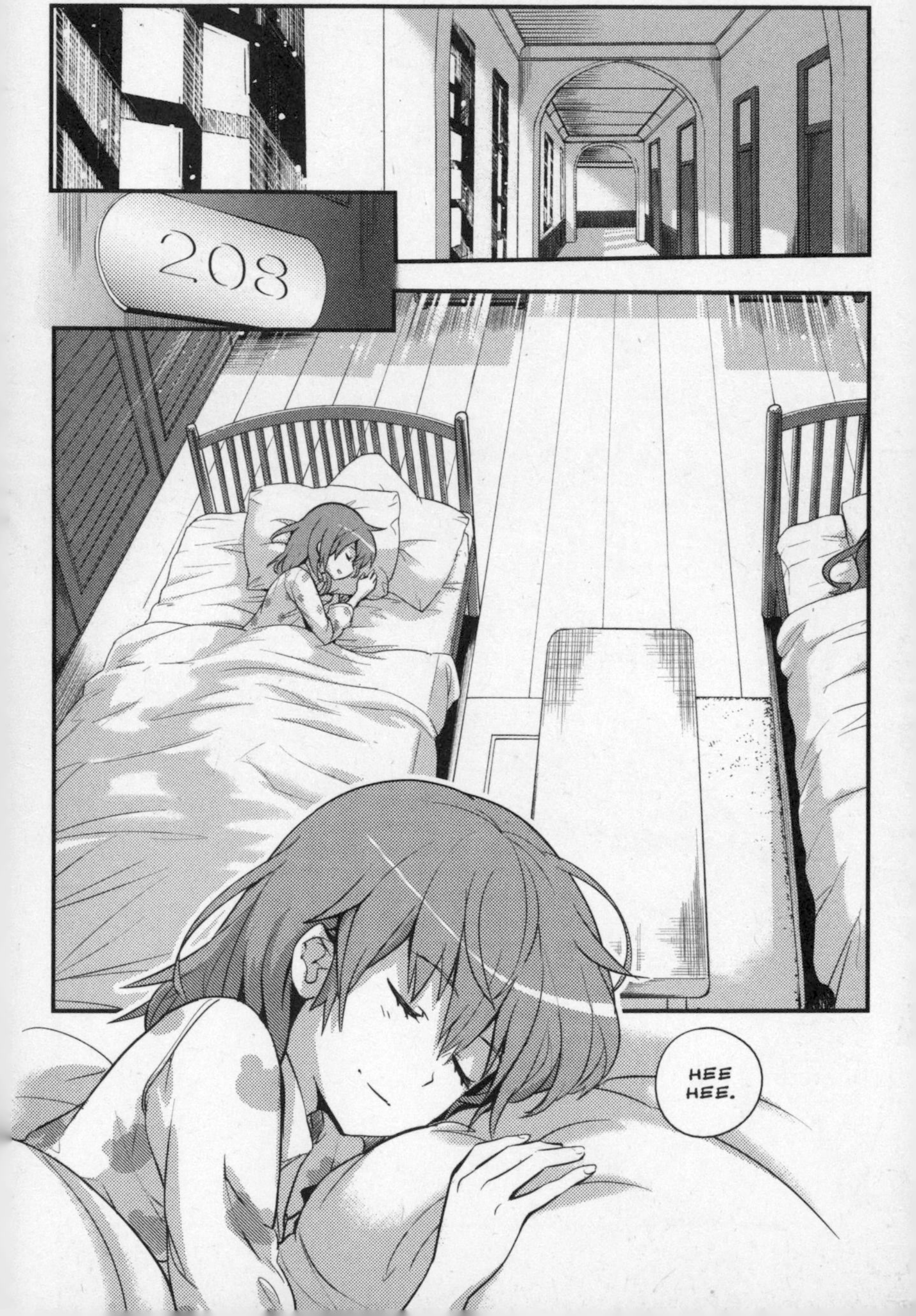
208
HEE HEE.

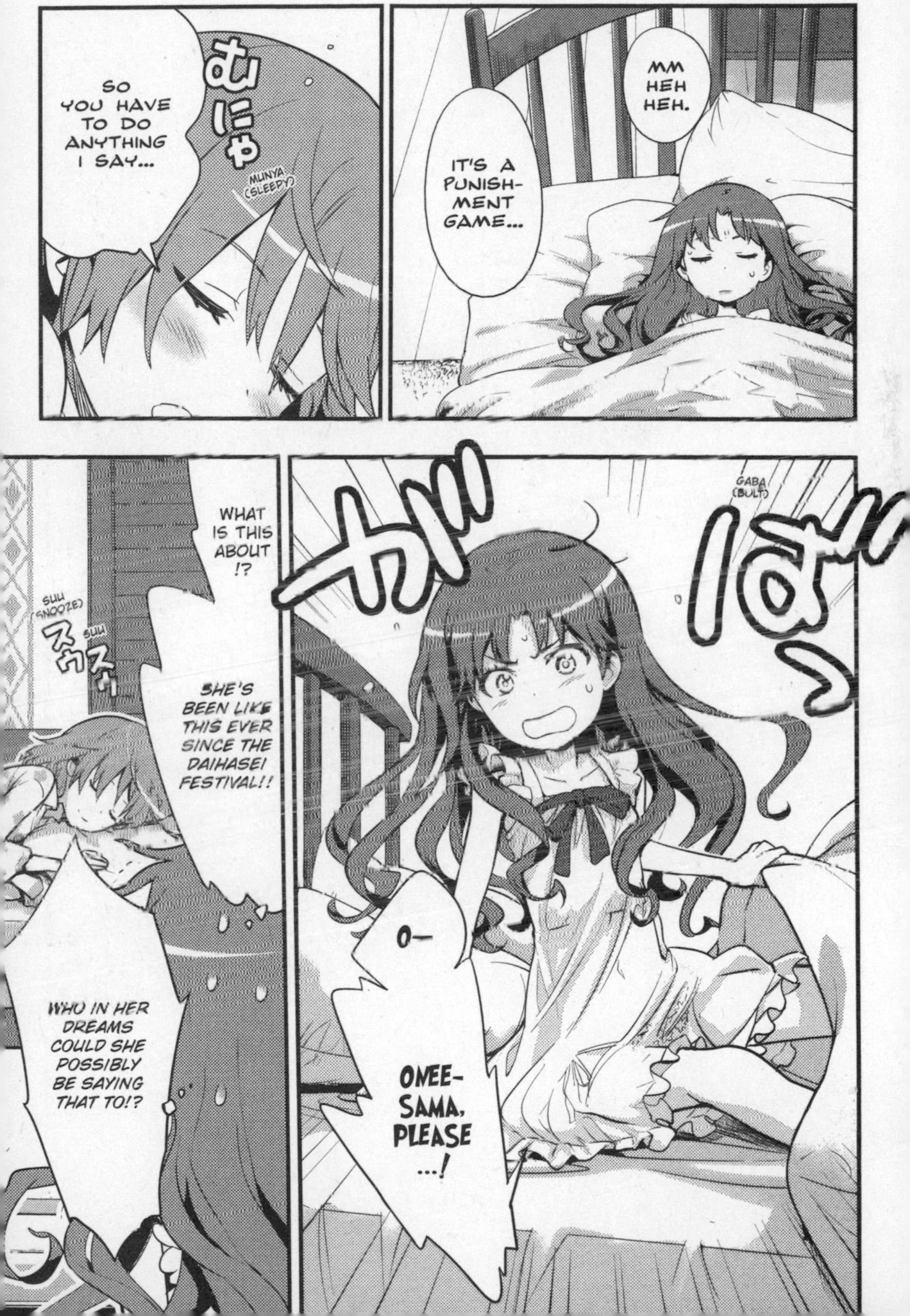
MM HEH HEH.
IT'S A PUNISHMENT GAME...
SO YOU HAVE TO DO ANYTHING I SAY...
むにゃ
MUNYA (SLEEPY)
がばっ
GABA (BOLT)
O—
ONEE-SAMA, PLEASE ...!
WHAT IS THIS ABOUT !?
SUU (SNOOZE) スゥ
SUU スゥ
SHE'S BEEN LIKE THIS EVER SINCE THE DAIHASEI FESTIVAL!!
WHO IN HER DREAMS COULD SHE POSSIBLY BE SAYING THAT TO!?

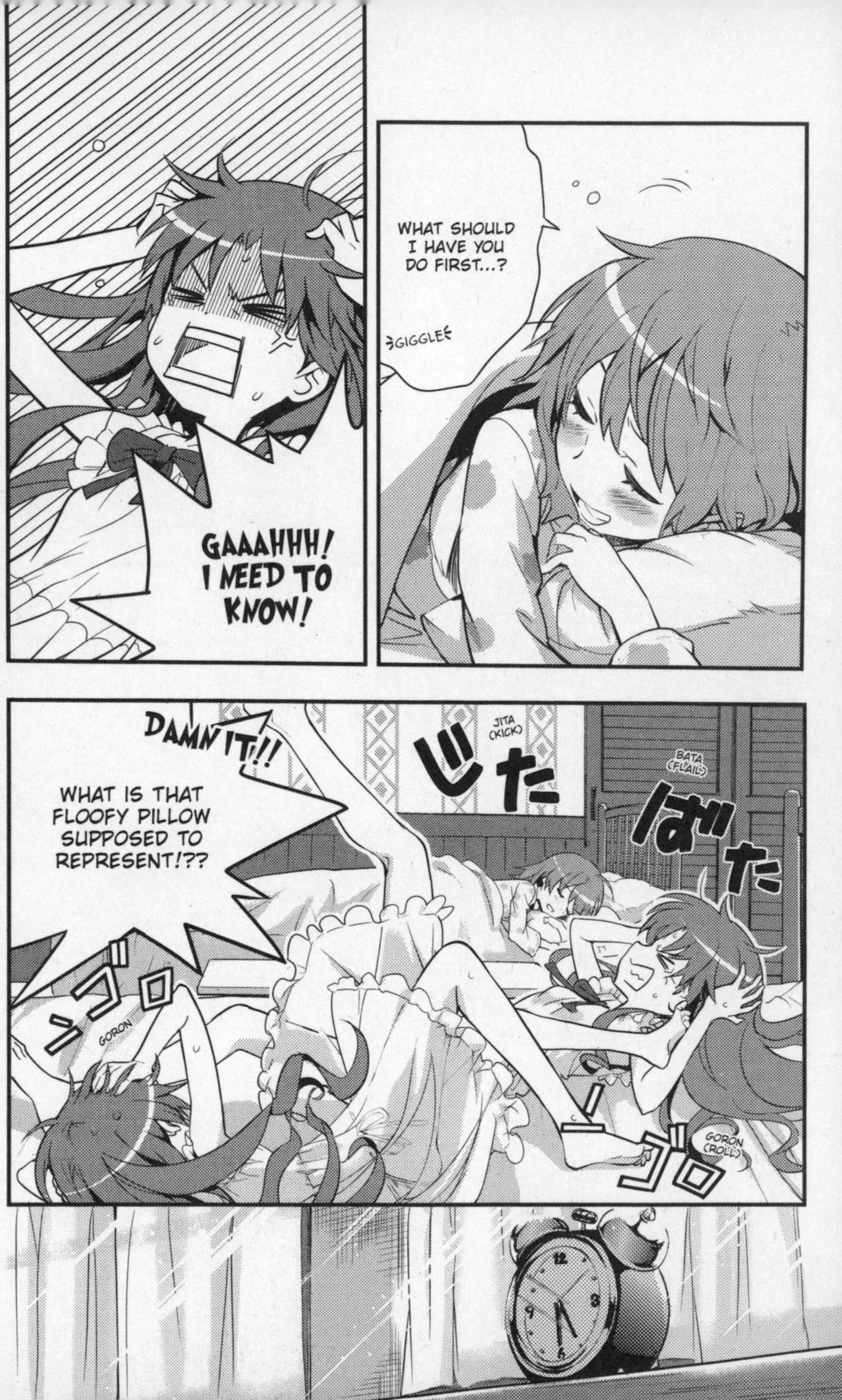
WHAT SHOULD I HAVE YOU DO FIRST...?
GIGGLE
GAAAHHH! I NEED TO KNOW!
BATA (FLAIL)
JITA (KICK)
DAMN IT!!
WHAT IS THAT FLOOFY PILLOW SUPPOSED TO REPRESENT!??
GORON (ROLL)
GORON

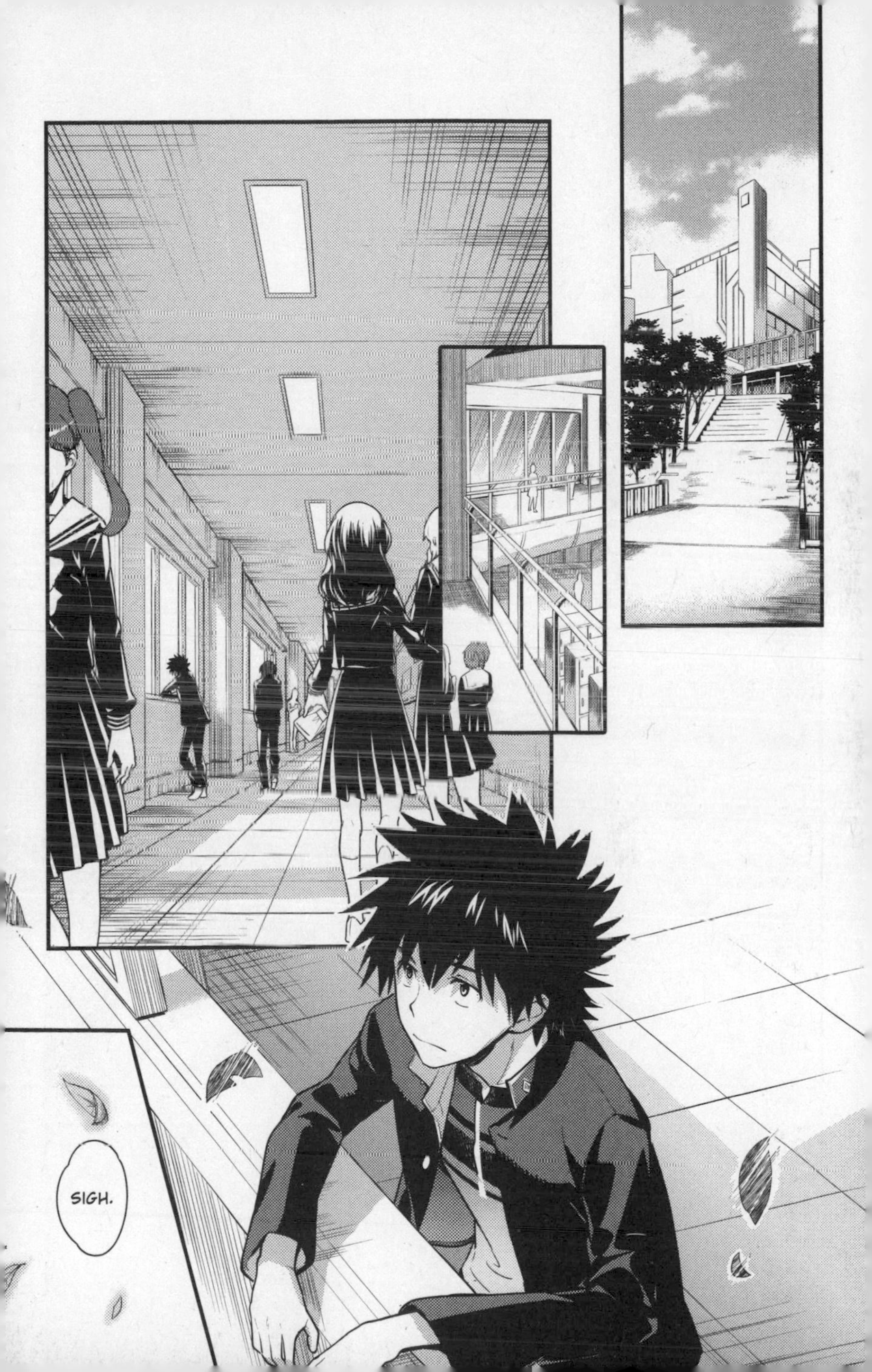
SIGH.

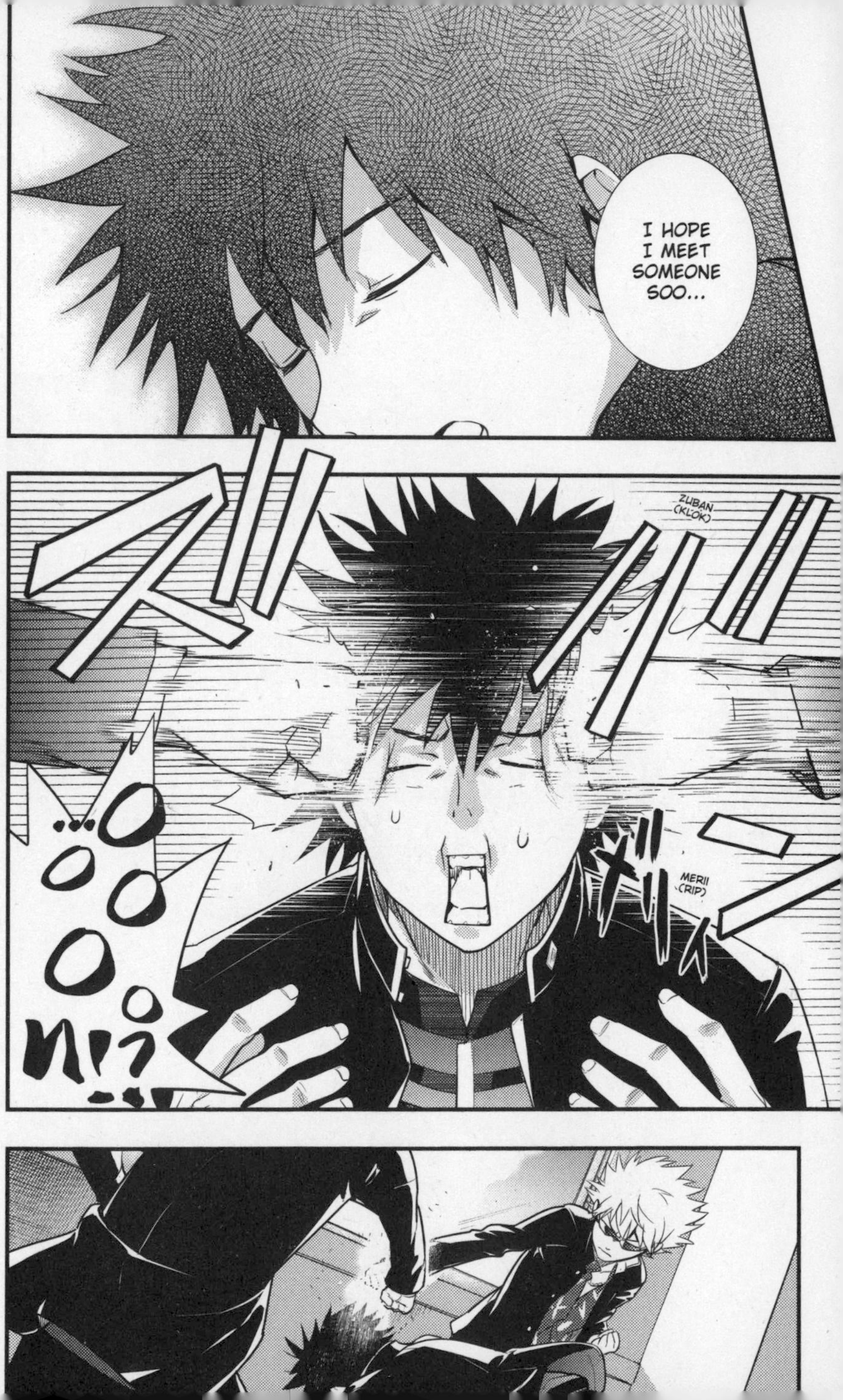
I HOPE I MEET SOMEONE SOO...
ZUBAN (KLOK)
MERII (CRIP)

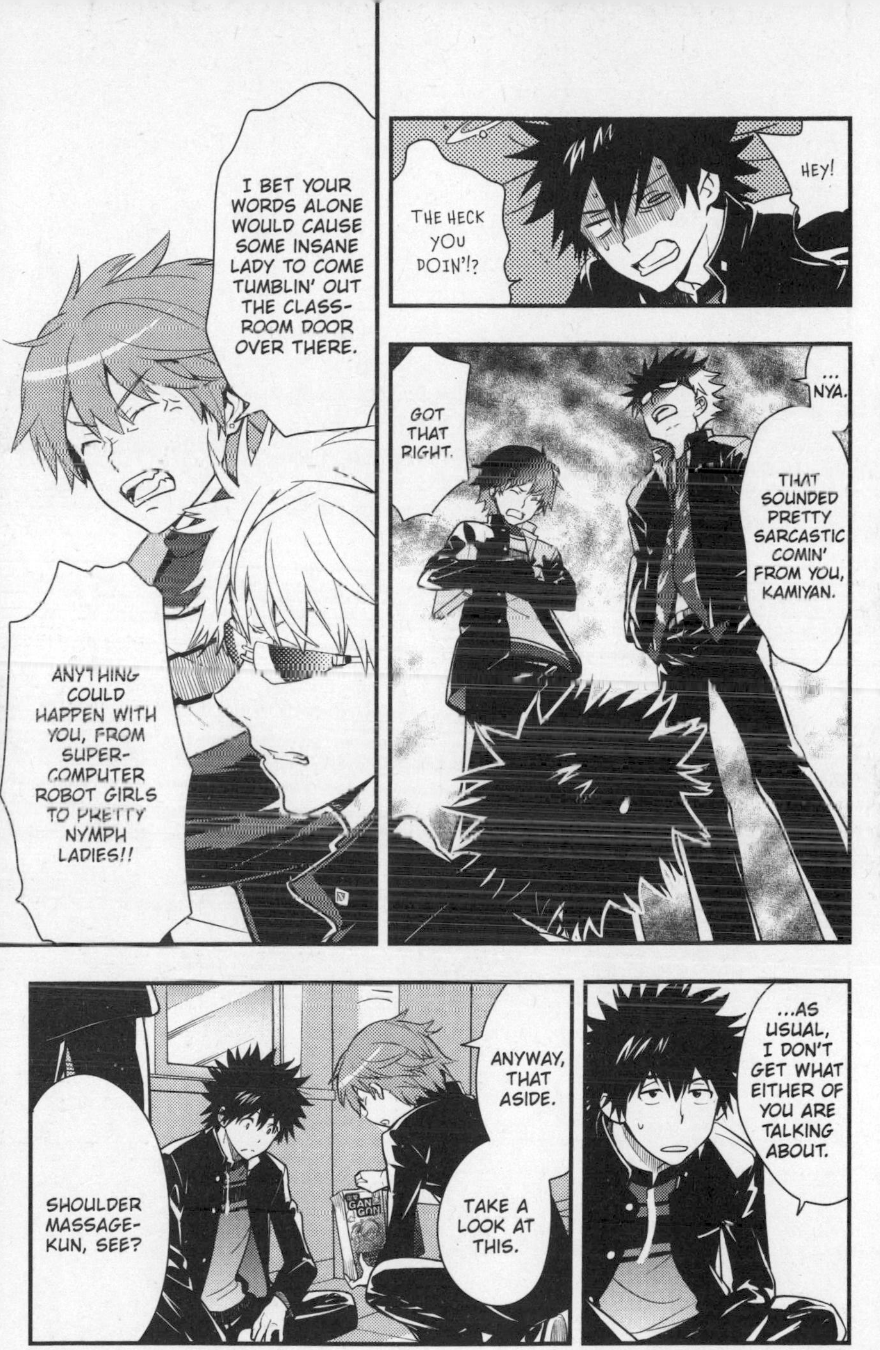
HEY!
THE HECK YOU DOIN'!?
...NYA.
THAT SOUNDED PRETTY SARCASTIC COMIN' FROM YOU, KAMIYAN.
GOT THAT RIGHT.
I BET YOUR WORDS ALONE WOULD CAUSE SOME INSANE LADY TO COME TUMBLIN' OUT THE CLASS-ROOM DOOR OVER THERE.
ANYTHING COULD HAPPEN WITH YOU, FROM SUPER-COMPUTER ROBOT GIRLS TO PRETTY NYMPH LADIES!!
...AS USUAL, I DON'T GET WHAT EITHER OF YOU ARE TALKING ABOUT.
ANYWAY, THAT ASIDE.
TAKE A LOOK AT THIS.
SHOULDER MASSAGE-KUN, SEE?

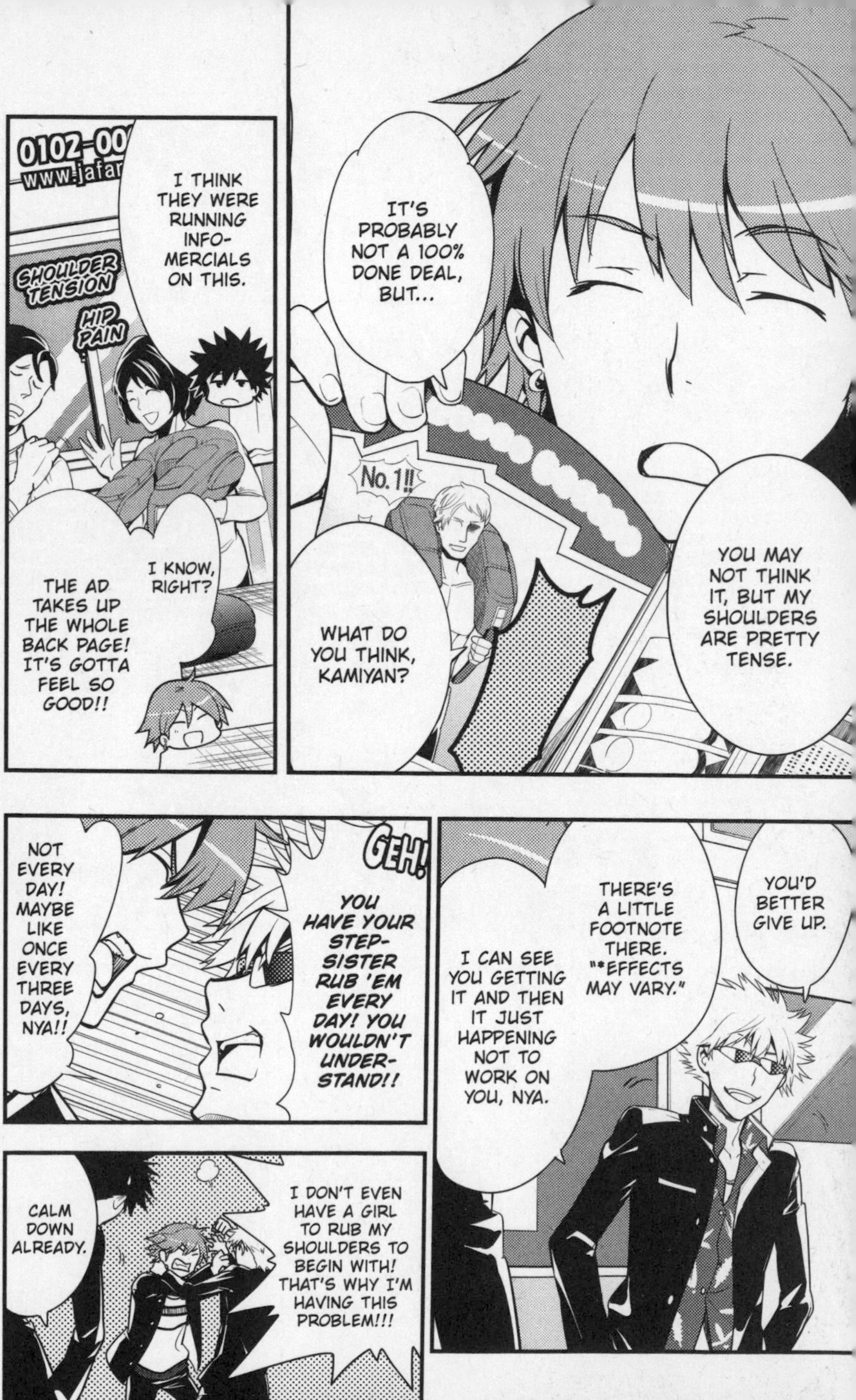
IT'S PROBABLY NOT A 100% DONE DEAL, BUT...
YOU MAY NOT THINK IT, BUT MY SHOULDERS ARE PRETTY TENSE.
No.1!!
WHAT DO YOU THINK, KAMIYAN?
0102-00
www.jafar
I THINK THEY WERE RUNNING INFO-MERCIALS ON THIS.
SHOULDER TENSION
HIP PAIN
I KNOW, RIGHT?
THE AD TAKES UP THE WHOLE BACK PAGE! IT'S GOTTA FEEL SO GOOD!!
YOU'D BETTER GIVE UP.
THERE'S A LITTLE FOOTNOTE THERE. "*EFFECTS MAY VARY."
I CAN SEE YOU GETTING IT AND THEN IT JUST HAPPENING NOT TO WORK ON YOU, NYA.
GEH!
YOU HAVE YOUR STEP-SISTER RUB 'EM EVERY DAY! YOU WOULDN'T UNDER-STAND!!
NOT EVERY DAY! MAYBE LIKE ONCE EVERY THREE DAYS, NYA!!
I DON'T EVEN HAVE A GIRL TO RUB MY SHOULDERS TO BEGIN WITH! THAT'S WHY I'M HAVING THIS PROBLEM!!!
CALM DOWN ALREADY.

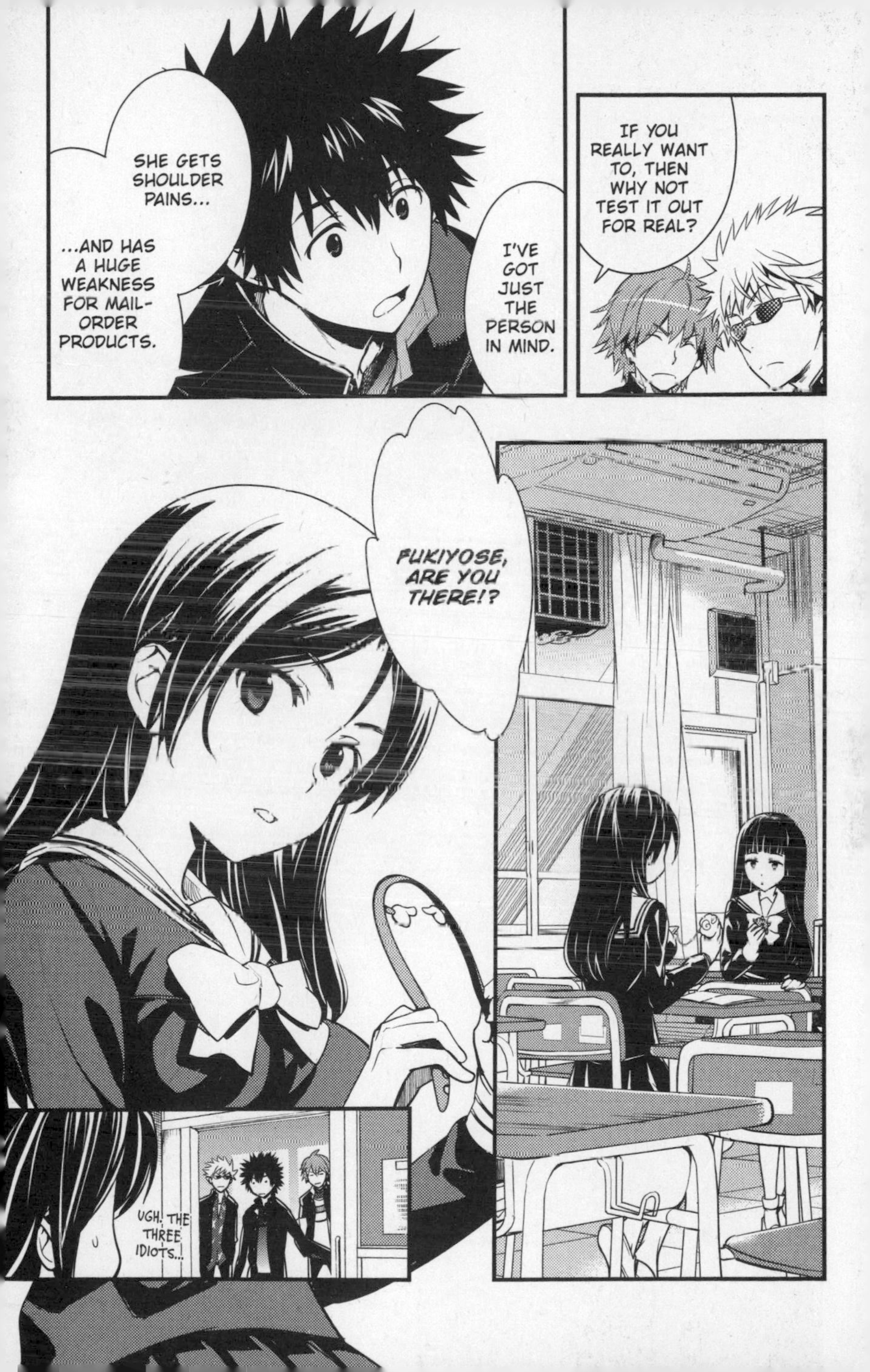
IF YOU REALLY WANT TO, THEN WHY NOT TEST IT OUT FOR REAL?
I'VE GOT JUST THE PERSON IN MIND.
SHE GETS SHOULDER PAINS...
...AND HAS A HUGE WEAKNESS FOR MAIL-ORDER PRODUCTS.
FUKIYOSE, ARE YOU THERE!?
UGH! THE THREE IDIOTS...

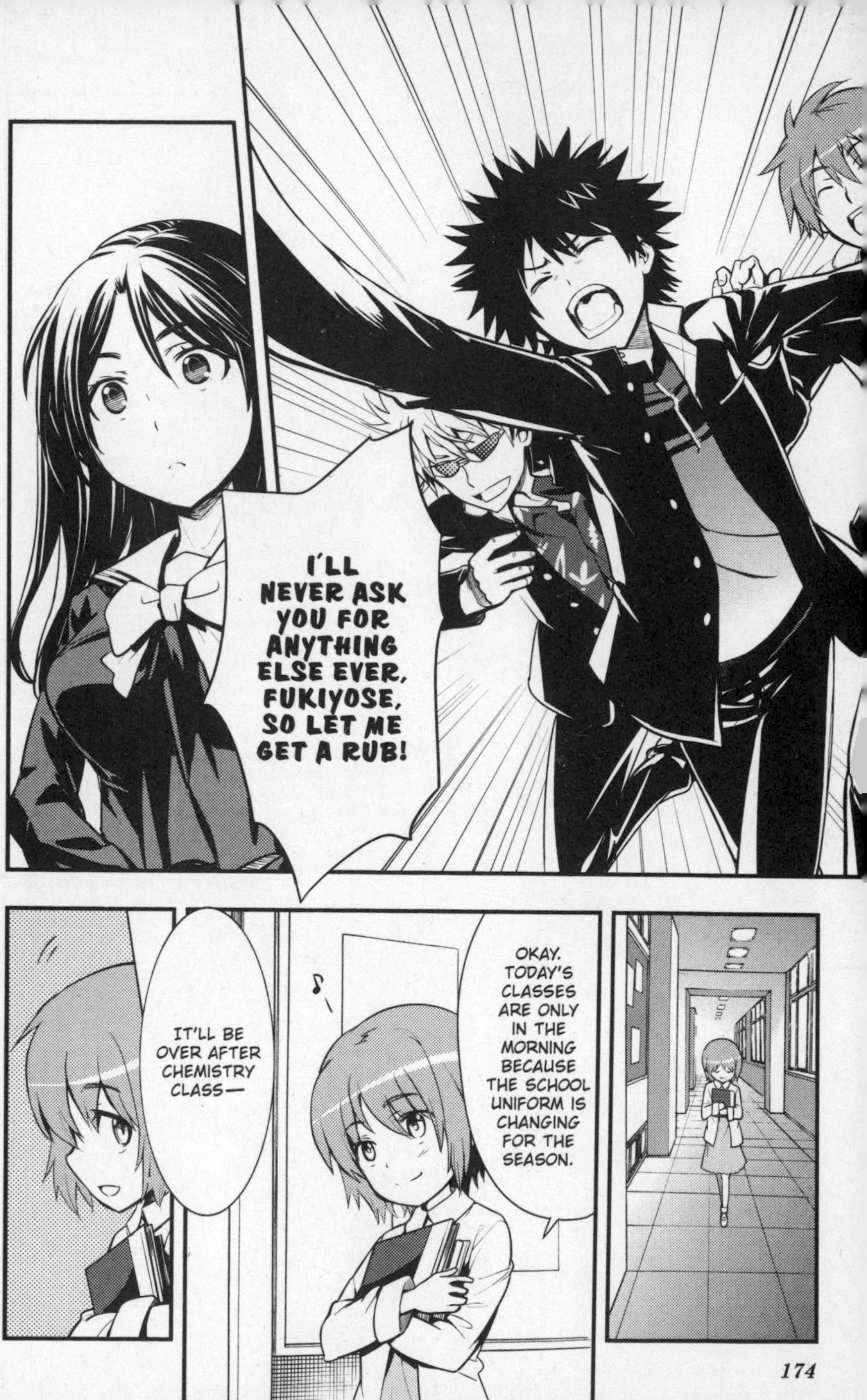
I'LL NEVER ASK YOU FOR ANYTHING ELSE EVER, FUKIYOSE, SO LET ME GET A RUB!
OKAY. TODAY'S CLASSES ARE ONLY IN THE MORNING BECAUSE THE SCHOOL UNIFORM IS CHANGING FOR THE SEASON.
IT'LL BE OVER AFTER CHEMISTRY CLASS—

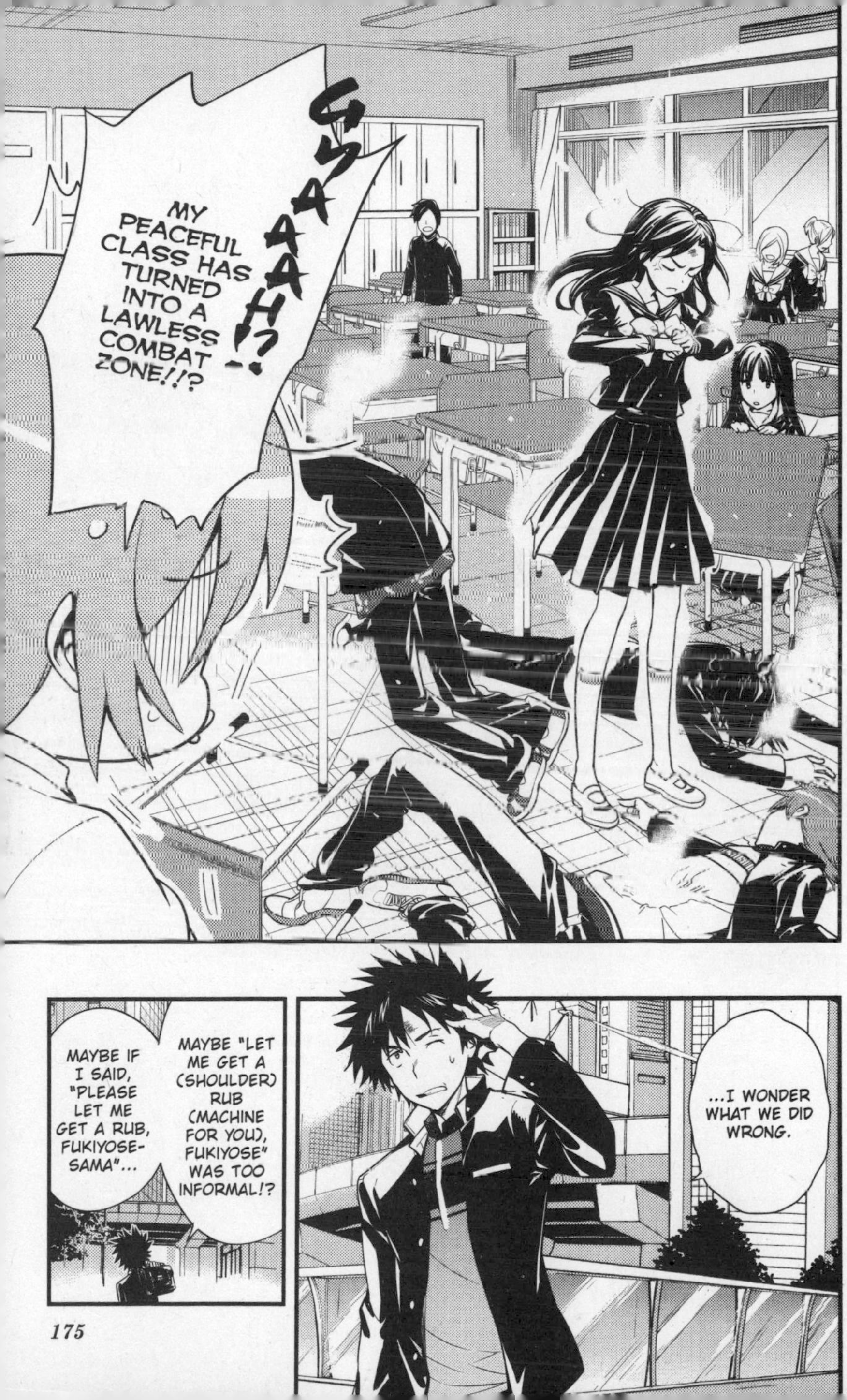
GYAAAH!?
MY PEACEFUL CLASS HAS TURNED INTO A LAWLESS COMBAT ZONE!!?
...I WONDER WHAT WE DID WRONG.
MAYBE "LET ME GET A (SHOULDER) RUB (MACHINE FOR YOU), FUKIYOSE" WAS TOO INFORMAL!?
MAYBE IF I SAID, "PLEASE LET ME GET A RUB, FUKIYOSE-SAMA"...

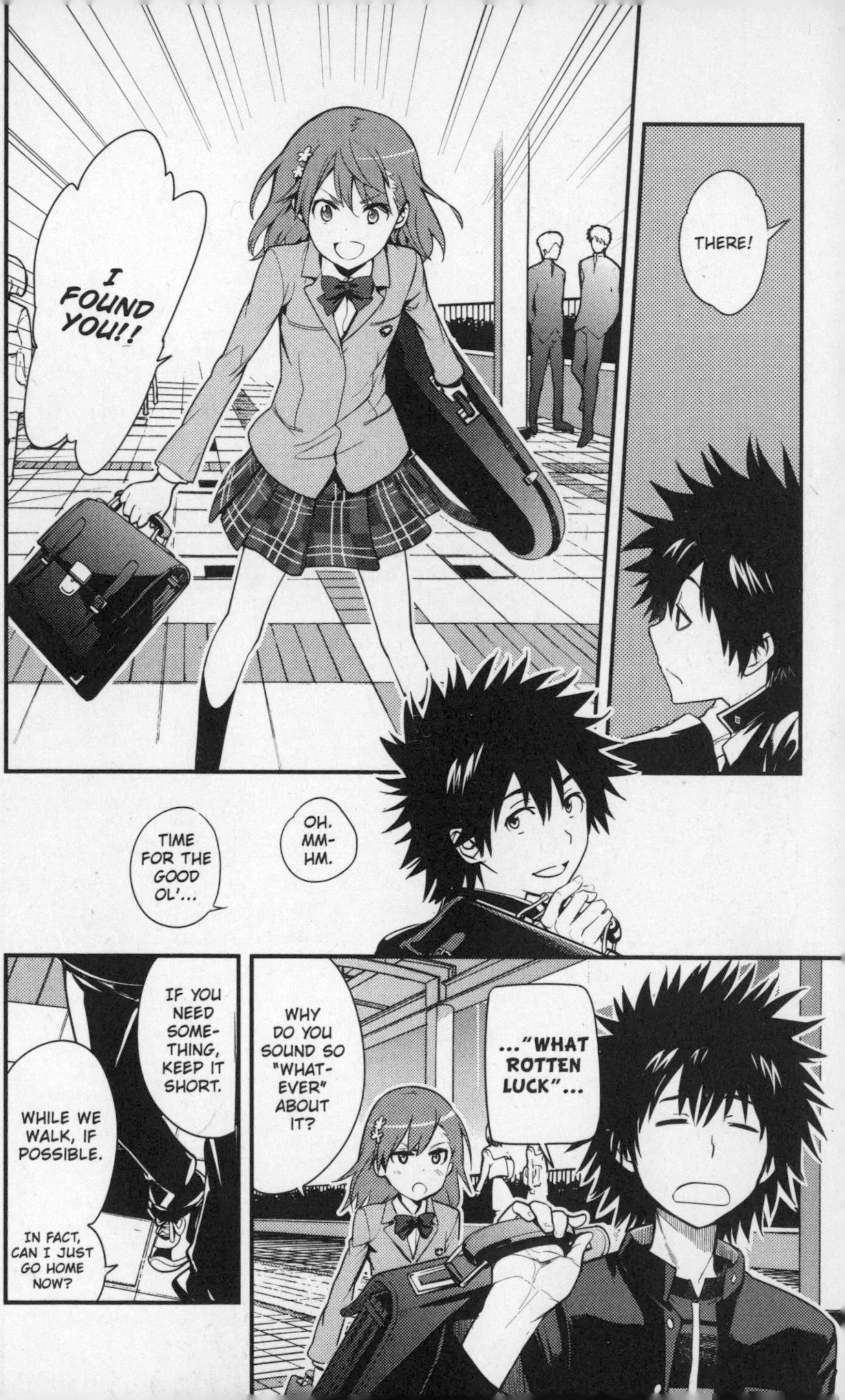
THERE!
I FOUND YOU!!
OH. MM-HM.
TIME FOR THE GOOD OL'...
..."WHAT ROTTEN LUCK"...
WHY DO YOU SOUND SO "WHAT-EVER" ABOUT IT?
IF YOU NEED SOME-THING, KEEP IT SHORT.
WHILE WE WALK, IF POSSIBLE.
IN FACT, CAN I JUST GO HOME NOW?

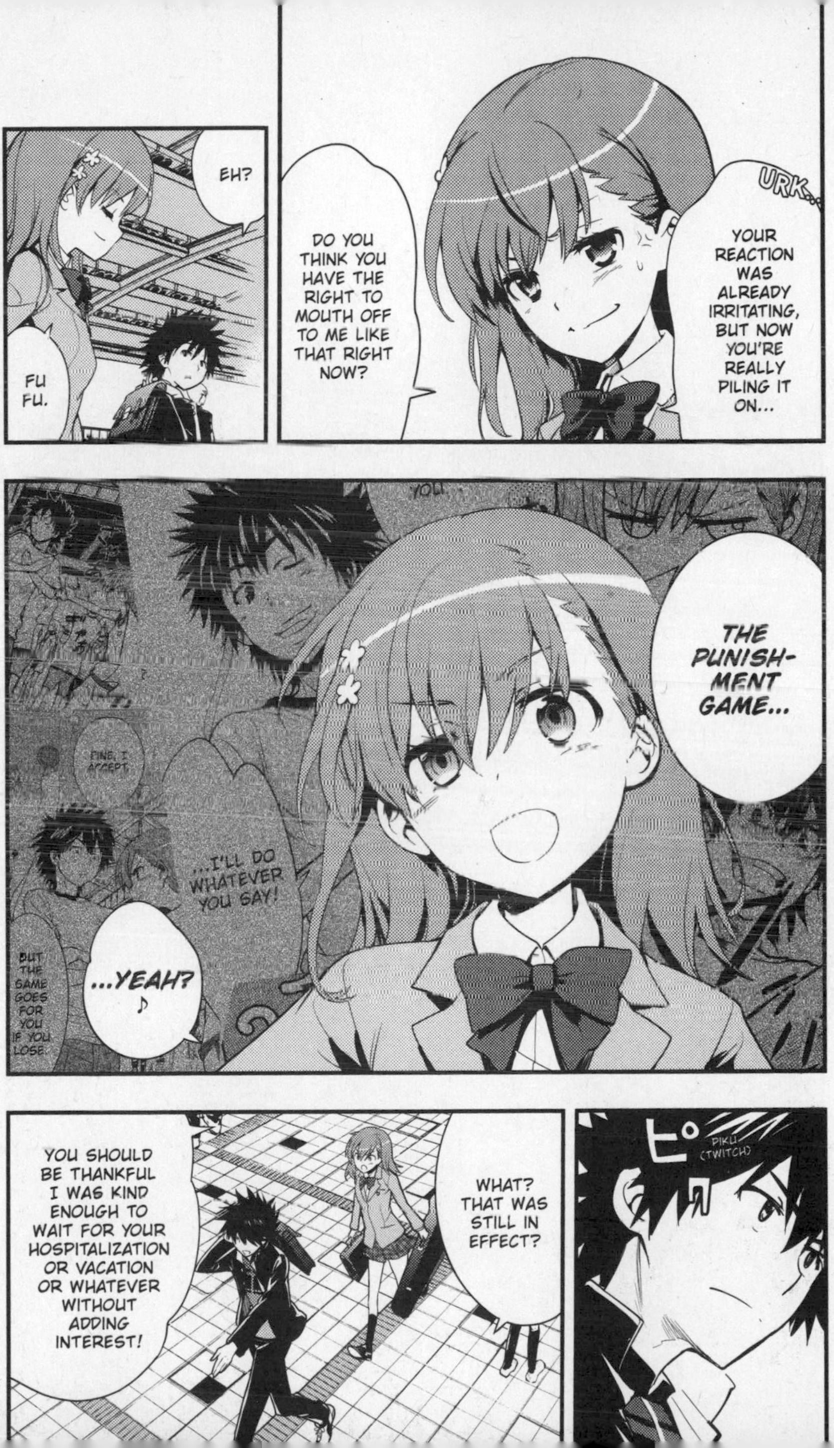
URK...
YOUR REACTION WAS ALREADY IRRITATING, BUT NOW YOU'RE REALLY PILING IT ON...
DO YOU THINK YOU HAVE THE RIGHT TO MOUTH OFF TO ME LIKE THAT RIGHT NOW?
EH?
FU FU.
YOU...
THE PUNISHMENT GAME...
FINE, I ACCEPT.
...I'LL DO WHATEVER YOU SAY!
...YEAH? ♪
BUT THE GAME GOES FOR YOU IF YOU LOSE.
ピクッ
PIKU (TWITCH)
WHAT? THAT WAS STILL IN EFFECT?
YOU SHOULD BE THANKFUL I WAS KIND ENOUGH TO WAIT FOR YOUR HOSPITALIZATION OR VACATION OR WHATEVER WITHOUT ADDING INTEREST!

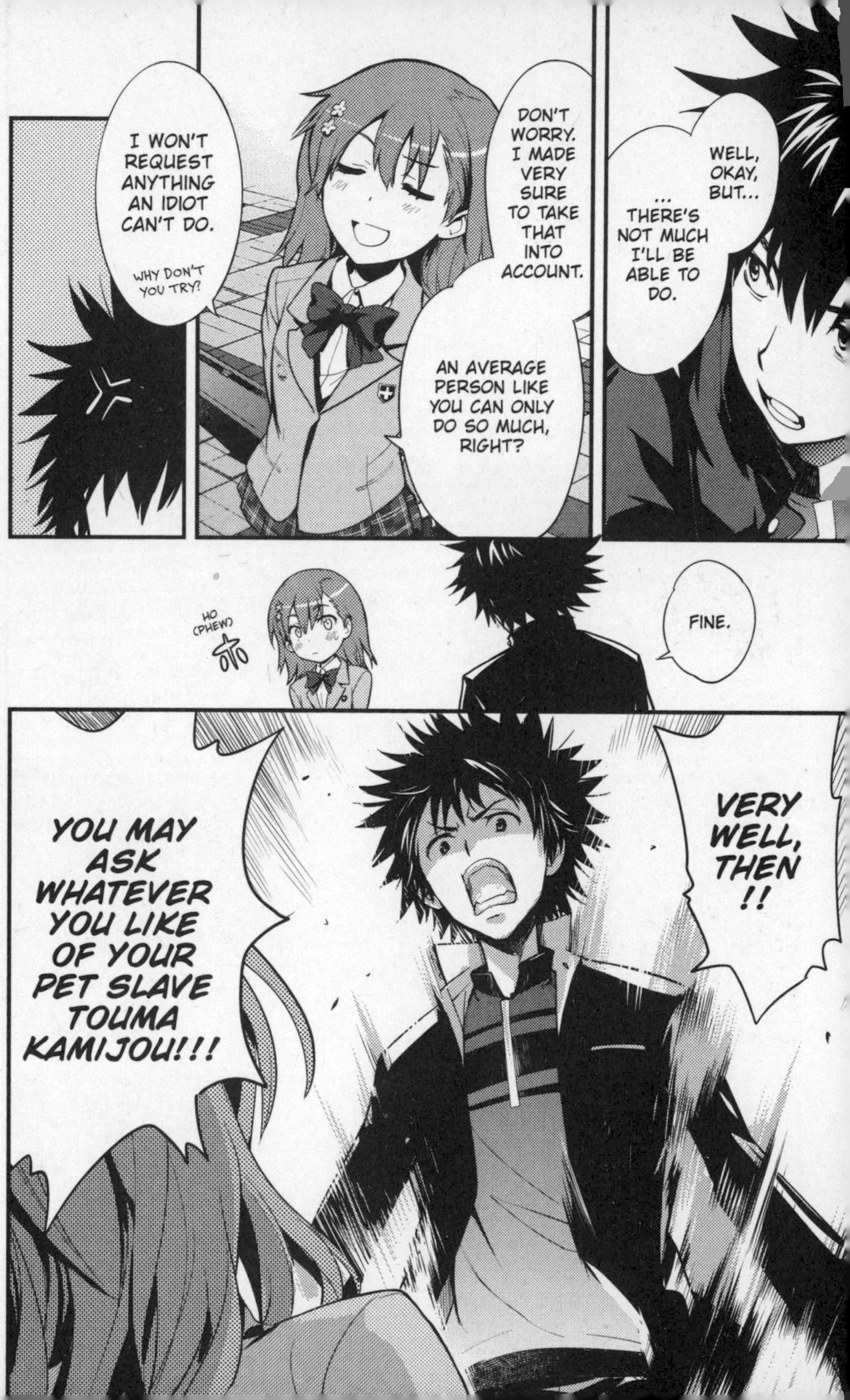
WELL, OKAY, BUT...
...THERE'S NOT MUCH I'LL BE ABLE TO DO.
DON'T WORRY. I MADE VERY SURE TO TAKE THAT INTO ACCOUNT.
AN AVERAGE PERSON LIKE YOU CAN ONLY DO SO MUCH, RIGHT?
I WON'T REQUEST ANYTHING AN IDIOT CAN'T DO.
WHY DON'T YOU TRY?
FINE.
HO (PHEW)
VERY WELL, THEN!!
YOU MAY ASK WHATEVER YOU LIKE OF YOUR PET SLAVE TOUMA KAMIJOU!!!

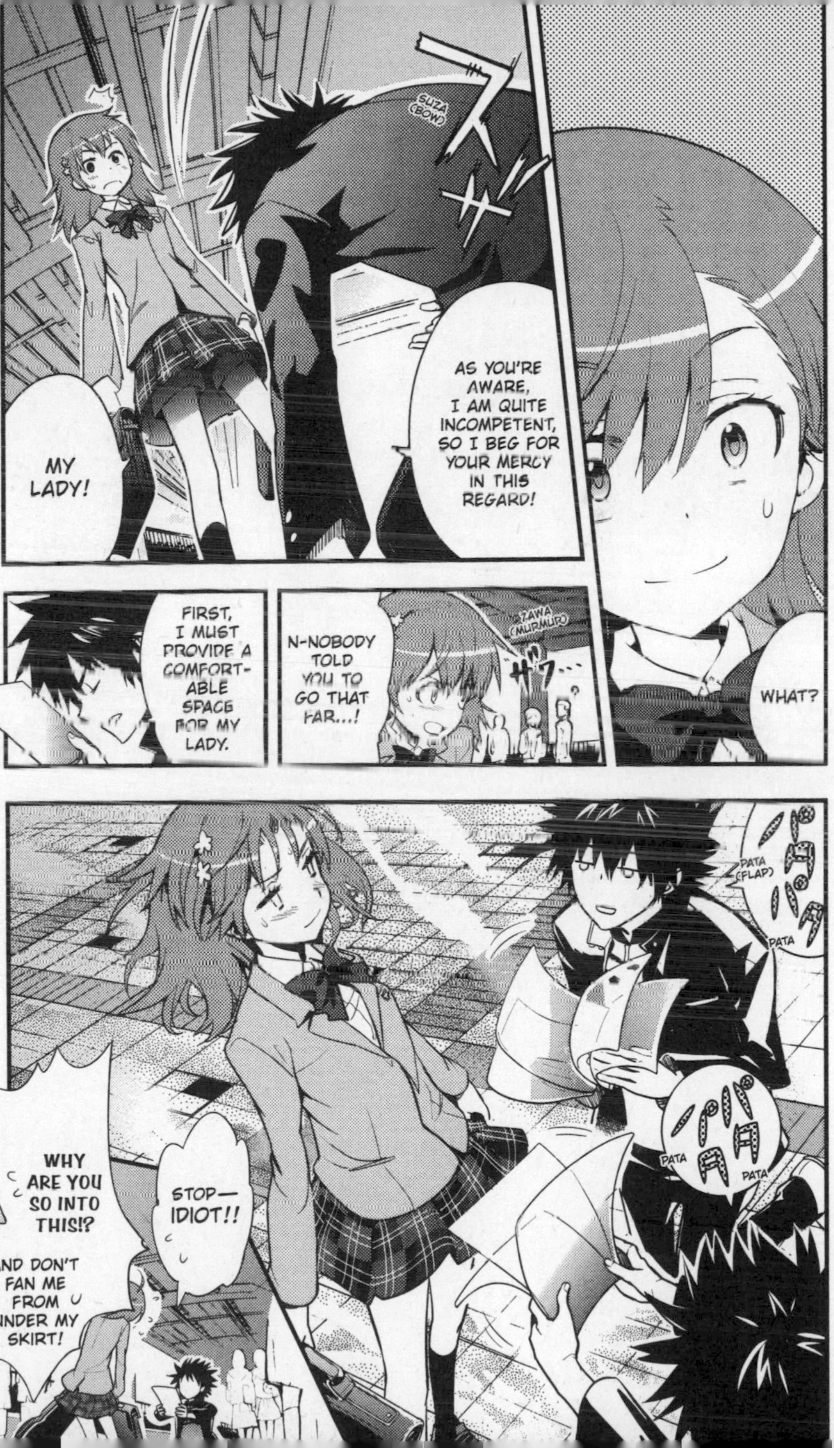
WHAT?
SUZA (BOW)
AS YOU'RE AWARE, I AM QUITE INCOMPETENT, SO I BEG FOR YOUR MERCY IN THIS REGARD!
MY LADY!
ZAWA (MURMUR)
N-NOBODY TOLD YOU TO GO THAT FAR...!
FIRST, I MUST PROVIDE A COMFORT-ABLE SPACE FOR MY LADY.
PATA (FLAP)
PATA
PATA
PATA
STOP— IDIOT!!
WHY ARE YOU SO INTO THIS!?
AND DON'T FAN ME FROM UNDER MY SKIRT!

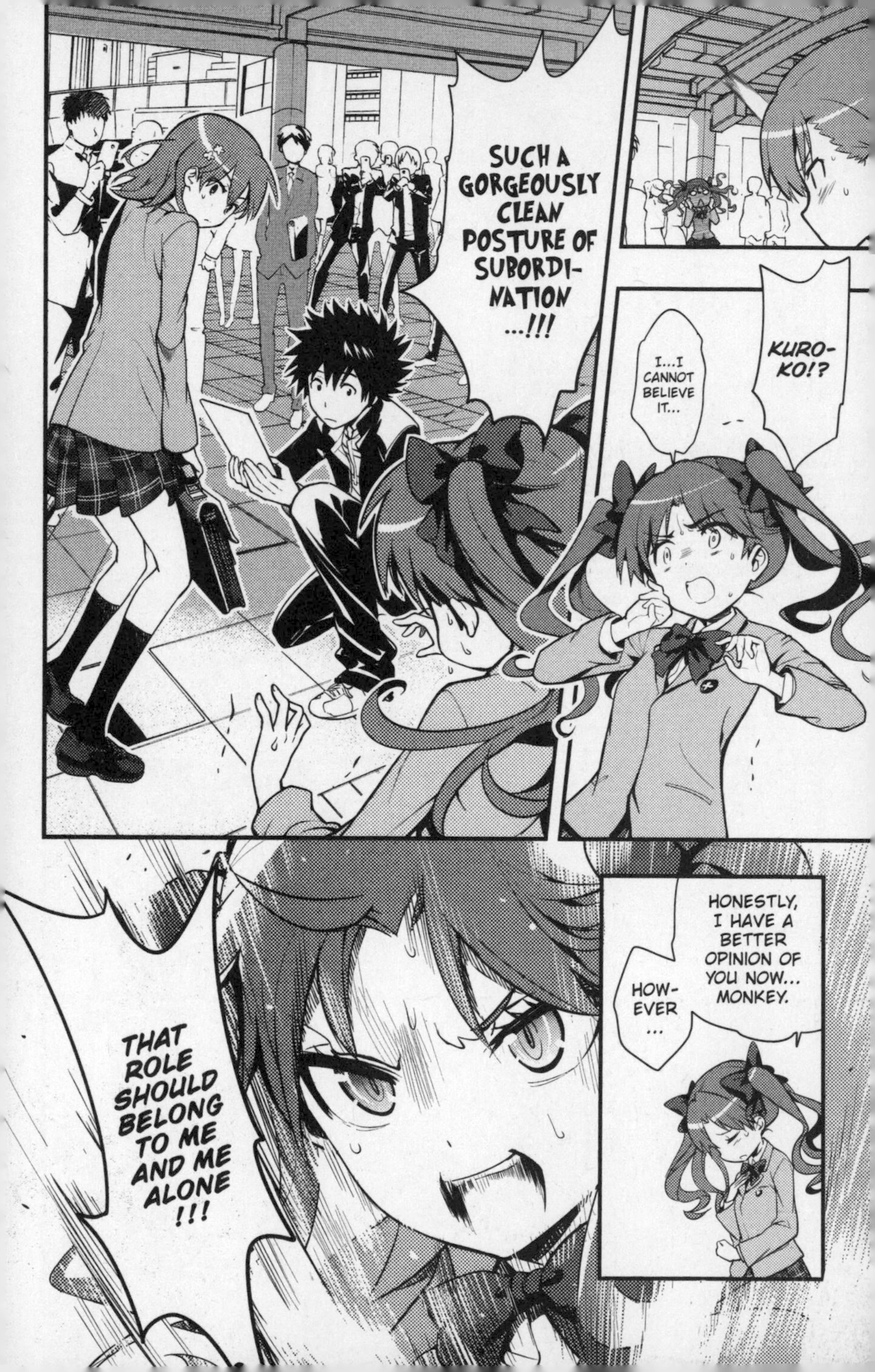
KURO-KO!?
I...I CANNOT BELIEVE IT...
SUCH A GORGEOUSLY CLEAN POSTURE OF SUBORDI-NATION ...!!!
HONESTLY, I HAVE A BETTER OPINION OF YOU NOW... MONKEY.
HOW-EVER ...
THAT ROLE SHOULD BELONG TO ME AND ME ALONE !!!

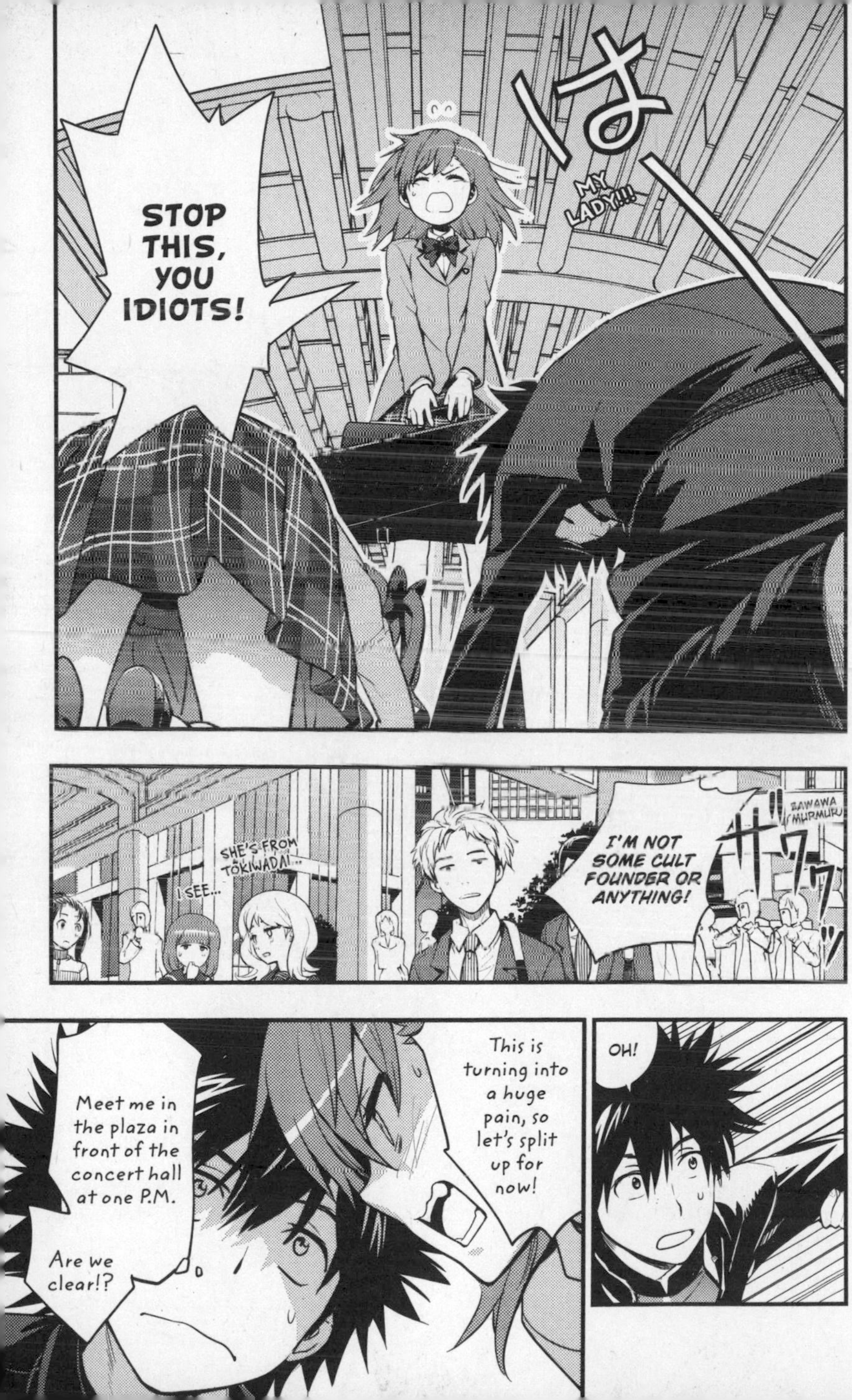
さ
MY LADY!!!
STOP THIS, YOU IDIOTS!
ZAWAWA MURMUR
I'M NOT SOME CULT FOUNDER OR ANYTHING!
SHE'S FROM TOKIWADAI...
I SEE...
OH!
This is turning into a huge pain, so let's split up for now!
Meet me in the plaza in front of the concert hall at one P.M.
Are we clear!?

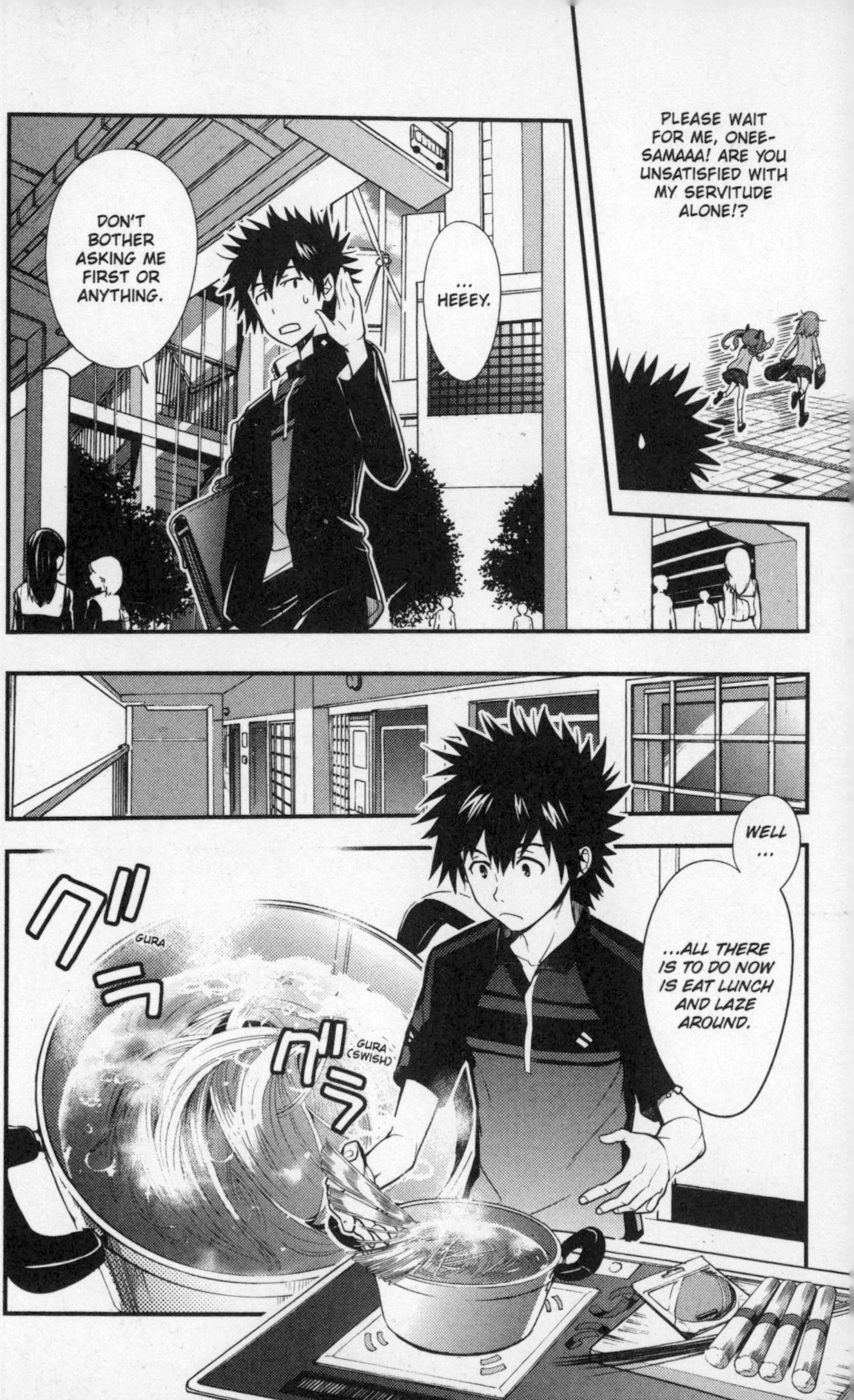
PLEASE WAIT FOR ME, ONEE-SAMAAA! ARE YOU UNSATISFIED WITH MY SERVITUDE ALONE!?
... HEEEY.
DON'T BOTHER ASKING ME FIRST OR ANYTHING.
WELL ...
...ALL THERE IS TO DO NOW IS EAT LUNCH AND LAZE AROUND.
グラ
GURA
グラ
GURA (SWISH)

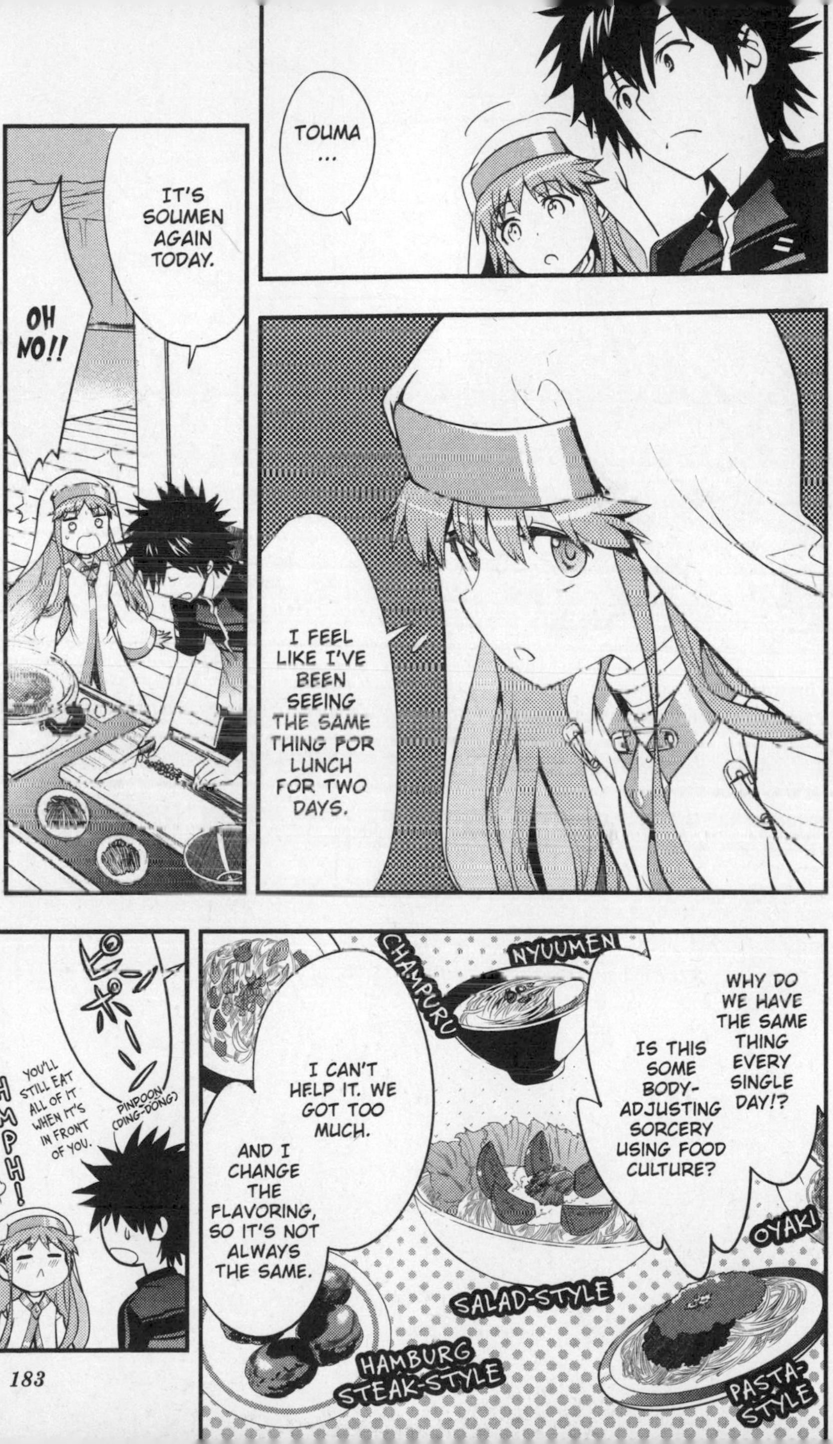
TOUMA ...
I FEEL LIKE I'VE BEEN SEEING THE SAME THING FOR LUNCH FOR TWO DAYS.
IT'S SOUMEN AGAIN TODAY.
OH NO!!
WHY DO WE HAVE THE SAME THING EVERY SINGLE DAY!?
IS THIS SOME BODY-ADJUSTING SORCERY USING FOOD CULTURE?
NYUUMEN
CHAMPURU
I CAN'T HELP IT. WE GOT TOO MUCH.
AND I CHANGE THE FLAVORING, SO IT'S NOT ALWAYS THE SAME.
OYAKI
SALAD-STYLE
PASTA-STYLE
HAMBURG STEAK-STYLE
ピンポーン
PINPOON (DING-DONG)
YOU'LL STILL EAT ALL OF IT WHEN IT'S IN FRONT OF YOU.
HMPH!

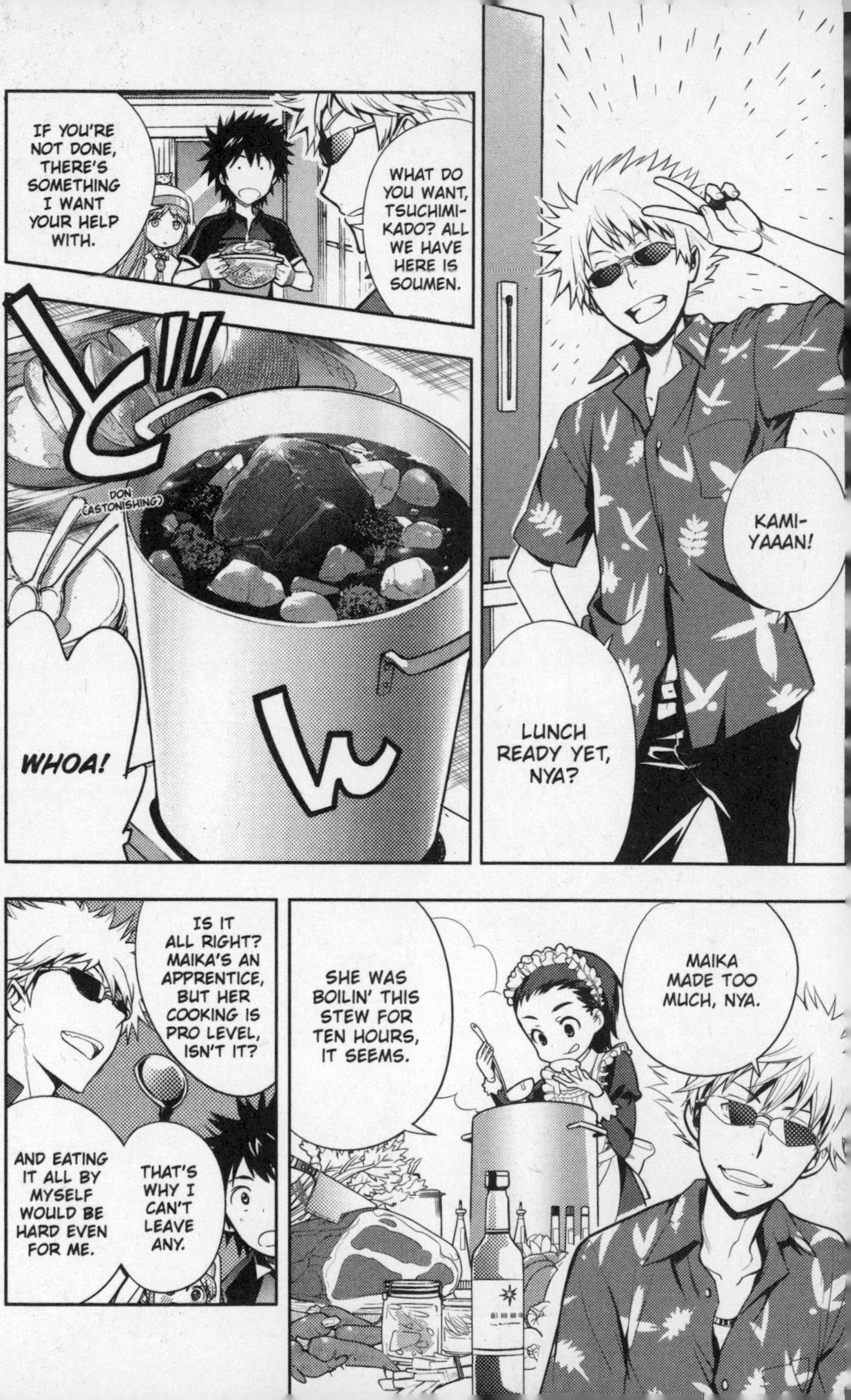
KAMI-YAAAN!
LUNCH READY YET, NYA?
WHAT DO YOU WANT, TSUCHIMIKADO? ALL WE HAVE HERE IS SOUMEN.
IF YOU'RE NOT DONE, THERE'S SOMETHING I WANT YOUR HELP WITH.
DON (ASTONISHING)
WHOA!
MAIKA MADE TOO MUCH, NYA.
SHE WAS BOILIN' THIS STEW FOR TEN HOURS, IT SEEMS.
IS IT ALL RIGHT? MAIKA'S AN APPRENTICE, BUT HER COOKING IS PRO LEVEL, ISN'T IT?
THAT'S WHY I CAN'T LEAVE ANY.
AND EATING IT ALL BY MYSELF WOULD BE HARD EVEN FOR ME.

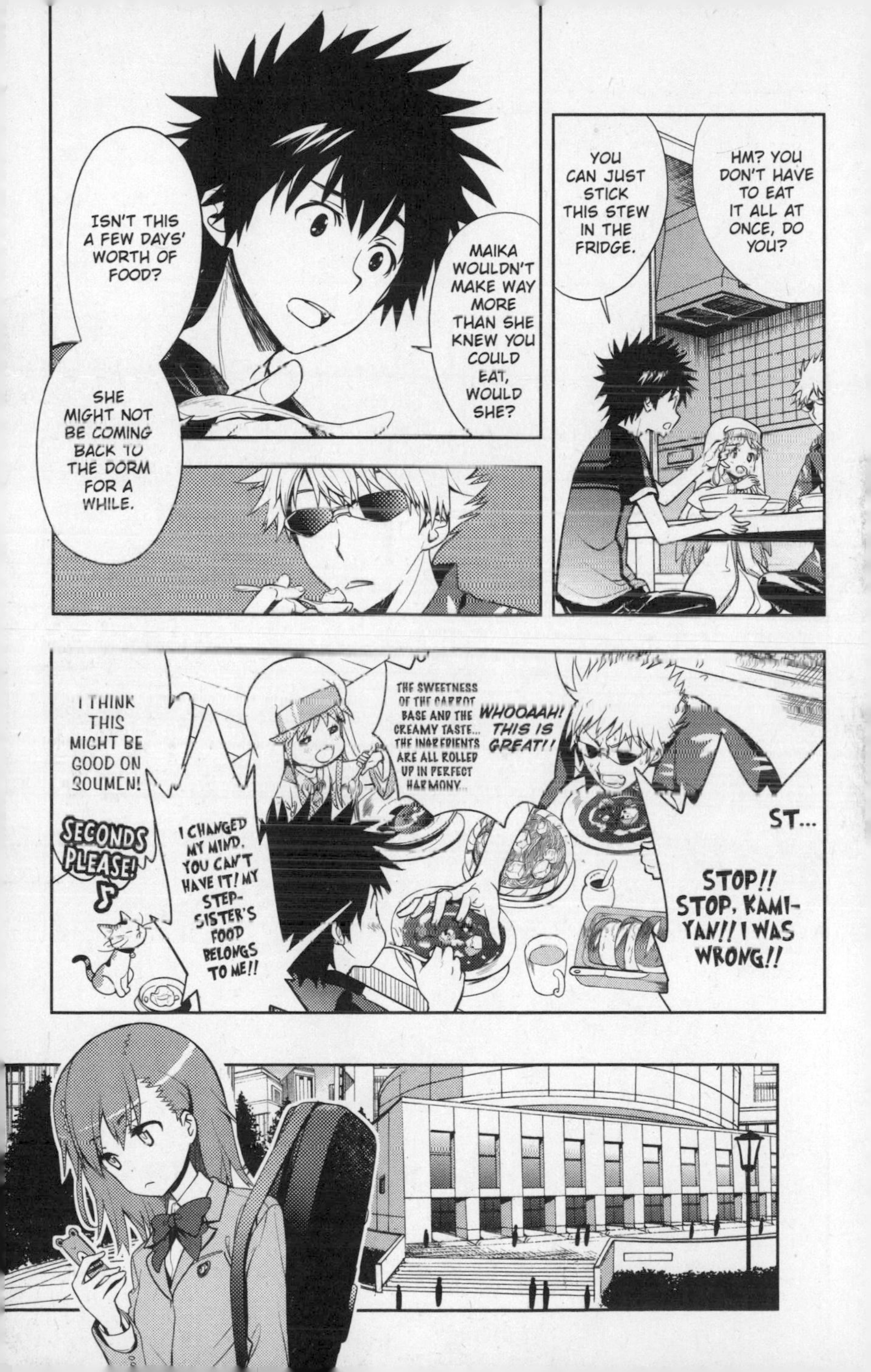
HM? YOU DON'T HAVE TO EAT IT ALL AT ONCE, DO YOU?
YOU CAN JUST STICK THIS STEW IN THE FRIDGE.
MAIKA WOULDN'T MAKE WAY MORE THAN SHE KNEW YOU COULD EAT, WOULD SHE?
ISN'T THIS A FEW DAYS' WORTH OF FOOD?
SHE MIGHT NOT BE COMING BACK TO THE DORM FOR A WHILE.
WHOOAAH! THIS IS GREAT!!
THE SWEETNESS OF THE CARROT BASE AND THE CREAMY TASTE... THE INGREDIENTS ARE ALL ROLLED UP IN PERFECT HARMONY...
I THINK THIS MIGHT BE GOOD ON SOUMEN!
SECONDS PLEASE! ♪
I CHANGED MY MIND. YOU CAN'T HAVE IT! MY STEP-SISTER'S FOOD BELONGS TO ME!!
ST...
STOP!! STOP, KAMI-YAN!! I WAS WRONG!!

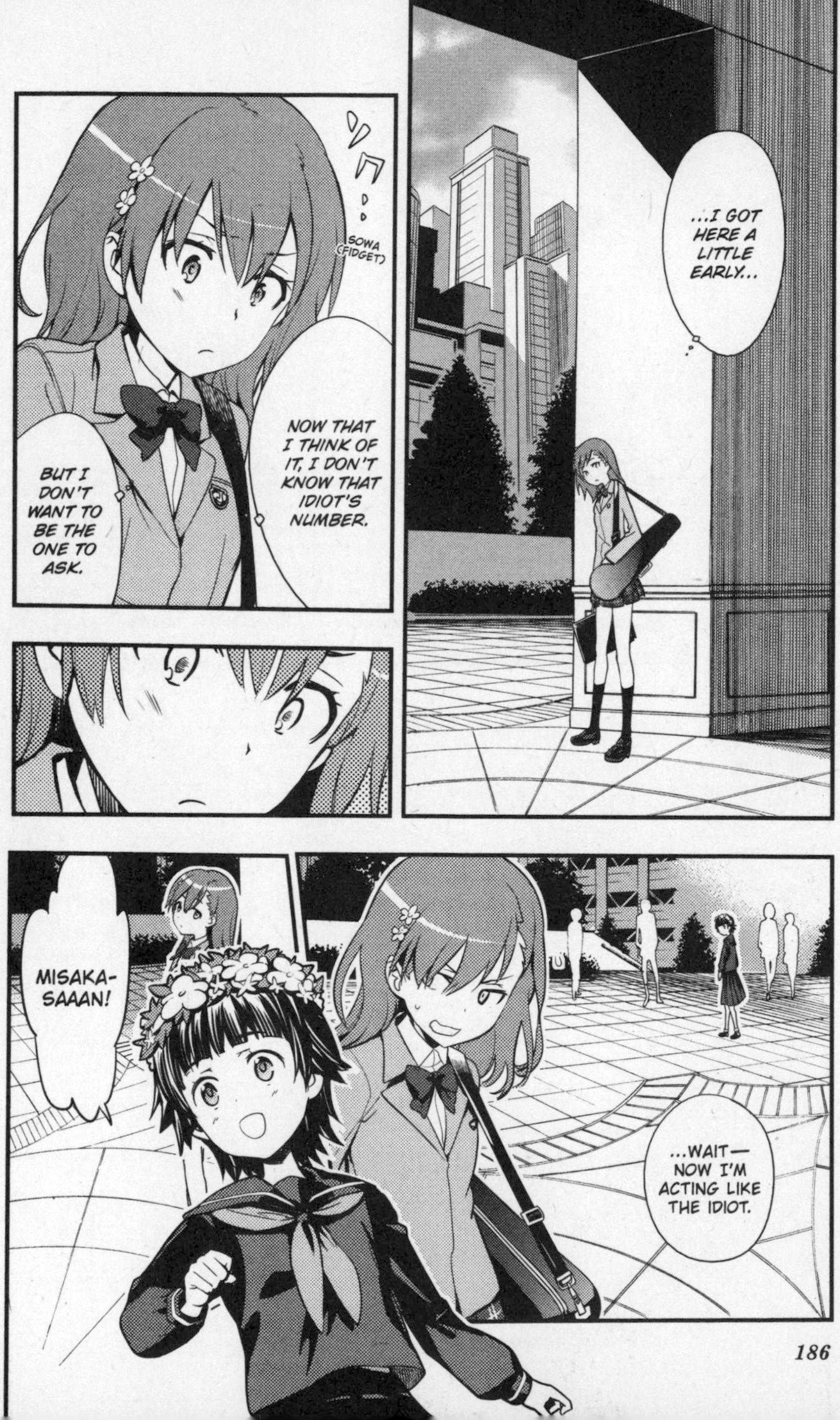
...I GOT HERE A LITTLE EARLY...
ソワ
SOWA (FIDGET)
NOW THAT I THINK OF IT, I DON'T KNOW THAT IDIOT'S NUMBER.
BUT I DON'T WANT TO BE THE ONE TO ASK.
...WAIT— NOW I'M ACTING LIKE THE IDIOT.
MISAKA-SAAAN!

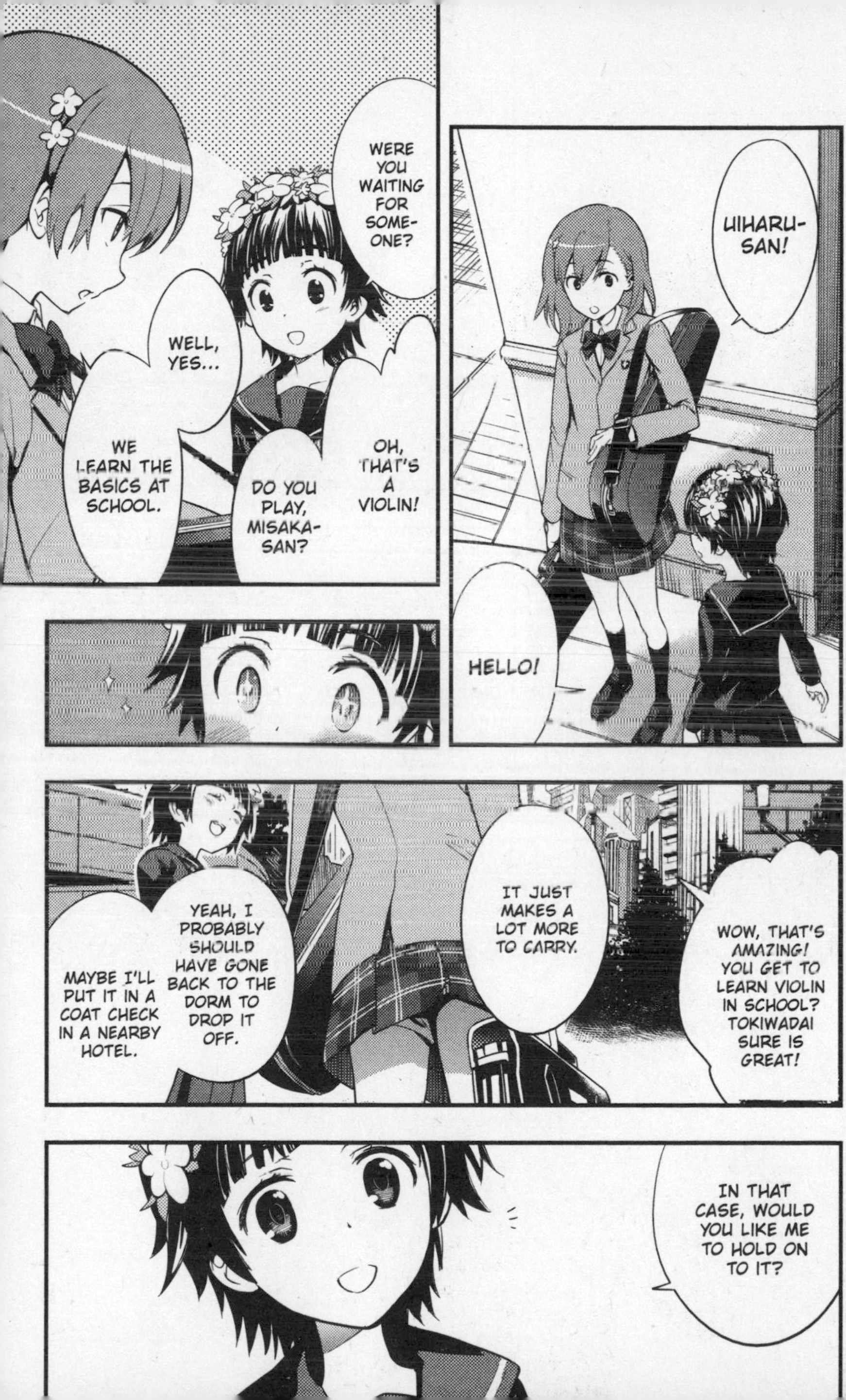
UIHARU-SAN!
HELLO!
WERE YOU WAITING FOR SOME-ONE?
OH, THAT'S A VIOLIN!
WELL, YES...
DO YOU PLAY, MISAKA-SAN?
WE LEARN THE BASICS AT SCHOOL.
WOW, THAT'S AMAZING! YOU GET TO LEARN VIOLIN IN SCHOOL? TOKIWADAI SURE IS GREAT!
IT JUST MAKES A LOT MORE TO CARRY.
YEAH, I PROBABLY SHOULD HAVE GONE BACK TO THE DORM TO DROP IT OFF.
MAYBE I'LL PUT IT IN A COAT CHECK IN A NEARBY HOTEL.
IN THAT CASE, WOULD YOU LIKE ME TO HOLD ON TO IT?

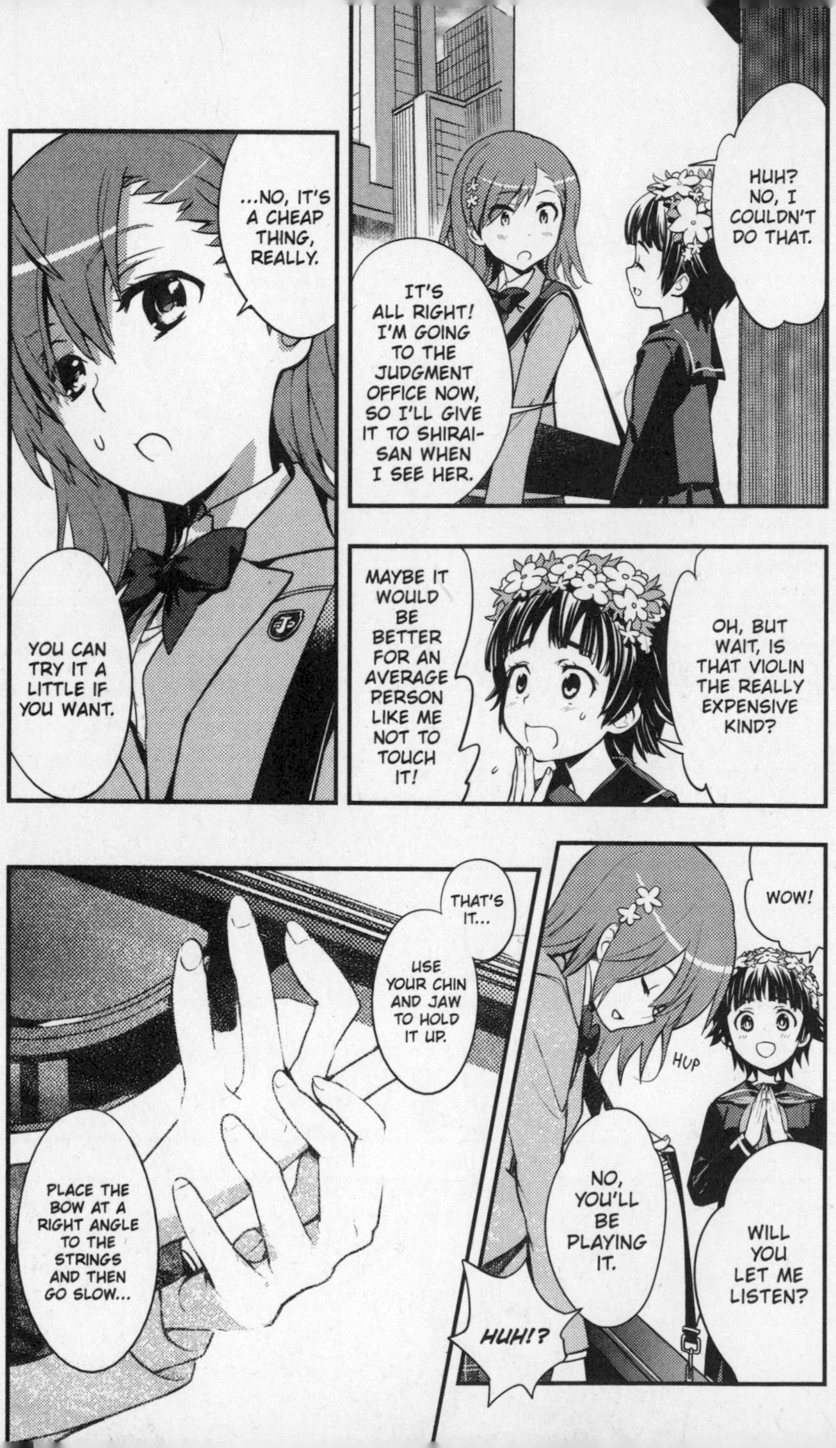
HUH? NO, I COULDN'T DO THAT.
IT'S ALL RIGHT! I'M GOING TO THE JUDGMENT OFFICE NOW, SO I'LL GIVE IT TO SHIRAI-SAN WHEN I SEE HER.
OH, BUT WAIT, IS THAT VIOLIN THE REALLY EXPENSIVE KIND?
MAYBE IT WOULD BE BETTER FOR AN AVERAGE PERSON LIKE ME NOT TO TOUCH IT!
...NO, IT'S A CHEAP THING, REALLY.
YOU CAN TRY IT A LITTLE IF YOU WANT.
WOW!
WILL YOU LET ME LISTEN?
HUP
NO, YOU'LL BE PLAYING IT.
HUH!?
THAT'S IT...
USE YOUR CHIN AND JAW TO HOLD IT UP.
PLACE THE BOW AT A RIGHT ANGLE TO THE STRINGS AND THEN GO SLOW...

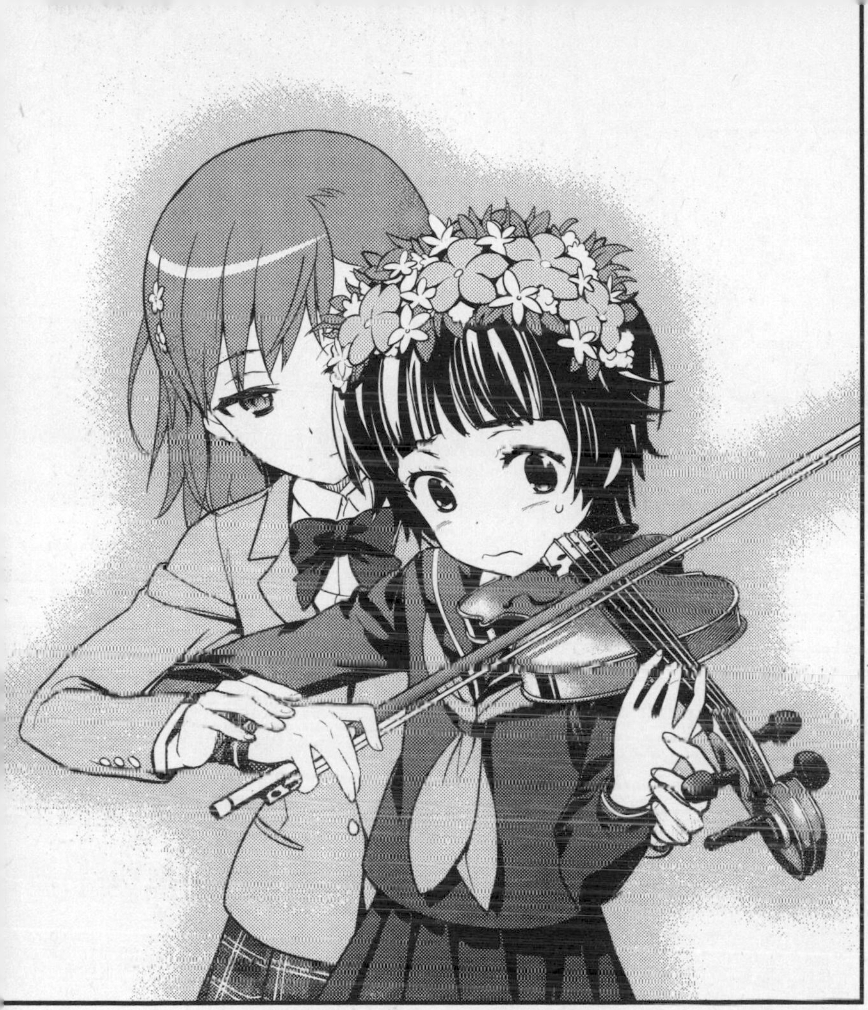

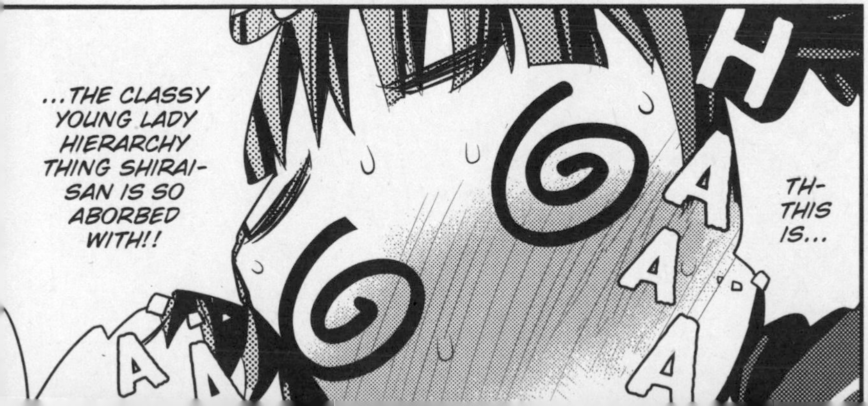
TH- THIS IS...
HAAAA
...THE CLASSY YOUNG LADY HIERARCHY THING SHIRAI-SAN IS SO ABORBED WITH!!

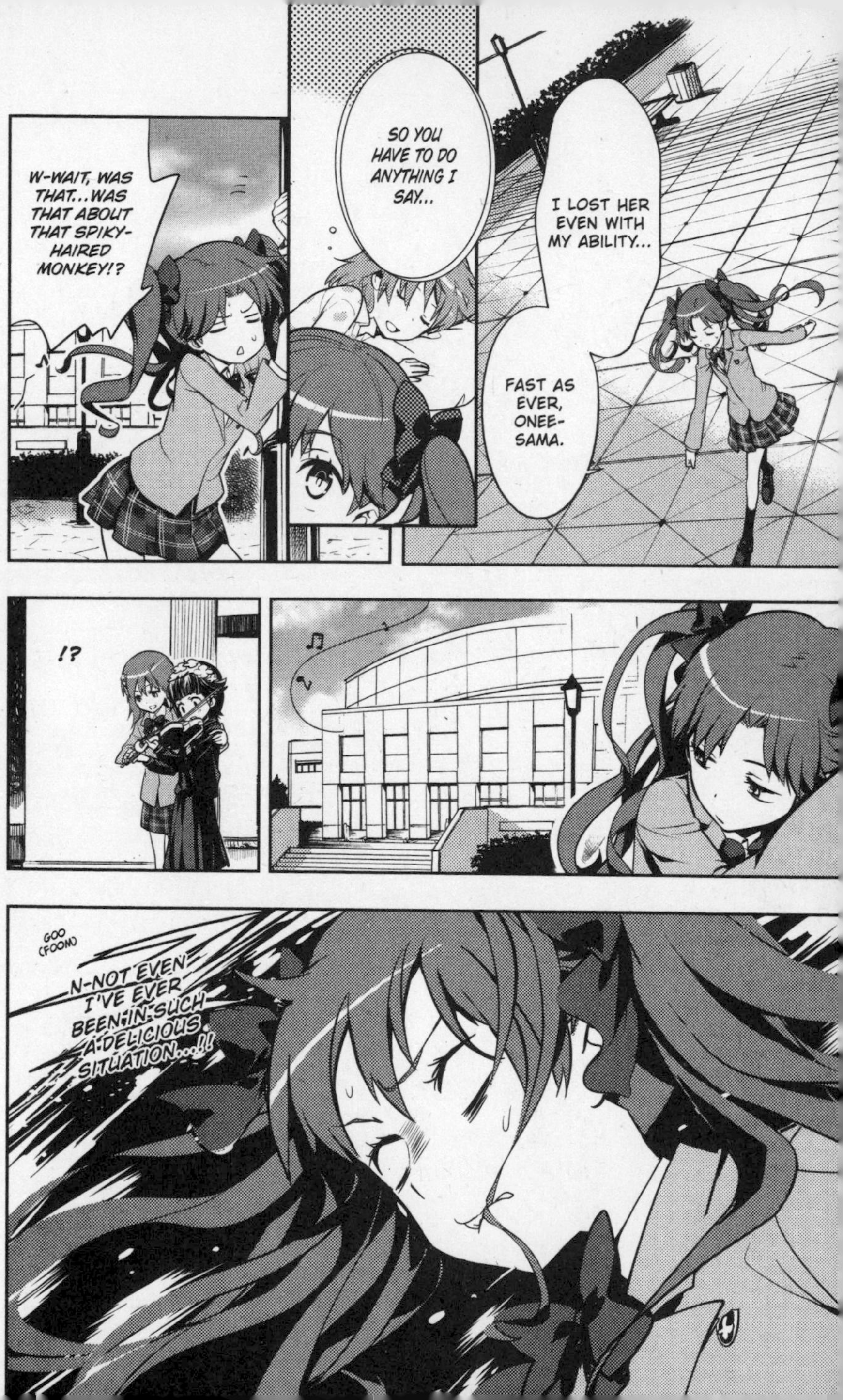
I LOST HER EVEN WITH MY ABILITY...
FAST AS EVER, ONEE-SAMA.
SO YOU HAVE TO DO ANYTHING I SAY...
W-WAIT, WAS THAT...WAS THAT ABOUT THAT SPIKY-HAIRED MONKEY!?
!?
GOO (FOOM)
N-NOT EVEN I'VE EVER BEEN IN SUCH A DELICIOUS SITUATION...!!

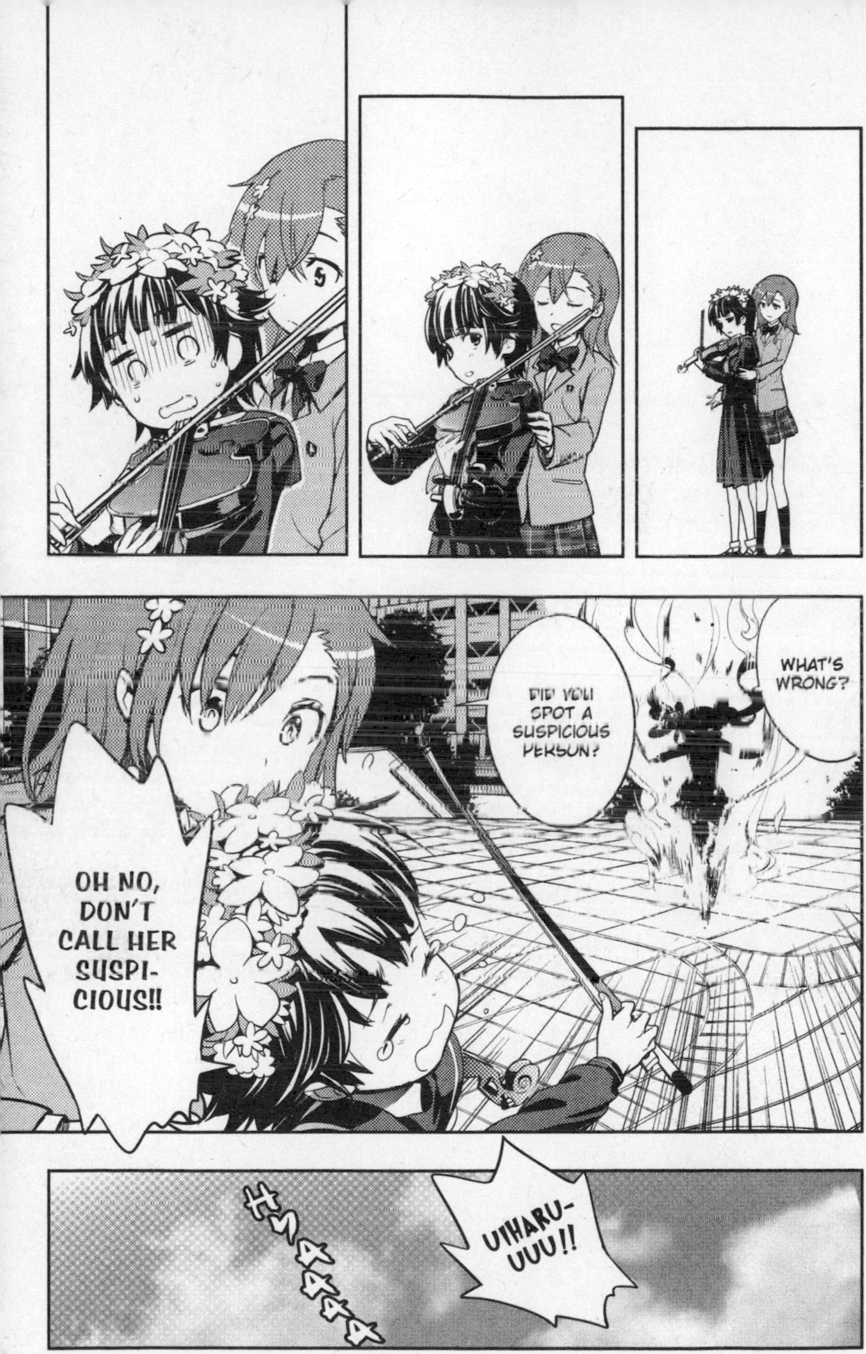
WHAT'S WRONG?
DID YOU SPOT A SUSPICIOUS PERSON?
OH NO, DON'T CALL HER SUSPICIOUS!!
UIHARU-UUU!!

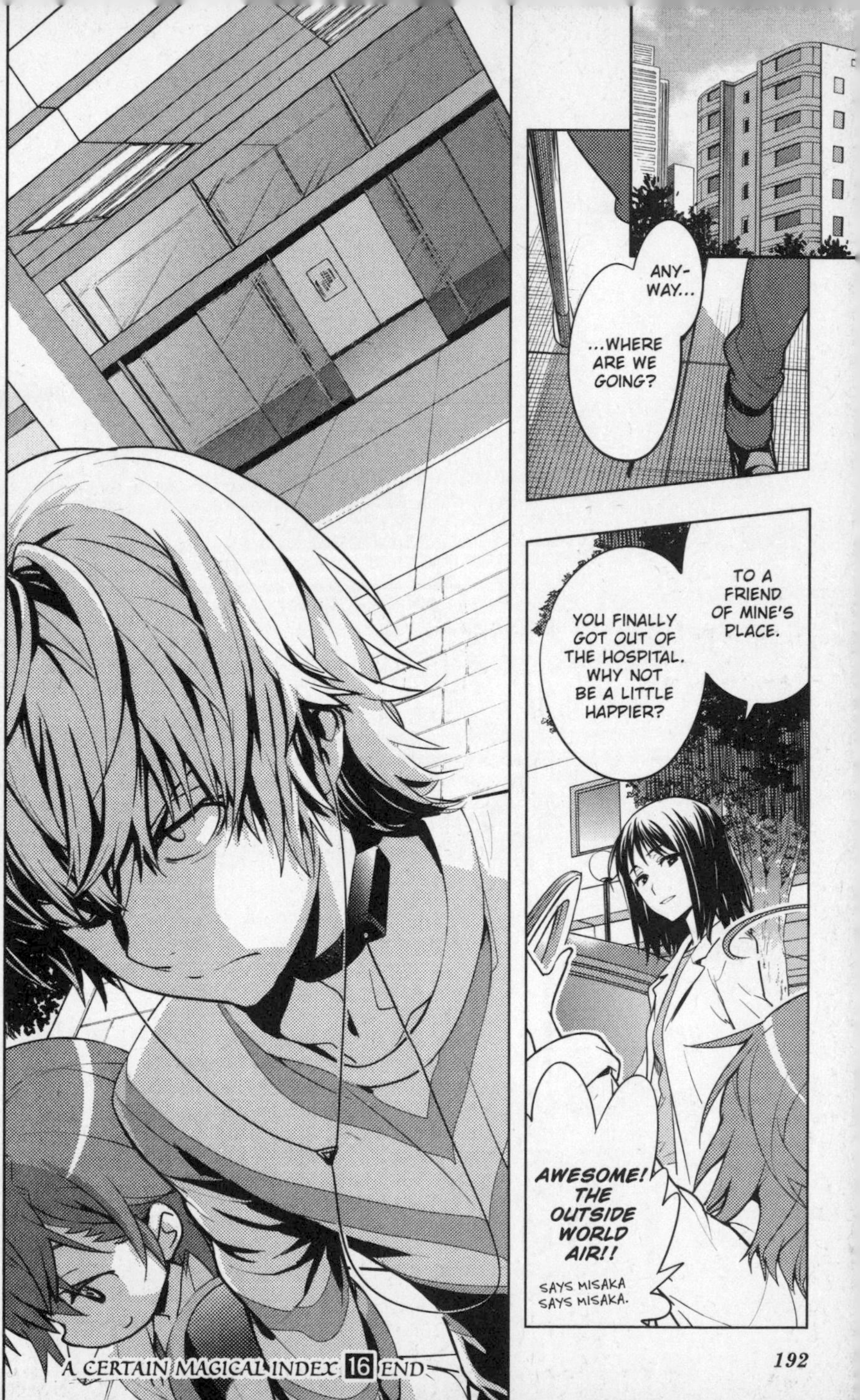
ANY-WAY...
...WHERE ARE WE GOING?
TO A FRIEND OF MINE'S PLACE.
YOU FINALLY GOT OUT OF THE HOSPITAL. WHY NOT BE A LITTLE HAPPIER?
AWESOME! THE OUTSIDE WORLD AIR!!
SAYS MISAKA SAYS MISAKA.
A CERTAIN MAGICAL INDEX 16 END

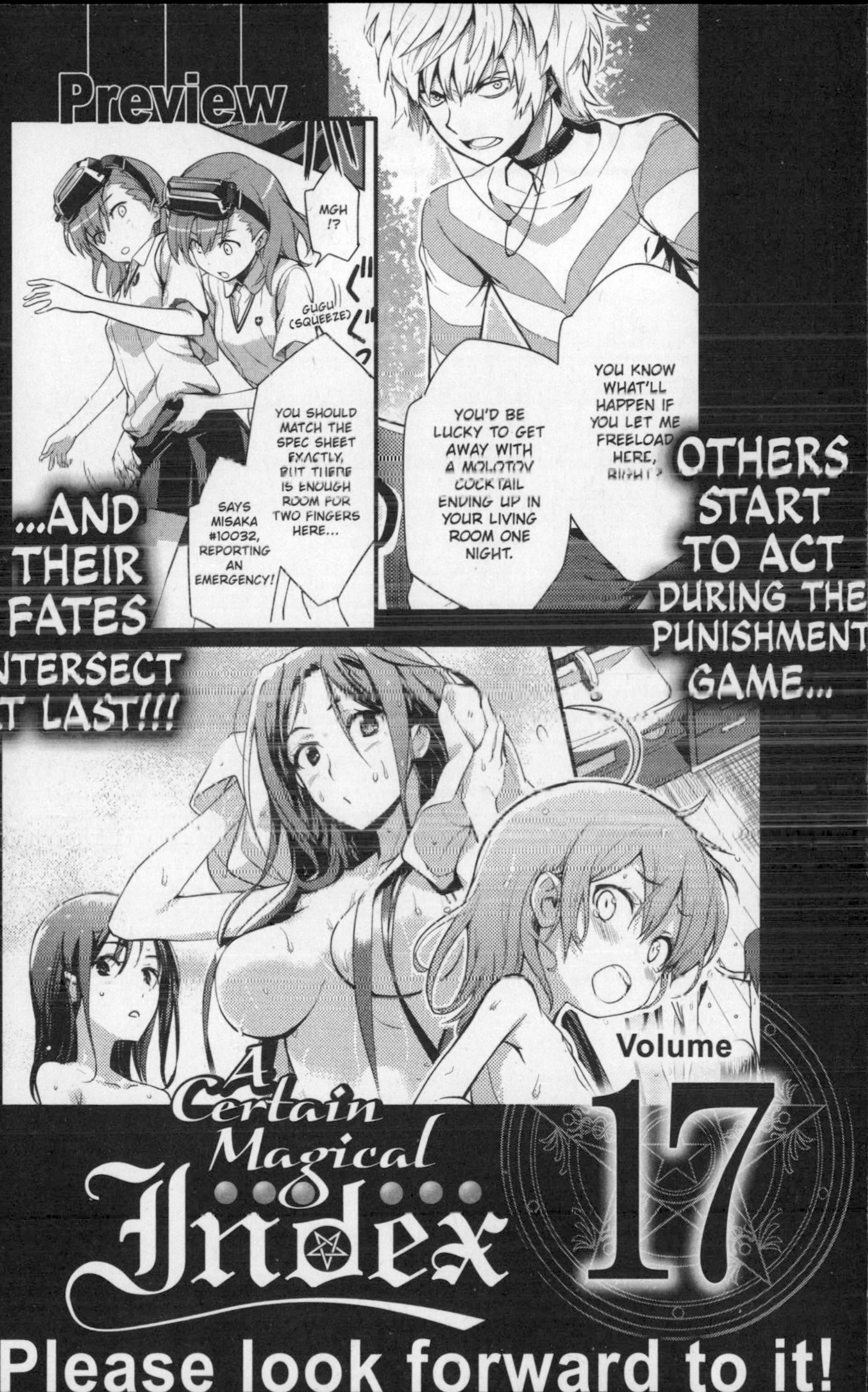
Preview
YOU KNOW WHAT'LL HAPPEN IF YOU LET ME FREELOAD HERE, RIGHT?
YOU'D BE LUCKY TO GET AWAY WITH A MOLOTOV COCKTAIL ENDING UP IN YOUR LIVING ROOM ONE NIGHT.
MGH !?
GUGU (SQUEEZE)
YOU SHOULD MATCH THE SPEC SHEET EXACTLY, BUT THERE IS ENOUGH ROOM FOR TWO FINGERS HERE...
SAYS MISAKA #10032, REPORTING AN EMERGENCY!
OTHERS START TO ACT DURING THE PUNISHMENT GAME...
...AND THEIR FATES INTERSECT AT LAST!!!
A Certain Magical Index
Volume 17
Please look forward to it!

L INDEX ⑯

Kazuma Kamachi
Kiyotaka Haimura
Chuya Kogino

Translation: Andrew Prowse

Lettering: Brndn Blakeslee

TOARU MAJYUTSU NO INDEX Vol. 16
© 2015 Kazuma Kamachi
© 2015 Chuya Kogino / SQUARE ENIX CO., LTD.
Licensed by KADOKAWA CORPORATION ASCII MEDIA WORKS
First published in Japan in 2015 by SQUARE ENIX CO., LTD.
English translation rights arranged with SQUARE ENIX CO., LTD.
and Yen Press, LLC through Tuttle-Mori Agency, Inc.

English translation © 2019 by SQUARE ENIX CO., LTD.

Yen Press
1290 Avenue of the Americas
New York, NY 10104

Visit us at yenpress.com
facebook.com/yenpress
twitter.com/yenpress
yenpress.tumblr.com
instagram.com/yenpress

First Yen Press Edition: January 2019

Yen Press is an imprint of Yen Press, LLC.
The Yen Press name and logo are trademarks of Yen Press, LLC.

Library of Congress Control Number: 2015373809

ISBN: 978-1-9753-5445-9 (paperback)

10 9 8 7 6 5 4 3 2 1

WOR

Printed in the United States of America